This book is due

Event
Entertainment
and Production

The Wiley Event Management Series

SERIES EDITOR: DR. JOE GOLDBLATT, CSEP

Event Entertainment and Production

Mark Sonder, MM, CSEP

WILEY

JOHN WILEY & SONS, INC.

This book is printed on acid-free paper.♾

Published by John Wiley & Sons, Inc., Hoboken, New Jersey
Published simultaneously in Canada

For general information on our other products and services or for technical support, please contact our Customer Care Department within the United States at (800) 762-2974, outside the United States at (317) 572-3993 or fax (317) 572-4002.

Wiley also publishes its books in a variety of electronic formats. Some content that appears in print may not be available in electronic books. For more information about Wiley products, visit our web site at www.wiley.com.

Library of Congress Cataloging-in-Publication Data:

Sonder, Mark.
   Event entertainment and production / Mark Sonder.
      p. cm. — (The Wiley event management series ; 1294)
   ISBN 0-471-26306-0 (Cloth)
   1. Entertaining—Planning. 2. Special events—Planning. 3. Business entertaining.
I. Title. II. Series.
   GV1471.S66 2003
   394.2′068—dc21

                                                                            2003006735

Printed in the United States of America

10 9 8 7 6 5 4 3 2 1

This book is dedicated in loving memory to my friend Kenneth A. Cranford, who had wanted to see his name and music published. Well, my good friend, at least your name is prominent in this book. Thank you for all you contributed to this book and to my life.

Kenneth A. Cranford (September 6, 1952–September 30, 2002)

Contents

Foreword

Wolfgang Amadeus Mozart once described his creative process as *gleich alles zusammen*. According to Mozart, he experienced in his imagination the notes "all at the same time together." *Event Entertainment and Production* represents creative process, for here, in one volume, you will be able to experience the techniques, ideas, strategies, and formulas in this field. In fact, this book is one of the most comprehensive compendiums of entertainment and production art and science that has ever been assembled.

The author has drawn from his rich and varied background as both a musician and a producer to create a set of tools that will assist you in improving the quality of your entertainment and production for any type of event. Whether you are responsible for a small meeting or a major festival, all of the resources you need to make the best decision, to bring the greatest value, and to receive the applause you deserve are included in this book.

The innumerable checklists and examples of contracts and schedules, as well as other helpful information, will make this book one that you will refer to and use over and over again throughout your career. The first-person interviews with luminaries in the field of entertainment and production, furthermore, will allow you to step behind the scenes and learn from the experts in this growing field.

Economists have identified the entertainment industry as one of the fastest-growing fields in modern commerce. This book is your passport to this global industry, and your tour guide is one of the most respected leaders in the field.

Perhaps what separates this book from all others is the author's ability to incorporate his personal passion and love for entertainment, especially for music, within the essential technical details that form this work. His devotion to his chosen profession is refreshing and inspiring and will certainly motivate you to achieve greater outcomes in your own career.

Mozart understood that behind every note of music there is, first and foremost, a muse that brings inspiration, contemplation, and, ultimately, illumination of new ideas. This book represents a modern muse in our profession of event management. As you read and benefit from these valuable pages, may you experience *gleich alles zusammen* and, like Mozart, experience all of the notes at the same time together in one magnificent melody that carries your career forward to new and greater heights.

Dr. Joe Goldblatt, CSEP
Series Editor, The Wiley Event Management Series

Preface

"Nobody's going to read that 500-page John Adams book, but people still want to know what they missed and what they should retain."

—JUSTIN KESTLER, OF SPARKNOTES,
ON STUDY GUIDES FOR CONTEMPORARY BOOKS

When I lived in New York City, our local newspaper, *The New York Times,* had as its slogan for the Sunday paper, "You may not read it all . . . but it's nice to know it's all there!" In this book I have strived to have it all there. Start, not necessarily at the beginning, but by using this book as a reference. Once you begin reading what you want to know, you will want to read on for what you have missed.

In many ways, this is a book furnishing information for those aspiring to enter the world of event entertainment and production. In other ways, it is a road map, charting a journey into an industry that is relatively new, constantly changing, and not as strictly defined as others are. If you have decided that you want a career in this industry, you should know that there is no single career path to follow. There are many ways to enter the field, and many different career paths available, and a variety of areas in which you can focus your talents and interests. This book is not a step-by-step guide to a career in event entertainment and production; it is an overview of the industry and its many components, including information and insights from a variety of industry experts and experienced professionals.

People want entertainment for a myriad of reasons: an amnesia cocktail to quell the stress of modern living, a substitute for the vanishing nuclear family, or a distraction from the reality of life-changing domestic and world events. Event patrons, meeting participants, and incentive winners are no different; they expect top-shelf thrills for their dollars. Hence, the face of event entertainment is changing at full speed, beginning with changes in the way the industry operates. The information presented here is an overview of event entertainment and production, along with a look at some of the other components central to the future of the industry.

Part One considers the event entertainment and production industry and explores the reasons event entertainment is such a big business. Chapter 1 describes the size and scope of the industry, growth projections, and the importance of themed locations and venues. As each generation's musical tastes change, event entertainment has to keep up with those changes. The chapter discusses Generation Y's effects on event entertainment as an example of the industry's ability to reinvent itself.

Chapter 2 reviews parades, fairs, and festivals, as well as themed events that simultaneously contain historical, cultural, ceremonial, religious, patriotic, and social aspects. It also travels the world to uncover some global opportunities in event entertainment.

If you are interested in entering the event entertainment industry, it is because you love entertainment and want to be part of it, whether that includes being a performer or delivering performances to an audience. Perhaps you are a musician and want to build a career around music, expanding your interest from playing music to being part of a group of professionals who help to bring music and other forms of entertainment to an event. That career path includes many options, which are discussed in Chapter 3.

Event entertainment is constantly reinventing itself to meet the changing demands and tastes of its audience. Chapter 4 looks at new product development, industry trends, and the increasing popularity of event sponsorships.

Part Two moves from a discussion of the industry to the actual planning and research phases. Chapter 5 begins the journey into the event entertainment planning process, beginning with a historical perspective. Sometimes creating the "new, fresh, and different" means reviving an old idea and putting a fresh spin on it. Historical data can also provide valuable information for planning a current event. Looking at the past will help you accurately assess the needs and resources required for your event. Successful event entertainment production focuses more on planning than on the actual event. If the right questions are asked, then the right preparations will be made, and you will understand and be ready for the event's needs and potential risks, allowing the event itself to flow efficiently.

Chapter 6 continues the focus on researching and designing events, beginning with a review of the creative process, including a discussion on brainstorming. It explores various ways to recreate others' events, using an "adopt and adapt" approach. The chapter also considers events whose themes have been borrowed from film, television, and the theater.

Although events often appear to flow effortlessly, they involve months of planning and the efforts of, sometimes, hundreds of people. Strategic planning for event production and entertainment is the theme of Chapter 7. You will learn how to build a Production Book or "bible" for each event, how to develop production schedules, scripts, cue sheets, timelines, and other event elements that are invisible to the audience but crucial to production.

Budgeting is an important aspect of event planning and production, which is discussed in Chapter 8. Different types of events, such as for-profit and nonprofit, have different financial objectives. These may be tangible, such as raising money, or intangible, such as generating future sales or creating goodwill. This chapter focuses on financial planning and management. Did your event meet its objectives? That question is answered through postevent evaluations, and the measurement tools of the trade used in such evaluations are discussed here.

Part Three focuses on coordination of the various elements of production. Chapter 9 begins with a discussion of how to select and contract production and entertainment vendors. Whom do you call when you need entertainment and production personnel? Once you have established your goals, professional music purveyors can provide valuable assistance in selecting the ideal musical accompaniment for your event. They can also give recommendations as to the lighting, placement, attire, and speaker systems that will best enhance the mood and image you want to achieve. A variety of production resources are considered, including destination management companies, and you will discover how to legally contract for their services. This chapter also discusses the differences between contractors and employees and why this distinction is important.

Once you have contracted with your entertainment and production support vendors, you will need to know how to manage them. This is the subject of Chapter 10, which looks at various types of managers and management companies, allowing you to understand how to work with them. It also takes a look at hiring speakers and headliners. These individuals have special requirements and needs, and the chapter provides information and tips you can use to ensure that they are happy.

Keeping your audience's attention at an event means that all of the elements must flow smoothly and continuously, including sound, lights, and other special effects. Although you will hire professionals for the production, you will need to monitor these elements for quality control. This is the subject of Chapter 11. Luck is not responsible for keeping the myriad of technical details running in a smooth and cohesive flow; it is totally dependent on planning, production, and quality control.

Risk is an inherent part of every event, whether it is a small private event or a large public extravaganza. Chapter 12 introduces risk assessment, the portion of the planning process in which potential risk elements are individually identified and contingency plans are developed to prepare for them. Every part of an event has a risk factor, from music licensing to the technical elements of production, the entertainment, and the audience.

Do you know that the music used at an event requires licenses and as the event planner, you are responsible for obtaining those licenses? Chapter 13 discusses the rights of musicians and songwriters, music licensing issues, music licensing agencies, such as Broadcast Music Inc. (BMI) and the American Society of Composers, Authors and Publishers (ASCAP), and the penalties that can be assessed against you for playing unlicensed music at your event. Language from the BMI and ASCAP agreements is included, as well as a description of how these agreements apply to the events industry.

Part Four explores strategies for becoming successful in the event entertainment and production industry. Chapter 14 discusses best practices for various types of for-profit and nonprofit events, including fund-raising events, product launches, and ceremonies. It also takes a look at incentive programs, used by many organizations to reward top-performing employees, which present new and exciting opportunities in event entertainment.

Today's events may not include live musical entertainment, a headliner, or even a speaker. Multimedia presentations are increasingly the entertainment focus of events, and Chapter 15 presents a how-to discussion on executing audiovisual, slide show, and other multimedia events. The Internet offers a new set of opportunities for multimedia presentations, and this chapter also discusses Webcasting and video on demand and how you can introduce these elements to your clients to enhance their multimedia event.

What is the future of event entertainment and production? Chapter 16 explores the many new and exciting technologies available today and those that are on the cutting edge. It looks at how hotels can use live music to enhance profitability and entertain their guests. Entertainment is a key element in *branding strategies,* the new buzzword in marketing. The chapter also discusses how upbeat rhythms and lyrics can emphasize corporate or association messages to generate excitement about products or events.

From students in meeting and event management institutions, to musicians, hospitality professionals seeking certification, and seasoned meeting and association planners and special event producers—this book is written for all who are interested in and can benefit from learning the best practices in event entertainment and production for meetings and special events. In addition, the benefits will include stronger returns on the efforts invested in such endeavors and a greater appreciation for this creative art form.

This book will take you toward your destination, each chapter beginning with an insightful quotation and a list of topics for discovery. In addition, you will find illustrations and checklists to aid in your entertainment operations and logistics, real-life stories of what people have learned before you, and "Scripts for Future Study," providing additional resources on the topics covered. "Exit Stage Right," at the end of each chapter, will tell you what is coming up next on your journey.

As Joe Goldblatt, CSEP, expounds in his *Special Events: Twenty-first Century Global Event Management,* there are five critical stages for all events. This book will take you through those stages—research, design, planning, coordination, and evaluation—within the framework of the four phases of management: administration, coordination, marketing, and legal, ethical, and risk management. The entertainment and production industry is a huge business. The importance of this business and its effect on the meetings and events industry today and tomorrow is stressed throughout the chapter.

May this book give you the freedom to pursue your dreams and goals in event entertainment and production. Legendary guitarist Carlos Santana accepted his nomination at his induction ceremony into the Rock and Roll Hall of Fame by saying, "May the music set you free."

Acknowledgments

I want to thank—

Ingelore B. Wenig—my mom, my first mentor, who taught me to listen to music at an early age and who has been a constant source of support and inspiration.

Ernest Sonder—my Dad, who passed away in 1995, who preferred that I go to a liberal arts college and not a music conservatory, but who always supported me in whatever my interests were.

Roxanne Sonder—my wife, with whom I always hear music.

Dr. Joe Goldblatt, CSEP—for being a pioneer in the event industry and a treasured mentor, who asked me to write this book.

John Wiley & Sons—for being the first publisher to publish a book on event entertainment and production for the meetings and events industry.

Jill Zeigenfus, MTA, a graduate of The George Washington University, who is my copyeditor and has helped me through the entire process of writing this book. She collected my words and made them sing, providing significant contributions to this book through her insights and knowledge of the industry. I am sure she will become an events industry leader as she pursues her career.

Jennifer Hoffman—for being my proofreader and first editor. We met at an association event. You have to be in it to win it! And I won it with her help!

The late Jay Magazine, friend and colleague. Windows on the World 9/11/01. One of the very first people I met in the industry.

I am also grateful to still other mentors—

Bill Henry, 1984 and 1988 U.S. Paralympic Cross Country Ski Team member; my roommate for the fall training camp with the U.S. National and Olympic team in West Yellowstone, Montana, friend, and coach.

Robert Sivek, CSEP, The Meetinghouse Companies, Inc., in Elmhurst, Illinois, for showing me the way at the beginning of the last decade.

Chris Spelius, 1984 U.S. Olympic Kayak Team member; we shared two Chilean kayak expeditions together.

Finally, there are many who have contributed not only to this book, but also to the profession as a whole. I could not have completed this book without their input and support, and I am sincerely grateful to each of them.

Richard Aaron, CMP, CSEP	Stanley Aaronson, CSEP	Aerosmith Sylvia Allen

Alliance Service Network
Meredith Anderson
Wendy Anderson
Jim Andrews
Dave Backer
Andrew Ballard
Joyce Banelli
John Baragona
Brenda Beckelman
Rita Bedritis
Kathy Bee
Pat Benatar
Tony Bennett
Mort Berkowitz
Peter Berliner
Ben Bernstein
Sandy Biback, CMP, CMM
The Big Bad Voodoo Daddy
Blondie
Blood Sweat and Tears
Blue Water Media
Marcy Blum
Toni Bodenhamer
Martin Boyle
Boys Choir of Harlem
Boyce Brawley
Jackie Brett
Jennifer W. Brown, CMP
Kent Bush, CSEP
Mark Butts
Don Campbell
Richard Carbotti
Jane Celler
Cher
Bob Cherny
Keith Clark
Nicole Clark
David Clayton-Thomas
The Coasters
Michael Cohen

Jim Cohn
Kip and Tiffany Colligan
Frank Como
Alice Conway, CSEP
Lauri, John, and Bits Cranford
Paul Creighton
Nicolas Daeppen
Jan Davis
Tom DeLuca
Robert DeMaria
Democratic National Convention
Clem DeRosa
Blanca Diaz, CMP
Frank Dickson, CMP
Bo Diddley
David DiPaulo
Mary Ellen Dobrowolski
Joel Dolci, CAE
Dan Doyle
The Drifters
Joan L. Eisenstodt
Bob Ellis
Diana Ellis
Maria Erspamer
Dr. David Fardon
Fairfax County Republican Committee
Famous Music Publishing
Blair Farrington
Eunice Farrington
Phyllis Firebaugh
Benoit Flippen
John Foster
Buddy Fox
Paul Frank
Sue Frank-Serphos
Willie Garcia Jr.
Greg Gibadlo

Marc Glaser
James Goldberg, Esq.
Dr. Joe Goldblatt, CSEP
Bob Goyena
Rob Goyena
Adele Gutman
Wally Hallas
Jimmy Heath
Chris Heide
K. Mary Hess
Tyra W. Hilliard
Jennifer Hoffman
Richard Hopkins
Dana Hornstein, CMP
Lee J. Howard
Oren Jaffe, CMP
Ray Jaskey
Joan Jett
Joshua Jones
Mark N. Jordan
Deborah Joy
Marvin Kaplan
Glenn Kasofsky
Andy Kerr
Randy King and Son
Gladys Knight
Emily Kresser
Carol Krugman, CMP, CMM
Trace Kuhn
Sherry Lane
Ellen Larkin, CMP
Ralph and Ricki Lauren
Bill Lee
Robin Lerner
Wendy Leshner
Stephen Liaskos
Al Lieberman
Ira Lieberman
Rebecca Linder
Marie Long
Mark Lorimer
Margaret MacDermott
John K. Mackenzie

Ian Maksik
David Markham
Katherine Markham, CHME
Paula Marshak
The Marvelettes
Doug Matthews
Universal - MCA Music Publishing
Carla Hargrove McGill
Eric McNulty
Joanne Mera
Phyllis Mikolaitis, CSEP
Paulette Miller
Ronnie Milsap
Kaz Miyamoto
Jim Monroe, CMP, CSEP
Jack Morton
Jan Moxley
Brian Mullen
Marty Mullen
Frank Nardoza
Bob Nargassons
National Park Service in the Shenandoah Mountains
New York Republican Committee
Karl Nybergh, CMP
NYC & Co.
Pat O'Brien
Lana Ostrander
Michael Owen
Marianna Paolini, CMP
Paramount Pictures
C. B. Park, CAE

Keith Patrick
Jared Paul
Chris Pentz, CMP
Lisa Perrin
Len Piotrowski
Dakota Pippin
Mary Power
Catherine Price
Ray Pulver
Annie Revel, CSEP
Steve Revetria
Van Allen Rice
Bob Robustelli
Stephanie Rodnick
Ira Rosen
Deidre Ross
David Rubin
Carl Ruh
Salsa Picante
Mark Sanders
Gael Sandoval
Susan Sarro
Jean-Michel Savocca
John Schrotel and Sons
Steve Schwartz
Fred Seidler
Bobby Short
Tia Sillers
Julia Rutherford Silvers, CSEP
Robert Sivek, CSEP
Stephen Sondheim
Stan Soper, Esq.
Mark Steele
Dick Steiner
Detective Brad Stevens

Kathryn Summer
Shelli Sutton-Steinberg
Rita Tateel
Thoth
TimeSaver Software— Room Viewer
Suzanne Tobak
David Tutera
Patrick Tuttle
Frank Vagnozzi
Clint vanZandt
Becky Ventorini
ViewPoint International Event and Destination Management Company
Laren Ukman
Lesa Ukman
Jeff Wagner
Neil Waltzer
Elaina Ward
Washington, D.C. Convention and Tourism Corporation
Diana Webb
Kenneth L. Weissman
Andre Wells
Jim West
Rich Westerfield
Wayne Wilentz
William Morris Agency
David Williams
Jill M. Zeigenfus, MTA
Jennifer Ziehl
Jill Zitnik

PART ONE

The Entertainment and Event Production Industry

CHAPTER 1

The Entertainment Economy: Big Business

He who mingles music with gymnastic in the fairest proportions, and best attempts them to the soul, may be rightly called the true musician.

—PLATO, THE REPUBLIC, *III, 411*

IN THIS CHAPTER YOU WILL DISCOVER

- The size, scope, and growth of the entertainment and production industry.
- How to bridge the generation gap for entertainment at events.
- How to use theme-prepared destinations for events across the globe.

In *The Art of the Show*, the author describes the historic roots of expositions. "The exposition has deep roots that can be traced to fairs almost at the beginning of time. The biblical Book of Ezekiel documents the fairs and markets of Tyre, a Phoenician city on the Mediterranean Sea. 'Tyre, at the time of the prophet, was already a city over 2000 years old' (Hanlon, 1982, 2).[1] The ancient Greeks tell of fairs being held in conjunction with their celebrated Games. 'At Delphi, Nemaea, Delos or the Isthmus of Corinth, a fair was held almost every year. The Amphytctionic fairs were held twice a year' (Walford, 1883, 3)[2]" (Morrow 1997).

According to *A History of Western Music,* "Both Plato and Aristotle were quite clear as to what they meant by the 'right' kind of person; and they were agreed that the way to produce him was through a system of public education in which two principal elements were gymnastics and music, the one for the discipline of the body and the other for that of the mind" (Grout 2000). This book hopes to improve the reader with that other discipline, "that of the mind."

As noted previously, when music joins education, the "right" type of person is created. Consistent with this concept, history has shown that participating in music is known to have broad positive effects on learning, motivation, and behavior. Don Campbell further confirms this in his book *The Mozart Effect:*

> *The College Entrance Examination Board reported in 1996 that students with experience in musical performance scored fifty-one points higher on the verbal part of the SAT and thirty-nine points higher on the math section than the national average. In a study of approximately 7500 students at a medium-size university between 1983–1988, music and music education majors had the highest reading scores of any students on campus, including those in English, biology, chemistry, and mathematics. Walt Disney film scores and New Age music had the most positive impact on the mood of 255 first and second graders, with classical music coming in third. Other studies showed that playing music lessened children's inappropriate behavior on a school bus, and that scheduling arts activities, including music, on Mondays and Fridays reduced student absences on those days. Researchers reported that light pop music, primarily songs by the Beatles, reduced the rate of inappropriate or disruptive behavior in young children in a special preschool class. Most people graduate from school and join the workplace, where music can also be beneficial. Music in the workplace has been shown to raise performance levels and productivity by reducing stress and tension, masking irritating sounds, and contributing to a sense of privacy.*

[1]From Hanlon, Al. 1982. *Trade Shows in the Marketing Mix, Revised Edition.* Shrewsbury, MA: Wordsworth Publishing. Joseph Hepburn, Archives Researcher, The Franklin Institute. Personal correspondence, 1969.

[2]From Walford, Cornelius. 1883. *Fairs Past and Present: A Chapter in the History of Commerce.* Reprinted edition. 1968. New York: Augustus M. Kelley Publishers.

The Convention Industry Council's (CIC) APEX Terminology Initiative defines a number of key words:

> *Entertainment:* Activity performed for the amusement and enjoyment of others.
>
> *Meeting:* A gathering for business, educational, or social purposes. Associations often use the term to refer to a combination of educational sessions and exhibits. Includes seminars, forums, symposiums, conferences, workshops, and clinics.
>
> *Special Event:* A one-time event staged for the purpose of celebration; a unique activity.

Does event entertainment reflect the culture of the attendees, at least the culture in which people see themselves? Do the tunes that are performed define the attendees? Do they listen to these tunes at home or go to the concerts, movies, or the theater, where they hear them in their original contexts? Do people read the books, wear the clothes, or drive the cars shown in those music videos, major motion pictures, or Broadway shows? What music and entertainment at events are really doing is selling freedom for attendees. The meeting and event industries should tap into a source of great creativity for their functions. That source is entertainment.

We humans are herd animals. We want to feel that we belong to a set group, that we are traveling with the in-crowd. It takes but a few people to start a village. It takes villages of consumers to create a movement. The event entertainment business is animated by trends, trends in our own culture.

It has been heavily documented that music plays a prominent role in promoting consumerism. In department stores, in supermarkets, in car dealerships, music increases sales. So, too, music and entertainment can play a prominent role in events. In his book, *The Entertainment Economy: How Mega-Media Forces Are Transforming Our Lives,* Michael Wolf states that the entertainment industry is a $480 billion business with a possible growth of 50 percent per year over the next five years. Americans spend 58 percent of their waking time interacting with media. This makes entertainment the world's largest economy.

Entertainment Everywhere

During a field trip to Rio de Janeiro, Brazil, students (future event professionals) from The George Washington University were able to study and witness an international citywide event, Carnaval. Their education started immediately upon entering the airplane. Directly in front of each seat was an individual video screen. One can be entertained on a long trip with movies, games, and other interactive devices. Some foreign airlines even offer in-flight gambling. Revenues of $500+ million per year are generated from this type of gambling.

Taking your family out for a drive? Minivans are now equipped with built-in entertainment centers with VCRs, CD/DVD players, and consoles. If you take your family shopping, you will find that many retail establishments have added the total entertainment experience on their floors, which is proven to yield higher revenues. Enhancing the entertainment experience will more likely lead to a new client, whether a retail establishment or convention center; thus, a meeting planner recommending an entertainment experience may ensure a greater return on investment. Enter an upscale apparel store. See the lights, hear the music, touch the furniture, listen to the helpful staff (which could be considered walk-around entertainment), smell the sweet aromas, look, see, and touch the products. Retail establishments now have signature products. The store is now the gatekeeper to a consumer purchaser of long-term allegiance to the retailer's brand. The brand has now established itself not just as a product, but as a way of life. How would you like to set up your company or association's brand with the assistance of entertainment? This book will assist you in accomplishing that task.

A person who enjoys a certain event entertainment experience can be associated with a particular lifestyle, interest group, attitude, educational level, buying behavior, voting habits, and even a set of beliefs. An organization in the twenty-first century must be available in every medium and in every platform. Companies and associations need to seek out new and unique distribution channels. Talent rules. A franchised player on a baseball, football, or basketball team, like a franchised entertainer for a record company, defines the value of the brand. This person is *marquee property,* of exceptional skill and popularity, and whose name is well-recognized. Your CEO may be this person, or it may be the employee or salesperson of the year. Who is your marquee property? Who is your franchised employee?

There are many forms of talent, many genres and categories of music and entertainment. John Sparks, the American Symphony Orchestra League's vice president for public and government affairs, observed that people often contradict themselves. People claim to have many musical tastes, even though, Sparks reports, "98 percent of their musical diet is a single genre." If that is, in fact, the case then you, as meeting and event planners, have a huge complex task on your hands: to accommodate a variety of musical tastes or to find out if that 98 percent agree on a single genre. Sparks continues, "The big problem is not that the major market share out there is primarily devoted to the most popular, commercially viable genres of music, such as rock, country and western, rap, hip-hop, or Latin/salsa. The real problem is that each audience for these forms listens only to one genre, or perhaps two. There may be a determined indifference to, or fear of, other musical forms—and that is what's threatening." (Sparks 2001).

Conduct an individual study on this observation the next time you are in your car and surfing through the radio stations. Do you usually take a tour to see what is being programmed? Do you listen to all the formats? Or do you quickly listen, make an even quicker determination of likes or dislikes, and switch briskly to something you personally like to listen to? This time, pay attention to a variety of stations. As an event planner, you need to know what people are listening to. Do your attendees or registrants prefer a different genre of music or another spoken language? Do they have a diffferent orientation from yours, or possibly a different cultural upbringing? How quickly do you usually "turn" the station and hit the scan button on your radio? The Reverend Jesse Jackson has always called for diversity in his Rainbow Coalition. Can you say that you have this rainbow of diversity in musical appreciation?

Music is a huge part of the world economic value. Retail record sales in the United States were $12.24 billion in 1997, which is about one-third of the $38 billion world record sales, according to the book *This Business of Music (2000).* In 1998, the Recording Industry Association of America (RIAA) Consumer Profile reported that rock, country, and rhythm and blues were the clear favorites of most consumers. It is interesting to note that in procuring music for meetings and events, event managers find that these are also the types of music most often asked for.

Entertainment by the Numbers

According to the *2002 Event Solutions Fact Book: An Annual Statistical Analysis of the Event Industry,* there are roughly 20,000 entertainment companies serving the event industry in the United States. These companies have an average gross revenue of $45 billion, which represents about 12 percent of the total event industry revenue of $389 billion. Michael J. Wolf, in *The Entertainment Economy,* (1999) says that entertainment is a $480 billion industry with a possible growth of 50 percent per year over the next five years. These numbers relate to more than just events. They represent the complete entertainment industry. With these two numbers to compare, it appears that events are a major part of the entire entertainment industry.

The article "Forecast 2002: What's Next for Special Events?" indicates that 7 percent of revenue comes purely from the entertainment event segment and predicts that this entertainment segment will grow by 11 percent in one year. (Hurley 2002). If we were to take a look at opportunities for entertainment at events in the United States, we would find that there are 4.68 million events per year, or 12,840 events every day. The *2002 Event Solutions Fact Book* goes on to say that entertainment companies performing in this arena, on average, have been in business for 14.8 years and have 21.4 employees.

Among entertainment companies, 80.6 percent have their own Web sites. According to *The Meeting Professional,* 75,000 new Web pages are posted each day and 500 million people worldwide will be on-line by 2003 (Chatfield-Taylor 2002). The *2002 Fact Book* reports that, of these entertainment companies, only 22 percent have Web sites from which customers can order their products or services directly. You can expect that entertainment companies today have computers, use the Internet, and have cell phones. More than 60 percent have CD-ROMs, but fewer than 10 percent use any type of management software. Going on the road? About 57 percent of entertainment companies use laptop computers, and 20 percent use handheld palm devices. As time and technology march on, expect all these numbers to rise for entertainment companies and for all companies involved with the meeting and event industries.

Where can you find your favorite entertainment purveyor, and where does it operate? According to *The 2002 Fact Book,* only 16.4 percent are local and 27.8 percent work regionally; 34.4 percent work across the United States and 21.3 percent work internationally. Although the meeting and event industries are predominately staffed by females, the entertainment world is 54 percent male and 46 percent female, with 43.5 percent in the 41 to 50 years age bracket.

What is the primary method for obtaining new customers? Fifty-eight percent of entertainment companies report that client referrals are the ticket. A distant second, at 10.1 percent, say it is national advertising. "The big spenders, in terms of percent of gross sales, are entertainment companies, which spend a sizable 7.6% on marketing" (*2002 Event Solutions Fact Book*). Although 30.2 percent of entertainment companies have a total gross income of less than $250,000, 31.8 percent have more than $1,000,000 in gross revenues and the average for all entertainment companies is $2,800,000.

> In 1999, 33 million tickets were sold to symphony concerts in the United States. In addition, countless numbers of school children heard free concerts given by the local orchestra in their school or local concert hall. The artistic goals and playing standards of every orchestra have been driven upward by the spectacular improvement of the players and the greater discrimination of an audience exposed to the high performance levels of electronic reproduction. Cities that only a few years ago had a semi-professional orchestra that gave a few poorly prepared concerts in an inappropriate venue now have a fine professional orchestra playing a generous schedule of fine concerts in a good sounding, well located concert hall to a broad-based and enthusiastic audience.
>
> —JOSEPH SILVERSTEIN, COMMENCEMENT ADDRESS, MAY 19, 2001,
> CLEVELAND INSTITUTE OF MUSIC

According to Blair Tindall, $1 million was spent on-line for single-ticket sales for the Boston Symphony Orchestra in the three months from its launching in May through July 2001. This 3-month period saw $2.5 million more in total on-line sales for the 2000–01 season. For the Chicago Symphony Orchestra's 2001–02 season, 400,000 registered on-line for season renewals, and 70 percent of the Dallas Symphony Orchestra on-line ticket buyers are new to the orchestra for 2001–02. The San Francisco Symphony's on-line single-ticket sales for the 2000–01 season were double those for 1999–00. The Cincinnati Symphony's on-line sales increased 75 percent during the same time frame, and the Chicago Symphony's on-line sales totaled $800,000—up from $220,000 for the previous season (Tindall, 2001). These figures indicate the broad scope and growth of the event entertainment and production industry. Ticket sales are one tool to measure industry size and growth.

Generation Y: Bridging the Generation Gap for Entertainment at Events

Baby boomers are people born between 1946 and 1964. These people make up approximately 28 percent of the population in the United States, or roughly 78 million people. They are economically empowered, as they include the people now heading up the Fortune 1000 companies. They represent 51 percent of the wealth in the United States, or $2.6 trillion. Now that they feel they have paid their dues, they and their companies have the money to party!

Fast forward to Generation Y. These are people born between 1977 and 1997. They personify multitasking: using the television, DVD player, stereo, and the Internet, all while calling friends on the cell phone. Some may feel this is sensory overload, but this generation sees the context as wallpaper. They have their own music, dress, and Web sites. Watch out for them—they are coming!

The February 2002 issue of *The Meeting Professional* posed the question, "How do you bridge the generation gap when planning entertainment for meeting attendees?" June Marra, CMP, of Pharmacia Corporation in Mississauga, Ontario, Canada, answered,

> *I never use extremes. If we are in the Bahamas, I use local talent that would probably not appeal to any of us on a regular basis but gives attendees the flavor of the area and is more for education than entertainment. While art galleries and sculptures may not appeal to 50% of the attendees, when we go to a gallery and have the artist or sculptor there as a guest to explain the works, it is perceived as having more value. The same is true with sporting events. One of the best events I held had an Olympic theme with an Olympic athlete at every table to serve as a host. The guests were blown away by the stories they heard, even if they did not have any interest in the sport.*

In communicating with large groups of people, several factors come into play, which include demographics such as the audience's age distribution, cultural heritage, interests, and education level. Each of these factors will affect how the audience perceives and interprets the message you are trying to convey. Although it is nearly impossible to tailor a message that will relate positively to each audience member, there are some basic principles of communication that can be followed to ensure that, as much as possible, the message is being understood and perceived positively.

As members of your audience hear your message, they are interpreting it based on their own beliefs, perceptions, and needs. If you are receiving feedback, what is it saying about the needs that are being met and those that are not? It is the needs that are not being met that will convey the best information about your message and are the best indicators of how to tailor your message to meet your audience's needs.

Cultural differences abound within any large audience, so the message should be as culturally generic and unbiased as possible. Although you may not personally agree with a certain culture's beliefs or attitudes, displaying an attitude that is nonjudgmental and accepting will ensure greater audience acceptance.

A nonjudgmental, open attitude will encourage your audience to return the sentiments, and its members will be willing to respond to your message with a higher level of acceptance. Whether you agree with what they do or say on a personal level, to encourage open dialogue and participation, you must abandon judgment and closed-mindedness—and you may learn something in the process.

Audience members will value consistency more than any other quality. They will know and appreciate you for your consistent values, presence, and message, and this will lead them to trust you. Establishing trust with your audience will then allow your message to be heard with expectant ears, because its members know you and know that what you say is true. Even if they do not like what you say, as long as it is consistent and honest, they will listen.

The downside of today's fast-paced communication environment, in which audiences are bombarded with hundreds of thousands of marketing messages every day, is that messages must be formatted to move quickly, so that they can be seen or heard and understood in 30 seconds or less. The objective of every message you send is to capture your audience's attention, generate interest in your subject, and provide enough information so that these people understand the message clearly, want to know more, trust and believe you, and follow through. This is a lot to accomplish in 30 seconds, especially when you are competing with thousands of other messages and trying to reach a very large audience. Thus, it is important to follow basic communication principles, which are more common sense than established procedures, so that those messages that are marketed to mass audiences achieve their desired results. Otherwise, the results could be disastrous. Remember that the Internet has created a global audience, facilitating communications around the world. Listen to your audience, respect and support the beliefs and differences of its mem-

and be consistent, and your message will be heard, understood, and ʳed.

ᴬⁱan L. Eisenstodt, president of Eisenstodt Associates, LLC, Conference ǫement and Consulting, believes there are certain aspects of events that ɂ impacted by generational issues. She shares a few items:

Knowing that an audience might have a great generation mix helps a planner understand more about how to structure a meeting, including meal and recreation planning and speaker selection. It helps a property understand that it might need brighter lights in its guest rooms for older generations of guests.

For association planners, understanding generational differences can mean the difference between a growing, vital organization and one that is withering. Many X- and Y-gens are not "joiners," and thus many associations are going to go out of existence unless they capture the interest of Xs and Ys now.

Joan Eisenstodt and Ann Fishman conducted a workshop for state chapter administrators of a major medical association to help them understand how to attract different generations to their brand. Last spring, Ron Zemke, one of the authors of "Generations at Work," and Joan Eisenstodt held a session for the Greater Washington Society of Association Executives (GWSAE) entitled "It's Not Your Grandfather's Annual Meeting Any More," which dealt specifically with meetings. They found that the audience could offer many examples of what can be improved when generations are considered.

Understanding the audience makeup is important in planning a meeting. It helps in selecting a site, planning sessions and recreation, selecting speakers, and presenting marketing materials.

The Destination as Entertainment: Using Theme-Prepared Cities Around the Globe

Special entertainment beyond the usual dance band or string trio brought in to provide background music can also be a factor in the selection of a site.

—ALAN L. WENDROFF, FUND-RAISING CONSULTANT,
LECTURER, AND WRITER

How many events are created "from scratch," with thousands of dollars spent, for example, on transforming a ballroom into a magical diversion? The concept is what is important here, not the actual act of doing it oneself, but as Alan Wendroff suggests, music can influence site decisions. It is the escape mechanism we all search for—that is the destination. As an event moves around a region or a country, why not utilize what is already set up for you in a particular town, city, or region? Why reinvent the wheel when so much may already be in place? Why reinvent Broadway if your event is already in New York City? Take your attendees to a real Broadway show.

A concern may be that you want to have control over your guests for networking, award banquets, or seminars. That concern can be lightened by utilizing the many entertainment experiences in theme-prepared chain venues such as the Hard Rock Café, Planet Hollywood, Dave and Buster's, the Rainforest Café, and the House of Blues, to name a few. In regard to hotels, Ian Schrager's properties come to mind—the Delano in Miami, the Mondrian in Hollywood, or the Royalton in New York City. These types of venues ooze with entertainment.

Judy Jacobs writes in *Meeting News,*

> *St. Louis is relying on the likes of Johnnie Johnson, the St. Louis Symphony, and late jazz great Miles Davis to help promote the city as a meeting destination. The three musical icons are part of the St. Louis Convention and Visitors Commission's (CVC) campaign to encourage planners to take a new look at the city. The CVC sent a select group of planners CDs of the works of these St. Louis musicians who have helped put the city in the forefront of American music. While the mailings covered most of what St. Louis has to offer, it is music and the role it played in the city's history that set the city apart. Carole Moody, the president of the St. Louis Convention and Visitors Commission well understands the power of marketing through emotion by using music to promote her destination. According to Moody, "We take Johnnie Johnson, who wrote a lot of Chuck Berry's [another St. Louis resident] music, to perform at promotions and according to the St. Louis Blues Society, there are more working blues musicians in St. Louis than anywhere else in the world."*
>
> *St. Louis, in fact, played a starring role in the history of American music. It was in the river city that Scott Joplin composed some of his most famous ragtime tunes, and where blues musicians from the Mississippi Delta adopted elements of ragtime to create the distinctive musical style known as St. Louis blues. And it was St. Louis that was, along with Memphis, the birthplace of rhythm and blues in the 1940s and 1950s, with locals Ike and Tina Turner leading the way. Meeting and convention groups can incorporate an exhibition entitled* A Miles Davis Retrospective, *hosted by the Missouri History Museum into their programs. They can handle from 12–600 guests.*

In her article Jacobs also reminds us about the Scott Joplin House State Historic Site, located in midtown St. Louis. The city opened a new venue, the Rosebud Café, in February 2001. It is not a working restaurant but a recreation of the historic St. Louis café where the best ragtime musicians performed at the turn of the century. "The Rosebud," Jacobs explains, "is in a two-story building on a site next to the home where Joplin lived from 1900 to 1903, the most musically productive years of his life. In addition, planners may want to consider Powell Symphony Hall, a music-inspired venue with a classical bent. What now serves as home to the city's acclaimed St. Louis Symphony originally opened in 1925 as a movie and Vaudeville palace. The facility includes a 2,700-seat auditorium [and] a grand foyer accommodating up to 400 guests." St. Louis has been able to effectively advertise its unique entertainment options in order to attract meeting planners to the city.

In an October 1999 address to the City Club of Cleveland, David Cerone, president of the Cleveland Institute of Music, noted,

Cities must consistently renew themselves and must be comprehensive in what they offer their citizens. Cities cannot stress stadiums over schools. They must stress stadiums and schools

and great musical organizations
and responsive government
and great museums
and thrilling architecture
and first-rate libraries
and theater
and teaching and research hospitals
and financial services
and a diverse religious community
and philanthropic individuals, corporations, and foundations
and health and human services
and a strong public transportation infrastructure
and yes, great airports!

So whether you go to Chicago for the blues, Las Vegas to ride the gondolas at the Venetian's Grand Canal Shoppes, Nashville for Opryland and country music, Australia for Abba, opera, or "Waltzing Matilda," Cuba for Gloria Estefan's "Mi Tierra," Israel for history, Germany for Bayreuth, Poland to experience "feast music" (Polka music enjoyed with food), or Russia to visit the Hermitage, you will find that your destination has its own unique entertainment experience to offer your attendees.

Certainly, a casino night works in Las Vegas, a Western party is perfect for Scottsdale, and a luau is a natural in Maui. But what happens when a majority of the attendees have been there—and done precisely that—one too many times? Or perhaps the meeting is being held in a place with no natural theme tie-ins and few natural charms. Such a destination may then pose a challenge.

In March 2002, *Meetings and Conventions* asked a number of event planners to share their thoughts. The following are their responses:

- *Utilizing a museum theme.* Around the perimeters of a ballroom are "living works of art"—groups of actors who keep very still, each group standing or sitting within a large gold frame atop a riser. The evening also can feature tableaux of famous works of art, each a replica of a painting or sculpture featuring actors made up and costumed to resemble the subjects of the original pieces. The various scenes are narrated by a host, who gives the audience some background on the works and the artists who created them. A classical music quartet, or even a small symphony, adds the perfect musical note for the evening.
- *The Sopranos.* Throughout the venue, guests interact with people made up as *Sopranos* look-alikes, get customized license plates supposedly made by penitentiary inmates, collect fake IDs and passports, or grab a cigar from the stogie stand. Centerpieces are lower halves of torsos—both trouser-clad males and shapely feminine legs decked out in various moll-style getups. Entertainment is supplied by a band or a deejay playing Frank Sinatra, Dean Martin, Bobby Darin, and, of course, the *Sopranos* theme song. Italian food—heavy on the red sauce—and wines complement the event.
- *Fiesta Latina.* The next best thing to being in an exotic place is enjoying the foods and music of the culture. And those pleasures can be replicated practically anywhere. The Fort Lauderdale–based special events firm Comcor, Inc., invites groups to savor the many delights of Latin American nations such as Brazil, Cuba, Mexico, and Peru. For entertainment, music can run the gamut from Brazilian jazz to hot Cuban beats, from mariachi brass to soft woodwinds from Peru.

"If You Ask Me," a column appearing in the March 2000 issue of *MIC* asked, "What's your best attendance-boosting strategy?" Joan Ann Dougherty of Austin Meeting Services in Melville, New York, responded, "My best strategy is a great location where families can tag along such as Orlando or Las Vegas, where there is great entertainment."

In the March 2000 issue of *Meetings South,* contributing editor, Judy Jacobs wrote, "Planners who strive for the new and unusual are sure to be a success—you can take it to the bank." She went on to write about the experience one witnesses at a specific destination. "Groups who meet in Texas prefer an authentic experience, and no venue is more typically Texan than a cattle ranch."

Jacobs gave another example of the destination as entertainment. "Daytona, Florida, offers a souped-up special venue in the form of the Daytona International Speedway, home of the famed Daytona 500 and Pepsi 400 races, among other events." According to Holli Harris-Hyatt in the same article, "Daytona USA is the only theme park of its kind in the country, so that gives meeting planners something that's entirely unique. It's not the 'same old, same old.' "

A popular destination is Nashville, Tennessee, home to a number of country music stars. If you speak with a local destination management company, it can arrange for you to meet a celebrity right in his or her own home. Of course, you can always, through your favorite music purveyor, book that name entertainer to perform at your event for all of your group. In Atlanta, Georgia, according to Vicki Foley, sales manager of the Atlanta History Center, "the most typical theme is Southern, with a Southern menu and people dressing up as Scarlett and Rhett to greet."

Contributing editor of *Corporate and Incentive Travel* Marie Doyle (2002) observed, "No matter what exciting, exotic location your group may be in, a meeting room is a meeting room. But a function in an unconventional setting will add pizzazz to an event and make it a truly memorable experience." Why not use your destination city as the entertainment and make it "a truly memorable experience?

Karl Nybergh, CMP, Ellen Larkin, CMP, and Willie Garcia Jr., all partners in American Meetings and Conventions (AM&C), headquartered in Miami, Florida, have thoughts on their location as a destination: "From the Dolphins to the Marlins, to the ocean and South Beach, to warm winter days and nights, Miami has it all." Meredith Anderson, Registered Meeting Planner, vice president, and Shelli Sutton-Steinberg, director of special events at ViewPoint International Destination Management Services located in New York City, Washington, D. C., and Los Angeles, say, "Let us show off our destinations to you for the delivery of the total entertainment experience."

Scripts for Future Study

BOOKS

(2002). *Sports Sponsorship and Brand Development: The Subaru and Jaguar Stories.* New York: Beck-Burridge, Martin, and Jeremy Walton Palgrave.
   Written by a British professor and a freelance writer and originally published in the United Kingdom in 2001, this book looks at the European motor sports campaigns of Subaru and Jaguar.
(2001). *Brand Warfare: 10 Rules for Building the Killer Brand.* D'Alessandro, David F. New York: McGraw-Hill Professional Publishing.
   David D'Alessandro has transformed John Hancock from a clubby, play-it-safe mutual company to a leading publicly traded financial services group where accountability, integrity, and growth are hallmarks. Marketing has played a critical role in the company's transformation. Unlike other life insurance companies, Hancock is led by a CEO who understands branding and embraces big ideas. D'Alessandro, who engineered Hancock's double-digit growth rate at a time when

many of its competitors were going under, is almost as well known for his pioneering moves in the world of sports marketing and sponsorship. Under his direction, Hancock became the first major sponsor—and savior—of the Boston Marathon, the first to completely rename a college football bowl game for the sponsor, the first in the insurance category to become a worldwide Olympic partner, and the first sponsor to stand up to the International Olympic Committee (IOC) in the midst of its bribery scandal over bribes and say: "This will not stand. Change your ways or suffer the consequences." Anyone in marketing, advertising, sponsorship, or communications should read *Brand Warfare*.

OTHER PUBLICATIONS

Entertainment Marketing Letter is a monthly newsletter published by EPM Communications. It provides industry data, such as cost analyses of entertainment marketing, a calendar of events, industry news and trends, and listings of contacts at key companies. Phone: 212-941-0099.

PROMO, a monthly publication, defines promotion trends, presents critical how-to information and case studies about promotion, and serves as a meeting ground for companies and professionals in the industry. Visit www.promomagazine.com.

INTERNET RESOURCES

American Meetings and Conventions, Inc. (AM&C), www.amcfl.com, is a full-service destination and meeting management company located in Miami, Florida. As one of the leading destination management companies (DMC) in the state of Florida, AM&C takes pride in its ability to provide the customer with high-quality, imaginative, well-organized, and cost-effective programs in the areas of destination management, conferences, conventions, trade shows, special events, and association management.

Association of Destination Management Executives (ADME), www.adme.org. Founded in 1995, the ADME is a relatively new, yet fast-growing organization. Its mission is to increase the professionalism and effectiveness of destination management through education, promotion of ethical practices, and availability of information to the meeting, convention, and incentive travel industry and the general public.

Exit Stage Right

As you proceed to Chapter 2, you will be introduced to international destinations and entertainment opportunities around the world. The chapter also discusses parades, fairs, and festivals, some of the most common international events.

CHAPTER 2

Global Opportunities for Event Entertainment and Production

There was a sound of revelry by night,
And Belgium's capital had gathered then
Her beauty and her chivalry, and bright
The lamps shone o'er fair women and brave men.
A thousand hearts beat happily; and when
Music arose with its voluptuous swell . . .

—GEORGE NOEL GORDON, LORD BYRON:
CHILDE HAROLD'S PILGRIMAGE, CANTO I, ST. 2

IN THIS CHAPTER YOU WILL DISCOVER

- How to develop themes and venues for parades, fairs, and festivals.
- Basic considerations for public events and how to organize them.
- Audience expectations for parades, fairs, and festivals and the factors you should consider in meeting these expectations.
- Opportunities to practice event management through international festivals and fairs.

Music is a voluptuous sound that can be heard around the world through entertainment at events, especially at parades, festivals, and fairs. These types of events can create multifaceted entertainment productions that will attract large crowds, support communities, and provide opportunities for business growth and tourism. They are events that require a great deal of planning, coordination, and communication on many levels. Because of the increased security and liability concerns, many city governments are hiring professional event planners to orchestrate these events, creating even more opportunities in this industry. Whether you are planning a small community parade or are participating in some of the world's most celebrated parade events, the key elements to delivering a successful event are planning, organization, and communication.

Parades, Fairs, and Festivals

Parades, fairs, and festivals are particular types of themed events that may simultaneously contain historical, cultural, ceremonial, religious, patriotic, and social themes. Although they differ to a certain degree in form and content, they share several characteristics. First, they are all events that are open to the general public. They will thus generate large crowds and require special planning and coordination. Second, unlike private events, they occur in large public venues and require communication and planning with local governmental agencies and may also require special licenses and permissions. Third, they can have historical roots within a community, such as the Tournament of Roses Parade in Pasadena, California, a 113-year-old tradition. This element of tradition means that there will be strong emotional ties to the event that will have to be considered and respected in the planning process.

Despite their similarities, each of these event types has a particular inherent thematic element. Many parades are family-oriented events that offer free entertainment to the general public, centered on a procession of both individuals and groups of people, sometimes in costume, with bands and/or other music, baton twirlers, and visual elements such as large balloons. There are exceptions to the family theme, such as the New Orleans Mardi Gras parades that encourage drinking, revelry, and feasting prior to the 40-day Catholic Lenten fast. Internationally, parades may commemorate special religious holidays or saints' birthdays, such as the Day of the Dead in Mexico. Various entries that may be in a parade are shown in Figure 2-1.

Fairs and festivals are other entertainment options within this genre that feature themed entertainment for the general public. Fairs have not varied much from their roots over the centuries and are generally oriented toward agriculture, featuring crafts, agricultural displays, food, and entertainment. This genre includes state and county fairs, which are regular annual events often dating back to the time of a community's settlement.

- *Marching Musical Units*—School Bands, Drum Corps, Independent Bands.
- *Floats*—Creatively built and decorated moving vehicle. Professional and amateur-built floats are accepted.
- *Specialty Acts*—Drill and Dance Teams, Clowns, Balloons, Antique/Specialty Vehicles.
- *Equestrian*—Equestrian Teams, Horse-Drawn Carriages.
SPECIAL GUESTS—Invited Guests, Dignitaries, Celebrities.

Figure 2-1

Types of Entries Considered for a Parade

(Reprinted with permission of Convene Magazine, *published by Professional Convention Management Association. Copyright 2003 PCMA. www.pcma.org)*

A festival as defined in *the International Dictionary of Event Management, 2nd edition* (2000), is "a public celebration that conveys, through a kaleidoscope of activities, certain meanings to participants and spectators." They can mark religious or other cultural events, focus tightly on a central theme, such as music, crafts, food, or wine, and may last more than one day, such as the Greek Bacchus festivals, which may last two or three days. Understanding the thematic element inherent in events of this type is important, as the audience will expect a specific type of event if it is promoted as a parade as opposed to a fair or festival.

These types of events can also be combined. For example, a parade can end with a fair or a festival, and a fair or festival can feature a parade as part of its activities. Combining event types can extend a parade into an all-day celebration for the audience, which can generate additional revenue for the parade and benefit local businesses and other groups. Ray Pulver of Upbeat Parade Productions gives an example of how a parade can become a multipronged event. He describes how California's Oakland Tribune Holiday Parade has created a successful combination of events by inviting the public to an "inflation celebration" the evening before the parade, where they can watch the large balloons for the parade being filled. The parade organizers bring in crafts and food vendors and encourage people to stay and mix with the parade participants. On the following day the parade is held from noon to two o'clock, ending in a small festival on the waterfront, where participants are entertained by various performers and can purchase food and souvenirs from vendors. Then, at dusk, there is a lighted yacht parade on the bay that ends the event. The parade therefore becomes a multiday, all-day event that benefits many vendors and businesses in the area. It is also used to promote tourism in the area, and the parade planner works closely with the region's tourism board, thus increasing event attendance.

There is also an expectation of continuity with a fair or festival or a parade, which may have been attended by several generations. Any of these events can be held on a regular basis, annually, seasonally, or coinciding with another relevant event. Most important, parades, festivals, and fairs are all about having fun, and that concept is central to the planning process.

CREATING PARADES, FAIRS, AND FESTIVALS

There are few events as inspiring as a parade, with its music, costumes, floats, balloons, and crowds. Parades are American institutions that embody generations of culture, tradition, patriotism, and family values. Long-standing parades, such as Macy's Thanksgiving Day Parade and the Pasadena Tournament of Roses Parade, have not changed in theme, venue, style, or content during the generations they have entertained, yet they retain their popularity.

Although parades (and fairs and festivals) may appear to be inherently uncomplicated to the viewing crowd, in truth, the planning process is very complex and involves the efforts of thousands of people coordinating with government agencies, business owners, residents, and city departments and staff. Ray Pulver estimates that a parade with 100 entries will have more than 5000 participants. It has become such a complex process that many parade organizers hire professional event planners to coordinate their efforts.

Creating New Themes

What does it take to create a new parade, fair, festival? Parades traditionally have patriotic, religious, or cultural themes, so how can you create a tradition for a community? To create a fair or a festival, determine what is currently popular, in demand, or interesting about the community. Use that information to create an event that will inspire, inform, educate, or just satisfy curiosity. Ira Rosen, president of Entertainment on Location, says that it is possible to create a successful parade event for a community by developing a theme for the parade around an already popular concept, such as Christmas, and then enlisting a media company, such as a television or radio station or a newspaper, to act as sponsor and heavily promote and advertise the event. Rosen's company was responsible for the recent introduction of a Christmas parade in San Juan, Puerto Rico, complete with marching bands, baton twirlers, floats, balloons, and Santa Claus. The parade was very successful and is destined to be a yearly event.

Funding a Parade, Fair, or Festival

Parades are not known as big money makers but they can, with proper planning, be self-funding and even profitable. Ray Pulver says that corporate sponsorships are an important source of funding for parades, as well as other events. Companies realize many benefits from sponsoring these events, as they include a display of community involvement, an opportunity to market their business, and team building among employees through their efforts in constructing floats. According to Pulver, companies such as Home Depot, Southwest Airlines, and AT&T generously sponsor many community (and larger) parades, fairs, and festivals, alongside local businesses.

Further sources of revenue include paid admissions, entry fees for floats, food and souvenir concessions, and partnerships with other events. Television coverage can also generate revenue for a parade and larger parades can tie a television package into the entry fee. In some cases, without corporate sponsorships a small community's parade tradition could not continue. According to Toni Bodenhamer of Toni Bodenhamer & Company, an event and parade planner in Santa Rosa, California, a decrease in volunteer availability and an increase in security costs and liability insurance expenses have forced parade organizers to seek corporate sponsors as sources of funding on an even greater scale.

Organizing a Parade, Fair, or Festival

"Parades appear to have an invisible structure," says Toni Bodenhamer. "They appear to be magical, as they come out of nowhere and then go away." Generally, the sense of an invisible structure is a compliment to the planner's efforts. Small parades may take as much as a year or more to plan, and larger parades, such as the Macy's Thanksgiving Day Parade, may take two to three years. A parade planner should allow a minimum of 12 months to plan, says Ira Rosen. Although a parade can be delivered in less time, the coordination effort suffers and that can cause problems. The parade planner must coordinate with a city's events department, police, fire and emergency services, the departments of public works, transportation, and sanitation, and local residents and businesses. Such coordination can ensure that the parade does not conflict with other events, that there is adequate police availability for crowd control and other security services, that the parade route is not encumbered by road construction, buses, or garbage trucks, and that traffic control systems are in place. Finally, local residents and businesses on the parade route must be notified so that they know that their streets may be blocked or closed for a few hours.

This level of coordination takes time and planning, so adequate lead time is essential. Ira Rosen states that city departments can be very cooperative as long as they are given adequate time to accommodate requests. And, because parades are annual events, establishing strong relationships with clear communication is essential to ensuring that each parade is successful. The same holds true for fairs and festivals and any event that is open to the general public.

Ask the Old-Timers

Many parades, fairs, and festivals have a long-standing tradition and a host of participants who have been with the event for many years. For example, at the Waterford Fair, held annually in Waterford, Virginia, a particular craftsperson had been attending the event regularly for 56 years. Such participants can be a valuable source of information for you, as the event planner, as they can advise you on any number of issues that can help you make the event more successful, including crowd sizes, the popularity of certain events or items, weather patterns, or any problems that have occurred in the past. If data from earlier event planners is unavailable or unreliable, the assistance of veteran participants will be even more valuable.

Permission, Protection, and Port-A-Potties

Because all of these events are venues that are open to the general public, the event manager must ensure that proper licenses are obtained and that any applicable local ordinances and laws are respected. In addition, any restrictions regarding alcohol, noise, or curfews must be observed. If an event is to be held on an annual basis, it is not advisable to cause problems for the community and expect to be invited back. Depending on the popularity and size of the parade, community officials, emergency and police personnel, and sanitation crews will be part of the planning process. As can be expected, the larger and more popular the event, the more people will be in attendance, increasing the need for everything from police to sanitary facilities to street cleaners.

Every public event requires some type of security presence, providing crowd control and oversight. In the past, off-duty police officers or police volunteers who used vacation time to work a parade or a fair may have provided this service. Today, labor contracts and liability risks have made this practice obsolete. Event planners must now hire security for their events, adding to their costs. Detective Brad Stevens, a 20-year veteran of the Fresno, California, Police Department concurs: "Parade permit holders are utilizing event planners now for all elements of coordinating and producing our parades." The liability insurance that event planners must provide has tripled or quadrupled in cost in recent years, says one parade planner, adding even more to a parade's financial burden.

Parades, fairs, and festivals can generate huge crowds of people who will, at some point, have to respond to the "call of nature." Providing adequate sanitary facilities ensures that event attendees will spend their time enjoying the event, not waiting in line to use the facilities. Accurately estimating these requirements may be difficult, but in this case, it is better to err on the side of caution. Ira Rosen suggests that an experienced parade planner will be able to estimate crowd sizes with 80 percent accuracy and should then overestimate port-a-potty needs by 50 to 60 percent. He indicates that it is better to send back unused Port-A-Potties than to have the event sponsor receive complaints about the lack of facilities, which will also reflect badly on the event planner.

When Mother Nature Is Uncooperative

It would be nice if every event had perfect weather, but that is not always the case. The possibility of inclement weather is an inherent risk with every event, so it needs to be part of the contingency plan. Is the event to be held rain or shine? And do all event participants know and expect that? Ray Pulver moved his event planning business from Massachusetts to California and was surprised to learn that California event participants did not march in the rain. While working in Massachusetts, he had held events in all kinds of weather, including rain, snow, and sleet. He made sure that his California parade participants understood that his events were held rain or shine and that they were expected to march in the rain or any other inclement weather.

If this is true of your event, then it should be included in all of the advertising and explained to all event participants. Plans must be made for inclement weather, including how bad the weather has to be for the event to shut down. If the weather turns cold, is there someone who can sell hot chocolate? Will there be a place for attendees to find shelter, including parents and small children? If you are lucky, the event will occur under perfect skies. If not, you need to be prepared for anything Mother Nature may send your way.

Parade Traditions

We're resilient; this is New Orleans. But how are we just going to wait for days and days until the next parade? We need our fix.
—Arthur Hardy, publisher of a Mardi Gras guide, upon the city's decision to stop Mardi Gras parades during Super Bowl weekend

Arthur Hardy accurately describes the sentiments of every parade junkie, who lives for the mix of sound, color, and emotion that is a parade. What makes parades so special? Perhaps it is because many parades, such as those of Mardi Gras, represent a continuity of culture, history, and tradition that is representative of our communities, those places to which we can always return with the wonder, anticipation, and excitement of our childhood years. It is often possible to bring our children and grandchildren to the same parades that we participated in as children. Parades can have many different themes, as seen in the wild abandon of Mardi Gras, the small family-oriented community celebration of Tibloe Days in Bonner Springs, Kansas, or the carefully orchestrated Macy's Thanksgiving Day Parade.

Parades are a quintessentially American type of celebration. They have come to represent a sense of community, as eloquently expressed by Toni Bodenhamer, a parade and event planner in California, "Parades are a way for a community to get together and clap for each other." Ira Rosen says that, if anything, parades are more popular than ever, and the summer of 2002 saw larger-than-normal crowds. He attributes the phenomenon to a post–September 11, 2001, increase in patriotism, civic pride, and a desire of community members to reestablish traditions and relationships within their communities.

Parades, fairs, and festivals provide unique opportunities for the event planning industry, because they will probably not be one-time events, as are many of the events you will plan. This means that the theme, structure, and timing of the event will not change. Whether you are planning a new parade or producing one that has been a regular community event for the past hundred years, it will basically remain the same in the future. Once you have developed a theme and the timing for a new parade, fair, or festival, it can become an annual event that will not change substantially from year to year or event to event. For these types of events in particular, audiences look forward to and plan to attend the next event before the current one is over. They also have an expectation of continuity and will expect the theme, venue, and event participants and features to remain constant (for example, the same craftsperson or the same types of crafts, foods, and music).

In the United States there are a number of noteworthy parades, including the Shriner's Parade in Philadelphia, the Rose Bowl Parade in Pasadena, the Macy's Thanksgiving Day Parade in New York City, and, of course, there are the parades for the "World Champion" professional sports teams. Yet perhaps none is more prominent than the 12-day parade we call Mardi Gras in New Orleans. New Orleans held its first Mardi Gras parade with floats in 1839 to celebrate food and fun before commencing the 40 days of Lent. Its two major modern parades, Endymion and Bacchus, feature a combined total of 75 floats and 60 marching bands.

According to the Associated Press, "Super Bowl XXXVI has been allowed to shatter a central feature of its [the Super Bowl's] distinguished and delirious history. The Carnival season, the ancient and chaotic period of besotted parades leading up to Mardi Gras, has been cut in half by a football game." In 2002, for the first time in 145 years, there was a weeklong break within the 12-day continuous round of parades and parties that precede the Lenten season in New Orleans while the National Football League concluded its business of selecting a champion. The bifurcation became inevitable after the league canceled games the weekend after the September 11 terrorist attacks, forcing it to postpone the Super Bowl by a week and impinging on an unusually early Mardi Gras season. Sam Scandaliato, a captain of a parade crew, says, "For us, the Super Bowl is just the halftime show. Then the game goes on." This is an excellent example of a community's attachment to a parade. Mardi Gras is a New Orleans tradition, one that its citizens were not willing to sacrifice in the face of another great American tradition, the Super Bowl. Yet although we consider parades to be part of American culture and tradition, they enjoy worldwide popularity. Many international parades and festivals are centuries-old traditions within their communities, such as Carnaval and Oktoberfest (Firestone 2002).

International Opportunities in Event Entertainment

According to a *Convene Magazine* survey, half of the responding associations consider holding future meetings outside the United States, a figure that remains constant from year to year. However, among associations that describe themselves as "international" or "national," the figure climbs to 65 percent.

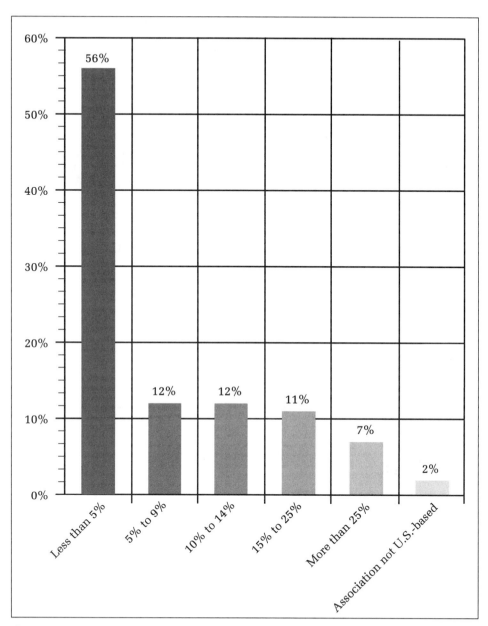

Figure 2-2
What Percentage of Your Membership Is Based Outside the United States?
(Reprinted with permission of Convene Magazine, *published by Professional Convention Management Association. Copyright 2003 PCMA. www.pcma.org)*

What has changed is where they are focusing their attention. Asia, which only a year ago was being considered by 37 percent of respondents, saw a precipitous drop to 22 percent. South America and Eastern Europe also experienced severe declines. Although Western Europe, Mexico, the United Kingdom, Australia, and Bermuda retained their relative positions, the Caribbean was the only international destination to post an actual year-to-year gain.

Figures 2-2 through 2-8 provide statistics on the probability of associations holding events outside the United States. Although it seems that many organizations are still resistant to this possibility, there is an increasing trend toward international participation at events in the United States. It is equally important for event planners to understand the implications of holding an event abroad as it is for them to consider the needs of foreign visitors at events. As the use of technology increases and global travel becomes more common, it will be increasingly important for event managers to take advantage of opportunities in international events as a way of reaching a larger audience.

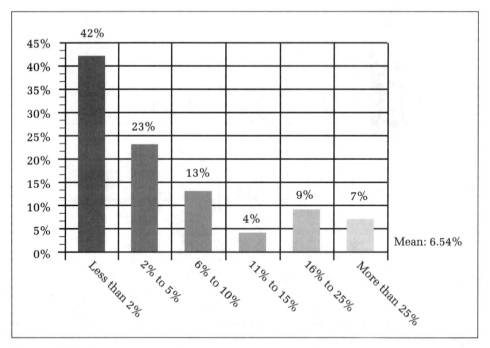

Figure 2-3

What Percentage of Registered Attendees at Your Largest 1999 Event Was International?

(Reprinted with permission of Convene Magazine, *published by Professional Convention Management Association. Copyright 2003 PCMA. www.pcma.org)*

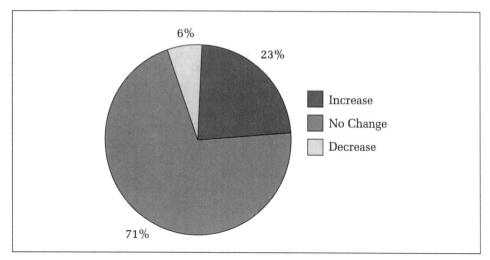

Figure 2-4
How Did the International Attendance at Your Largest 1999 Event Compare with That in 1998?

(Reprinted with permission of Convene Magazine, *published by Professional Convention Management Association. Copyright 2003 PCMA. www.pcma.org)*

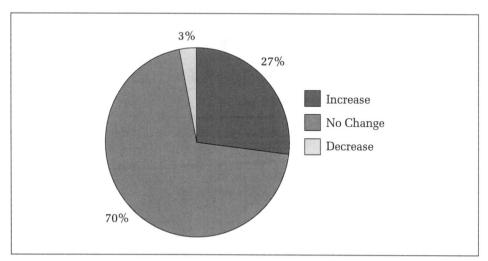

Figure 2-5
What Was Your Projection for 2000 International Attendance (versus 1999)?

(Reprinted with permission of Convene Magazine, *published by Professional Convention Management Association. Copyright 2003 PCMA. www.pcma.org)*

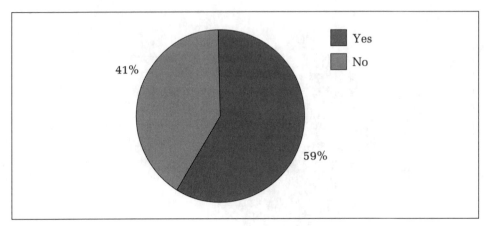

Figure 2-6
Has Your Association Ever Held a Meeting Outside the United States?
(Reprinted with permission of Convene Magazine, *published by Professional Convention Management Association. Copyright 2003 PCMA. www.pcma.org)*

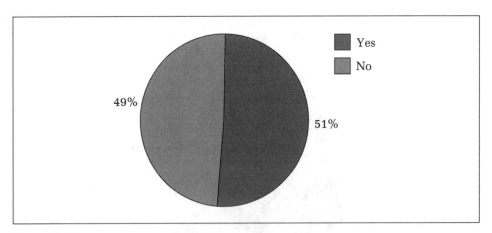

Figure 2-7
Does Your Organization Plan to Hold a Future Meeting Outside the United States?
(Reprinted with permission of Convene Magazine, *published by Professional Convention Management Association. Copyright 2003 PCMA. www.pcma.org)*

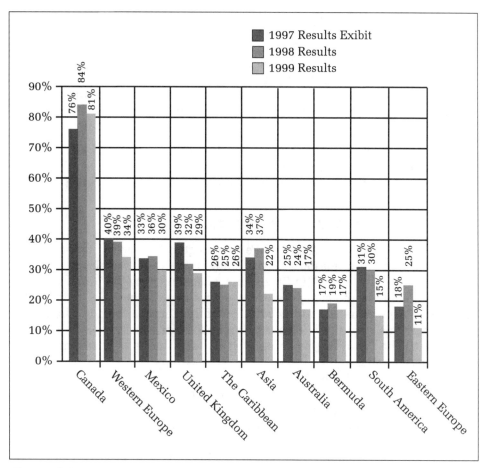

Figure 2-8
Which Destinations Are You Considering for a Future Meeting?
(Reprinted with permission of Convene Magazine, *published by Professional Convention Management Association. Copyright 2003 PCMA. www.pcma.org)*

International Events

In his book *Event Management and Event Tourism*, Donald Getz states,

> *The meetings and conventions, and trade and consumer shows held at special purpose facilities are major elements in a destination's event portfolio. But these facilities also have potential as*

international festival and special event venues, and there is much scope for packaging special events around conferences, meetings, and expositions. Without doubt, convention-goers examine the recreational and entertainment potential of a destination before deciding to attend, and organizers often choose their sites with this in mind. What better way to attract major conventions and meetings, therefore, than to add festivals and events directly to the package?

This section explores some specific examples of international events that have received major recognition for their entertainment. They illustrate the variety of events that exist and can give you ideas for themes for your own events.

CARNAVAL IN RIO DE JANEIRO, BRAZIL

As a faculty advisor with The George Washington University, the author accompanied a group of master's degree students to Rio de Janeiro to study international citywide events. In Brazil, this meant studying the "Carnaval." The Winners' Parade is the signature event with all of the best floats and entertainment. This parade was for the winners of the Carnaval parade held a week earlier and consisted of five Samba Schools. It started just after sundown and lasted until the following morning. It truly was the best entertainment the country had to offer.

Near Rio de Janeiro is the Maracan Football Stadium, a sports arena that can be readily adapted for various types of events, using modular units to create different settings. This is a large venue with a capacity of 120,000. "As the largest market in South America, Brazil represents the next logical step in the global expansion [of the entertainment industry]," said Brian Becker, chairman/CEO of Clear Channel Entertainment. "Brazil is a country with a rich culture of supporting live music, sports, and other events, and we look forward to bringing international stars and local talent to Brazil's stages, as well as exposing Brazilian artists to audiences around the world for many years to come."

OKTOBERFEST IN GERMANY

Oktoberfest, a procession of national costumes, has been taking place regularly since 1950. There are 7500 costumed participants from every federal state in Germany, as well as groups from Bulgaria, France, Italy, the Netherlands, Austria, Switzerland, the Czech Republic, Hungary, and the Ukraine, who march through Munich to the Oktoberfest Pavilion. The German ARD public TV channel broadcasts the event live to stations all over the world. It is a major attraction not only among the local communities, but for tourists from all over the world.

THE BIGGEST ROCK CONCERT EVER IN BRITAIN

Buckingham Palace celebrated 50 years of the rule of Queen Elizabeth II with an all-star rock concert featuring Sir Paul McCartney, 12,000 invited subjects, and an estimated one million people who lined the streets to watch the show on large screens to witness this historical performance. This was a monumental combination of event entertainment and production, with complex logistics involved to bring in the superstars of entertainment and show the live event to the approximately one million people.

EUROPEAN SONG CONTEST, HOSTED BY ESTONIA

In 2002, the 47th annual Eurovision Song Contest was held in Tallinn, Estonia's 10,000-seat Suurhall, bringing groups from 24 countries who competed for the votes of as many as 300 million television viewers in their quest to be named the tops in pop. This annual contest has become must-see television for millions in Europe and beyond. On an international scale, this event could be billed as the Olympics of the European music industry, providing media attention and promoting tourism to the host area, generating millions in revenues for local businesses, including hotels, restaurants, and shops.

OLYMPIC OPENING CEREMONY: HIGHEST-RATED EVER

"We have to be concerned about not focusing too much on America. We have to emphasize the rest of the world. The world expects an international event," said Don Mischer, producer of the Olympics' opening ceremony, concerning the impact of September 11, 2001. A quarter of the country watched NBC's first broadcast of the 2002 Winter Olympics, making it the highest-rated opening ceremony ever. Each night during the February 2002 Olympic Winter Games in Salt Lake City, different bands took center stage at the Olympic Medals Plaza for a free one-hour concert. These artists included a superstar lineup of today's rock, pop, and country talent, including the Dave Matthews Band, Foo Fighters, Barenaked Ladies, Sheryl Crowe, Smash Mouth, Brooks and Dunn, Train, Creed, Marc Anthony, 'N Sync, and Martina McBride.

ICELAND AND THE DOMINICAN REPUBLIC

The Society of Incentive and Travel Executives (SITE) announced two emerging destinations, Iceland and the Dominican Republic, as the settings for the 2003 SITE University and International Conference. SITE University will be held at the Melia Caribe Tropical in Punta Cana, Dominican Republic, and the SITE 2003 International Conference will be held at the Hotel Esja in Reykjavik, Iceland. "Both the Dominican Republic and Iceland are poised and ready to move their products into the glare of the incentive spotlight," says Peggy

Whitman, president of SITE. "Firsthand inspection of promising incentive destinations is an important element and a critical draw for our delegates. I am confident that these destinations will pass muster with our discerning group."

SYDNEY, AUSTRALIA

The International Special Events Society (ISES) chose Sydney as the venue for its global Conference for Professional Development (CPD) in August 2002. It was the first time in the society's 15-year history that the conference had been held outside North America. With the downturn in international visitor numbers since September 11, 2001, the conference spotlighted Sydney as a major international destination, following the success of the 2000 Olympics. According to the Bureau of Tourism Research, the business events industry in Australia is conservatively estimated at $7 billion per annum. On the highly competitive global scene, Australia is ranked fourth worldwide as a convention destination, as shown in a recent International Congress and Convention Association (ICCA) survey.

JOHANNESBURG, SOUTH AFRICA

The City of Johannesburg in South Africa, supported by the Gauteng Tourism Authority, has make a strong bid for Indaba 2004 to 2006. Should Johannesburg be successful in its bid, Indaba—South Africa's premier travel tourism trade show—will be hosted at one of the city's three premier convention centers: Sandton Convention Centre, Gallagher Estates, or the Expo Centre. Johannesburg is confident about its ability to host an event of this size and stature in the future.

DUBAI

Dubai's appeal to meeting planners and industry professionals goes well beyond the convention center's superb high-tech infrastructure and bricks-and-mortar capacity. The Dubai International Convention Centre will be managed by the Dubai World Trade Centre team, an organization that has been at the forefront of the region's exhibition industry for more than two decades. It promises to be a popular location for many international events in years to come.

THE 2008 OLYMPICS—OPPORTUNITIES IN CHINA

Event professionals looking for the latest and greatest emerging location need look no further than Beijing, China, home of the 2008 Summer Olympics. Many hospitality players are already planning to move in, including most of the major hotels and event people working for the World Trade Organization (WTO). A recent study by Jones Lang LaSalle Hotels of the last four summer Olympic host cities—Barcelona, Seoul, Atlanta, and Sydney—shows that all experienced growth in room supply in the two years leading up to the Games and during the years the Olympics were held. Much of the new supply was concentrated in the international-standard segment of 4- and 5-star ratings.

MONTREAL

From November 6 to 11, 2005, Montreal will host the World Travel Congress 2005, a major convention and exhibition of the American Society of Travel Agents. Some 6,000 delegates are expected from all over the world, who will be addressing issues affecting the world travel industry. The Society is the world's largest and most influential travel trade association, with more than 24,000 members in more than 140 countries. This will be an excellent chance for the city to introduce a wide range of industry professionals to its meeting and event facilities.

THE MOULIN ROUGE

Since 1889, the Moulin Rouge, celebrated throughout the world for its cancan dancers and immortalized by Henri de Toulouse-Lautrec, as well as by a major motion picture, has presented spectacular revues featuring feathers and spangles, fabulous decorations, original music, and the most beautiful girls in the world. Many stars of the world have gone through their rites of passage in Paris. Ella Fitzgerald, Liza Minelli, Frank Sinatra, and Elton John have all performed at the Moulin Rouge, as well as many prestigious French artists such as Maurice Chevalier, Jean Gabin, Edith Sparrow, and Yves Montand.

In Conclusion

As evident in the preceding descriptions of past, present, and future events across the world, event entertainment and production is certainly not limited to North America. As the world becomes smaller as a result of technology, an increasing number of event planners will be needed worldwide. Use the resources in the following "Scripts for Future Study" section to learn about new venues and events that will take place in the future so that you, too, can participate in them.

Scripts for Future Study

BOOKS

The following books were written by Roger E. Axtell and published by John Wiley & Sons, Inc.:

Do's and Taboos of Hosting International Visitors (1990)

Do's and Taboos around the World (1993)

Do's and Taboos of Using English around the World (1995)

Gestures: The Do's and Taboos of Body Language around the World (1997)

Cantwell, Robert (1993). *Ethnomimesis: Folklife and the Representation of Culture.* Chapel Hill: University of North Carolina Press. Examines Washington, D.C.'s annual Festival of American Folklife in terms of stereotyping within American history and culture.

McDonnell, Ian, and Johnny Allen (2002). *Festival and Special Event Management.* New York: John Wiley & Sons, Ltd. Written for students of festival and special event management, their teachers, and producers of festivals and events.

Rizzo, Leonard J. (1997). *The Key to Success in Running an Outdoor Festival.* Saint Joseph Publishing. Written for the volunteer director who has never produced a festival.

Taylor, Nelson (2000). *America Bizarro: A Guide to Freaky Festivals, Groovy Gatherings, Kooky Contests, and Other Strange Happenings across the U.S.A.* New York: Griffin Trade Paperback. Celebrates the country's wackiest, most off-the-wall events.

Van, Richard L. (1992). *The Complete Guide to Special Event Management.* Edited by Dwight W. Catherwood. New York: John Wiley & Sons. Inc.

National Trust for Historical Preservation. *Main Street Festivals: Traditional and Unique Events on America's Main Streets,* by Amanda B. West. New York: John Wiley & Sons, Inc. More than 700 special events held on the country's 300+ Main Streets—from Rodeo Stampedes to fruit festivals and winter carnivals. The special events featured in this guide capitalize on local history, popular culture, provincial character, and seasonal themes.

INTERNET RESOURCES

www.unlv.edu/Tourism/etiquette. Etiquette, networking, and protocol, from the University of Nevada at Las Vegas.

www.debretts.co.uk/people/address.asp. Hints on proper international etiquette.

Bank-holidays.com. Provides information on international banking holidays and other major events such as elections, strikes, and riots.

The Association of Festival Organisers (AFO), www.mrscasey.co.uk.

The Association of Irish Festival Events (AOIFE), AOIFEonline.com.

The Italian Music Association, www.assomusica.org.

The European Arenas Association (EAA), www.eaaoffice.org. The EAA represents 18 prestigious arenas in 14 European countries, with a seating capacity of at least 8000 and maintaining high quality standards in all areas.

European Festivals Association (EFA), www.euro-festival.net. The EFA is an organization that coordinates the important festivals in Europe.

The International Association of Convention & Visitor Bureaus (IACVB), www.iacvb.org, represents more than 1050 professional members from more than 450 bureaus in 26 countries. IACVB's member bureaus represent all significant travel/tourism-related businesses at the local and regional levels. They also serve as the primary contact points for their destinations for a broad universe of convention, meeting, and tour professionals.

The International Association of Fairs and Expositions (IAFE), www.fairsandexpos.com, is a voluntary, nonprofit corporation, organizing state, district, and county agricultural fairs, expositions, associations, corporations, and individuals within one large association. Begun in 1885, the IAFE represents more than 1400 fairs in North America and around the world, as well as more than 1500 members from allied fields.

The International Entertainment Buyers Association (IEBA), www.ieba. org, is the only professional nonprofit association dedicated to entertainment buyers; it boasts more than $350 million per year in talent-buying power.

The International Festival and Events Association (IFEA), www.ifea.com, has provided cutting-edge professional development and fund-raising ideas to the special events industry for 45 years. Through publications, seminars, an annual convention and trade show, and ongoing networking, IFEA is advancing festivals and events throughout the world through its membership of 2700 professionals.

Venue Management Association (Asia Pacific) Limited (VMA), www.vma.org.au. The VMA was established to provide information, education, coordination, and management assistance for public venues in the Asia Pacific market.

Victory Corps, www.victorycorps.com. Provides float supplies for parades and has a free e-book containing 136 pages of information for parade planners.

Exit Stage Right

Now that you have an idea of the size and scope of the industry and the many destinations used for entertainment around the globe, how do you become a leader in the event entertainment and production world? Please read on to Chapter 3 to discover how to become a leader in this exciting field.

Becoming a Leader in the Event Entertainment and Production Fields

I think the thing about honors is that you should never ask for them and you should never expect them, but I think you should accept them if they're given to you. It's like a compliment. You should never be churlish about compliments and you should accept them in the same way you should learn to deflect criticism and be impervious to it.

—Sir Mick Jagger on receiving his knighthood from Her Royal Highness Queen Elizabeth II

IN THIS CHAPTER YOU WILL DISCOVER

- How to start your career as a performer.
- How to enter the business of event production.
- How to become a contractor.
- How to make a successful career change to the event planning industry.

Award-winning pianist and conductor Seymour Lipkin once gave this direction to musicians of The National Orchestral Association, "Whenever you pick up your instruments, play them well." The best way to become a leader in the event entertainment and production industry is to always play your instrument well! Whether your instrument is an orchestral one, a rock guitar, a writing instrument like a pen or a calling instrument like a telephone, whenever you do something . . . do it well.

Everyone, at some point, is exposed to entertainment. Entertainment is a fundamental aspect of life on earth. From radio, television, commercials, movies, CDs, comedians, character artists, sound and lighting techniques—from childhood through adulthood, entertainment is part of our daily lives; it defines our culture and is part of our history. Who hasn't heard of or seen The Beatles, The Rolling Stones, *Star Wars,* or *Titanic?* A look at today's television ads will reveal how important music is to the advertising industry. We can say, probably without reservation, that everybody loves music. Although individual tastes in music may differ, most people have their favorites and still remember the words and music to the tunes they grew up with. Who hasn't picked up the air guitar lately, drummed on a desk, or sung in the shower?

The quotes at the beginning of the chapter exemplify the approach that two well-known figures used in order to become successful in their careers. Whether you commence your career as a performer or you start as an intern at a major music agency, the words of Sir Mick Jagger and Seymour Lipkin continue to ring true. Although everyone may love entertainment music, not everyone wants a career in the entertainment industry. But, for those who do, entertainment is more than a form of diversion or leisure, it is a passion. Entertainers want to perform, to be known for their art, to be remembered for the memories they create for their audiences. Not everyone reaches the level of recognition achieved by the Beatles, Meryl Streep, or Jay Leno, but many entertainers have a unique style for which they want to be known and recognized. Their ultimate performance goal may be to perform at a local event, open for a big-name rock band, or to appear in television and movies.

How do aspiring performers get to Carnegie Hall, or to the ultimate performance venue of their dreams? Today's answer may be "go to mapquest.com and plot out your course," but the traditional answer still holds true: practice! There is no easy way, course, or path to becoming a leader in the entertainment industry. Although many look at Bruce Springsteen, Garth Brooks, or other top-name entertainers with envy, they forget that their paths began with learning their instruments, daily practices, rehearsals, and playing their own brands of music, which often met with considerable public resistance. Today they are megastars, and we avidly listen to their music, often singing along to words and tunes that are now part of our culture. Although some may argue that there are those who were born to lead, in the entertainment industry and elsewhere, others contend that leadership takes time, maturity and, even in the face of some lucky breaks, a willingness to take a risk, to grab at opportunities and let the force of their desire dispel any fears they have, to achieve a position of leadership. The point is that nothing in life is free; if you want to be at the top of your game, you need to work hard, practice, and set a path for your success. If you are interested in entering the event entertainment industry, it may be because you love music and want to be around it. Perhaps you are a musician and want to build a career around music, expanding your interest in playing music to becoming part of a group of professionals who help to bring music and other forms of entertainment to an audience. When you have reached a certain point in your professional music career, you may wish to start to consider getting into the business of planning and producing music and other entertainment. It is often the musician who becomes a producer or manager in the event entertainment industry, but that is not the only path into the industry. That path may include many options, which are discussed in this chapter.

Ten Questions to Consider When Entering the Entertainment and Production Industry

Who becomes successful in the music industry? There are no clear roads one must take, or particular characteristics one must have, to be a success. Sometimes it takes being in the right place at the right time, or doing something differently. Despite a long and successful career in the music business, the late, great Frank Sinatra had only one song that made it to the top 40, "My Way." Yet no one would question the fact that he was a very successful singer. There is no single or secret formula for success. If there were, everybody would be Mick Jagger or Faith Hill, or Frank Sinatra or Jack Morton, or a member of the George Bush Sr. family, or a Certified Special Events Professional (CSEP). However, there are some people who can "smell the food before it is cooked." These people have an uncanny ability to make any venture successful, whether it is a Steven Spielberg guiding us through decades of major motion pictures with his finger on the pulse of American viewers, perceiving wishes and fantasies, or a Steven Wynn, Mr. Las Vegas, with his bigger, higher, more in-your-face type of interactive quality entertainment.

Although they are not the only issues that you must consider, think about the questions in Figure 3-1 if you want to pursue a career in music or in the event entertainment industry.

To make a name for yourself, you will have to show that you can not only do the work, but also excel at it. You have to be creative, original, and committed, even if you are the only person who can see the value of your ideas. In addition, you must be able to sell yourself and your ideas to potential

1. What are your goals in life, what do you want to do, and how hard are you willing to work to get there?
2. Are you willing to work more than eight hours a day, sometimes seven days a week, if necessary, to realize those goals?
3. Do you have the economic resources to stop what you are doing now to pursue your goals, or can you continue to work on "what is paying the rent" until your goal is attained?
4. What are your strengths (S) and weaknesses (W); what opportunities (O) and threats (T) can you identify? What is the outcome of your SWOT analysis?
5. Are you comfortable working by yourself? Can you work alone without back office support? Can you also work effectively as part of a team, owning a small part of a much larger process, or are you more comfortable being in charge?
6. Are you disciplined enough to focus positively on one goal and see it through to a positive outcome, when everyone else around you is focusing on only the negative aspects of the situation?
7. Do you have the fortitude to forge ahead, despite and in the face of any and all obstacles? Do you have sufficient knowledge, maturity, and experience to properly execute the goals you have in mind?
8. Do you have a "Plan B" for both support and financial stability?
9. Is your goal clearly presented in a mission statement or a vision strategy? Is this vision practical? If not, is the world ready for a new idea?
10. Is anyone or any organization accomplishing "your goal" already? If so, do you have an advantage over these people or organizations? Can you exceed their efforts with your own original plans and ideas? Can you follow through with your plans, even if you are the only one who believes in them?

Figure 3-1
Ten Questions to Consider If You Want to Pursue a Career in the Event Entertainment Industry

clients in order to make a living and to stay in business. Does this sound impossible? Consider, for example, the Beatles, who are now music legends but were once considered radicals for everything from their long hair to their "strange" music. They had a vision, and they stuck to it despite the odds.

Methods of Entering the Industry

Emulation has its merits. Great artists in interviews are often heard expounding the virtues of an older and sometimes not-as-great artist who was their model, whose technique, musicality, or business acumen inspired them. They try to learn the tricks from their masters. For instance, blues great B.B. King's "masters" were T-Bone Walker, Johnny Moore, and Django Reinhardt. Eddie Van Halen followed Eric Clapton and Jimi Hendrix. George Thorogood tried to be like John Lee Hooker. The great voice of Credence Clearwater Revival, John Fogerty, admired Scotty Moore, Charlie Patton, and Little Richard. This may be a way to start when you are young. Some may call it "copycat syndrome"; in the entertainment biz, we call it paying your dues. Even today's superstars had their own humble beginnings.

Doing It. If you wait until you think you are totally prepared, you may never take the first step. The most difficult part of entering the music industry is getting that first gig, making that first demo tape, signing your first contract. In fact, the most difficult part of any process is taking the first step.

If you are not the type who is comfortable jumping into a situation without first preparing yourself, there are many options available to lay a foundation for success in this industry. Some of these will take time, such as obtaining the right education and certifications; others will require you to learn to network and build a base of contacts, being a constant presence with the people in the industry or field that you have chosen. The criteria for success do include what you know, but whom you know and who knows you are also critical to achieving your goals.

Formal education acquaints you with the academic resources and knowledge that serve as a foundation for professional growth. There are a variety of options, ranging from high schools of performing arts, to advanced degree programs in a wide array of subjects, to event management certification programs. If you have the time and money, you should avail yourself of the opportunity to lay or reinforce your foundation. "Some schools provide opportunity for students to gain actual work experience as part of their educational preparation. The value of work experience in education has long been recognized and is now emphasized in the counseling of youth" (Microsoft Encarta 1998).

Networking is an informal system whereby persons having common interests or concerns assist each other, as in the exchange of information or the development of professional contacts. Any experienced event entertainment planner—indeed, anyone in the business—will tell you that success is based on building the right relationships. From knowing the right acts to match with the right event to getting the calls to produce an event, all depends on whom you know. In this industry in particular, you will not be able to do it all by yourself. Someone is going to have to buy into your vision, to give you that first job, to let you show what you can do. Networking, then, is a critical component of your business. Your network of contacts will become your most valuable asset in building your business. You must meet with other people who share your goals and who recognize your talent. They may get their breaks before you do, and when that happens, they may be gracious enough to bring you along with them. There are likely to be many associations for your specific genre. Go to meetings, get involved, and meet people. It may take time to build these relationships, but this is the best way to get to know the people who can help you meet your objectives.

Today there is less focus on the "hard sell" and greater emphasis on creating partnerships. In the April 1, 2001, issue of *Successful Meetings*, Tom McDonald writes,

> *No one wants to be hustled anymore. We are being accosted face-to-face, through e-mail, via phone, fax, radio, and television. There is too much selling going on. To survive, most of us have drawn up the bridge and gone inside. Now, in order to sell people anything, you had better have their permission first. Here are three tactics that will help you move a product, service, or idea in a sales-hostile environment.*
>
> **1.** Get noticed. *Value is always in the eye of the beholder. If you do not already know someone, you do not have much value going in. You have to get known first. I have found that the best way is through surrogates, such as business colleagues who already have a good working relationship with me. When I am eyeing a potential customer, I ask a mutual colleague to introduce me—usually by phone—and suggest a timeframe to do it in. Use your business buddies cautiously, however; after all, they have a real job, and it isn't marketing you. I use this strategy thoughtfully—and always respond if I'm asked to do the same—and have never been turned down by anyone. Having someone's permission to call will help you receive a cordial response on the other end.*
>
> **2.** Build trust. *Once you get noticed, the partnering campaign has only just begun. Your potential partners are already defensive after years of dealing with salespeople. To earn their trust, you have to take small steps. What can you offer prospects that will address their needs, wants, hopes, or fears? The idea is to win them over by not selling yet. For example, you could send them an article that helps them to be more successful, or give them an unsolicited lead. Always do what you say you will do, when you say you will do it. Over time, trust will develop, as it does in any personal relationship. But without this step, the drawbridge stays up and nothing gets sold, ever.*
>
> **3.** Set up a network. *With the Internet, it is easier than ever to start a permission-based network. Simply put, this means building an e-community among your business colleagues. You do this by creating dialogue: start with a survey of their thoughts on a particular topic, or share late-breaking information with them. However you create this community, always use "opt-in" offers, meaning that if they want what you are offering, they respond. Never use "opt-out" offers—those in which you keep sending them some-*

thing unless they unsubscribe. This is the height of intrusive selling and really has no place in our permission-now-required environment.

Public Relations and Marketing

Get your word out with the "new" communications method for the new century, putting your own spin on your own story. Event designer extraordinaire David Tutera does. All celebrity artists, authors, and actors do. Why not you? In this age of global communications and the World Wide Web, it is increasingly easy to get your message out. You can build your own public relations engine, or you can hire someone to do it for you. Your own Web site can tell the world what is unique, different, and special about you, your story, and your accomplishments. Can you use the Internet to build a network of potential clients, partners, and businesses? Then do it. The problem with this approach is that there are millions of other messages battling for the Internet audience's attention. You must devise a message that will rise above those of the competition, get noticed, and garner positive response without annoying your already communication-saturated audience.

Inside Connection

If you have connections, use them; fairness is not an issue here. This is a competitive world, and you had better believe your competition is going to link to any inside connections they can find. Many great visionaries never reached the public spotlight they deserved because they could never get their ideas to market. Call on your family and friends; that's what they are there for. Don't abuse your connections, though, as you may have to use them more than once in your career. Remember to thank everyone who helps you by giving credit where it is due and when it is appropriate, and by returning the favor when you are asked to do so.

Right Place/Right Time

Dr. John and the Medicine Show had the idea in their tune, "It Must Have Been the Right Time/But It Must Have Been the Wrong Place." Plan for your opportunities and carefully work out your strategies. Being in the right place at the right time means knowing who will be there and what they can do for you. You will obtain this kind of information as you develop your contact network. Keep your eyes and ears open for opportunities. Sometimes these opportunities are just random luck. But don't just sit around and wait for luck to take its place on the sofa next to you. These opportunities are generally the result of planning, diligence, and making an effort to know the right people who will be in the right place at the right time.

Hard Work

Work is a physical or mental effort or activity directed toward the production or accomplishment of a particular end. Most people learn to work the traditional way, in the school of hard knocks. Many an artist knows and lives the old saying that what he or she accomplishes derives from a mere 1 percent inspiration and 99 percent perspiration. Just imagine how many of the truly inspired have fallen into the abyss of failure and anonymity because they lacked the discipline, the tools, the fire-in-the-belly to compete and to succeed. Hard work includes perfecting your skills, knowledge, and expertise in your chosen career, diligently building your network, and always taking the extra steps to accomplish your tasks. Hard work means giving more than 100 percent, every day, to everyone you work with or work for, doing whatever it takes to achieve your goals.

Longevity

No one wants to be known as a "one-hit wonder," so how do you ensure the longevity of your career? Attaining longevity in the music or event entertainment industry involves knowing your market and your customer, being creative, and knowing how to respond to, foresee, or create trends. Study those who are masters at recreating themselves, such as Madonna. Getting to that point, however, can take time and may mean doing things that are less exciting or glamorous. Attaining longevity means being willing to start from the beginning and doing what it takes to learn everything you can about the business, providing exemplary customer service, and treating those around you with the same deference with which you want them to treat you.

Do your goals include a long-term plan? Can you see yourself doing what you have described as your career objective for the long term, say 10 or 20 years? If you want to have a long career in this business, especially in today's market, you have to be able to reinvent yourself in response to changing tastes and trends. As you will see in regard to the companies mentioned later in this chapter, longevity takes hard work, commitment, and time. Just ask the CEOs of the companies that have been around for 40 to 60 years or more. They often started their careers working in the mailroom or as administrative assistants (such as Carly Fiorina, now CEO of Hewlett Packard) and worked their way up through the ranks. They did not start at the top, and, most likely, neither will you.

Starting as a Performer

It should always remain crystal clear that without performers, music, theater, dance, comedians, entertainment, production, events, and meetings would not exist. Performers are the absolute core of entertainment. One cannot "start" as a performer; being a performer seems to be "in the blood" of these artists. It is something they are drawn to for some inexplicable reason. Like a bee to honey, these people want to hone in on their craft to become the best that they can be. Shakespeare wrote about the seven ages of life's stage:

> All the world's a stage,
> And all the men and women merely players:
> They have their exits and their entrances;
> And one man in his time plays many parts,
> His acts being seven ages. At first the infant,
> Mewling and puking in the nurse's arms.
> And then the whining school-boy, with his satchel,
> And shining morning face, creeping like snail
> Unwillingly to school. And then the lover,
> Sighing like furnace, with a woful ballad
> Made to his mistress' eyebrow. Then a soldier,
> Full of strange oaths, and bearded like the pard,
> Jealous in honour, sudden and quick in quarrel,
> Seeking the bubble reputation
> Even in the cannon's mouth. And then the justice,
> In fair round belly with good capon lined,
> With eyes severe and beard of formal cut,
> Full of wise saws and modern instances;
> And so he plays his part. The sixth age shifts
> Into the lean and slippered pantaloon,
> With spectacles on nose and pouch on side,
> His youthful hose well saved, a world too wide
> For his shrunk shank; and his big manly voice,
> Turning again toward childish treble, pipes
> And whistles in his sound. Last scene of all,
> That ends this strange eventful history,

Is second childishness and mere oblivion,
Sans teeth, sans eyes, sans taste, sans everything.

—As You Like It, *II, VIII, 139*

"There is no script for being a great leader, and no way to play act in the role" (Mackoff and Wenet 2001). To have the skills to be a performer in the creative arts is a gift. It is also a calling. "Beginner" performers are often delighted to be working, in any type of work environment, with or without compensation, grateful for the privilege of showcasing their talents. That is a good way to get started in a specific field, but once a performer achieves professional status and a certain amount of recognition, that person no longer needs to give his or her skills and talent away. Unless the performer learns to act as a professional and treat his or her skill set as a business-generating opportunity, that performer can become easy prey for contractors, agents, and managers.

How to Become a Contractor

Once you have been a performer for a number of years and have achieved some professional recognition, you will begin to make contacts with others in the industry, including other entertainers, musicians, managers, venue owners, and agents. Your contacts can become a valuable resource to develop a network of resources you can use to develop a contracting business, as an agent or manager. Once you become a contractor, your performer friends will either love you or hate you. Love you, because they hope you can get them jobs. Hate you, because they think you have now sold out. No longer will you share the plight of a performer, chasing after gigs. You are now the contractor, the agent, the boss person, and the employer. Contractors and agents may have gotten a bad rap in the industry. True, they make money from other people's talents, but they can make the perfect match between performer and buyer as well. They have many resources from which to draw. They are masters of the Rolodex, and with that they have bridged the gap between the people who have and the people who need. They are the conjunction point that binds the performer and the buyer.

How do you become a contractor? By not saying "No." Your answer to the first person who asks, "Can you get this for me?" should be "I will help you" or "I will try to help you." Some performers, anxious to make money or to develop their resumes, have blind faith in contractors. This faith may, at times, be misplaced, as they may choose the wrong contractor or one who does not specialize in their genre or who is not able to obtain the right kind of work for them. Contractors have their own sets of strengths and weaknesses and, as in many other industries, have their own specialties. Their strengths may include being able to make connections; their weakness may lie in not having the right kinds of connections for everyone. Sometimes the best way to help a prospective client is to send that person to someone who is more qualified to assist him or her.

You become a successful contractor by building a growing clientele of performers and entertainment buyers. To build your business, you need to accept opportunities as they come to you and provide the best service you can. Maintaining your reputation is important to the success of your business. The entertainment industry is relatively small and very closely knit; everyone knows everyone else. As you become recognized for providing reliable service, you will receive more calls for your services. Over time, you can establish an office, start a corporation, hire someone to market your services, and then you are off and running.

Some "Rules" to Live By

Some entertainers enjoy their work and do not seek to expand into becoming contractors, agents, or managers. Others, although they enjoy performing, may find that the demands of this line of work, including constant travel, being away from family and friends, never being home for holidays, and, in some cases, the constant pressure of ever-changing public demands and tastes, take their toll. Sometimes the step toward becoming a contractor is a step toward achieving balance in the performer's life. Despite long and successful careers, many top entertainers and others at the head of their professions look back at their lives and realize the considerable sacrifices that they made to achieve their goals, often with a sense of regret. Balance is important in the achievement of longevity in the entertainment and production industry. Work time must be balanced with family time; travel time must be balanced with time at home. Former Senator Jesse Helms said, when he announced in August 2001 that he would not seek reelection, "Being part of the Senate is not just another job, but I had to choose between that and my family." Thus, a person in the entertainment and production industry or at one of the highest levels of elected office must look for the equation that will work to live life in balance and harmony.

There are many highly successful performers, songwriters, and entertainers who never achieve this balance, yet they succeed in spite of it. But only they know the true price they have paid for their success. Those who have developed successful careers in the event entertainment industry understand what it takes to reach that level. They know that there are some rules to live by that can ease the process. These rules can become guidelines that will help you to set your professional boundaries and establish good working habits that enhance your reputation. To get started in this industry, you may eagerly take any assignment that is handed to you, in an effort to gain experience and recognition. At some point, however, you will have to learn to prioritize your time and your obligations and accept assignments that best fit your individual skills, rather than any job that adds to your bank account. You need to become known as a professional and establish yourself as someone who can do the job, whether that means doing it yourself or finding someone who is more competent or skilled at the task than you are. Here are some things to consider when starting your career:

- The more "stuff" you put up with, the more "stuff" you are going to get.
- You can go anywhere you want if you look serious and carry a clipboard.
- If it weren't for the last minute, nothing would get done.
- Following the rules will not (always) get the job done.
- When confronted by a difficult problem, you can solve it more easily by reducing it to the question, "How would Captain Kirk handle this?" Taking a different or humorous perspective often helps in a time of crisis.

How to Make a Successful Career Change to Event Planning

If you have gone from being an entertainer to a contractor, becoming an event entertainment planner is the next step in the industry. How do you get there? Kenneth L. Weissman, former Wall Street executive turned entrepreneur, offers the following advice:

> *Laying the foundation for financial independence early in one's career can dramatically offer increased mobility and flexibility for that time when you might need or desire it most. Adopting a disciplined approach to saving and investing money from the start [read: first paycheck] not only propels you on your way toward developing a core financial base, which you should regard as untouchable, but also can allow your savings to leverage the time-benefit of compounding. Take full advantage of tax-advantaged programs, corporate matching, and employee savings programs to the extent available. Remember: The "early years" represent what might be the single easiest time of all for you to reserve as much disposable income as possible, before life's responsibilities take hold. So save early, and save big. Over time, your fiscal resourcefulness will become a multidimensional enabler, helping you achieve your long- and short-term goals.*

Save a lot of money, and enjoy the luxury of taking big risks without necessarily having current income is the message from Kenneth Weissman. Those who may be less fortunate must create opportunities for themselves. If you believe that becoming an event entertainment planner is the next logical step for you, use these steps to assess whether you are ready for this role:

1. Do you have a network of contacts in place that you can use to build your business?
2. Do you have the right skills and experience to provide the services you will be contracting to deliver to your clients? If not, do you know the people who can help you either find or provide these services?
3. Have you answered the ten questions asked at the beginning of this chapter?

Optimism in the face of uncertainty is a difficult art. The terrain of life is varied and mysterious. I cannot always see the path ahead. At times, my view is shadowed by doubt, constricted by fear. The open vistas of optimism are closed to me. In such shortsighted times, I must practice the discipline of positive attitudes. I must consciously choose to expect a benevolent future despite my shaken faith. Grounded in the routine of each day's unfolding business, I must act in alignment with my coming good. This means I say, "yes" to opportunities for new adventures and acquaintances to enter my life. I say, "yes" to unexpected doors opening. Rather than cling to my known life, I allow that life to alter and expand. I choose to take positive risk. I step out in faith despite my misgivings.
—JULIA CAMERON 1999

The event entertainment planner, as CEO, or chief entertainment officer, must create an experience, inform and amuse, and build a destination. Then the CEO must reinvent and recreate the experience for the next audience. Furthermore, and most important, a CEO needs to engage the emotions, content, and experiences, using every available avenue and opportunity to entertain the audience. David Tutera says, on going from designer to producer, "We must create fantasies that are magical and memorable for our clients. We must reeducate to show them new cultures." Education and cultural enlightenment aside, what we produce must entertain. The television and the radio must entertain before they can inform, including programs ranging from "The Factor" with Bill O'Reilly to those of the "shock jocks" Howard Stern and Don Imus. These people have defined their brands, and year after year they redefine and reinvent themselves.

TALENT RULES

A franchised player on a basketball team can have the same value as a franchised entertainer for an event. This person becomes marquee property and defines the value of the event's brand. Defining an event's brand with the name of an exceptional popular entertainer enhances the perceived value of both the organization and the event. He or she becomes the "calling card," or the attraction, for the event. Capturing the celebrity mystique and associating it with product marketing has become the new branding methodology. Examples include Aerosmith paired with Dodge, Britney Spears with Pepsi and James Earl Jones with Verizon. In the entertainment economy, celebrities are the universal language and currency.

PROFIT OR LOSS AT AN EVENT

We generally think of profit and loss in financial terms, and although the measure of an event's success may include a monetary element that can be measured in dollars and cents, it also includes more intangible elements. These intangibles can include whether the event's attendees had fun and were truly entertained, whether the client's intangible goals were met, either at the event or for a longer term, or other elements that fall into the gray areas of perceptions, feelings, and beliefs. The profit or loss of an event, both tangible and intangible, can be guided in a positive or profitable direction by paying attention to the following issues: Does the entertainment reflect the culture of the attendees, or at least, the culture in which people see themselves? Do the tunes that are performed define the attendees? Do they listen to these tunes at home? Do they go to the video store, movies, or theater where these songs can be found in their original contexts? Do they read the book, wear the clothes, or drive the cars featured in those music videos, major motion pictures, or Broadway shows, sharing the thoughts and philosophy of their creators? The impresario (event entertainment producer) who is able to deliver the right answers to these questions will be a true leader who generates positive profits and returns on investment.

Today's event attendees have a limited amount of time and short attention spans, and they are impulsive and unpredictable consumers. Initially content to be entertained, attendees now expect to be "wowed." If you wow them, you will get a call to repeat your performance. If you are called back enough, you can take your first steps to becoming an impresario.

Consistently meeting profit and loss objectives will keep you in the business and in business. An example of a company with longevity is Jack Morton Worldwide, which opened its doors in 1939. In the more than 60 years that it has been in business, this company has learned to create and recreate its vision to meet the needs of several generations of clients. This ability has been used to assist the firm's clients in many ways—for example:

Jack Morton Worldwide worked with Lifetime to create a marketing initiative that toured 12 markets across the U.S. over four months. Interactive stations were underwritten by participating sponsors, and offered information on personal finance, home, health, and beauty

as well as product samples and multimedia extensions of Lifetime's programming and public advocacy.
                                              —JACK MORTON WORLDWIDE, 2002

Another way a contractor can graduate to impresario is to own more than one entity, to branch out and acquire more than one company—for example:

> *Production Design Group (PDG), a Jack Morton Worldwide company, created a broadcast environment balancing the familiar and innovative qualities of the MSNBC brand, and the distinct cultures of the two great brands whose partnership created MSNBC—Seattle-based Microsoft and New York-based NBC. The environment incorporates more than 200 workstations, robotic monitors for visually dynamic camera work and a 22 by 28-foot digital "weather wall." The MSNBC Broadcast environment received a 1997 Emmy Award.*
>   —JACK MORTON WORLDWIDE, 2002

An Almost 50-Year-Old Start-Up Company

Another example of a real impresario in the event entertainment and production industry is Frank Dickson, CMP, whose long and varied career has changed many times to meet the changing industry and audience demands.

Maestro Ray Bloch led the orchestras on the Ed Sullivan and Jackie Gleason shows on CBS television. In 1954, Charles E. Dickson and Ray Bloch joined together to launch what eventually became Ray Bloch Productions (RBP) (www.rayblochproductions.com). The company became the leader in booking and producing major headline entertainment for corporate business meetings and special events. RBP grew, took on more employees, and opened multiple offices in the United States. Frank Dickson, Charles's son, joined the company in the late 1960s and assumed the role of president in 1974. By the early 1980s, RBP had branched out to become a full-service corporate communications provider with several offices coast to coast.

During his many years with RBP, Frank Dickson grew the company to national recognition with several U.S. offices, expanding its services to encompass music, entertainment, speakers, production, graphics, film, video, exhibit management, meeting planning, and industrial theater. In 1996, Production Group International (PGI) acquired RBP and the original name was eventually retired. Over the next two years, Dickson and Jeremy Driesen, director of sales at the company, became increasingly disheartened about the industry consolidation, the large companies that grew out of that consolidation, and the deterioration in customer service that ensued. Simply put, they thought it was time to go back to the small company with the unflagging commitment to customer service. So, in 2000, Driesen and Dickson partnered to reopen Ray Bloch Productions. The company has returned to its roots and now provides professional, cost-efficient, creative, and compelling results for a group of clients who want extraordinary, highly personalized service with direct access to key personnel.

Dickson received his master's degree in marketing from New York University's Graduate School of Business. He spent the first 15 years of his professional career as professor of marketing at his alma mater, Fairleigh Dickinson University, including one year as an exchange professor to Bangkok University in Thailand. He has written many articles on meetings and special events and a book, *Successful Management of the Small and Medium Sized Business*. He also developed the Meeting Planner's Music Library.

Dickson was among the first to be designated a Certified Meeting Professional (CMP) by the Convention Industry Council and served for several years on the CMP's board of directors. *Meetings and Conventions* honored Dickson on two occasions, naming him an "industry leader." He also received recognition from *Meeting News, Corporate and Incentive Travel, Performance,* Meeting Planners International (MPI), and the American and New York Societies of Association Executives (ASAE and NYSAE). In 1998, Dickson was named NYSAE's "Outstanding Associate Member."

Dickson received a Crystal Award from the Society of Incentive Travel Executives (SITE) for outstanding events and was among the inaugural group made an Associate Fellows of the ASAE. He served as chairman of the Associate Fellows. His educational roots are strong, and he has conducted classes and given speeches for ASAE, MPI, Meeting World, Affordable Meetings, Event Solutions, IBM, Armstrong, Merrill Lynch, CIGNA, and McDonalds, to name a few.

Dickson personally serves as a consultant and producer for such companies as Merrill Lynch, PepsiCo, John Hancock Financial Services, and First Union Securities. He has served on the board of trustees of Valley Forge Military Academy and College and on the board of directors of the New York Society of Association Executives and the NYC & Co.

In Conclusion

This chapter has covered the various avenues available for becoming an event entertainment planner. You can start as a performer, moving to contractor, agent, or manager, and then to planner, or you can start at any step on that path, learning the business through experience and networking effectively to develop the contacts you will need to build your business. This is a small, relationship-based industry, and getting to know the right people is important to your success. Also important is being able to deliver the right vision and meet your clients' and audiences' expectations. Is it possible to change your vision and still deliver an experience that "wows" your audience? This chapter has provided examples of award-winning companies in this industry that have achieved longevity. They attribute their success to their ability to consistently meet changing demands and provide excellent customer service. That is, in essence, what makes the difference between the player and the impresario in this industry.

Scripts for Future Study

For further information on networking and changing in selling behavior, consult the following resources:

PUBLICATIONS

Godin, Seth (1999). Permission Marketing. *New York: Simon & Schuster.*
Harvard Management Communication Letter *(February 2001).*

INTERNET RESOURCES

Jack Morton Worldwide, www.jackmorton.com
Ray Bloch Productions, www.raybloch.com

Exit Stage Right

The next chapter explores opportunities for future growth and development in event entertainment. It looks at what is new, fresh, and different in the industry and how you can use and even create your own image or trend to differentiate yourself from the competition. It also explores marketing trends, including sponsorships that can help you promote and fund your events.

CHAPTER 4

Opportunities for Future Growth and Development

I would rather play "Chiquita Banana" and have my swimming pool than play Bach and starve.

—Xavier Cugat

IN THIS CHAPTER YOU WILL DISCOVER

- How to create a career path in the entertainment and production industry.
- Popular trends in entertainment and production and how to create new ones.
- Why and how you should utilize sponsors for entertainment.

In 1844, at a time when religion was a central part of daily life, Karl Marx wrote that religion was the opiate of the masses, blinding them to their own power and allowing them to be led at will by clerics. His purpose in writing this was to suggest that the masses turn their loyalty to the state, which would provide for their good by ensuring egalitarianism and an equitable distribution of wealth. The social attitudes of that period reflected a general practice of giving allegiance to a higher authority, whether that authority was religion, a king, a country, or an employer. Social ills were ignored, and human rights was a vague theory and not a general practice. If we look at the music of that period, we may find that it reflected these social attitudes. It was light, silly, and did not speak of the discrimination, indignities suffered by workers, rampant abuse of women and children, political and corporate scandals, and social inequality that marked the period.

If religion was the "opiate of the masses" in Marx's time, then music has taken its place today. Music does more than entertain and amuse us; it is a vehicle that is used to express the sentiments that we cannot or do not openly voice in opposition to or in support of prevailing social conditions. Music speaks to the soul and the emotions. As a social barometer, it is the most telling indicator of the social, political, and economic mood of the times. Whether we want to hear it or not, it is all around us, a constant presence in malls, elevators, and many public places. We can listen to a wide variety of music stations on our car radios or play our own musical preferences from CDs, DVDs, and, for the time being, audiocassettes. Music is an important part of films and entertainment events. We unconsciously hum tunes, repeat lyrics, and adapt themes, and even our vernacular, from the music that we hear every day.

Popular music will reflect and will change with the social, and even economic, times. Consider, for example, the music of the 1920s, which included ragtime and the Charleston and reflected the popularity of flappers. This was a time of economic growth and social change in the United States; women were cutting their hair and shortening their skirts, and the economy was booming. It was replaced by the big band music of the postwar 1940s, which echoed the return to economic growth and renewed interest in dancing and fun. The rock and roll movement of the 1960s, introduced predominately by Elvis Presley, the Beatles, and the Rolling Stones, heralded even more social change, and the free love, sex, and drug revolution was born. For the first time in a long while, couples danced apart, adapting their movements to their own rhythm. Vietnam heralded even more changes to the music scene as, for the first time en masse, popular music was used as a form of protest against an unpopular war. The lyrics of Credence Clearwater Revival (CCR) and Crosby, Stills, Nash, and Young, for instance, reflected the unfairness of the draft, whereby the sons of the privileged could avoid going to war, and the social and economic burden that the war placed on the lower and middle classes. These are powerful lyrics that do not leave anything to the imagination.

Bob Dylan is another singer/songwriter whose music expressed the social and political unrest of the period. His folksy style did not have the same musical "punch" as the drums and electric guitars of CCR, but his messages were no less direct and hard-hitting. His tunes reflected the vast sea of change that faced the people of that time, its inevitability, and the fact that change was something that had to be accepted and adapted to. Dylan is a prolific songwriter whose work reflected his interpretation of the times. His songs are still in the mainstream today and are regularly used to underscore social themes, appearing in political venues and advertising when the objective is to issue a strong statement about a subject.

The disco music of the 1980s reflected the excesses of that period, and the easier listening of the 1990s allowed us to regroup, reconsider, and sing along with the tunes of that period. The introduction of rap music and its violent, fast-moving lyrics and repetitive beat were the African American community's response to decades of discontent and discrimination, and the artists that produced rap music led lives that were reflective of their genre. Some are now dead, in prison, or have changed their focus and are now more interested in being part of a solution instead of just recording the problems, leading efforts to help their communities. Still others have moved on to Hollywood, capitalizing on their popularity to make a living in the film industry.

Some artists, such as Madonna and the Rolling Stones, have been able to change the focus of their music to reflect the times and retain popularity across several generations of music listeners. These artists are still performing today, to sell-out concert crowds, and their albums still generate record sales. To engage them for a special event costs millions. The Beatles were also able to sustain their level of popularity, from the early rock and roll beats of the 1960s to the more thoughtful, protest-driven music of the 1970s. Although the Beatles no longer perform, their music is a part of our history and is known the world over. This ability to transcend change and maintain superstar stature in the music community is a rare talent, and it remains to be seen whether current artists can duplicate it.

Music is still an important element of society, and songwriters are not only lyrical poets, they also reflect the opinions and emotions of the world they live in. On an international level, tastes in popular music differ widely. Disco and techno music are very popular in Europe and Asia, whereas Australian musical tastes are oriented toward the more satirical lyrics. Americans tend to appreciate a variety of music styles, with rapidly changing tastes that constantly seek new forms of satisfaction. As a world society, we have become inoculated against violence, and it takes more to shock us than ever before. As events are just a microcosm of society, the events industry has witnessed the same phenomenon—that it takes more and more to "wow" our guests and attendees. Although we readily accept the new and different in music, we also tire of them more rapidly, putting pressure on artists and music labels, as well as the industry's own music purveyors, to innovate, introducing a succession of artists and music to satisfy the public's—and our clients'—insatiable appetite for entertainment.

As you consider a career in the meeting and event industry, your social and political views will color your musical choices. Will you expand on what is currently musically popular, or are you prepared to take a stand and create something new? The passion of musicians such as Bob Dylan and Xavier Cugat is reflected in their work and in the type of music they wrote and played.

Are you prepared to "walk your walk" and produce event entertainment with integrity? Some artists, such as Vanilla Ice and Milli Vanilli, created imaginary personas to gain popularity, only to become musical pariahs once they were exposed. The meeting and event industry is a dynamic, difficult environment, now run by financiers instead of planners. The music industry has endured the same fate. It wants to sell records, not win popularity contests, and is less interested in a song's social message than whether it will make money.

Creating a Career Path: An Exploration of the Many Directions in This Expansive Industry

If being an egomaniac means I believe in what I do and in my art or music, then in that respect you can call me that. . . . I believe in what I do, and I'll say it.

—JOHN LENNON

John Lennon obviously was passionate about his music and his work, and his career was one of the most successful in the music business. The following sections present accounts of a career and the journey from individual musician to a big corporate entertainment company. Both show effective means of entering the industry, and both require high levels of commitment, dedication, and hard work.

BEING A MUSICIAN

The first three chapters discussed event entertainment and production from the perspective of the event entertainment company or its clients. However, it is the actual musicians and entertainers who make the whole system "work." To provide an understanding from the perspective of a musician, Dave Rubin examines the mind of the musician and offers tips for a working musician. Rubin is senior editor at *Guitar One* magazine.

Professional musicians desiring to make it pay can be an odd lot. Ambitious to the point of obsession about their careers, they often harbor deeply rooted feelings of paranoia about an industry that does not understand their true creative nature. Why can they not be rewarded for going before the public and baring their sensitive souls? After all, they worked hard to perfect their craft, sacrificing family, friends, and even health, to reach a rarefied level of artistic expression. Many talented individuals are unaware of the unnecessary obstacles they place before themselves on the road to fame and for-

tune, glamour and girls (or guys, as the preference may be), wealth, and world renown. Well, a decent living at least.

Right from the downbeat it helps to know what the available opportunities are for gainful employment in the special events industry. Peruse the following list of suggestions and commit it to memory. These are some viable options for the commercial (not a bad word) musician:

- Private events. *Many individuals and corporations still enjoy the immediacy of a live band or solo musician. Despite the economic downturn in the beginning of the new millennium, ready cash is still waiting for those interested in these (usually) low-pressure gigs.*
- Industrial shows. *A market rebound is inevitable, resulting in a return to work in this vast arena. Remember, today's and tomorrow's future executives were raised on rock and pop music and often play an instrument (mostly guitar) themselves, so they like to see someone come in and jump, jive, 'n wail.*
- Hotel bars and lounges. *There is nothing like a good piano man or guitar picker to add that special touch for the businessperson wishing to relax or prowl.*
- Weddings, bar mitzvahs, and the like. *Deejays have really cut into this sector of the industry, so you have to be quite dedicated to pursue this avenue. However, the pay can be excellent.*
- Political rallies and fund-raisers. *Here again, the candidates, their staffs, and constituencies are getting to be of an age where they expect to hear classic rock and contemporary rock and pop. These jobs are somewhat "seasonal," as election campaigns come around only every two, four, or six years.*

How do you successfully compete in these potentially lucrative markets? Four main areas need to be addressed: material, gear, presentation, and promotion.

- Material. *Rule "numero uno" for the modern working musician is that you must play music for the* people, *not just tunes that provide room for exposing your blistering chops. Give them what they want, and you will have leveled the playing field in terms of competing with deejays. Standards, swing, 1950s rock 'n' roll, Motown, and classic rock are just the beginning. If you are able to throw in a little grunge, country, and appropriate hip-hop, you expand your audience incrementally.*
- Gear. *The latest digital hardware and software are definitely required to produce a reasonable facsimile of the hits people want to hear. Amplifiers (amps), pedal boards, and actual acoustic and*

electric instruments you play are still the backbone of pop music, but a small group (quartet or less) particularly needs accessible synthetic help to achieve that polished and produced sound so prevalent over the airwaves today. Speaking of amps, the modeling types allow guitarists to accurately reproduce the sounds of all the popular rigs, from Marshall to Fender to Vox and beyond. Outboard units are less expensive and present the option of keeping one's favorite old tube combo amp. Keyboardists will want the latest sampling signal processors, naturally.

- Presentation. *Remember, you are in the entertainment business, so entertain. Always dress sharp and put on a show for the folks. Once again, you are competing with deejays who do all kinds of nonsense to keep the party going. Giveaways, dance contests, humor, and lots of attention to the guest of honor will increase your marketability at weddings and bar mitzvahs.*

- Promotion. *Last but hardly least, promotion is probably the most important factor in this age of image. Get your public relations kit together with a great photo and video, a pro demo that you can sell (or give away), and eye-catching graphics featuring a band logo. Do not hesitate to play a number of selected auditions and benefit gigs in order to get your band in front of the public. Get a Web site with the most "bells and whistles" you can afford, as the Internet will certainly grow in importance as the big engine that drives the information age.*

FROM MUSICIAN TO AN INITIAL PUBLIC OFFERING

Your career is your business, whether musician or corporation, so why not treat it as such? If your idea, concept, business product, and practices are filling gaps in the public eye, why not take your company public? David Bowie was able to do this successfully, creating an enterprise that capitalizes on his unique style and his music. Martha Stewart, although not a musician, is another example of someone who has parlayed a unique style into a successful brand and a very successful business. Of course, there are many negatives as well; the greatest may be that you now have to answer to your stockholders instead of holding the company privately and making all of the decisions yourself. However, the positives may outweigh the negatives, as a successful initial public offering (IPO) may yield many dollars in your new bank account, enabling you to go much farther with your ideas and future plans.

In regard to going from individual entertainer to an entertainer for the masses, some people may ask, "How do you do it—to create a career path?" Some may answer, "By not having no in your vocabulary." Jim Shea Jr., 2002 gold medal winner, an American Olympian in the skeleton, speaking about the first time he rode the sled, said, "I asked, 'How do you steer it?' Somebody said, 'Shut up and go down.' I asked again. And he said, 'Shut up and go down.'" As you ride the sled of life, it will be clear to you that many people "know what they are doing" in this industry. Emulate them, learn from them.

BECOMING A PROFESSIONAL

The profession you have chosen may become more tangible with the acquisition of a professional certification. Working toward certification (discussed at greater length in Chapter 16), is a direction in which to proceed in many career journeys, whether as a supplier or as planner. Jim Monroe, CMP, CSEP, a design director and event manager in Dallas, Texas, observes, "As a supplier, I became certified so potential clients would recognize my familiarity with their fields and my commitment to professionalism. We work in multidisciplinary fields, where competence in one or two disciplines does not guarantee we will understand or achieve our clients' goals and objectives."

As one of the first professionals to be awarded the CSEP (Certified Special Event Professional) in 1993, in a group of 17 people, the author obtained this designation to expand his career path, and by being the first to receive this certification, was able to become a pioneer in the industry. It is important to speak the language of meetings, conventions, trade shows, expositions, and special events, as well as the language of music. Today's music industry is a business, whether it involves creating music, booking headline entertainment, promoting and selling CDs, promoting or producing concerts, or having a corporate entertainment and production company. Obtaining professional certifications allows a musician to own more than a music company—it allows him or her to create a company that handles and produces corporate entertainment events, a destination management company, a special event venue, and a meetings and events management firm. The value of experience in the music industry adds to the professional's ability to understand the full scope of the industry and provides a more well rounded resume.

Megan Rowe reported, in Primedia Business Magazine, "Despite questions about the value of certification, more planners are piling on the initials." Sandy Biback, CMP, CMM, of Imagination + Meeting Planners Inc., and Meeting Essentials A–Z, in Toronto, Canada, chimed in and explained,

The recertification is based on the work you have accomplished in the last five years. So it is an accumulation of your work in the industry. Most professions have to recertify in some way. I understand the CMM (Certified Meeting Manager, a professional designation conferred by Meeting Planners International), is also looking at a recertification program. I have to agree; for those inside and outside the industry, when you have those initials after your name, it is assumed you know 'stuff.' Just last week I met with [the representative of] a new venue, and when I handed him my card, he did a double take and said I must be very experienced (Well, yes, I am, but when he saw the 'letters,' it opened the door to my telling him about my career). It also opens the door with potential clients. Neither the CMP (Certified Meeting Professional, conferred by the Convention Industry Council) or the CMM is perfect, but they are better than nothing! And they have improved professionalism and awareness a great deal (Rowe 2002).

Reinventing the Industry: New Product Development—Old, Stodgy, and Tired versus New, Fresh, and Trendy

"No one was there to confuse me, so I was forced to be original."
—COMPOSER JOSEPH HAYDN, SPEAKING WITH THE PRINCE OF ESTEHAZY
ON HIS WORKS WHILE UNDER THE PRINCE'S EMPLOY.

"If you ask, 'Would you like to hear something that is essentially the same as you have always known, or instead hear something new and different?' most respondents will answer—or at least be tempted to answer—that they want the new and different. But they do not mean it. Most of us are lifetime adherents of what we liked (were exposed to) first, and our occasional departures from that cul-de-sac of taste only give us the good feeling that we are not narrow." So writes John Sparks, vice president for public and government affairs for the American Symphony Orchestra in *Symphony* magazine (2001). Twentieth-century American composer Charles Ives would agree with Sparks's twenty-first-century point of view. "Beauty in music is too often confused with something that lets the ears lie back in an easy chair," said Ives.

If you are very creative and fearless, creating a "new" wheel may be the objective. If not, a new spin on the old wheel may be enough. Perhaps you have devised a new, unique, and reproducible product or service that you can now offer to the industry. Everyone is always looking for the next new something in event entertainment and production. The big questions are, Can you present it with integrity, and Can you maintain it? And, most important, are you willing to keep on producing it until it gains acceptance? Nirvana's sounds were first popular with Seattle's grunge crowd before it became a mainstream band. And although the Grateful Dead had its following, not everyone appreciated its unique style. Grunge, punk, rap, hip-hop, all of these styles gained favor with a particular audience before hitting the mainstream. What was the secret to their big break? And what did they do in the months, and even years, before they gained popular acceptance? The short answer is they kept on doing what they believed in. The long answer is that they kept doing the same thing, every day and every week until their names were associated with a particular rhythm, style, or sound that people began not only to appreciate, but to really like. Just as there are people who do not like classical music, which has been around far longer than today's music, there are also people who will not like other particular types of music. But each type of music will appeal to someone. Cultivating that appeal takes perseverance, timing, and luck, not to mention knowing the demographics of the guests or attendees. A notable entertainer who has mastered these lessons is Madonna, who has consistently reinvented her music and style, coming up with new, fresh, and reproducible ideas every few years. Some people like her and some do not, but her ability to consistently provide new sounds has garnered a personal fortune of more than $500 million.

The late Kurt Cobain, of Nirvana, and the late Jerry Garcia, of the Grateful Dead, came up with why they felt the sounds of their bands were new, different, fresh, and reproducible. Kurt Cobain said, "We sound like the Bay City Rollers after an assault by Black Sabbath. And we vomit better on stage than anybody." Jerry Garcia described the Dead Head movement of his band, "It's pretty clear now that what looked like it might have been some kind of counterculture is, in reality, just the plain old chaos of undifferentiated weirdness."

Just remember that weirdness has a price and that price may include labeling. If you are known for producing the wild and weird, then your guests, attendees, or registrants will not appreciate your desire to become more staid and normal and may drop you for some even wilder and weirder planner. As you set a style, sound, and genre for your music, be sure that it is something that you can consistently produce and, as necessary, update. Can you create new sounds and lyrics that maintain your style and genre, but provide new forms of entertainment for your attendees? That is what you will have to do to stay viable as both a musician and a planner. And, on the topic of expanding your planning and music career into a business, will your musical style lend a certain ambiance to your events that will be underappreciated by many? For example, it would be hard to imagine an event production company owned by the rapper Eminem. What types of events would he produce, and who, besides his current fans of Generation Y, would they appeal to?

DIFFERENTIATION MAY BE THE KEY

Setting yourself or your company apart from the others by differentiating yourself from the competition can be very effective. If we pull back the curtains of corporate America, we will find the president and chief executive officer of Handspring Corporation, Donna L. Dubinsky, recounting how her company makes a distinction from the competition, "When we started Handspring three years ago, we set out a clear strategy: Enter the market quickly, build critical mass by offering innovative and differentiated products, create a leading brand, and gain scale. At the same time, we started investing in what we believed to be our ultimate future, that of integrated wireless communicators. We have accomplished all of these goals." Keep in mind that as part of your long-term plan, you will also have to factor in the presence of competitors who will imitate your style or any other unique factors, especially if they are successful. Will you parlay your rapid success into another venture, go for a buyout, or just take the money and get out while you are still ahead? How you will address your competitors and stay one step ahead of them?

If you want to see the future, look at those whom some may describe as being "way out." These are people who are performing now what will be "mainstream" in the future. Thoth is a New Yorker, half Jewish, half African-American, who clearly defines this category of being on the cutting edge. Music has always been in his life, as his mother is a very accomplished timpanist, performing with the New York City Opera and the San Francisco symphony. His present life was chronicled in the award-winning documentary, "Thoth," seen on HBO in 2002. He wrote to me,

> I call myself a prayformance artist and I prayform what I call soloperas. Solopera *is a word I coined myself; it comes from "solo" meaning alone, "sol" meaning sun, and "sol" a homonym for soul, which is merged with "opera" meaning a dramatic performance put to music and the plural form of "opus" which means work. A prayformance is part vocalizing, puzzle, aerobics routine, monologue, language deconstruction, alchemy, theater, healing ritual, sacred dance, all accompanied by solo violin and complex percussive rhythms. It draws from the mythological world of the Festad about which I have been writing since a child.*

Thoth is an artist with his own unique genre that combines art and entertainment (see Figure 4-1). Is it reproducible? Yes, but although it may be reproduced, it may be sustainable only to the point that meeting and event audiences continue to appreciate his form of entertainment. Does he draw an audience that is truly interested in and follows his work, or just those who are curious? Do people go to see him just once, or does he have an audience that consists, at least in part, of repeat visitors? For the moment, his appeal derives from the exuberance of his performances and their uniqueness. Is his appeal sustainable? Time will tell, but creating this type of unusual performance is inherently risky in that the artist may have to consistently draw a new audience to each performance. Eventually, everyone who is interested will have participated and the demand for performances will be exhausted. Until then, his is the most original form of entertainment to hit the meeting and events industry.

REINVENTING YOURSELF

David Tutera, event designer turned producer, has reinvented himself many times. What he can do for his clients is "to create fantasies for them. We are

Figure 4-1
Thoth Prayforming at New York City's Bethesda Terrace Arcade
(Photo courtesy of Thoth)

creating fantasies magical and memorable." His forecast is for people to get over the obstacles they have imposed on themselves, to get from designer to producer. His motto is, "If it's been done before, redefine it or don't do it!" Tutera gave additional advice at the 2002 Event Solutions Expo: "Allow something to happen every 30 minutes in your event. Have your client experience all five senses. Keep your presentation of event entertainment crisp and clean." Is an event really in need of music? Can we ever afford not to have entertainment at a celebration or special event? The Sony Music Custom Marketing Group, like Tutera, also has a wonderful motto, "Everybody, everywhere likes music! That's what makes it a powerful motivating force." The event may create the illusion, but the music sets its tone and mood. What would film be like without music? Music has become such an integral part of filmmaking that film soundtracks are released simultaneously with a film's theater release. Films are also instrumental in promoting or reviving music. The recent film *What Women Want* featured a scene with Mel Gibson dancing to Frank Sinatra's "I Won't Dance," creating an instant demand for this Frank Sinatra recording from an audience that had never really heard his music.

WHAT IS REALITY?

"The success of shows like *American Idol* and *Joe Millionaire* on Fox and *The Bachelorette* on ABC was so impressive that numerous executives said they were now ready to embrace plans for a radical restructuring of the network business, which previously had been talked about only as dimly possible, long-term adjustments," wrote Bill Carter in his article "Reality TV Alters the Way TV Does Business" in the *New York Times* (25 January 2003). Sandy Grushow, chairman of the Fox Entertainment Group, in the same article on the popularity of reality shows, chimes in: "The audience is never wrong. They have a huge appetite for this and we've got a responsibility to satisfy that appetite."

Why and How You Should Utilize Sponsors

According to the International Events Group (IEG), a Chicago-based research and consulting firm, sponsorship is a cash and/or in-kind fee paid to a property (typically in sports, arts, and entertainment, or for charitable causes) in return for access to the exploitable commercial potential associated with that property. Organizations sponsor or tie into events in order to gain awareness from or a closer affinity with a target audience. The IEG Sponsorship Report *(19th Annual Projections Report)* states that North American companies alone are expected to spend $10.52 billion in 2003, a 9.1 percent increase over spending in 2002. As shown in Figure 4-2, sports continue to dominate this industry, with a 67 percent share of total sponsorship revenues. Entertainment tours and attractions enjoy a 10 percent share, and festivals, fairs, and annual events account for another 8 percent. Cause marketing, which entails companies tying into charities, accounts for 9 percent, and the arts 6 percent.

A major cost of event marketing is the sponsorship fee. Sponsors pay an agreed-upon amount to have their names linked to an event or cause. The sponsor hopes that it can have an impact on its target market, both at the event and before and after, as a result of publicity. Yours does not have to be a large national company to benefit from event marketing. It is often beneficial for

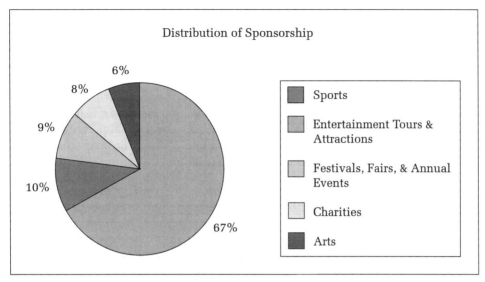

Figure 4-2
Distribution of Sponsorship

small regional companies to tie into local events, whose costs are often quite affordable. Moreover, event marketing is not only for consumer-oriented companies. Despite the size of the market, there is not much empirical research on the effectiveness of event marketing (Brickman 2002).

IEG states,

> *Without emotion, a product or service is just like every other product or service. Effective marketing is no longer tied to eyeballs but rather to heartstrings. Whether it is through sports or entertainment, arts or causes, companies are creating loyalty by tethering their products and services to the issues, events, and organizations their customers care about most. Companies do not use sponsorship to replace advertising. The benefits sponsorship offers are quite different and the medium typically works best as part of an integrated marketing communications effort. Advertising is the direct promotion of a company through space or airtime bought for that specific purpose. Advertising is a quantitative medium, sold and evaluated in terms of cost per thousand. Sponsorship, on the other hand, is a qualitative medium; it promotes a company in association with the sponsor.*

EVENT SPONSORSHIP

We have all witnessed the degree to which corporate tie-ins have become a staple of superstar concert tours. After the failure of concert tours for record companies in the 1980s, corporate partnering became the only way to make them profitable. *Adweek* reports that research by Chicago's PS Productions revealed that "marketers of products as diverse as soap and salad dressing saw sales gains of between 52% and 1,454% during sponsored events," according to Selling-Communications, Inc.

Event sponsorship continues to grow due to the increased need by marketers to find more effective ways to influence consumers. Industry publication such as *Meetings and Conventions Magazine* regularly reports that this is one of the major trends in the convention and exposition industry. According to Martha Cooke, Senior Associate Editor at the magazine,

> *Dollars might be tight, but companies are still spending money on sponsorships. In fact, industry and trade associations raked in $290 million from sponsors last year, an increase from $270 million in 2001, according to IEG, a Chicago-based research and consulting firm. The challenge for the show manager is to offer attractive sponsorship opportunities, price them right, and convince potential customers to buy. Most of us are accustomed to seeing a sponsor's logo printed on attendee materials, splashed across a Web site, or mentioned before a presentation. What is this kind of tangible recognition worth?*
>
> Priced right. *For professional or business-to-business shows, all types of recognition, from traditional signage to electronic displays or audio announcements, can be priced from five cents to one dollar per attendee who will see or hear the promo, say experts. Groups with greater buying clout command premiums at the higher end of this range. "For consumer events, the value is lower—between one-quarter to one-half of one cent per attendee exposed. If a show has both consumer and B-to-B constituencies, find out how many of each is expected to attend, and price accordingly," advises Laren Ukman, managing director of IEG Valuation Service, a division of IEG. "At B-to-B shows," she explains, "you might have a smaller audience, but you can command higher fees because the attendees have greater purchasing power." This is where an audit comes in handy, since it gives the event manager the tools to show a potential sponsor her group's professional clout and buying power.*
>
> Good visibility. *While items like banners or tote bags will be seen by all, more specialized sponsorships such as information kiosks or product demonstrations might not be attended by everyone. The number of attendees who will be exposed to the message should determine sponsorship value. Signage is worth more if attendees see it for an extended period of time. A banner hanging over the podium at a seated lunch commands a higher price than the same size banner at the entrance to the venue, since attendees only pass under*

*that sign briefly at the start of the day. IEG's Ukman says a sponsor-ship with those kinds of intangible benefits should be priced at be-tween 1.2 and 3.5 times the amount of the tangible assets alone.
Pick a party. A better idea, suggests Ukman, is to let each sponsor host a function at the show, such as a breakfast, coffee break, or cocktail reception.*

An option that appeals to Nancy Frede's budget-conscious clients is sponsoring volunteer speakers for an event. There is no speaker's fee to pay, just the price of attaching the company name to a session. Sponsors not only get exposure from seminar signage but can place handouts on seats or tables, Frede says (Cooke, March 2002, courtesy of Meetings & Conventions, *a publication of NORTH-STAR Travel Media, LLC.).*

Once a company identifies the benefits that they want to gain from a sponsorship opportunity, they must then plan the implemen-tation process that will achieve their goals. The Sales Marketing Net-work (www.info-now.com) has determined through extensive research that there are fundamental guidelines that should be followed to en-sure a successful sponsorship program. According to the Sales Mar-keting Network, the following ten steps should be followed when launching a sponsorship program:

1. *Determine your company's specific marketing objectives. Is this sponsorship merely a matter of good will or tied to a strategic objective? Is this sponsorship tied to a specific sales promotion or incentive? Define as best you can the image your company generally tries to portray through its marketing. Objectives should be highly specific and measurable.*
2. *You need to carefully define your target audience. What demo-graphic or interest groups are you trying to reach, and where are they located? What are their expectations of the event and how will you use those expectations to appropriately position your product?*
3. *Carefully define how your company will use this event with its employees and key customers. Can they attend and, if so, under what circumstances? Can the event be a team building exercise for your employees, or a show of community involvement for your company by allowing employees to participate as volun-teers?*
4. *Decide whether or not to use an event agency or consultant. To get someone to handle your business, you will generally need a budget in the tens of thousands of dollars to get someone's atten-tion. Make sure you are dealing with an expert in the particular type of event you want to sponsor. Look at the agency's other*

clients and track record and make sure you spell out precisely what you expect the agency to do. If you are planning to hire the services of an entertainment or sports celebrity, you will want to work with an attorney who knows the issues involved, such as what happens if your celebrity does not show.

5. *Select an event that appeals to your target audience and relates to your company's objectives and positioning. Try to match demographics and image to your company's goals. Are these goals product or revenue specific?*

6. *Carefully analyze the specific types of sponsorship packages offered. Review publicity plans, ticket sales outlets, lead times involved, category exclusivity clauses, use of logos, on-site signage, and how your company's name will be advertised. Ask about opportunities to bring guests, obtain special seating, and get tickets imprinted with your logo. Ask the organizer for publicity clips from former events, as well as photographs or ads, showing the way sponsors are presented.*

7. *While many organizers have standardized packages, do not be afraid to negotiate a deal specific to your needs. Maybe your company wants more event signage and less in the way of amenities.*

8. *Take advantage of the event in your advertising, sales, and marketing efforts. The more committed your company, the more commitment you will get from customers and employees. Do not forget to include mention of these events on your corporate web site, and have a link to your web site from the event's web site.*

9. *Take full advantage of the event itself. Invite as many customers, distributors, agents, and employees as possible. Stage a reception or have a special seating area for your guests. Make sure your sales staff can invite key accounts.*

10. *Before, during, and after the event, keep a logbook detailing every form of exposure generated by the event, including the number of guests, newspaper clips, television/radio mentions, photos of on-site signage, samples of event marketing materials, and guides—everything that can help you quantify the exposure generated by the events. Consider a customer or employee survey of your event sponsorships. If you have web site links from the event's web site, add a counter to the link to determine how many additional web site visits the event generated (Brickman 2002. Reprinted with permission from the Sales Marketing Network at www.info-now.com) (See Figure 4-3.)*

But where can you find these sponsors? According to Sylvia Allen and C. Scott Amann, in their book *How to Be $ucce$$ful at ponor$hip ale,*

	Sponsorship	Charitable Contribution
Publicity	Highly public.	Usually little widespread fanfare.
Source	Typically from marketing, advertising, or communications budgets.	From charitable donations or philanthropy budgets.
Accounting	Written off as a full business expense, like promotional printing expenses or media from placement of print, radio or TV expenses.	Write-off is recently limited to 75% of net income. This limit was recently increased 20%. As a result, accounting/tax considerations are less likely to influence the way a corporation designates funding of a not-for-profit organization.
Objectives	To sell more products/services; to increase positive awareness in markets and among distant stakeholders (customers, potential customers, geographic community).	To be a good corporate citizen; to enhance the corporate image with closest stakeholders (employees, shareholders, suppliers).
Partner/ recipient	Events; teams, arts, or cultural organizations; projects; programs. A cause is sometimes associated with the undertaking.	Larger donations are typically cause-related (education, health, diseases, disasters, environmental), but can also be cultural, artistic, or sports-related. At times funding is specifically designated for a project or programs; at times it is provided for operating budgets.
Where most funding goes	Sports get the lion's share of sponsorship dollars—about 65%.	Education, social services, and the health sector get 75% of charitable donations.

Figure 4-3
Structure of Publicity Exposures

1. Local electronic retailer
2. Local beer bottler
3. Local soft drink bottler
4. Local banks
5. Local restaurant association
6. Local retailers' association
7. Car dealers
8. Automobile aftermarket
9. Long distance carriers
10. Mobile telephone companies
11. Network marketing companies (Amway, Nu Skin, Mary Kay, etc.)
12. Craftspeople
13. Antique dealers
14. Fresh produce dealers (mini-farmer's markets)
15. Local radio
16. Local cable
17. Local newspapers
18. Food vendors
19. T-shirt vendors
20. Flea market vendors

Figure 4-4
The Allen-Amann Model of Guaranteed Places to Look for Sponsorship
(Reprinted from How to Be $ucce$$ful at ponor$hip ale *by Sylvia Allen and C. Scott Amann, which is available through Allen Consulting Inc., 732-946-2711 or www.allenconsulting.com.)*

(1989) there are 20 "guaranteed" places to look, as shown in the Allen-Amann Model in Figure 4-4.

THE SIX REASONS WHY COMPANIES SPONSOR

The following are the most common reasons that companies use sponsorship, according to IEG's *Complete Guide to Sponsorship:*

Entertain Clients: *Many companies sponsor for hospitality opportunities. For example, golf tournament sponsors offer their key clients pro-am spots, giving sponsors the opportunity to spend a few hours with important customers and solidify business relationships. Events make great settings for this informal networking. They are unique and desirable, two things that are absolutely necessary to entice a business contact to join you during non-business hours.*

Heighten Visibility: The wide exposure events enjoyed in both electronic and print media provide sponsors with vast publicity opportunities. For many companies, the cost of purchasing the TV and print exposure their sponsorships garner would be unaffordable. For example, for the cost of a 30-second spot on the Super Bowl telecast, a company can sponsor a team on the NASCAR Winston Cup circuit, which delivers more than 30 hours of TV coverage.

Shape Consumer Attitudes: *Brands with huge ad budgets and high unaided recall do not need sponsorship to generate visibility. Instead, they often sponsor for the lifestyle association the sponsored property represents. They are looking to the event to have a rub-off effect on their image and ultimately their sales. Miller Lite's sponsorship of pro beach volleyball is an example of an image-driven tie. By becoming synonymous with beach volleyball, the brand is identified with a lifestyle emulated by its young adult target market. "Consumer attitudes are the hardest thing to change," said a Miller marketing executive. "And the more our brand is part of events that are part of a consumer's lifestyle, the more we can affect his or her attitude toward the product." Depending on the type of event sponsored, they can also generate an enormous amount of goodwill, an intangible benefit that cannot be bought, but that is very valuable to a company.*

Business-to-Business Marketing: Incenting the Trade: *Competition for shelf space is one of the biggest issues facing companies today and many are using sponsorship to win the battle. For example, many of the companies sponsoring stock car racing do so to offer retailers perks such as driver appearances at stores and event tickets in exchange for incremental case orders and in-store product displays. Sponsorship of all types can be used to incent wholesalers, retailers, dealers, and other intermediaries in the distribution channel.*

Merchandising Opportunities: *As consumer buying decisions are increasingly being made in-store (80% of all product choices are now made at the retail level), marketers need to have relevant promotions for consumers at the point of purchase (p-o-p). A sports or entertainment tie can bring excitement, color and uniqueness to a p-o-p display and can be merchandised weeks or months in advance. The opportunity to have items available as giveaways or for sale is valuable because this type of merchandise is immensely popular with consumers and can be used to provide a key point of difference when offered in conjunction with an in-store promotion.*

Drive Sales: *Purchases, not perceptions, pay the bills, and companies increasingly use sponsorship as a hook to drive sales. For example, Visa conducts a national usage/fund-raising effort around its sponsorship of the Olympic Games and the U.S. Olympic Team. Visa promotes its association by offering to make a donation to the team each time consumers charge a purchase to their Visa card. During a recent Summer Olympics, Visa's sales volume rose 17%—well over the company's projected 11% increase. Visa does not increase its marketing spent during Olympic years; rather it gains extra mileage from those dollars. That kind of cost efficiency is critical in today's budget-trimming corporate climate.*

Local sponsorships also can drive sales. For example, the Olive Garden Italian Restaurant chain used sponsorship of the Florida Marlins to attract consumers to its outlets. Its regional office developed a neighborhood baseball clinic in conjunction with the team sponsorship and saw guest counts increase by 5% to 9% in participating areas during the promotion. Similarly, Southwest Airlines Co. used its sponsorship of the State Fair of Texas to increase ticket sales. More than 15,000 passengers took advantage of Southwest's offer of free admission to the fair with a ticket receipt. Sponsorship offers the possibility of achieving several goals at once; most companies expect the medium to deliver a combination of the above benefits.

The goodwill generated by this type of sponsorship is an added benefit, something that is not as easily measured, but that is extremely important to any business. On a much smaller scale, local businesses such as dry cleaners, music stores, and delis will sponsor a local children's sports team as a show of goodwill and as a means of advertising their business. The sponsor's name appears in bold letters on the jersey and is visible by the team members, their parents, and the opposing team's players and parents during a game. The benefits of this type of sponsorship are measured by assessing increases in revenue generated after the sponsoring begins. It is an excellent means of showing community support.

In Conclusion

There are two universal languages, body language and music.
—Dr. Jackie Rankin, body language expert,
speaker/trainer/author/jury consultant

To be successful, we must not only introduce innovative products but also build on our manufacturing excellence, bring new capabilities into the company, and continue to attract and retain the best employees.

—Intel 2000 Annual Report

Music is a universal language, and this language can be spoken fluently at your meetings and events. It is unique in its ability to cross social, cultural, economic, and political boundaries. Music evokes a wide range of emotions;

it can be used to express opinions and passions and is a barometer of the social, corporate, economic, and political times. Musicians and songwriters have a rare ability to capture the essence of a moment in time and make it a permanent part of history. The songs of many of the greats, such as the Beatles, the Rolling Stones, Madonna, Bob Dylan, and Eminem, were a defining part of the social fabric of their time and are still popular today. There are many avenues available to those who wish to make a career of their music, which include being an entertainer and parlaying a musical career into a corporate event and production company.

Each year, thousands of aspiring musicians try to "make it" in the music industry. Although there are only a few who are world renowned, there are many successful musicians who make a career by providing musical entertainment for events. Becoming an accomplished musician takes hard work, commitment, and practice. Becoming a superstar takes timing, luck, and perseverance, as well as the ability to create something new, fresh, and reproducible. Can your music be accepted by the mainstream? Can you create something that will be popular today, and then create additional sounds that attendees at a conference will appreciate? Are you an artist whose music is so original that you appeal only to a small group of people? Will you be accepted on the corporate and association circuit? Can you maintain this level of output for the long term? How often can you reinvent yourself or your music to keep it in the ever-changing mainstream? This will be the litmus test of a successful musical career.

If you decide to expand your musical interests into producing events for others, obtaining professional certifications is one way to enhance a career in the event industry. It shows your customers that you have taken the extra steps to truly learn your craft. As a meeting or event planner, you will deal with many business owners who will appreciate the professionalism and expertise signaled by a professional designation.

Whether you are a musician, another type of entertainer, or an event entertainment producer, corporate sponsorships are an increasingly popular form of marketing for events ranging from association meetings and conventions, to fairs and social events. Sponsorships provide the funds for the events, as well as marketing and advertising venues for the sponsors, and have shown phenomenal growth throughout the 1990s. As mentioned earlier, they can generate increased revenues, provide exposure, and generate goodwill for the company. Events of all types now feature sponsor logos on everything associated with them, from programs to plastic cups. There are essential steps to follow to ensure that a sponsorship will yield the intended results, whether they include greater product or corporate exposure, higher revenues or increased market share.

The event industry can provide a wealth of career options with multiple avenues of expression. Whether you are a musician interested in developing a career in this business or wishing to broaden your skill set to produce events for others, it is a dynamic industry that allows you to express your creativity so that attendees can be entertained and have fun. The event industry is all about entertainment, yours and your guests'.

Scripts for Future Study

BOOKS

Beck-Burridge, Martin, and Jeremy Walton (2002). *Sports Sponsorship and Brand Development: The Subaru and Jaguar Stories*. New York: Palgrave-Macmillan.
Written by a British professor and a freelance writer and originally published in the United Kingdom in 2001, this book looks at the European motorsports campaigns of Subaru and Jaguar.

Graham, Stedman, Joe Jeff Goldblatt, and Lisa Delpy (1995). *The Ultimate Guide to Sport Event Management and Marketing*. Chicago: Irwin Professional Publishing.
This book walks the novice or expert through the planning and execution of sports events. It discusses all the elements involved in marketing such an event: finding sports figures, contract negotiations, outdoor versus indoor events, key strategies, and how to manage the media. In addition, it gives examples of event marketing, tips on how to enter the field, and offers appendixes with sample agreements.

IEG's Complete Guide to Sponsorship (1989). Chicago: IEG, Inc.
In addition to giving you the essential building blocks, *IEG's Complete Guide to Sponsorship* goes a step further and shows you how to apply them, with checklists for you to use and real-life examples that illustrate principles in practice.

IEG Sponsorship Sourcebook (2003): *The Comprehensive Guide to Sponsors, Properties, Agencies and Suppliers*. Chicago: IEG, Inc.
This one-stop reference guide indexes 4500 of the most active sponsors and what they sponsor; 2200 sponsorship opportunities and who their sponsors are; and 550 industry agencies and suppliers. Includes a CD-ROM version with complete contact information.

Reed, Mary Hutchings (2001): *IEG's Legal Guide to Cause Marketing*. Chicago: IEG, Inc.
An essential tool for understanding the rules and requirements of not-for-profit organizations and sponsorship. Don't sit down at the negotiating table without this one-of-a-kind resource.

OTHER PUBLICATIONS

The Sponsorship Report is a biweekly newsletter geared primarily to people who make event marketing a full-time profession.

Entertainment Marketing Letter is a monthly newsletter published by EPM Communications. It provides industry data, such as cost analyses of entertainment marketing, a calendar of events, industry news and trends, and listings of contacts at key companies. www.epmcom.com.

PROMO Magazine (monthly magazine) defines promotion trends, presents critical "how-to" information and case studies about promotion, and serves as a meeting ground for companies and professionals in the industry. Free for qualified subscribers, or by paid subscription. www.promo-magazine.com.

ORGANIZATIONS

International Events Group (IEG) is a for-profit organization that provides information on sponsorships in sports, arts, entertainment, causes, and events. Its comprehensive services include an industry newsletter, sponsor locator service, books, conferences, workshops, consulting, and nearly 30 boilerplate contracts for a variety of sponsorship situations.

Promotion Marketing Association (PMA) has an annual event on entertainment marketing. Members don't necessarily specialize in event marketing services.

Exit Stage Right

In this chapter you learned about opportunities for future growth and development in the event industry. Chapter 5 begins the discussion on researching, designing, and planning for event entertainment and production.

PART TWO

Researching, Designing, and Planning Production and Event Entertainment

How to Research the Needs and Resources for Your Event

After silence, that which comes nearest to expressing the inexpressible is music.

—ALDOUS HUXLEY

IN THIS CHAPTER YOU WILL DISCOVER

- What questions to ask before you sign onto an event.
- How historical data facilitates the event planning process.
- How associations and convention and visitors bureaus (CVBs) are good starting points in researching an event.

As the preceding quotation suggests, music can be a powerful tool in expressing an event's messages of meaning to the attendees. But before music can be chosen for an event, you must conduct research to accurately assess the needs and resources required for the event. It is critical to ask the right questions before you sign onto an event so that you will know exactly what to expect, what will be expected of you, and of the event, and to ensure that your event meets the client's expectations. Then, once you have the contract, the insights provided in this chapter can help you to plan for every aspect of the event. Successful event entertainment production focuses more on planning than on the actual event. If the right questions are asked, then the right preparations will be made, you will understand and be ready for the event's needs and potential risks, and the event itself can flow efficiently. This is what the professionals do; they ask detailed questions, ensure that they have the appropriate answers, and use that information to develop their plans. Event entertainment requires that many, sometimes hundreds, of individuals work as a team, and choreographing their activities would be impossible without detailed planning. Because event entertainment planning is a relationship-driven industry, your career and your future in the industry depends on developing and maintaining a reputation for producing flawless, professional events.

Questions to Ask Before Planning an Event

Experienced event entertainment planners rely on historical data to ask the right questions. The information from previous events provides valuable insights into venues, sponsors, subcontractors, suppliers, and even in providing reasonable estimates and costs to clients. They are also aware of, and learn to use, member-driven resources, such as convention and visitors bureaus, whose purpose is to provide information and support for events. Experienced planners have learned to maximize their efficiency by utilizing available, dedicated, and experienced resources to help them plan and deliver successful events. A typical Event Sheet with standard questions is shown in Figure 5-1.

How is one supposed to do, if one does not know? Through knowledge? experience? certification? internships? partnering? listening? watching? asking questions? The answer is all of the above. In your data collection or research phase when planning an event, the "correct" questions must be asked. These questions relate to the event's many components, including music, lighting, sound systems, venues, and entertainment. They will help you to identify the many elements you will have to coordinate to make the event happen as planned. They will also help you to coordinate the many different tasks and people who will be part of the production process.

Upon successful completion of the questioning process, the answers must be analyzed in order to achieve successful planning of your meeting or special event. In this portion of the chapter many professionals share their insights into what questions they ask to be able to analyze the answers and begin planning a successful event. Note that even the professionals take time to ask relevant questions and get answers before they start planning an event.

EVENT SHEET:

EVENT: _____

DATE: _____

TIME:_____

PLACE: _____

NUMBER OF GUESTS:

VENUE: (CONTACT INFORMATION)

SEATING:

DÉCOR:

VENDORS:

MUSIC:

ENTERTAINMENT:

REQUIREMENTS:

CONTRACTS:

PERFORMERS:

CONTACT INFORMATION:

TOTAL AMOUNTS AND PAYMENTS:

FOOD AND BEVERAGE:

    CONTACT:

    SETUP TIME:

    REQUIREMENTS:

Figure 5-1
An Example of the Questions on an Event Sheet

The questions they ask have been developed from experience, and many of these are derived from past errors of omission. Learn from their example and experience, and take the time needed to ask the right questions, and get the right answers, before you start planning your event. When planning an event in your locale, or in a distant city, keep in mind that there are municipal organizations whose purpose is to provide services to meeting and event planners. Get to know them and use them effectively. They will save you time and effort and help you to ensure that your event is a success.

Some people use mnemonic devices to organize the design and planning phase of their events. Richard Aaron, CMP, CSEP, president of BiZBash.com Idea Center, utilizes the word "VERVE" in his seminar, "Creating Winning Events for Today." This device stands for Visualize, Energize, Ready the plan, Validate, and Expect the impossible. Each element represents a phase of the event planning process and has its own set of processes and questions to complete. Breaking down the process into workable pieces helps the planner to work on concept development, planning, and implementation in stages and even, if necessary, to delegate portions to other parties.

Other industry professionals echo the need for planning, preparation, and attention to detail. A notable experienced venue manager and event planner is Fred Seidler, the director of sales at the Metropolitan Pavilion and a veteran in the New York City special events industry. He has worked at some of the city's hottest night clubs and concert arenas, as well as having been a stagehand in Florida, Texas, and New York. He has worked on tour with major musical acts, including soul great Teddy Pendergrass. This exciting national tour gave Seidler some insight into the mechanics of producing a nightly concert on a single-engagement basis. The production involved working with tour personnel and venue staff and mastering the delicate balance between them that is needed to produce a musical show. He shares his insights on what it is like to work in a world-class venue and how to produce a great event and offers special tips on coordinating a multievent function.

Metropolitan Pavilion has been fortunate to have some fantastic musical acts perform here in just the few short years since we opened. Tina Turner sang here for the opening party for O, The Oprah Magazine, *and since then there have been several more performers, including Natalie Cole, Art Garfunkel, and Ashanti. Recently the owner had nearly 600 New York City special event professionals and city dignitaries here for a networking event that featured the hottest Cuban jazz you will ever hear from a new group, the New Standards Band.*

Setup of a Venue
Obviously, event planners booking a loft area for an act must consider the room's structural aspects. You cannot simply come in and set up a system arbitrarily. It is critically important to give the planning and setup more time than you think you might need, or else a whole host of things can go wrong, such as areas of dead sound, unintended reverb, or feedback problems. They should also coordinate a preshow site inspection by the sound and production company to determine the unique acoustics of the venue. The venue's facilities manager must tell them in advance if any renovations are planned, since a modification of the location can have a major impact on the quality of the sound.

At Metropolitan Pavilion the musical acts are seldom stand-alone events; they are generally part of a larger experience for the

evening that includes a presentation, a dinner, or dancing. There-
fore, the audiovisual team cannot just work from the floor plan; they
need to walk the space. Also, they need to understand what the vari-
ous parts of the whole special event consist of and which parts must
get priority, and then execute the setup accordingly. Will someone be
presenting an award from the same stage the band is on? If so, how
will you get everyone's attention if people are dancing first? What
should you do with the lighting at that point?

Sponsorships
Many events at Metropolitan Pavilion have corporate sponsors, espe-
cially events for associations and not-for-profits. A particularly suc-
cessful sponsorship strategy is to have the liquor at the event do-
nated. In exchange, the liquor company can highlight its brand.
Another idea is simply to offer sponsors opportunities for signage or
ads in a program in exchange for assistance with the event. A recent
big-ticket event had a merchandise and information table, and one
of the items it sold was a gorgeous four-color coffee table book. One
of the event's cosponsors helped defray the book's printing cost. In
exchange, the president of the sponsoring company wrote a foreword
to the book, and his company had a full-page ad inside the back
cover.

Always pursue sponsorships and present potential sponsors with
a proposal for involvement. You might be surprised at the level of
interest you get. Start by clearly showing the potential sponsor the
benefits it can derive. But then also communicate your flexibility.
The sponsor might have its own ideas of how it can help.

According to Seidler, planning a successful event hinges on paying attention to an array of small details, details that can impact the quality of the
event. This further underscores the importance of asking the right questions
and getting those questions answered so that a missed detail does not become
a source of problems at the event.

The following are a number of questions to pose regarding event entertainment and production before beginning to plan the event (Price 1999; courtesy of Catherine Price):

- *Questions in preparing entertainment for a meeting:*

These questions will help to determine type of entertainment that
the event's hosts are planning so that additional questions can be
asked to ensure successful production.

1. *Will we have entertainment?*
2. *Has a budget been provided for entertainment?*
3. *What type of entertainment relates best to the theme of the*
   event?

4. *What type of entertainment relates best to the participants?*
5. *What type of entertainment might be offensive to the partici-pants, sponsor, or companions?*
6. *How much lead time is necessary to prepare entertainment?*
7. *Will the entertainment be provided through a professional agency?*
8. *How many times, and when, will entertainment be used?*
9. *What entertainment equipment does the site have?*
10. *What are the union requirements?*
11. *Are there any nearby attractions for entertainment?*
12. *Does the site or surrounding area offer any unique entertainment opportunities?*

- *On Site:*

These questions relate to the planned entertainment and the venue's ability to accommodate the many factors surrounding its production.

1. *Who has responsibility for coordinating the entertainment?*
2. *What is the back-up position if the entertainment is a no show?*
3. *Will the entertainers require rehearsal space and time?*
4. *Is a special setup required?*
5. *Will the entertainers require dressing rooms?*
6. *Will the entertainers require refreshments, food, or other amenities?*

- *Site Entertainment Factors:*

This list contains all of the physical elements that you need to con-sider when doing your site inspection to ensure that the entertain-ment planned for the event can be accommodated by the venue, both physically and in terms of available staff.

- *Loading dock availability*
- *Is the site prepared for the rider requirements?*
- *What entertainment equipment does the site have?*
- *Dressing rooms*
- *Rehearsal date and time confirmed*
- *Rehearsal room assigned*
- *Room availability confirmed*
- *Other personnel required*
- *House electrician*
- *Musicians*
- *Entourage*
- *Sound engineer*
- *Stage crew*
- *Lighting director*
- *Union requirements*

Questions to Ask During a Site Inspection

What do you ask during a site inspection? The following guidelines were compiled with the assistance of Jennifer W. Brown, CMP, partner, Meeting Sites Resource, Newport Beach, California.

GENERAL INFORMATION

Acquiring general information includes getting appropriate telephone numbers of the venue's staff. This will prevent you from losing time searching for their contact information should you have an emergency. Although it seems to be a minor detail, you will be glad to have this information if you ever need it. Be sure to ask about renovations. Many events are planned months in advance, and planned renovations could be completed before your event, meaning that the venue that you first inspected could look vastly different from the one you work in six to twelve months later.

MEETING AND BANQUET SPACE

Meeting and banquet rooms can appear deceptively large when they are empty or not configured according to the requirements of your meeting. Therefore, get enough details about the space to ensure that you know exactly what you have to work with. Although many properties have upgraded their wiring to accommodate today's telecommunication needs, some have not. Ask the right questions about the venue's wiring and technical capacity while there is time to make required modifications.

- What is the name and square footage of each meeting room?
- Can floor plans be provided with details on dimensions, ceiling heights, seating capacities, and breakout configurations?
- Does each room have temperature controls?
- Is lighting adequate? Are there tracks mounted for spot lighting?
- How many air walls (single and double) does each room have, and do they adequately block out sound?
- Is there a stage? What size is it?
- Is there a sound/projection booth?
- Are there hang points in the ceiling?
- Is there on-site audiovisual support? Can a list of equipment and pricing be provided?
- Will the property provide security for meeting rooms?
- What is the drayage policy?
- How many restrooms are near meeting rooms?
- Where are the elevator banks? What is the freight capacity?

OTHER INFORMATION

A meeting or event's attendees count on the planner to handle the details, including where they will park their cars. Have these details ready for them to ensure that they can be present on time and ready to enjoy the event. Also ask what other types of events the venue is hosting, and find out whether their attendees present problems for your event. An event that requires silence for speakers or specific event activities should not be held next to a room housing an extremely boisterous event.

- What types of theme parties are offered?
- Are outdoor spaces or other areas available for special events?
- Is there a business center? What services are offered, and what are its hours of operation?
- Is on-site parking available? How many spaces are there? What are the parking rates?
- Is valet parking offered? What is the rate?

The client should provide some general information about the event during the initial planning session. This information includes the number of expected attendees, the length of the meeting, and the catering requirements. As meeting planner, you should then request more specific information so that you understand the client's expectations and can meet them. With respect to the attendees, find out whether, in addition to the planned attendance, walk-ins are allowed and how many are anticipated. A meeting can last several hours, a half-day, or all day, which will determine the catering requirements. Will there be a continental breakfast, lunch, dinner, or a combination of both? When should such meals be served? The venue manager should be present during all planning discussions, as he or she will be an integral part of the planning and production process.

The meeting space is where the meeting will be held, and the attendees may be there for several hours or all day. It is important that they are comfortable, can easily and quietly enter and exit the room, and are not distracted by noises from the hallway or adjacent rooms. While conducting the walk-through, pay attention to the room's lighting and ceiling height and note any obstructions to access. The meeting must be compliant with the requirements of the Americans with Disabilities Act (ADA), and there should be no code violations. Are the tables and chairs in good condition? What is the condition of the air walls? Is ventilation adequate? There will probably be a speaker or some type of presentation at the meeting, so be alert to any distractions that could be caused by noise from other rooms, hallway traffic, or door movement. Is the room large enough to accommodate all of the attendees, and will there be adequate access to emergency exits and restroom facilities? Does the meeting require teleconferencing and Internet access and are these facilities available and working? It is a good idea to test electrical and phone outlets prior to the meeting.

Are there any contractual, union, or other policies that you need to be aware of, and what are the costs associated with them? Some venues have established exclusive contracts with specific vendors, and anyone planning events at these venues must honor those contracts. The associated costs may be higher than those of your preferred vendors, and this information must be established early in the planning process so that your client is aware of them. They may also impact the meeting's budget.

The audiovisual (AV) requirements are another part of the planning process. If the venue has AV equipment available for use, is it in working order and is it compatible with the speaker or presenter's equipment? Is there backup equipment available in the event of a malfunction? Speak directly with the audiovisual company's representative and get a sense of its service level and customer service capabilities. Make sure to agree on costs, how billing will occur, and how the company handles cancellations. Get everything in writing, and be sure to put copies in your Production Book. See Chapter 15 for more information on multimedia presentations.

If the meeting venue has a convention services manager, establish communications at the beginning of the planning process. This person will be your "go-to" source for any issue concerning the meeting and will also know the venue's policies and procedures with respect to on-site events. Discuss the details and requirements of the meeting with this manager so that he or she is aware of your requirements and can work with you to ensure that they are met.

If there is an exhibit hall as part of the meeting, establish communications with the decorator. He or she will have experience in working with the staff that will service the event and will be a source of information and support when working with the drayage company, engineers, electricians, and audiovisual staff. The decorator will also know the catering staff and all on-site personnel. Establishing a strong rapport with all on-site staff members at the beginning of the planning process will ensure that they have had input into the event planning process, which can help to avoid problems later. Their history and experience with previous events at the venue will be an invaluable resource to you.

GROUP DYNAMICS

Because of the large number of people who are usually associated with planning an event, it is often important to consider group dynamics. Especially of interest are the types of behavior group members may develop while handling various tasks along with their membership in the group. Identifying group behaviors and addressing any observed problems or issues will be critical to ensuring that they do not interfere with the planning and implementation of an event. The efficient production of any event depends on the ability of each person to accomplish his or her required tasks, and it is the sum of those tasks that makes the event a success. If negative group dynamics are allowed to develop, they will interfere with the flow of the event planning and development process, especially the entertainment element. So, as part of the planning process, take time to identify the group's dynamics and address any problems you uncover.

Task Functions

Task functions illustrate behaviors that are concerned with getting the job done or accomplishing the task the group has before it.

- Does anyone ask for or make suggestions as to the best way to proceed or to tackle a problem?
- Does anyone attempt to summarize what has been covered or what has been going on in the group?
- Is there any giving of or asking for facts, ideas, opinions, feelings, or feedback, or searching for alternatives?
- Who keeps the group on target? Who prevents topic-jumping or going off on tangents?

Membership

A major concern for group members is the degree of acceptance or inclusion in the group. Different patterns of interaction may develop within the group, which give clues to the degree and kind of membership behaviors and attitudes.

- Is there any subgrouping? Sometimes two or three members consistently agree and support one another, or consistently disagree and oppose one another.
- Do some people seem to be "outside" the group? Do certain members seem to be "in"? How are those "outside" the group treated?
- Do some members move in and out of the group—for example, lean forward or backward in their chairs or move their chairs in and out? Under what conditions do they come in or move out? *(Annual Handbook for Group Facilitators, 1972).*

David Cerone, president of the Cleveland Institute of Music, addressing the City Club of Cleveland in October 1999, offered some words of inspiration that can be applied to the event planning process.

> *Consistency and Comprehensiveness!! I believe that these two words are imbedded in greatness. These are two words which are an integral part of my educational philosophy, management style, and performance approach as a concert violinist. Two of the most difficult, time-consuming, demanding, frustrating, and rewarding qualities any human being can ever hope to attain, qualities which are valued in the pursuit of most anything.*
>
> *We can make machines which are Consistent, but they are usually not very Comprehensive in their chores. They can produce a*

widget, a bowl, a toy, an airplane rivet, a car part, a baseball bat, or a golf tee. But, machines do not make paintings, they do not write plays or compose symphonies, and they can't make a Stradivarius. These are things that are made by people, people who have spent many years mastering the fundamentals of their craft in an effort to bring Consistency and Comprehensiveness to their work. They master these qualities first—thereby empowering themselves to attain excellence.

What are the steps we take to develop Consistency and Comprehensiveness? I will use the study of violin playing as an example. First, we must understand that it is a long process. The process must start early. It takes years of commitment, daily application, and discipline. For the violinist, it requires:

1. *Mastery of scales and arpeggios*
2. *Control of vibrato*
3. *Development of a sure bow stroke*
4. *Educating the ear*
5. *Engagement of the eye in the note reading process*
6. *Engagement of the mind in interpreting the composer's musical messages*
7. *Studying the history of music*
8. *Knowing about the physics of sound and how it relates to the process of musical communication*
9. *Feeling secure enough in all these areas to be musically spontaneous*

David Cerone makes clear that the key to delivering excellence is experience and a level of commitment that entails seeking perfection in all you do. Whether you are playing a violin or planning an event, knowledge and experience constitute the foundation for successful delivery of a performance or a task. Although not every event you deliver may be perfect (and each event will have its imperfections), it is important to learn from these experiences and use them for future successes. Once you have learned from your mistakes and have planned enough events to be experienced, you will learn to accept the spontaneity that occurs in every planned event with the grace of a master.

Historical Data: To Know the Present Is to Study the Past

We examined historical weekly returns over the previous 10 years to calculate our value at risk.

—THE COCA-COLA COMPANY ANNUAL REPORT

For any business or organization operating in the Internet Age, information is currency. The ability to realize the potential of your information assets—turning data into intelligence—will be vital to the evolution and success of your business.
—MICROSTRATEGY 2000 ANNUAL REPORT

We are not creating but reinventing with everything we do. According to the first law of physics, matter is neither created nor destroyed; it merely changes form. This means that there is truly nothing new under the sun, that everything we do today is just a repetition of something done in the past. How does this apply to event entertainment? As the preceding quotations from Coca-Cola and MicroStrategy illustrate, knowing the details of past events provides you with data you can use in planning future event entertainment. The Production Book or "bible" that you developed for previous events will contain detailed information on venues, support staff, the contractors you used, problems you had—with people, equipment or locations—and a myriad of other details. This information will be a valuable reference tool for you at many stages in the process, including the pre-event stage, during the bidding and costing process, during the planning stage, and during the event itself.

Do professionals use this data? "Absolutely," says Steve Revetria, director of sales and marketing for Giants Enterprises in San Francisco, California. Revetria is a 12-year veteran of the event entertainment production industry and has produced everything from small corporate events to World Series parties to a Rolling Stones concert. He is responsible for events in Giants Stadium, but also utilizes other venues around the San Francisco Bay area. He keeps detailed files on every event, including contracts, phone conversation logs, copies of every activity and supplier related to the event, and the likes and dislikes of the headliners and other event entertainment VIPs. After an event has been delivered, known issues are highlighted and then incorporated in a standard operating procedures manual that provides guidelines for the production of future events. The standard operating procedures manual is a dynamic document, developed with historical data derived from past events. It is the benchmark that Revetria uses to assess the feasibility and potential of future events.

Jared Paul, director of entertainment for Washington Sports, in Washington, D.C., has been in the event entertainment industry for six years, getting his start by producing musical events while in college. He indicates that historical data allows him to assess the value and feasibility of proposed events. This data provides him with valuable information on whether a proposed event will meet the client's expectations and whether it is a good fit for the venues for which he produces events, which include the MCI Center in Washington, D.C., and George Mason University's Patriot Center. The MCI Center alone averages more than 250 bookings per year and coordinating those events' production requirements means meticulous attention to a wide variety of details. Paul maintains hands-on records of every detail relating to each event, with backup copies. Because he outsources all of an event's production re-quirements, these historical records provide him with detailed information about suppliers and other service providers who were used in the past and who may be candidates for future events. He knows, for example, which sup-pliers deliver and which ones don't, whom he can trust to produce and whom he needs to avoid. In this case, the records become an important reference for assessing an event's risk factors and determining which of them he can con-trol by using service providers who have been dependable in the past.

Historical data can also provide significant information on the financial viability of an event. It allows Steve Revetria and Jared Paul to quickly assess whether an event will meet their respective venues' financial goals and whether an event will deliver a profit. They can review their historical records to as-sess how many attended similar events in the past, levels of ticket sales, the types of concessions that were provided, and the returns that were generated. Because they produce event entertainment for specific venues, their goal is to book as many appropriate events as possible and meet their operational ob-jectives. Their access to historical figures allows them to have a means of checks and balances to evaluate and contrast their respective objectives.

Both of these event entertainment producers also collect information on events produced by other event planners in different venues within their mar-keting areas. Keeping these records provides them with marketing information they can use to propose their venues to organizations that have used other venues in the past. Using their historical event data, they can then submit pro-posals that include information on the types of clients, events, and entertain-ment that have been successful in the past, cost and profit data, and other rel-evant information, which may result in their gaining additional clients.

The importance of historical data in event entertainment planning having been established, the following guidelines can be used in developing and uti-lizing your own historical reference system. First, you should keep a separate production manual for each of your events. This manual is the record of your event and will contain information on every detail of the event's entertain-ment production. After each event, review the Production Book and note any elements that were very successful and those that did not generate the ex-pected results. Here are some questions to ask yourself:

- What were the points of failure in the event?
- Who was responsible, and how did he or she react to the situation or remedy it?
- Did the suppliers or service providers deliver great service? Which ones did not? Which ones exceeded expectations?
- What could I have done differently, or would I have done differently, for this event?
- What will raise "red flags" in future events of this type?
- What have I learned from this event?

The post event evaluations will provide additional insight into the identification of successes and opportunities for improvement. You can consolidate this information in a separate document to become a reference for future events. Learning from the past helps you to avoid mistakes in the future. Steve Revetria has some important advice in this area: "Relationships are so important in this industry. It is a small industry in which everyone knows everyone else and word spreads fast. Experience helps, but it is your reputation that really counts." Jared Paul adds, "Mistakes will be made, and experience and great relationships help you to remain calm and to show professionalism. After all, the show must go on."

Member Driven Resources: An Examination of Associations and CVBs

One of the benefits of experience is knowing whom to turn to for help with your event entertainment planning. Convention and visitors bureaus (CVBs) occupy a special niche in this business. Municipalities understand the value of tourism to their communities, and the focus of the efforts of every convention and visitors bureau is to attract meetings and conventions and the participants who attend them. They are an excellent resource for meeting and event planners because they have the contacts and resources in place to facilitate event planning. No one understands the situation better than a person who has worked on the hotel side, then switched over to the CVB side. Greg Gibadlo is such a person. Gibadlo served as vice president, Convention Development, at NYC & Company, Inc., Convention and Visitors Bureau; as vice president, Convention Sales, at the Washington, D.C., Convention and Visitors Association, and spent more than 20 years with Hilton Hotels Corporation, holding positions that include director of marketing, the New York Hilton and Towers; director of marketing, Waldorf-Astoria, and director of marketing, Eastern Region, Hilton Hotels Corporation. He states:

> *Convention and visitors bureaus were established in the early 1900s. The first one was founded in Detroit when a number of businessmen noticed that groups of doctors and others came to town for their business, spent a lot of money in the local establishments, and left. The money stayed with a variety of services, restaurants, attractions, and shops. They decided that attracting these conventions was good for their economy, and the concept of convention bureaus came into existence.*
>
> *These bureaus were originally separate organizations or attached to a local chamber of commerce, as was the case in Washington, D.C.; however, as they grew, their scope evolved into a function of*

tourism development beginning in the '60s and blossoming in the late '70s. The newest trend has been their involvement in the special events industry. Surely some bureaus, such as Atlantic City's, with its Miss America pageant, have utilized special events for many years to attract tourism and gain needed publicity, but these were usually one-time events run by local promoters under the auspices of the bureau.

The special events industry has matured, now recognized as an industry that generates monies, jobs, and good relations within a community. Convention and visitors bureaus have restructured and reorganized to provide insight and other assistance, including introductions, as they had originally done for the convention planner or group tour producer. New York City has a special events department headed by a senior vice president, which signifies its commitment to this facet of the hospitality industry.

The services provided cover a wide area. In some cities promotional funds can be advanced if a concept is thought to be exciting and prospects for success are judged to be worth the risk. In most cases the organization will open doors with various departments of the local or state government to ease the planners' process. Information about the venues is made available and introductions are easily arranged. There is a level of comfort established for all concerned when the bureau (or whatever the organization is titled) is intertwined with the event planner and the local community. The bureau can be the catalyst for extraordinary events. It has the experience, knowledge, and contacts needed by the event planner. It is an expert in recognizing the needs of the community and the prospects of mutual success for itself and the planner.

It is recommended that the event planner responsible for creating a memorable function should contact a service manager at the convention and visitors bureau. Introductory information, with the appropriate detail, should be communicated concerning the planner's requirements and objectives. The service manager will have introductory information available, as well as an extensive list of opportunities. Most bureaus have a methodology available to communicate to its members as directed by the planner, and this referral system offers the advantage of speedy, unbiased communication under the approval of the planner, which enhances the process. Complete details from the event planner are helpful, and a personal conversation between the event planner and the service manager will clarify the planner's requirements.

Most cities have an organization with these responsibilities. The International Association of Convention and Visitors Bureaus, located in Washington, D.C., can provide information on the locations of CVBs throughout the world. Its Web site may be accessed at www.iacvb.org.

Whereas a destination city has its own specific convention and visitors bureau, professional associations have chapter affiliations in the major marketplaces. Many planners are members of various associations, all of which print their directories as a benefit of membership. If you are planning an event in a location unfamiliar to you, a vendor affiliated with an association in that location will probably be a strong candidate for an initial interview. If you do engage such a vendor in one capacity or another, you are, at least in theory, protected by the association's Code of Ethics. This may be better than a Yellow Pages approach. If in doubt, contact the local convention and visitors bureau, which should be able to provide you with a list of approved vendors for event production.

"Meeting production is such a competitive business it generates very aggressive selling practices," says John K. Mackenzie. He offers some tips on screening out those wanting to use your business to learn theirs.

Finding a Producer

CONFIRMING PRODUCER CREDENTIALS

Visit the producer: *Producers (or sales reps) are happy to visit you. In my experience, office and staff size control the amount of business a producer can handle, but have little to do with quality or ability.*

Awards: *Bronze, silver, and gold award plaques on the reception room wall? Could mean a lot. Could mean nothing. It depends on the source of the awards. Some competitions and festivals are more concerned with collecting entry and judging fees than they are with originality and quality.*

Listening vs. talking: *How well does the producer listen and let you talk about your plans and problems? Motor-mouth producers may be more interested in their work than yours.*

Production procedures: *The question, "If you got my business, what's the first thing you'd do?" can elicit interesting (revealing) responses.*

Check references: *Generally useless. I would question the ability of anyone dumb enough to list a reference that did not provide good feedback.*

Time in business: *A production firm in business for 10 or 15 years is doing something right, and you gain some assurance they will not go under in the middle of your job. (Although the attrition rate in this business is legendary.)*

Repeat clients: *The size of a client list provides an indication of diversity. But, in my opinion, size is not as important as the number of clients who have been there more than once.*

Specialization: *If your meeting concerns something like* Managing Risk Assessment for Subordinated Debentures, *or* Clinical Characteristics of Serotonin Uptake Inhibitors, *you may need a producer with special experience.*

Grace under pressure: *Try this one sometime: While talking with a producer, ask the following (with a straight face), "What's the worst mistake you ever made?" The pro will smile and answer. The pretender will smile and waffle.*

—MACKENZIE, 2002, REPRINTED FROM THE WRITING
WORKS AT WWW.THEWRITINGWORKS.COM

When you don't know—ask. When you do know—listen. When you research—collect all of the data. All businesses in the meetings and events field need resources from which to function and do their jobs efficiently. Start your file system now and add to it with each event you deliver. You never know when you will need someone's products or services, and it is better to deal with vendors you know and trust than to constantly start new relationships. In this industry, experience is the best teacher, so along with your file system containing vendor information, keep notes on each event you plan. Be sure to note any problems you had and what you would do differently. This is your personal file, so be honest with yourself. Review this file prior to planning your next event and use it to develop your list of questions. Did you ask enough questions while planning your last event? Did the one question you did not ask cause you problems? If so, then be sure to include that question on your list. Remember that even the experienced professionals keep lists and use them when they plan events, and that they developed their lists from their own experiences.

In Conclusion

Even people you have known for years can change their attitudes and behaviors when they are involved in a group. Groups can take on their own personalities, and negative group behaviors can create serious problems for your event. The checklist of group behaviors provided in this chapter can be used to observe how your group behaves so that you can address any troubling issues before they create problems for your event.

Everything old can be new again, so keep history in mind when planning your event. Historical data is an important tool in all aspects of event production, from bid generation to planning and delivery. The production manual you create for each event will be useful in evaluating and fulfilling an event's requirements, from bidding the event to knowing which vendors and service providers would be most appropriate for the event (and which ones to avoid), to identifying and preparing for risk factors. Some event entertainment planners also research events held at other venues and use this information to market their venues to other organizations. There are many resources available to meeting and event planners who are working in a distant or unfamiliar city. The local convention and visitors bureau is one such resource, whose sole purpose is to attract meetings and conventions and the people who attend them. It will be an invaluable aid as you plan your event, providing contacts and assisting with event coordination.

Finally, as the saying goes, "If it sounds too good to be true, it probably is." Use careful screening procedures to qualify any prospective vendors or service providers. Use the various interview and question checklists provided in this chapter to ensure that you get the best service and results from everyone with whom you work. Use historical data as an assessment tool in planning and managing your events. Although your clients may appreciate your successes, they will also remember your failures. Your reputation and your career depend on your ability to provide dependable, consistent results for every client.

Scripts for Future Study

Member-Driven Resources Related to the Event Industry

American Society of Association Executives (ASAE)
1575 Eye Street, NW
Washington, DC 20005
Phone: 202-626-ASAE
www.asaenet.org

Convention Industry Council (CIC)
801 Greensboro Drive, Suite 30
McLean, VA 22102
Phone: 800-725-8982
www.conventionindustry.org

Hospitality Sales and Marketing Association International (HSMAI)
1300 L Street, NW, Suite 1020
Washington, DC 20005
Phone: 202-789-0089
www.hsmai.org

Insurance Conference Planners Association (ICPA)
Unit 106, 260 W. Esplanade N.
Vancouver, BC, Canada V7M 3G7
Phone: 604-988-2054
www.icpanet.com

International Association of Exhibition Management (IAEM)
5001 LBJ Freeway, Suite 350,
Dallas, TX 75244
Phone: 972-458-8002
www.iaem.org
International Association of Convention and Visitor Bureaus (IACVB)
2025 M Street, NW, Suite 500
Washington, DC 20036
Phone: 202-296-7888
www.iacvb.org
International Special Events Society (ISES)
The membership of ISES encompasses professionals from a variety of special events disciplines, including caterers, meeting planners, decorators, corporate and social event planners, audiovisual technicians, party
   and convention coordinators, educators, journalists, hotel sales managers, and many more. ISES provides education and networking for its
   members to promote professionalism in the special events industry,
   which benefits the public. (www.ises.com)
Meeting Professionals International (MPI)
4455 LBJ Freeway, Suite 1200
Dallas, TX 75244
Phone: 972-702-3000
www.mpiweb.org
National Speakers Association (NSA)
1500 South Priest Drive
Tempe, AZ 85281
Phone: 480-968-2552
www.nsaspeaker.org
Professional Convention Management Association (PCMA)
2301 S. Lake Shore Drive, Suite 1001
Chicago, IL 60616
Phone: 312-423-7262
www.pcma.org
Society of Government Meeting Professionals (SGMP)
908 King Street
Alexandria, VA 22314
Phone: 703-549-0892
www.sgmp.org
Society of Incentive and Travel Executives (SITE)
21 W. 38th Street, 10th Floor
New York, NY 10018
Phone: 212-575-0910
www.site-intl.org

Exit Stage Right

Having researched the needs and resources for a meeting or an event, how do you manage the creative process? The objective is to produce entertainment that is unique and yet reproducible. In Chapter 6 you will discover how to create original events that can be customized and replicated again and again.

CHAPTER 6

Managing the Creative Process

Opera is where a guy gets stabbed in the back, and instead of dying, he sings.

—Robert Benchley

IN THIS CHAPTER YOU WILL DISCOVER

- The origins of themes in the creative world.
- The implicit and explicit meanings of themes.
- How to identify audience expectations.
- The various types of themed media.
- How to create a themed event.

Being creative involves more than coming up with a "new and fresh" idea. Within the events industry, it means being able to take that idea and turn it into something that is fun, exciting, and meaningful for the event hosts, sponsors, and audience; you need to "make it sing." A successful career in the events industry hinges on being able to produce a continuous stream of new and fresh ideas, or variations of old ideas, for events and productions through careful management of the creative process. An event producer does not reinvent the wheel to create a theme for every event. Rather, it is a process of finding a mix of something creative with what has worked in the past and what is currently popular in the mainstream. It also takes a creative process to put a fresh "spin" on the concept, along with good planning and management skills. Your best measure of success is seeing your theme repeated, with modifications, of course, by other event planners.

An article entitled "Entertainment Tie-Ins," appearing in *The Sales and Marketing Network* (2002), reports that new themes in entertainment are being adopted by other industries and that entertainment is crossing industry boundaries to become a critical element of the marketing and promotions industry:

> *Marketers with an eye for muscular promotions are turning increasingly to the entertainment industry for solutions. It's no surprise, given the increasing number of promotional options available in the industry and entertainment's ability to reach consumers of any age, ethnicity, or income level. Entertainment crosses over lifestyle categories like no other industry, giving marketers the ability to saturate a targeted demographic group at work, rest, and play, often over a period of many months. The export strength of American entertainment products often makes them ideal vehicles for building brand identity overseas through tie-ins. And, thanks to the extended life provided by TV reruns, movie video rentals, and concert films, entertainment can be the marketing gift that keeps giving for years to come.*

Themed Entertainment

We can thank Walt Disney for the birth of the concept of themed entertainment. Prior to the creation of Disneyland, entertainment venues followed the carnival model: a few rides, some games, and a chance for the local population to compete in various displays of craftsmanship, skill, and accepted competence. Once Disneyland came into being, however, a new world of entertainment was born. Entertainment now sought to transform the ordinary into the extraordinary, to create a world where, for a few brief, magical moments, the participant was taken out of his or her mundane existence into a fantastic extravaganza of sound, color, and illusion. That mystique can be experienced daily at Disney's MGM Studios with the feature show "Fantasma." A highlight of the show is a video display, but in place of a screen Disney uses fanned water to display the images. Take a look at special events right now, and you will find vendors offering exactly that. Disney remains a pioneer in event entertainment.

If Disney created the world of themed entertainment, then Hollywood became responsible for its mutation, as generations of "theme-saturated" audiences demanded more—more color, thrills, sounds, and lights. This movement has given rise to generations of vicarious thrill seekers, those who see entertainment as an escape from the banality of their existence and will pay large sums of money for their entertainment nirvana. This provides an endless stream of opportunity for event producers.

The "theme" juggernaut has invaded every aspect of American entertainment, encompassing radio, television, film, theater, and music. Here we must stress the categorization of this type of entertainment as an *American* phenomenon, because, as Disney discovered when it opened its EuroDisney theme park, Europeans are not as enamored of vicarious thrills as their American counterparts and they are not willing to pay exorbitant sums for the privilege of being so entertained.

The overriding presence of themed entertainment has created an audience type that wants to be entertained. The theme removes the mystery from the event and sets the mood. So, in one sense, the use of known themes removes audience expectation. For example, birthday party attendees have an expectation of the type and sequence of events they will experience. The event is expected to include some type of shared entertainment, a cake and candles, perhaps ice cream, light singing, and the opening of gifts. Remove any of these elements, especially an important one such as the cake, and everyone will talk for weeks about the birthday party at which cake was not served.

Every themed event has two main participants. On one side there is the event producer, whose objective is to parlay a vision to the participants, using a carefully controlled series of components and the addition of color, sound, light, texture, and any other media or effect that will complete the experience of the vision. On the other side are the event participants, the audience, or the attendees. They will experience the event or production through the filter of their perceptions and beliefs, which include their expectations of the event based on two criteria—the explicit and implicit elements of the theme. Whether their expectations are simple—to be entertained, or complex—to be entertained within a range of criteria, failing to understand and apply the concept of implicit and explicit themes in planning an event can result in disappointment for both the producer and the audience.

A theme is an idea or a subject that unifies an event. In the birthday party example, there are certain implicit or anticipated elements of the birthday theme, including the cake and gifts, which are extremely important in terms of audience expectations. They are, in fact, so important that the alteration or removal of any of them will result in the audience's declaring that the event, even in part, was a failure, notwithstanding the brilliance of the production of any other part of the event.

An explicit theme leaves nothing to the imagination. Thus, describing an event as an "extravaganza" will set the audience's expectation for the outrageous and spectacular, "tropical" will prepare them for sand, coconuts, and palm trees, "big band" will prepare them for swing music, the lindy, Glenn Miller, and so on. It is difficult to choose a theme that will not have some implicit or explicit elements. Even the type of product being promoted that a theme is created for will have some implicit elements, whether it is a meeting, celebration, trade show, or other event. The event producer needs to be aware of these elements and how the audience will interpret the production based on its expectations.

Adopt and Adapt: Creating through Other People's Ideas

The author first heard these words, *adopt and adapt,* and understood their meaning, from Julia Rutherford Silvers, CSEP. "Why create the wheel?" she asked. "Just take that wheel and roll with it, make it into something yours!" The question, then, is, How can you adopt and adapt an element, making it uniquely yours for your meeting or event needs? An example can be found in a General Mills cereal promotion that used popular music as a sales promotion. The power of music can be utilized to fuel your incentive programs and promotional needs, to increase sales, to grow brand awareness, to improve customer loyalty, or to say thank you to your customers and employees. How can you tie cereal brands and music together for a promotion? Read on and find out about a successful program developed by General Mills.

CASE STUDY: GENERAL MILLS AND GET MUSIC FROM BMG SPECIAL PRODUCTS

Objective: To develop an innovative, effective promotion to drive sales for 13 brands within the General Mills cereal portfolio

Program: The food manufacturer identified the use of music and the Internet as the way to excite its vast multibrand target market. Seven different exclusive CDs were produced, each featuring a different genre of music (country, pop, rock, etc.). The CDs were redeemable on-line via GetMusic.com. The program was featured on 80 million boxes of cereal, including Cheerios, Rice Chex, and Total Raisin Bran, and supported by 45 million free-standing insert units, TV spots, and in-store displays.

Offer: The offer consisted of a gift with purchase. Each box of a participating cereal brand contained a unique code and directions on how consumers could redeem their code for a CD of their choice via the on-line site GetMusic.com.

Music: The CD compilations were teen pop, adult contemporary, modern rock, R&B, country, classical, and holiday. Featured artists included

Carly Simon, 'N Sync, Sarah McLachlan, Alan Jackson, Britney Spears, Alabama, Natalie Imbruglia, Monica, and others.

Result: More than 2.5 million CDs were produced for this program, indicating that music could be used to successfully promote cereal products and that this type of marketing venue presented opportunities even though it deviated from this company's traditional marketing methods.

Why go to the trouble of choosing a theme? Why not just stage an event? Audiences now expect to be entertained with flair and, just as in the movies, they want previews too. The theme sets the stage for the production so audiences will know what to expect before attending the event. We have become so accustomed to having our entertainment handed to us that we can no longer wait to be surprised by the show. With so many existing themed events, things are bound to be done and redone ad nauseum. Where and how do you get new ideas?

Take the family theme in television shows as an example. In the 1940s there was *Life with Father,* a very popular radio show. *Leave It to Beaver* followed, along with *Bewitched, My Three Sons,* and the more risqué *I Dream of Jeannie.* Then we had *All in the Family, The Jeffersons,* and *The Cosby Show.* After a brief hiatus, enter *The Osbournes,* a look at a dysfunctional, but believable, family in the new millenium. All of these shows have a central theme—life in a family—although none of them portrays life as we know it within our own families, there is the occasional brush with reality that keeps us tuned in. *The Osbournes* is a prime example of the adaptation of a well-worn theme (the family television sitcom) from a wholesome, generic, if blasé, setting to one we can relate to in the twenty-first century. Children and parents now swear at each other, dysfunction is overt and central to the show's production, and the father figure is changed from the wise, benevolent patriarch to a caricature openly displaying the worst attributes of parenting.

Why choose a theme that is an adaptation of one that has already been used? First, because if the theme is fairly general and has been popular in the past, that popularity can be expanded upon. And second, because audiences want entertainment without analysis or thought. They do not want to have to think about or analyze what they are seeing or hearing. This is the buffet style of entertainment—everything is on the table and the audience takes what it wants; one price covers everything, from surviving in Thailand to being crowned an American idol.

A theme is a motif, an implicit or recurrent idea. According to Carla Hargrove McGill, vice president of industry relations at Hargrove Corporation in Lantham, Maryland, "A theme helps to create an event that will be long remembered. It puts guests in an excited, upbeat mood. It entices them to stay, mingle, have fun, and conduct business. Theme development and implementation can be exciting and rewarding. Themes can be developed in many different ways and derived from many sources, such as a company's message, special occasions, anniversaries, holidays, a particular era, cuisine, geography, movies, cities, and shows—anything you can think of."

Music is an excellent starting point in creating specific themes. Choose your favorite themes and see what tunes fit or, conversely, you can select some of your favorite tunes and think about the themes they may represent. Then, consider how, over time, these themes have come to relate to subjects in our lives that we now associate with them. Think about how they have become cultural icons and even part of our everyday language.

Using the right mix of targeted themes for your guests can really emphasize the purpose of your meeting or event. Be sure to choose a theme carefully, considering all of its implications, so that the message is clear and cannot be misinterpreted by the audience; a negative message has potential to create a media nightmare for you, the event, and any sponsors.

Techniques for Brainstorming: Bringing Creative Thoughts to the Forefront

Yes, we were playing out of tune and we were doing the same songs over and over again [at the last number of live concerts by the Beatles]. To keep myself entertained I'd play some of the songs like a rumba and no one would notice.

—RINGO STARR

The thought of Ringo Starr playing a rumba tune is antithetical to the themes associated with the Beatles—screaming girls, catchy tunes, the twist, rock and roll music that evokes the sixties. If Ringo Starr played a rumba, we probably would not even notice because of the theme implicit in the Beatles's music. Thus, if you intended to create a Beatles theme, there are elements inherent to that style that would have to be present. How do you hold those elements together and yet separate them so that you can create something new and different?

A technique called brainstorming, which involves unrestrained creative thinking, is a good way to begin. Brainstorming allows ideas to flow without critique or criticism so that the creative process can happen. Analysis and critique follow a brainstorming session, taking each idea and assessing its merit and potential. How do you start to brainstorm? Are there techniques that really work in trying to come up with new and exciting ideas? How can you manage your inner self and bring your creative thoughts to the forefront? In *The Mozart Effect* (1997), Don Campbell suggests putting on music; then he offers three tips for an individual brainstorming session:

Close your eyes and sit at ease. Allow the tension or negative thoughts to leave you by taking around seven deep breaths in and out. Think of a daily chore, and envision yourself carrying out that chore when the music commences. While keeping your thoughts going and your eyes shut, see yourself in a theme and variations position [separate, distinctive positions]. Write down 10 or so variations upon your daily chore.

Campbell is clearly suggesting a brain-music connection. "Often external music, movement, or images help bring the 'neurological music' back in tune. Music mysteriously reaches the depths of our brain and body that call many unconscious systems into expression," he continues. It is true that music can help us to relax and unwind, and this can unleash the creative process. The music that inspires you to be creative may even become a central part of your event.

A similar technique is suggested in the 2002 *CSEP Self-Study Guide* as one of a few that may be compatible with an individual's learning style in preparation for the CSEP examination. The International Special Events Society (ISES) recommends musical tools as a mnemonic device for musical learners, including "songs, melodies or rhythms. If you are good at remembering song lyrics and tunes, you might link terms or concepts to a favorite song by 'rewriting' the lyrics. You might relate terms or concepts to particular songs or jingles, such as protocol issues with the national anthem."

Brainstorming is not always done individually, however. Some useful tips for group brainstorming sessions come from Microsoft Corporation, a leader in the software industry. Microsoft offers the guidelines shown in Figure 6-1.

Group brainstorming is an effective way to generate a wide range of ideas in a "no holds barred" environment that encourages free thinking. Not all of the ideas and concepts generated during a brainstorming session may be useful or applicable, but it is likely that many will emerge that you can use to develop concepts and themes for your event.

What if you would prefer not to reinvent the wheel, but your mind is as blank as an empty canvas? In *Professional Event Coordination*, Julia Rutherford Silvers, CSEP, states,

I do my best brainstorming late at night, doodling my thoughts down on legal pads. I practice a sort of thesaurus brainstorming in which I write down the key event objectives, requests, and requirements and start listing synonyms, letting a free-writing exercise take me wherever it happens to take me. As the words start to fill up the page, patterns appear that suggest themes and options for the event. This is supplemented by watching and reading lots of varied materials. Frankly, television is a main source of creativity for me—not in a traditional sense, but by providing vast amounts of seemingly disparate reference points. Fresh ideas come from connecting two or more known things to create a new one. For example, when our local convention and visitors bureau asked my company to come up

1. Discuss the objectives of the exercise with the attendees. Make sure they understand the "big picture" goals and why they have been invited to participate, and define the goals for the session.
2. Meet at a different location for a change of pace and to reduce stress; make sure there are refreshments and music to greet the participants. Don't invite negative or stressful personalities. Their input will be more appropriate when a critical assessment of the ideas and concepts is required. At a brainstorming session, the smooth flow of ideas is crucial to the process.
3. Keep the tone positive by using a combination of humor and examples and stay focused on the objectives.
4. Set the guidelines for success at the outset; establish the need for creativity and positive idea generation. Make it clear to participants that those who are consistently negative will be asked to leave the session.
5. Be ready with all of the appropriate tools, including a white board, tablet, pencils, colored markers, and any other visual or other devices you will need to record the participants' ideas. Assign someone to take notes so that you can be sure to capture all information. If you will require a computer or Internet access, take care of those details prior to the session. Eliminate interruptions by asking participants to turn off their cell phones, and tell the venue management staff that you do not want to be interrupted.
6. The moderator is critical to the success of the brainstorming session and should be a person whom the group will trust, has expert knowledge about the subject matter, and is able to guide the group's efforts without leading or manipulating the conversation.
7. Decide on the best method to collect and display the group's ideas. They should be written large enough so that everyone in the room can read them and should branch off each other. Tape additional paper to the walls, if necessary, to create a visual display of the session's results.
8. Refine the session's output, consolidate it into a final idea or plan, and post it publicly. Or, if appropriate, have the team present the idea or plan. Follow through on the best ideas to create something new and fresh.

Figure 6-1
Guidelines for Brainstorming

> with an event that would garner media coverage, I brainstormed by putting together a story I had seen on an artist who created landscape sculptures and another one on the infamous crop circles. "Let's carve out a UFO landing strip on the west mesa!"

Silvers further states,

> Starting to delve into this idea, we noted that not only is New Mexico home to the legendary Roswell incident, Albuquerque is home to Lovelace Medical Center, where the first astronauts were tested (as humorously depicted in the film The Right Stuff). New Mexico also

*has the Alamogordo Space Center and, of course, the Los Alamos
and Sandia National Laboratories. The science fiction/science fact
theme started to take shape, and the end result was the Albuquerque
Intergalactic Reception, a one-night event, staged in 1994 atop the
Convention Center's parking structure, featuring a UFO landing strip,
a dozen exhibits—including the UFO Museum from Roswell, roving
lunar robots from Sandia National Lab Robotics Department, hands-
on zero-gravity activities and a scale model of the Mercury I space
capsule from Alamogordo, a sci-fi book fair (New Mexico has the
highest per capita ratio of science fiction writers in the United
States), a portable inflatable planetarium, telescopes provided by the
university's astronomy club, and a "Milky Way Mercado" of souvenir
vendors. Media releases were sent out, attached to "flying saucers"
(Frisbees), highlighting the unique "galactic" assets in New Mexico.
A local television station came on board as a media sponsor, promoting its participation with its extensive menu of science fiction
programming (and providing a celebrity guest appearance by the star
of one of its sci-fi programs). The event attracted nearly 2000 locals
and hundreds of thousands of dollars worth of media coverage.*

This is an example of using local lore, attractions, and themes to build a themed event. The foundation for the theme is there; all it takes is some creative work to find a "fit" between the venue and the event.

A final suggestion for managing the creative process is illustrated in Figure 6-2. Individuals and organizations are being prepared by changes in society to accept and support creativity, but organizations are going to have to change their practices in order to take full advantage of the creativity of their people. Group creativity begins with an idea—the vision of a single person. Usually, a creation is built around a mental template, structured from experience or training; pure creation occurs rarely, if it exists at all. The best individual creations are not spontaneous eruptions of an idea. They result from often frustrating trials that ingeniously combine known concepts and elements into original forms. In other words, creativity is hard work.

Harnessing collective creativity to produce useful, salable, and innovative products can be made a lot more effective by using a process that specifically addresses all the phases of a product life cycle and all the tools available to create and bring the product to reality.

Such a creative process can be visualized as a system of interrelated elements, as shown in Figure 6-2. The elements around the ellipse correspond to phases in a product life cycle, but the double-headed arrows indicate that they cannot just proceed in a step-by-step process. They must continually interact, and each element affects, and is affected by, the others. Each element is addressed, as well as the relationships between the elements and how to deal with the dynamic nature of these relationships as the process of creation goes along (Shirley 2001).

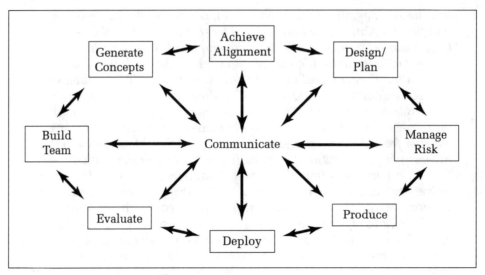

Figure 6-2
A Creative System
(Courtesy of http://www.managingcreativity.com/training.html)

Utilizing Motion Pictures, the Small Screen, and Broadway as Stimuli for Creation

Anytime a product can be seen as part of a movie, a TV program, or a theatrical show, there is an event product-placement opportunity. *Selling Communications* reports, "What used to be merely set dressing is now the basis for some of the biggest money deals in the industry. Witness the celebrated example of the BMW Z3. The German automaker paid to have its new sports car become James Bond's ride in the film *Goldeneye,* and the association between car and movie became the basis for BMW's entire launch campaign." (2002).

This is also a method of exploiting an existing theme to promote an existing event. The James Bond persona already implies the rich, nonchalant playboy who drives fast cars (the older James Bond movies always featured Bond driving a Jaguar), mingles with beautiful women, and lives a blessed, if dangerous, life. BMW's target market was the affluent male, possibly single, with the means to afford this lifestyle (if indeed, it could be lived) or at least to have some of its trappings. This theme, already established, was easy to leverage. The popularity of the long-running James Bond series meant that there was little risk in adapting the theme to the auto maker's marketing campaign. The same holds true for event entertainment. There is little risk that this motion picture theme idea will go away anytime soon.

The theme of the shows that the snack-food maker Gardetto's Inc. has chosen to advertise its products is important because they are long-standing programs with an established audience base representative of the people who purchase the company's products, or whom it wants to purchase its products. The message here is that if you want your event to be successful, choose your audience carefully and learn to leverage success, yours or someone else's. The audience probably won't even notice. The small screen has something to lend to meetings and events. At the Meeting Planners International (MPI) World Education Conference held in Las Vegas in 2000, TV anchor Carol Martin interviewed actor Danny Glover in a made-for-TV interview, yet this was seen live in one of MPI's general sessions—and it worked.

LOOK THROUGH THE WINDOWS AND SEE HUGE EVENTS

Some of the largest events, measured in amounts of money spent and numbers of people invited either live or over satellite hookups, have been the product launches of the Windows Operating Systems by the Microsoft® Corporation. Not only can they start you up on your computer and provide employment opportunities for meeting and special event companies, but now there will be a move into movies and television.

> At the National Association of Broadcasters industry conference in Las Vegas, the Seattle Microsoft Corporation announced plans to move forward into the market of movie and television distribution. The software giant disclosed that a number of "behind-the-scenes" audio and video production companies expressed their interest in making their products compatible with Microsoft's Windows Media Player format. While a less advanced system for playing music and videos already exists, the hope is that this technology, code-named Corona, will allow for cheaper movie distribution and TV transmissions. Companies like Adobe, Avid Technology, and Thomson Grass Valley Group agree that this advance in technology will provide a product that could prove an intense competitor with rival RealNetworks' RealOne player (Nelson 2002).

However, persuading the entertainment industry to adopt a new technology is difficult. With security the main issue, movie industry companies are wary about adopting new technologies. "The biggest concern that they have is that if the media content gets into a digital format, then it can be transferred anywhere on the Internet and they can lose control," said Phil Leigh, a digital media analyst with Raymond Jones and Associates. How to handle copyright and artist compensation also becomes problematic within an industry that has adhered to a singular and time-honored financial model since its inception. The Internet has forced some interesting changes on the music and film industry, with no firm resolution or solution in sight.

TELEVISION

Cable TV has figured out a way to combine television and music. Writing in the March 31, 2002, issue of the Sunday *New York Times,* Arts and Leisure Section, in "Letters to the Editor," Gerry Dorman of Lindenhurst, New York, responded to an article entitled "Turning a Television into a Music Box," authored by Terry Teachout in the March 10 edition of the *Times:* "I was surprised to see that there was no mention of Direct TV and EchoStar satellite television systems, which have been carrying Music Choice digital music programming for years. I have had Direct TV since 1997 and always listen to my favorites: the two classical channels as well as the jazz and Dixieland channels."

Thirsty for a good show and a beverage? The Florida Citrus Commission was spending $65,000 to market grapefruit martinis nationwide, after the drink, called the Ruby, was featured on the TV show, *Sex and the City.* This award-winning show has been the catalyst for sales of everything from books to clothing, shoes, jewelry, and accessories. This is an excellent example of how the power and popularity of a television show can drive sales of products and create new venues for themed entertainment. Look for more show-related sales generated by this television series, including perhaps the introduction of specialty items based on its characters' styles and tastes.

Be alert to Ozzie look-alikes and his legendary music in forthcoming event entertainment and production. *The Osbournes,* introduced as the latest in family show entertainment, is an adaptation of a theme that has existed in radio, television, and film entertainment for more than 60 years. Its mainstream popularity was a surprise to show producers, mainly because the Osbournes are not representative of the wholesome family that Americans like to think exists today. *The Osbournes* was produced by HBO, which does not have the same programming constraints as the network stations. However eccentric and dysfunctional the Osbournes may appear, they portray a realistic, if somewhat distorted picture of family life that, unfortunately or not, many families today can relate to. Being a show business family, their popularity is also due to our extreme voyeurism with anything having to do with the personal lives of the glitterati, another old, but timelessly successful theme.

MOTION PICTURES

Because of the 20th anniversary release of *E.T.: The Extraterrestrial* in March 2002, look for more E.T. walk-around characters at special events, not to mention the old reliable transportation vehicle, the bicycle, set in futuristic surroundings. With millions of viewers over two decades, this movie sets a wonderful tone for themed special events around the world. The major motion picture *Moulin Rouge,* as of the first quarter of 2002, had a reported revenue of more than US $170 million worldwide, according to Washington, D.C.'s WTOP all-news radio. This movie is tailor-made for special events. Now if we could just get Nicole Kidman to sing at this event, that would truly be a memorable moment of event entertainment!

What about utilizing a movie theater as a venue for special events? In an article in *Selling Communications,* a Primedia Business Magazine on www.info-now.com, this topic was investigated. After all, "movie theaters are larger than ever, now physically capable of giving third parties room to operate. Movie houses with 25 screens and stadium seating are popping up around the country with lobby restaurants, cappuccino bars, and merchandise stores. The old Odeons and Rivolis have morphed into mini-theme parks where marketers can score some space for themselves," writes Kilmetis. "That increase in real estate brings with it more expensive leases, so theater owners are bending over backwards to tap any and all alternative revenue streams."

Enter special events. Holding events in movie theaters is not a new concept. In the days of silent films, movie screenings were accompanied by pianists who provided musical backdrops that set the tone for the on-screen action. *The Rocky Horror Picture Show,* even after more than 20 years of screenings, is a testament to the continued popularity of the movie as an event. Have you ever been to a late night showing of this film? What would be the audience response to hosting a corporate or association special event in the theater during this movie, or a showing of your own corporate or association screening? This makes a lot of sense—everyone likes the movies, and the popcorn is less expensive than bringing in an off-site caterer.

BROADWAY

> *Bit by bit,*
> *Putting it together.*
> *Piece by piece,*
> *Only way to make a work of art.*
> *Every moment makes a contribution,*
> *Every little detail plays a part.*
> *Having just the vision's no solution,*
> *Everything depends on execution:*
> *Putting it together.*

"PUTTING IT TOGETHER"
MUSIC & LYRICS BY STEPHEN SONDHEIM
COPYRIGHT © 1984, 1985 BY RILTING MUSIC, INC.
ALL RIGHTS ADMINISTERED BY WB MUSIC CORP.
ALL RIGHTS RESERVED

The theater has been an integral part of music for centuries. Many of the master composers have experienced their greatest success in the theater, from Mozart and Wagner to Gershwin and Sondheim. Throughout the centuries, people have loved to hear music with their eyes. This is not just a part of history, however; this theme continues in popularity to this day.

That piece of real estate in New York City known as Broadway has seen the production of contemporary music's most treasured repertoire; it has been the working place for dozens of America's most gifted composers, lyricists, playwrights, producers, directors, and performers. Staged musicals of genuine quality demonstrate the endurance and staying power unique to most popular music today.

Paul Creighton of T. Skorman Productions in Orlando, Florida, says, "The 'Stomp' idea is still one of the most popular shows to use for general sessions. A three-person percussion show really wakes the crowd up and gets them in the mood for the start of their meeting. These musicians can incorporate different 'instruments' into their performance: garbage cans, BBQ grills, kitchen appliances and utensils, and even your company's product (within reason). It makes a powerful statement." Music has the ability to capture an audience's attention, mesmerize its members with sound and rhythm, and create a memorable event that will stay with them long after everyone has gone home.

Look for "boy bands" such as the Back Street Boys or 'N Sync for event entertainment, as well as themes like "My Big Fat . . . (whatever)" plus a continuance of Broadway themes. Witness total cross-pollination from pop star to the big screen to the Broadway stage.

The Associated Press, on July 23, 2002, announced that 'N Sync's Joey Fatone would join the cast of the hit Broadway musical *Rent* on August 5, 2002, at the Nederlander Theatre. Fatone was scheduled to appear in the role of struggling video artist Mark Cohen through December 22, 2002. Although Fatone appeared in several films, including the comedy *My Big Fat Greek Wedding*, *Rent* would mark his first foray into theater.

Stacy Garner of the *New York Times* writes, "These days, Broadway has been relying on the creativity of film directors to produce plays. Although many movie-made Broadway shows like *Big* and *Saturday Night Fever* were disappointments on the Broadway scene, many more movies are currently being made into musicals" (April 14, 2002).

The wonderful thing about event entertainment is that if it is working, your guests can be transported from their trials and tribulations to the world you have created for them, albeit for four hours, but a different world nonetheless. Thus, the goal of managing the creative process for meetings and events is to enrapture your attendees and to "Leave your troubles outside" (Joel Grey, in the Broadway show, as well as the motion picture, *Cabaret*).

In Conclusion

The best way to proceed after reading this chapter is to go to a movie, see a Broadway show, or watch some great television. Now that you have some background on the history of themed entertainment and an understanding of the creative process that is used to develop such events, pay attention to the elements involved. Can you identify the theme? Is it familiar to you? What is the audience's reaction and participation level? Do you know others who have seen this show or event? What are their reactions? Is it a show or event that others talk about long after it is over? As you watch commercials and advertising, notice how many of them have adopted themes from various other types of entertainment. You may even notice that your clients will ask you to consider themes for their events based on a favorite movie, a play, or even a song. As discussed in this chapter, themed entertainment—ranging from music to motion pictures to Broadway—is an audience favorite and themes are increasingly linked to various types of media. Old themes are modified and sometimes "modernized" to produce something new, exciting, and different that audiences will talk about long after the event is over.

Scripts for Future Study

BOOKS

Anupindi, Ravi, Sunil Chopra, Sudhakar D. Deshmukh, Jan A. Van Mieghem, Eitan Zemel, and Jan Van Mieghem (1999). *Managing Business Process Flows.* Upper Saddle River, NJ: Prentice-Hall.

Campbell, Don (1997). *The Mozart Effect.* New York: Avon Books.

Goldratt, Evivahu M., and Jeff Cox (1992). *The Goal: A Process of Ongoing Improvement.* 2nd rev. ed. Great Barrington, MA: North River Press.

Kotler, Philip, and Geoffrey T. Renshaw (1994). *Marketing Management.* 8th ed. Upper Saddle River, NJ: Prentice-Hall.

Westberg, Barbara (1990). *Programs for Ladies: Themes and Complete Programs for Banquets and Retreats, Adaptable for Special Services, Auxiliary Meetings, and Conventions.* Hazelwood, MO: Pentecostal Publishing House.

Exit Stage Right

Chapter 7 investigates strategic planning. From the first draft of your event through the evaluation analysis, this chapter deals with the operations and logistical handling of event entertainment and production.

CHAPTER 7

Strategic Planning for Event Production and Entertainment

Too many elements of the system are not trustworthy today. They have failed us because of self-dealing and self-interest.

—Arthur Levitt Jr., former chairman of the Securities and Exchange Commission, at a Senate hearing on Enron

IN THIS CHAPTER YOU WILL DISCOVER

- How to organize your strategic planning into one source, referred to as "the bible."
- How to use, make, and distribute production schedules.
- The art and science of strong script writing.
- How to write realistic cue sheets and distribute them.

The event production and entertainment industry is a fast-paced, exciting business that brings together the skills, experience, and efforts of sometimes hundreds of people to deliver something fabulous. The successful delivery of an event hinges on having a comprehensive strategic plan in place and then executing it. Coordinating the efforts of vast numbers of people, sometimes across geographic locations, requires attention to every detail. This is the nitty-gritty of event production and entertainment planning—not the most glamorous part, but certainly the most necessary. From a production standpoint, inadequate planning will make it difficult to deliver an event successfully. From a legal standpoint, you may have problems with licensing boards, liability, or even lawsuits if you do not deliver an event as promised. From a professional standpoint, event planners and suppliers who do not deliver events as promised eventually do not receive new bookings.

This chapter will discuss the organization of your strategic plan into one personal resource including production schedules, scripting, and cue sheets. From the first draft of your event through the evaluation analysis, this chapter deals with the operations and logistical handling of event entertainment and production. This chapter was partially written by Bob Cherny, sales manager of Paradise Sound & Light, Orlando's Premier Full Service Sound, Light and Staging Company, and former production manager for Disney Event Productions.

Your Bible: Organizing Your Strategic Planning into One Source

We are a passionate people in the meetings and events industry. We "do it" because we "get it" and we love it. When it happens fabulously, we want it to happen even bigger and better the next time, and we thrive on that feeling. To some, at first, this feeling is quite novel. Sometimes the feeling wears off and event planning can become a job. With the "it's just a job" attitude, a planner may become complacent. When that happens, the mind goes, along with the passion. Instead of looking forward to the often crazy weeks before an event with excited anticipation, you will begin to wonder how you will get through the next few weeks, or single engagement, without driving yourself crazy.

THE PRODUCTION BOOK

There is something that helps even the most passionate event planners cope with the crazy times. It is called "the bible," or the Production Book or Operations Manual. It contains all the information and details about the event within a three-ring binder with different tabs that separate the information. There should be three copies of each binder: two on the road, held by two different people, and one, known as the "one-off," left in the planner's office.

This strategy has a dual purpose: insurance and protection of the information. The bible is the most important part of the event, because it is the event's strategic plan, containing all the information needed for the event. If there is only one copy of this bible, how would the planner react if it were lost or stolen? Having three (or several) copies of your bible will protect you, your team, and your engagements. It if should happen that two copies are lost, the office will have a copy, and the event (and your neck) will be spared.

> The Production Book, *or Operations Manual, as it is referred to in the meetings industry, is your on-site reference and guidebook covering every important facet of the entire event. It should include anything and everything required for smooth operations at the event site, even if you are not able to be there in person. The Production Book should include all key information and documents related to the planning and operations of the event, as well as any documentation required to comply with governmental regulations.*
>
> The directory *consists of a contact list of all vendors and key stakeholders [in the Production Book]. The list should include names, all potential telephone numbers (and room numbers if the parties are at a hotel), and mailing and e-mail addresses. Don't forget to include your own contact information and to make certain your key staff have copies of the directory. Also include your organizational chart and staff schedules and instructions. Be sure to cross-reference your vendor lists by name and service.*
>
> Verification. *Everything from your initial proposal to the final contract, correspondence, vendor agreements and purchase orders, floor plans, confirmations, invoices, licenses, and certificates of insurance should be at your fingertips in case a question or dispute arises on-site. If allowed, put copies of all permits and waivers in your Production Book and keep the originals in a safe place in your office. You might also include copies of pertinent policies and regulations that you can present should there be a question about what will and will not be allowed or what should or should not be done* (EXCERPTS FROM PROFESSIONAL EVENT COORDINATION *BY* JULIA RUTHERFORD SILVERS *ARE REPRINTED COURTESY OF* JULIA RUTHERFORD SILVERS, CSEP).

There are as many ways of producing an event master record, or Operations Manual, or bible, as there are people who need it. The most common method is to use the traditional three-ring binder; however, as we become more technologically sophisticated, we are tempted to abandon this old friend in favor of more technological alternatives, such as laptops and personal digital assistants (PDAs). In my opinion, however, although as much as possible should be created and duplicated in your personal laptop computer and PDA, everything you need for your event should be in print form in your three-ring binder(s). Remember to back up all of the event information files on a diskette or network server. Better yet, make several diskettes and give one to each person who has a binder.

Developing a binder actually begins when you first get the call indicating that there may be an event in your future. It probably starts with a folder that you randomly throw things into as the documentation is created. Depending on the size of the event and your involvement with it, the folder may be adequate, but if you are the planner, that is unlikely. You may have to have several binders to hold all the information you will need to create the event and that will accumulate in the process. The hard part is to ensure that the pieces of the data most likely to change are duplicated in your laptop so that you can reprint them legibly and distribute them quickly. The laptop is an integral component of today's event production and entertainment management process. The laptop, along with the three-ring binder, and possibly your PDA, back each other up and track each other's changes. (Your PDA backs up your computer through a synchronization process.)

What is the function of a personal data assistant? The PDA has a limitless role in the strategic planning process. As stated earlier, the PDA should contain a copy of the information contained in your laptop. Desktop-to-Go and Documents-to-Go are two PDA software applications that synchronize with MS Word, MS Excel, MS PowerPoint, and MS Outlook files. The detailed schedules with notes of items of concern should be in the PDA, and you will use the PDA to jot down notes that you will need at billing time inasmuch as you will have it with you when you are, perhaps, sitting in the back of the bus on the way to the hotel from the final-night party. You can then studiously peck away with your stylus, entering final details, as the bus bounces you home or back to your hotel.

What goes into the three-ring binder, other than copies of everything? According to Bob Cherny, there are some specific items that it should contain:

- The site inspection forms you filled out on your first trip to the property
- Copies of the digital photos you made of everything you saw during the site inspection
- Copies of the contracts and proposals
- Event-specific contact lists
- Schedules
- Menus
- Maps
- Floor plans
- Renderings of the sets
- A picture of your spouse and/or kids (to cheer you on your way)

Tabs in the three-ring binder may include:

Travel	Travel information related to the event
Client	Contract, riders, and notes with client

Act	Contract, riders, and notes with act or entertainers
Pro Sch	Production schedules
S/L/B	Tech riders, etc. (sound / light / backline); for more complex events this section may be separated with separate tabs

Include blank lined paper at the very front, for writing notes, as well as at the back of the binder for additional notes. Carry a loose-leaf folder with a sleeve in the front and back of your binder or sheet protectors for last-minute distribution of information. To protect your assets, the first page of your newly constructed Project Book should read:

If found, please return to:
Company Name
Or call collect to:
Company Phone Number

Travel Arrangements: Do you know where your airplane/train tickets are? If you are the event leader, do you know everyone's itinerary, his or her travel agent and locator number, and, of course, the telephone numbers of all of the above? Make photocopies of all this information and three-hole punch them for inclusion in the binder under the tab "Travel." Do not forget to make a master sheet with everyone's information: name, airline, flight number, and departure and arrival times. Include emergency telephone numbers, such as the leader's home, cell, or beeper number, and the booking agency's number. In addition, include the hotel information, such as its name, address, telephone number, and method of transportation from the station or airport to the hotel. In addition, include the name of a limo company in case there is a transportation problem.

Rooming Manifest: Most event entertainment is planned months in advance, so the time to plan hotel accommodations for the events planning staff, entertainers, and other personnel is not the day or even the week before the event. Besides ensuring that rooms are available for everyone who needs one, make sure to consider:

- How many rooms will you need?
- How many beds are in each room?
- Who will be in those rooms?
- Who is paying for the room and tax?
- Who is paying for incidentals?
- What are the arrival/departure dates?
- How many smoking or nonsmoking rooms will be required?

Contracts

Make sure that a signed contract exists. You don't want to be left in Peoria without a gig or any money. Contracts are documents that protect *both* parties.

You cannot prove anything if it is not in writing, so protect yourself and your event and get everything in writing.

Event producers should have the following information:

- **The contract between a buyer and a corporate entertainment company**
  If a client is not following the terms of the contract, prove to that person, by the client's own signature, that he or she may want to remember what was agreed upon. This is to include not only terms, but also rider requirements and the method of and timetable for payment. Also have on hand the technical requirements such as sound (with input list), light, catering, and stage riders. All of that has, of course, been double-checked ahead of time with the subcontracted vendors in the town in which the event is to be held. Have their names and phone numbers available as well.

- **The contract between a corporate entertainment company and the headline entertainment**
  What can you expect from the headline entertainment? What must you supply for its members? What do they expect from you? How many sets will they perform, and how long will they be? Who collects the money for the job? How much is to be paid, and what is the accepted method of payment?

- **The contract between a corporate entertainment company and other vendors, technical people, and musicians**
  If these people are going to be at the job or will have a part in its success, before or after the job, you need to know about it and communicate that information to the leader or producer on-site.

- **The contract between a producer and the American Federation of Musicians (AFM) of the United States and Canada**
  This contract should be in effect for all, and if it is not, you may want to investigate this option, as it could mean more protection for you. Remember that you, and not your office, will be paying your own work dues through this contract. The form of the contract may be your local union's contract, or Form CP-1s for traveling musicians, with jurisdiction over the territory in which the engagement covered by a contract is to be performed. These specifics should be included in the information section of the Production Book.

Production Schedules: How to Make Them, When to Use Them, Who Gets to See Them

The Production Book should include a complete schedule of all event components and activities. This schedule could be in two different formats—

chronological in sequence or alphabetical by activity—or both, depending on the scope and complexity of the event.

The chronological schedule will help you monitor the progress of the event, and the alphabetical schedule will help you locate individual components. Create a "Program-at-a-Glance" overview chart of the entire event as a cross-reference tool, showing day, date, times, and site/room name. See Figure 7-1 for an example of a production schedule.

Frequently, production schedules are not made by production people, but are determined by the availability of the space. The following are the four most important pieces of information that go on every production schedule:

1. When is the room available?
2. When is the first event or rehearsal?
3. When does the last event end?
4. When do we need to be out of the room?

There is an inverse relationship between the time available to do a job and the number of people it takes to do it. If more time is available, fewer people are required and, frequently, the cost is lower. Advance planning by the technical crew significantly improves both the quality and speed of the work and has the net effect of holding the price steady. The first item on your production schedule is the timing of the request for proposals. Long lead times are better than short ones. The second item is the date they are due back. The third is the date you commit to award the bids. The next several steps are negotiated. You will need to work with your vendors to determine when all of their final plans, drawings, and specifications have been approved so that they can start building, if necessary
(EXCERPTS FROM PROFESSIONAL EVENT COORDINATION BY JULIA RUTHERFORD SILVERS ARE REPRINTED COURTESY OF JULIA RUTHERFORD SILVERS, CSEP).

Bob Cherny reminds us that the production schedule starts well in advance of the event and should include everything that impacts its look and feel except the food and the speakers' scripts. Every event should have a production schedule of some sort. Even "Load in at noon, show at 8:00, out at 11:30" is a production schedule. Obviously, the bigger the event, the more involved the schedule.

Preparation takes time. Subtract the time a task takes to accomplish from the time it needs to be finished to determine the time it should start. Then factor in other conflicting activities and adjust the schedule accordingly. Submit the schedule to all relevant parties and adjust as needed. Repeat this process until consensus is achieved. All involved should feel that they have sufficient time to complete their tasks in a manner that does justice to their skills and experience.

Who gets the schedule? Everyone whose name or job is on it. Everyone whose job is impacted by the schedule. Everyone who needs to be out of the

June Jam/Crime Stoppers
Production Schedule as of 4:00 P.M. EST, Tuesday, June 11, 2002

Producer:	Mark Sonder Productions (MSP)	
Contact:	Mark Sonder, CSEP	(cell number)
Contact #2	Stanley Aaronson, CSEP	(cell number)
Contact #3	Roxanne Sonder	(cell number)
Telephone:	(number)	
Cell:	(number)	
Fax:	(number)	

Date:	Saturday, June 15, 2002
Venue:	Fig Garden Golf Course
City/State:	Fresno, CA
Artist:	Big Bad Voodoo Daddy

Crime Stoppers:	Detective Brad Stevens (CS)
	Fresno Police Department
	Manposa Mall
	PO Box 1271
	Fresno, CA 93715-1271
	(telephone number)
	(cell number)
	Note: Jerry Dyer, Chief of Police
Fig Garden	Dave Knott (FG)
	President
	7700 N. Van Ness Boulevard
	Fresno, CA 93711
	(telephone number)
	(cell number)
Table Mountain Casino	Diana Ellis (TM)
	Marketing Department
	8184 Table Mountain Road
	Friant, CA 93626
	(telephone number)
Sound/Light	Rusty Rocha and "Static"
	Light & Sound Solutions
	4460 W. Shaw, Suite 196
	Fresno, CA 93722
	(cell number)
Staging	Mario Viramontes/Ike Pursel
	Expo Party
	PO Box 9321
	Fresno, CA 93791-9321
	(fax number)
	(cell number)

Figure 7-1

An Actual Production Schedule Used for a June 15, 2002, Event. This event, held in Fresno, California, was a benefit for Crime Stoppers, featuring Big Bad Voodoo Daddy.

Hotel Accommodations for MSP/BBVD: The Piccadilly Inn University (Andrew)
4961 North Cedar Street,
Fresno, CA
559-224-4200/800-468-3587

All dates are in the month of June 2002.

Day	Time	Action	Responsible
Pre-Show			
Wednesday, 12th	8:00 A.M.–4:00 P.M.	Initial setup of stage	Mario
	Early afternoon	Arrival in town of Mark Sonder	
	2:00 P.M.	Meeting with CS and TM	MSP/CS/TM
Thursday 13th	8:00 A.M.–4:00 P.M.	Stage setup	Mario
	11:00 A.M.	Mark Sonder on-site	MSP
Friday, 14th	10:00 A.M.–4:00 P.M.	Light and trusses setup	Static
		Power setup	Rusty
	10:00 P.M.	Arrival in town of Stan Aaronson	
Day of Show			
Saturday, 15th			
	11:00 A.M.	Arrival of BBVD airport	
	12:30	Arrival of Rusty	
	12:30	Setup of sound	Rusty
	1:00 P.M.	Lunch for BBVD crew	CS
	1:30	Setup of BBVD	MSP
	1:30	Setup of BBVD/4 guys	CS
	4:30–5:30	Sound/light check	ALL
	5:30–9:00	BBVD in trailers near stage	CS
	6:00 P.M.	Doors open	CS
		Dinner for BBVD & crew	
	8:00	Seated for dinner	FG/CS
	8:05	Table Mountain presentation	TM
	8:15	Auction commences	CS
	8:30	Follow-spot operators in place	
	9:00	BBVD starts show	MSP
	10:30	BBVD finishes show	MSP
	10:55	Surprise fireworks	MSP
	11:00	EVENT OVER	CS
Load-Out			
Saturday, June 15, 2002			
Load-out MUST be completed by the dawn's early light!			
	11:00 P.M.	BBVD breakdown	MSP
	11:30	Sounds starts	Rusty
	Midnight	Light starts	Static
	Midnight	Stage starts	Mario

Figure 7-1
(Continued)

Notes for all:
Mark Sonder Productions will ALWAYS have the Master Production Schedule. This schedule will change MANY times, possibly right up to show time.

Please e-mail any and all changes, as well as any questions, to me directly at *msonder@marksonderproductions.com.* In the subject matter write BBVD Fresno. Thank you to all. With all the experienced, knowledgeable people working on this event, it will be both seamless and flawless!!

Figure 7-1
(Continued)

way when the work is being done. How and when do people get the schedule? They get it electronically whenever a change is made to it, in advance of the event, and on paper once the event commences. One hopes this is the final schedule.

The following is an example of an inspection checklist. Not all of its elements may be relevant to your events, but these items should be considered when developing the checklist for your Production Book.

- Facility name, address, fax, e-mail, Web site, best information on the Web, best map on the Web
- Driving directions
- Facility manager, phone, fax, e-mail
- Administrative office contact, phone, fax, e-mail
- Business office contact, phone fax, guest fax, e-mail, services available
- Technical contact, phone, fax, e-mail
  What are the contact's levels of experience? Which tech areas are their strengths?
- Audiovisual office contact, phone, fax, e-mail
- Does the AV contact have the authority to assign staff to specific projects?
- Receiving office contact, phone, fax, e-mail
  Can you get your truck to the building? What hours does the dockmaster work?
- Electrician office contact, phone, fax, e-mail
- In-house or outside contract?
- Fire marshall contact, phone, fax, e-mail
- Telephone company contact, phone, fax, e-mail
- Local services

- Nearest IATSE Local no., phone, fax (Theatrical Stage Employees, Moving Picture Technicians, Artists and Allied Crafts of the United States, Its Territories and Canada, AFL-CIO, CLC)
What is the union rate per hour during the day, evening, and weekends?
What is the minimum call time?
What is the minimum number of people engaged for your meeting or event?
Are you allowed to run your own equipment? Can you touch your own equipment at all?
- Nearest Teamsters Local no., phone, fax
Do you need Teamsters to bring your equipment in?
What hours does the elevator operate, who has the only key, does the elevator work?
- Nearest "big box" general merchandise store, address, phone, directions
- Nearest full-service hardware store, address, phone, directions
- Nearest electronics store, address, phone, directions
- Nearest gas station with diesel fuel, address, phone, directions
- Nearest fast-food restaurant, address, phone, directions
- Nearest all-night restaurant, address, phone, directions
- Nearest decent restaurant, address, phone, directions
- Nearest decent moderately priced hotel, rates, address, phone, directions
- Loading area, number of docks, dock heights, levelers, access
- Room name, length, width, ceiling heights, ceiling loads, rigging details, lighting system, audio, power, floor load, loading access, fire restrictions
- Where is the power?
- How good is the installed sound system? Is there an installed sound system?
- Can you control the house lights, or must you have a tech do it? Can you use the building's sound systems to record your sessions?
- Is there a limit to the floor load?
- Can you rig in the ballroom? (This assumes that you are hanging things like lights.)
- What is the ceiling rigging load limit per point? Where are the points?
- Are there chandeliers or wall sconces in the way? What is the ceiling made of?
- Are the measurements on the facility floor plans accurate? (Generally they are close, but not always exact.)
- Are the room capacities listed in the sales brochure accurate? (They are frequently inflated.)
- How secure is the ballroom, really? (Generally, not very.)
- Who else shares the loading docks?
- Where are the dressing rooms for the talent? How are they equipped?

- What are the riser sizes? How quickly can they be set up and torn down? Are they draped? Is there a charge?
- Is there a charge for podiums? What condition are they in? Can you attach your logo?

If your meeting or event involves headline entertainment:

- How private is the facility?
- Can the staff be counted on to not tell your delegates where the celebrity's sleeping room is located?
- Are there dressing rooms for the performers?
  What condition are they in?
  Do they have mirrors, sinks, and showers?
  Are they shared with the house talent?
  What is the path from the dressing room to the stage?
  How close to the meeting room can you get a limo?

For remote or off-shore venues, you may wish to ask these additional questions:

- Can you ship equipment to the venue?
- How long does it take the equipment to get there and back?
- What is the boat schedule?
- What taxes are imposed on equipment shipped in for a convention?
- What documentation is required for customs on both ends?
- Is there available labor? Is it any good?
- Are trucks allowed on the island? Will the local roads allow a truck to get from the harbor to the venue?
- What is the power like? Is it U.S. standard, some other standard, or just plain unreliable? Is there enough of it where you need it?
- Does the hotel own scissors lifts and forklifts? Do they work?
- Can you get to the loading dock? Is there a dock? Is the dock on the ground level?

Figure 7-2 shows an actual checklist used for a concert by Huey Lewis & The News. Such lists can be used as excellent guides for different types of events, but should be customized to meet the specific needs of the event planner.

The checklist will give you some of the many details you need for the entretainment at your event. The next step is to put those details together into a script so that everyone's activities work together and flow smoothly. Every event runs from a script, a detailed description that lets all involved to know where they are supposed to be and what they are supposed to be doing. A well-prepared script removes confusion, improves communication, and increases your team's efficiency.

Please e-mail or print clearly and fax back to: *info@marksonderproductions.com* or 555-555-1212.

Venue_____ Day of Week _____ Date(s) _____

Venue Address _____

Capacity_____ Ticket Prices (if applicable) _____

Facility Manager _____ Tel _____ Cell _____

Box Office Manager _____ Tel _____ Cell _____

Technical Director _____ Tel _____ Cell _____

Backstage _____ Tel _____ Cell _____

Promoter _____ Tel _____ Cell _____

Promoter Rep _____ Tel _____ Cell _____

Production _____ Tel _____ Cell _____

Show Settlement _____ Tel _____ Cell _____

Advertising/Promo _____ Tel _____ Cell _____

Tickets _____ Tel _____ Cell _____

Security _____ Tel _____ Cell _____

Catering _____ Tel _____ Cell _____

Transportation Co. _____ Tel _____ Cell _____

Sound Check_____ Doors _____ Show Time _____

Support Act_____ Length of Support Show _____

Support Contact_____ Tel _____ Cell _____

Band Hotel/Name and address _____

Contact_____ Tel _____ Cell _____

Crew Hotel/Name and address (if different from above) _____

Contact_____ Tel _____ Cell _____

Miscellaneous Info _____

_____

In addition, please list e-mail addresses for all the above names. Thank you!

Figure 7-2
Mark Sonder Productions Information Contact Sheet

Scripting: The Art and Science of Strong Script Writing

The key to good scripting for the production schedule and the documentation derived from it is to employ the level of detail appropriate to the needs of the presentation (or event) at the time the presentation is being given. People will not know what is expected of them unless they are told what to do and when to do it. This does not mean that their every move must be described, just where they are supposed to be and what they are supposed to be doing. Once they know, they should have the experience and the expertise to fill in the details themselves. Knowing the timing of their activities is derived from the cue sheets, subsets of the production schedule that pinpoint the timing of the event's various activities.

Cue Sheets: Writing Realistic Cue Sheets and Disbursing Them

A cue sheet is a detailed subset of the total schedule and should not be viewed in isolation. The amount of detail on the cue sheet is determined by the needs of the event. Generally, the technicians will write their own cue sheets because each crew member needs different information. Although conventions frequently look like theater and "business theater" people would like us to think that conventions are theater, they are far more like rock concerts than carefully scripted drama. This is not to say that conventions and rock concerts are not planned. They are; in fact, rock concerts are generally very well planned. The planning for conventions, though, is different. The technology is different. The goals and expected outcomes are different.

Trying to apply what may have been learned in a theater class to convention planning functions is a dangerous endeavor. The basic concept of theater, that we are peering through the missing "fourth wall" and suspending disbelief about the goings-on in front of us, is simply not relevant to the convention experience. Perhaps the most obvious example of this is the audio component. Dramatic actors do not walk around with microphones in their hands; singers and motivational speakers do. Unless the scene involves a church, there is almost never a podium in a dramatic presentation. Have you ever seen a convention without a podium?

There is a temptation to confuse special events like Super Bowl halftime shows and Olympic opening ceremonies with concerts. As tightly scripted as they are, these special events are theater. Conventions are not theater. The tightly controlled world of theater is not relevant to way life works in the meeting and events industry.

Virtually everyone working on the event is an independent contractor or an employee of a subcontractor who has joined the team to accomplish this particular project, and when the project is over they will disband until the next project, when some of them will work together again. What this means to planning and running the event is that although all are given the same information, they will all use it differently according to their needs. Their needs are determined by what they will have to do to accomplish their individual parts of the show.

Even within the event, the needs will vary. For example, a stage manager might call the cues for the keynote speaker: "Slides go to conference logo, lights go to full stage wash, followspots pick her up as she enters, audio roll fanfare, fade out and fade in her wireless, followspots stay with her until her speech is over; we are scheduled for 40 minutes."

Of course, each of the people addressed in these cues would know in advance what they have to do because a line item for the speech, without the details, would have been in the event schedule. In contrast, a speech given by a vice president of marketing, with 400 slides, ten videos, and a dancing "mascot," would need a detailed script and lots of rehearsal. Although the stage manager would call the cues, the members of the crew would operate from individual detailed cue sheets that they wrote for themselves. During the event production, the stage manager's job is more about "when" than about "what."

Consider now the most critical part of larger events, rehearsal. Rehearsal is key to a smoothly run presentation. The author has seen the consequences when executives have been "too busy" to rehearse. Very few people can pull off a complex presentation without a rehearsal. Although not apparent to the audience, the lead-in for each cue must be brutally obvious. An industry favorite is a line such as, ". . . and now you can see the new campaign for yourselves. Roll the tape, please!" Rehearsals benefit every member of the production team, including the technicians and production staff. During rehearsals they can make any needed adjustments to their equipment and their own cue sheets and fine-tune their parts in the production. A smooth, trouble-free rehearsal will give the entire production team confidence that the day of the event will also run smoothly. The next item in the Production Book deals with communication, how you must communicate to everyone on the team, at any time.

Master Communication Tabulation

The master communication sheet should include, at a minimum, the company name, responsible person(s), short job description, and telephone number(s) of all the people that will make this event a success. Realize that there may be different information on your master communication sheet, depending on where you are on the organizational chart. You may be provided with information needed for those a few levels above you and everyone below you. All of this information should be on one page, with a page dedicated to each town or venue where you will be working.

In Conclusion

The Production Book is the most important tool in planning an event, as it contains all the information you, as planner, will need to do your job. Gathering this information can be time-consuming, and you may be tempted to cut corners. However, imagine the problems you could encounter if there were a misunderstanding about an out-of-town gig. It could mean your job, the jobs of your team, and jobs in the future. The key to successful entertainment and production is in management, through planning and attention to detail, and effective communication with all of the people who are involved in every aspect of the event. You need to know how you, as the planner, interact with the total product and how it interacts with you. Everyone's task is of vital importance. Plato has said, "The productions of all arts are kinds of poetry and their craftsmen are all poets." Whether you are responsible for event planning or production, or you are the entertainment hired for the event, this is your job; not just to plan, produce, or to play well on the gig, but to make sure you have covered all of the details and are in the right place at the right time.

Scripts For Future Study

BOOKS

Allen, Judy (2000). *Event Planning: The Ultimate Guide to Successful Meetings, Corporate Events, Fundraising Galas, Conferences, Conventions, Incentives and Other Special Events*. New York: John Wiley & Sons, Inc.

Fitt, Brian, and Joe Thornley (1997). *Lighting Technology: A Guide for the Entertainment Industry*. St. Louis, MO: Industry Focal Press.

Moody, James L. (1997). *Concert Lighting: Techniques, Art, and Business*, 2d ed. St. Louis, MO: Focal Press.

Moxley, Jan (1996). *Advance Coordination Manual*. Boulder, CO: Zone Interactive Communication.

Vasey, John (1997). *Concert Tour Production Management: How to Take Your Show on the Road*. St. Louis, MO: Focal Press.

Boehme, Ann J. (1998). *Planning Successful Meetings and Events: A Take-Charge Assistant Book*. (Take-Charge Assistant Series). New York: AMACOM.

Exit Stage Right

This chapter has discussed the tools that can be used to plan for the actual details of an event, Chapter 8 discusses the financial implications of an event. Although not all events need to earn a profit, they must all adhere to a budget, and it is very important for an event manager to understand how the entertainment portion of an event fits into its overall financial goals.

Financial Planning and Management: How to Measure the Return on Event Entertainment

Money makes the world go 'round.

—LIZA MINNELLI AND JOEL GREY IN CABARET

IN THIS CHAPTER YOU WILL DISCOVER

- How to demonstrate value through measurement and analysis of budgets, reports, and evaluations.
- How to measure your return on event entertainment (ROEE).
- How to save money and get the most impact from your entertainment dollar.
- How to identify hidden factors behind the costs of event entertainment.

If you are an event entertainment professional, the goal of every event you produce is to ensure that you meet your client's objectives and that every event is successful. But every event will have a more specific purpose or objective that you will have to meet, and as the preceding quotation from *Cabaret* implies, that objective is often a financial one. Your client may set such objectives, and you will have to keep them in mind when planning the event. Sometimes money will not be an object and you will be able to produce an extravaganza that your client and his or her guests will talk about for years. Generally, however, your event will have a budget and stated objectives that you will be expected to meet. In that case, you will have to understand how you can assess those objectives, before the event, state your goals to your client to win his or her business, and, after the event, measure how well you achieved the objectives.

Budgets: How to Measure the Financial Success of Entertainment at a Meeting or Event

Companies come and go. It's part of the genius of capitalism.
—PAUL O'NEILL, FORMER U.S. TREASURY SECRETARY,
ON THE COLLAPSE OF ENRON

The amount of money one needs is terrifying . . .
—LUDWIG VAN BEETHOVEN

Both composer Beethoven and politician O'Neill agree with Sally Bowles in *Cabaret,* that even with the gift of creation of fine arts, money seems to be a key element to stage those gifts. Sometimes money is not the issue in producing entertainment. For example, in the summer of 2002, Michael Jackson was offered a multimillion-dollar contract to perform for 60 to 90 minutes at the Georgia Dome for 86,000 people, plus a private jet for his own transportation and a host of other perks. That offer was declined by Jackson. The two surviving Beatles were asked to perform together and were offered more money than some countries' total gross national product. That offer was declined. The Swedish supergroup Abba was offered $1 billion for a reunion tour to play 100 concerts. That also was declined. Although these performers declined to perform for various personal and business reasons, money not being one of them, those who would have gained most from these events would have been the fans, the event producers, and the promoters. They were well aware of the value of a concert given by any of these superstars. For all of their potential nostalgic and entertainment value, the real purpose behind producing those events would have been to make money for the shows' producers and promoters.

Even if money is not the issue, your event will have to meet or exceed certain financial performance objectives. Sometimes those objectives will be tangible, such as revenue or sales, and sometimes they will be intangible, such as increased goodwill, exposure, or some other future benefit. Each event will have its own objectives, based on a combination of the needs and expectations of the client and the audience. If, for example, your event is for a charitable organization, it will want to raise money for its cause. If it is a corporate event, the company will have certain business objectives it wants to meet. If it is a public event, then exhibitors, concessionaires, attendees, and your entertainers will have their own objectives and expectations.

Accounting for and meeting the objectives of events is the bottom line, and although this is a fun, creative business, it is still a business. If your events do not meet their tangible and intangible objectives, including the financial goals, you will eventually go out of business. Figure 8-1 explains the five steps you can follow to determine your event's revenue objectives, calculate your costs, and derive the numbers that you will have to reach to meet these objectives.

Once you have established and are comfortable with the objectives for your event, you need to manage the money flow. Events are generally booked many months in advance, and in order to secure the booking, most of the providers and the venues that you will be using will require a deposit. Deposits may range from a percentage of the anticipated cost to a fixed fee; most entertainment companies require a 50 percent nonrefundable deposit, paid at the time of booking. There may also be additional expenses for the event on your behalf, such as purchasing sets, equipment, or supplies. The vendors will look to you, as the planner, for payment. You will have to be reimbursed by your client. In this business, corporations, associations, and other entities that procure entertainment for their events are quite smart and financially savvy. They know that if they want a product or service for their events, they will have to pay for them. Because you will be the contracting entity for these events, you will be responsible for managing the cash flow to the vendors and from your client by managing your receivables. Giving your client a schedule of receivables early in the planning stages will help the client to understand when certain items will have to be paid. For example, if the venue deposit is due six months before the event, the client can be prepared for that and be prepared to pay your invoice on time. The alternative is to surprise your client with unexpected invoices and then wait for payment.

Once you have developed the schedule of receivables, you must send out the invoices as soon as each item is "invoiceable." Theoretically, the sooner you send invoices to your client, the sooner they will be paid. There will be times when you will not receive payment from your client in time to meet the invoice's due date. Clients may not be late with payment intentionally; their work or travel schedules may interfere with their ability to approve invoices for payment, especially if they do not know that the invoices are coming.

1. Determine your financial goals for the meeting or event. Is it a host event? Are you looking to break even? Do you want to make a profit? If so, how much or what percentage?
2. Gather all of your "hard costs" expenses—that is, costs that are stable, that you are sure of, that will not change. If this is unclear, you can utilize the figures from the historical costs of this meeting or event or from similar events that you have produced in the past.
3. Estimate your variable costs expenses. These are the costs that rise or fall depending on the number of guests you will be having. There may be circumstances beyond your control that can influence these expenses. For instance, dates (some dates that are during peak seasons will incur higher travel, venue, and accommodation costs), locations (some locations cost more than others), number of attendees, speaker expenses, food and beverage events, promotional requirements, and sources of funds (e.g., sponsors, donors, or attendees).
4. Gather all of the income items for your meeting or event. These can include advertising revenues, concession sales, donations, exhibit/exposition booth rental fees, gifts in kind (fair market value), grants and contracts, interest income from investments, merchandise sales, registration fees, special event ticket sales, sponsorship fees, and vendor commissions.
5. Take the total of #4 (income) and subtract #3 (variable costs) and #2 (hard or fixed costs). Relate this number to your answer for #1 (your financial goal). This number represents the potential income for your event. If the number you obtain for your answer is negative, then you need to review your costs and determine where you can make changes. This does not mean "cutting corners," it means providing the best service and results for your client, based on the client's budget and objectives. Take a look at your established financial goal, item #1. From a critical perspective, is it attainable and reasonable? What is the client's opinion? If, in your professional and expert opinion, you are not comfortable with the financial objective and do not think that it can be met, you must tell your client. This adds another risk factor to your event, and you must work with the client to ensure that he or she has reasonable expectations that will come close to the actual outcome.

Figure 8-1
Five Steps to Determine an Event's Income Objectives

However, this may interrupt your event's cash flow and put you in the position of having to pay invoices out of your business account. To prepare for this eventuality, you should have a financial contingencies fund available. Managing money flow is a critical component of managing risk. If you are the employer, you must be able to pay your employees or independent contractors. In this industry, where good working relationships are critical to success, you do not want to earn a reputation for not paying your vendors in a timely fashion.

You should be able to provide your clients with financial statements for the entertainment and production portion of the event. Doing so shows professionalism. Use these statements within your own business; this is another tool that allows you to manage receivables and expenses. There are two different reports that you can use for financial reporting for yourself and for your client, the cash flow statement and the income statement. A cash flow statement is a standard business accounting report that shows money coming in and money going out, similar to a checking account register, providing you with a snapshot of your money or cash position at a specific point in time. It can be structured on a weekly, monthly, quarterly, or per event basis. An income statement is a report you can use in your business and for your clients. Whereas a cash flow statement indicates money flows, an income statement provides an overview of income and expenses over a certain period of time and groups items by their revenue or expense category, rather than showing line items, as in a cash flow statement. For example, an income statement may show an audiovisual and catering expense, whereas a cash flow statement would show the individual line item amounts for each vendor paid in those categories. Income statements can be generated on a monthly, quarterly, or annual basis.

For most events, you will need to know the approximate costs in order to establish a starting point for achieving the financial objectives. These can be determined by looking at historical data for similar events. Finding the "breakeven point" will tell you how much revenue you will need to earn to cover your expenses, as represented in the following formula:

$$\text{Breakeven point (BEP)} = \text{fixed costs (FC) plus variable costs (VC)}$$
$$= (\text{number of registrants}) \times (\text{registration fee})$$
$$\text{Fixed costs (FC)} = \text{the amount spent even if no one registers}$$
$$\text{Variable costs (VC)} = (\text{number of registrants}) \times (\text{cost per registrant})$$

Once you know your event's breakeven point, you can make assessments of your costs, marketing efforts, and promotions and know what it will take to make your event a financial success. Knowing the breakeven point will help you determine whether your event is financially viable. For example, if you are planning an event that will require at least 200 attendees in order to break even, you know that you will have to attract at least that many for the event to be financially viable, and more if it is to actually generate revenue. Ask yourself, is it possible to attract 200 or more attendees? If not, perhaps you need to reassess the event's objectives, details, or expenses and find less expensive alternatives. You may also need to increase your marketing and promotional efforts. Presenting clients with this information will help them keep their expectations for the meeting or event in line with projected results. Figure 8-2 is based on a hypothetical event, showing how the breakeven point is

All fixed entertainment costs (FC):

$ 6,000 lighting
  1,500 sound
  6,000 talent fees
  2,000 labor (stagehands)
  2,000 musicians
    200 ASCAP fees
 20,000 administration
    500 signs
_____
$39,200 = Total FC

All variable costs (VC) are per person:

$10 lunches for musicians, talent, and crew
  3 coffee breaks for musicians, talent, and crew
  5 printed programs for audience
 30 backstage passes
 15 radio rental
_____
$63 = Total VC

Substitute the event numbers provided into the following breakeven formula to determine the registration fee required to meet the breakeven point for this event:

(number of registrants) × (registration fee) = $39,200 (fixed costs)
                              + (number of registrants) × ($63/registrant).

Assume 600 people.
600 × registration fee = $39,200 + (600) ($63)
registration fee = ($39,200 + $37,800)/600
registration fee = $77,000/600 registrants
registration fee = $128.33

It is a good idea to perform this calculation assuming a variety of attendance levels; for example, assume 200, 300, 400, and 500 people to determine the best registration fee. There is an inverse relationship between the number of attendees and the registration fee—the more well-attended the entertainment event, the lower the registration fee. However, you should err on the side of caution. If actual registration is estimated to be between 300 and 400, you may want to use the 300-attendee figure to determine the registration fee, to account for no-shows and to ensure that you can meet your costs.

Figure 8-2
An Example of How to Find the Breakeven Point

calculated. Remember that fixed costs exist whether or not there are any attendees, so that number is a constant in the formula.

How Entertainment Companies Bill Their Clients

There are a number of ways an entertainment company may charge for its services, based on the scope of the work, its required performance and effort, knowledge, expertise, and experience. Most companies charge for their services in one of the following four ways:

1. *Consultant fee.* This will generally be a flat fee, based on providing an expert opinion, negotiating the rider requirements for a headliner, or performing another specific service that the meeting or event requires. This can be a payment per service or per quarter, year, or event.
2. *Fixed fee.* Generally paid to an entertainment company for a multiday program to handle all of the entertainment for all functions.
3. *Hourly rate.* Some entertainment and production houses may charge by the hour, but this is uncommon.
4. *Percentage of product or services sold.* This is probably the most commonly used method of payment to an entertainment company. Generally, a straight agency fee would be 10 percent. However, if the entertainment company is asked to do more than just the paperwork in regard to an artist, the percentage may start at 20 percent. Artists' managers may make up to 50 percent of their artists' fees, which is built into the price of engaging an artist. In comparison, most caterers mark up their products and services 300 percent.

It must be noted that when you hire an entertainment company, unless it is part of your company's payroll, you are hiring it as an independent contractor. The entertainment company may also utilize a combination of independent contractors and employees. Employees represent additional costs to the company, which are billed back to the hiring company as part of its costs. In the United States, these employee-related costs include the payment of federal income tax withholding, Social Security (FICA), Medicare, and federal unemployment insurance (FUTA). At the state level, additional amounts include state income tax, state unemployment insurance (SUI), state workmen's compensation insurance, and state disability insurance (SDI). Other licenses or permits may be required, depending on the company's core business.

There are other cost factors to consider that are part of the production of a publicly attended event. These include compliance with certain federal regulations such as those of the Americans with Disabilities Act (ADA), the

Occupational Safety and Health Administration (OSHA), the Federal Communications Commission (FCC), and the Bureau of Land Management (BLM). At the state level, there are additional tiers of compliance and regulation, including the requirements of CAL-OSHA (like the federal agency, but specifically for the state of California), public or state park property use requirements, adherence to the health and safety code, minimum wage/hiring requirements, the requirements of Alcohol-Beverage Control (ABC), and for public safety, as well as overtime calculation and payment requirements that may vary from state to state.

Understanding all of the cost factors that will add to your event's fixed costs is important in presenting a competitive price. But it is difficult to compete on price alone if you do not have a cost advantage. Your cost advantage decreases with each additional layer of contracting. For example, if you are buying from someone who is buying from someone else, you may not have a cost advantage once all of that entity's margins and markups are added into its price. Clearly, the more money you can save on products or services, the higher margin you may be able to earn or the lower the price you will be able to offer to your client. Conversely, the most expensive provider is not always the best, so price cannot always be a decision point. Use your network of contacts, other experienced industry professionals, and your production manuals from past events to hire the best professionals at the best rates.

Tips on Saving Money and Getting the Most Impact from Your Entertainment Dollar

You will get the impression that everything in an entertainment event costs something, and this is often true. Yet there are ways that you can save money and still provide high-quality food, fun, and entertainment for the attendees. Here are some tips to help you engage top-name speakers and headliners for your guests without breaking the bank.

Planning
- Book several dates. The concept here is "volume discounts." The more dates you book, at least in theory, the lower the cost per entity (or date), whether that entity is a headliner, a generic dinner dance band, character artists, or speakers. Booking several dates at the same time helps performers to fill their calendars, eliminating downtime, and helps to ensure that you are on their calendars.
- Offer several dates. If you can supply your favorite entertainment purveyor or speakers' bureau with several dates, it can respond with the

best dates for its artists. With a choice of dates, the suppliers can offer you dates in either peak, shoulder, or off-peak time periods, which can save you money.

- Book for more than one function at the same event. Again, the concept of volume discounts applies, but all of the bookings would be within one specific program. If you operate multiday programs, you may be able to utilize your talent in a "double-duty" situation. Talent agencies enjoy this arrangement as they can have the same people working multiple times over a period of several days. To them, this means money in the pocket now, as they will not have to wait for your next program 3, 6, or 12 months away.

- Hire musicians for less than four hours. Although in some metropolitan areas there may be a four-hour minimum for musicians, the smart local music houses offer a one-, two-, or three-hour rate, which is just perfect to set the tone, mood, or atmosphere for your cocktail receptions. When purchasing local or regional entertainment, ask the purveyor how many hours the price represents. If you cannot hire entertainers for less than their minimum, book them for the entire time even if you think it exceeds your requirements. Thus, should they have to play longer than you anticipated, you may not incur additional costs for overtime if the additional time falls within the entertainers' minimum. If you know that your meeting or event will definitely end at a specific time, have the entertainers come in early. This can allay nervousness about the possibility that they won't show up until the last minute, and if your attendees arrive early, the entertainers will be there and ready to perform.

- Avoid overtime. Overtime can cost you additional money, ranging from straight time to double time. Certain states, such as California, have very exacting overtime laws that are strictly enforced. Once your event runs into overtime, you will have to pay overtime rates to several groups, including the house electrician, food and beverage departments or caterers, and other labor at the venue. Keep to your production schedule or include an "overtime" line item in your budget.

- Get the best buys in headline entertainment. Payments for headliners start with a four-digit figure and can range up to a seven-digit figure. To get the most marquee value for your dollar, choose headliners that provide the music of oldies, jazz, and country artists. For years, these categories of musical entertainment have been the most "underpaid" and still deliver quality entertainment that is popular with many meeting attendees.

Budgeting

- Arrange to receive 10 percent off as your commission back to your company. Be inventive in your negotiation. For instance, work your best deal, then mention that your company works as a commissionable office. Although this method may work only with local or regional entertainment and not headliners, "a penny saved is a penny earned." Have the entertainment company or management lower your contracted rate by a stated percentage or have it make a donation, in the amount of your "commissionable rate," back to your organization.

- Your convention services manager may recommend the property's exclusive and often recommended orchestra, which is generally 15 percent more expensive than other local talent. This percentage is remitted by the exclusive orchestra back to the property for the right and privilege of being awarded the exclusivity. You may wish to think twice about utilizing such a recommendation.
- Licensing your music is less expensive than a lawsuit. See Chapter 13 for information on how to and why you should license music for your event.

Negotiating

- There is no justification for a line item that adds a 10 percent fee for musicians' union tax. This extra charge is included by various music offices even though musicians local unions in the American Federation of Musicians do not charge that much. Moreover, it is the responsibility of the local musicians to pay their own work dues, not the purchaser of the entertainment (this amount typically ranges from 0.5 to 3 percent).
- Do not pay for use of the venue's piano. A property should not use its piano(s) as a revenue stream. You should, however, be charged for the tuning of any pianos. Typical charges should be from $50 to $100.
- Allow artists to display, promote, and sell souvenir or promotional items. This comes under the heading of merchandising. From publications to T-shirts to compact discs, this is a money-making opportunity for them and can help offset some of your costs. For a guarantee of a lower cost of the artists, offer to purchase a specific dollar amount of their merchandise. Always make certain your client approves these purchases.
- Utilize your favorite music purveyor. Although it may seem to add another layer of purchasing, and therefore an additional expense, this move can actually save money in talent and production procurement. For example, a major event planner in Glastonbury, Connecticut, always engages Mark Sonder Productions (MSP) for production of sound reinforcement, lighting, and building a stage. She has called the staging company direct, the same one that MSP uses, for the same stage. Because MSP gives this staging company more engagements than the planner does, it is still less expensive than the planner's price booking directly even with the "middleman's" markup!
- If you do not ask, you will not get, so do not be afraid to ask for what you want and be prepared to negotiate where you can. If you present

your purveyors with reasonable and mutually beneficial options, you have to be prepared for a simple yes or no answer. If the answer is yes, you prosper. If the answer is no, the vendor saves face and everyone moves on. This approach may be difficult for some people and may clash with their personal philosophy or cultural background, but asking for a reasonable concession and being ready and willing to negotiate helps you and your client. If the vendor believes that you are a qualified buyer and that the deal can be consummated by saying yes right away, you may have a deal at a better price and perhaps more or better options. What do you have to lose?

The High Cost of Entertainment and Music for Nonheadliners

Music and entertainment for an event, although it generally adds the most value, usually takes the smallest percentage of the budget. A look at all of the costs associated with hiring entertainment for your meeting or event may explain why the price may seem to be high.

Entertainers: Although many music offices have a one-, two-, three-, and four-hour rate schedule, musicians are most often engaged for a four-hour minimum. Recently, the union has made allowances for engagements of less than four hours; however, the best value is usually to book for four hours.

Administrative Surcharge: An entertainment office has a 20 percent overhead cost for total union contract scale just to cover Social Security, unemployment and workmen's compensation insurance, other payroll taxes, and bookkeeping expenses.

Health Benefit Contributions: This is a per entertainer per engagement charge that is contributed to the health benefit plan set up by the union, and the music office pays the premium for the engaged musicians. The union charges a penalty for late payment, at a rate of 1.5 percent per month.

Pension Contributions: 5 percent of gross union scale wages including overtime, rehearsals, cocktail hour, mileage, and all premiums, which the music office pays to the local unions.

Leader's Premiums: 100 percent above scale to the leader of the band.

Subleader's Premiums: 50 percent above scale to the subleader of the band.

Conducting Premium: 25 percent of gross union scale for any musician conducting any part of an engagement.

Holiday Premiums: For Memorial Day, Independence Day, and Labor Day in the United States, as well as New Year's Eve.

Doubling Premiums: Musicians who play more than one instrument are paid a premium fee.

Rest Periods: Although there is no additional pay for rest periods, rest period pay applies if the entertainers do not get a break every hour on the hour. In that case, the music or entertainment office will assess a penalty of up to 75 percent of the hourly rate.

Cartage: Many event managers have had to pay cartage charges when hiring harpists or other musicians with large equipment. The music office pays cartage for amplifiers, drums, drum machines, vibraphones, a string bass, cello, tuba, sousaphone, baritone sax, a second sax (excluding soprano sax), synthesizers weighing at least 20 lb. or 36 in. or more in length, each case of folding music stands, and extension speakers.

Parking: Parking fees and charges for vehicles while loading or unloading are all subject to reimbursement to the entertainers.

Mileage: This is a wage payment for travel time outside any metropolitan area. This payment is itemized in categories such as car, train, and plane, plus an accommodation fee.

Transportation: You would think transportation is covered within the mileage classification, but it is not. This is an expense reimbursement paid to drivers for the use of an automobile outside a metropolitan area. The exception is air transport, for which the music office "shall provide first-class transportation (plane, bus, train, or chauffeured vehicle) for travel to engagements more distant than 150 miles."

Other Travel-Related Payments: Meal allowances, transportation from destination to airports, after-midnight or later engagements, and layovers are included in this category.

Overtime: If the engagement lasts more than four hours, overtime represents additional costs, sometimes more than the actual booking costs. Before you satisfy the crowd's request for one more song, check to see how much that song may cost.

Overscale: Some entertainers make overscale. Union wages are set as a minimum for the music office to pay. The operative word here is *minimum*. Saturdays, weekends in June, and all of December are all affected by the economic concept of supply and demand. Expect to pay a premium when booking entertainment during peak periods. Moreover, there are minimums at what are known as "Class A" hotels. These minimums establish a minimum number of musicians required to play in each room at these specific properties in large metropolitan areas.

Although the music office passes along most of these charges to the purchaser, realize that these represent hard (and fixed) costs that your music purveyor has to consider when booking the entertainment. Although it may appear that there is a charge for everything connected with booking entertainment, there is something that is free: the hours upon hours each entertainer spends practicing his or her art each day, for years, so that he or she can play/perform professionally for you at your next event.

Measuring Return on Event Entertainment (ROEE)

How can you change a meeting or events department whose expenditures always seem to be a drain on the company or association, to a profit-making department? You need to show your management or board of directors a positive return for their money from the events you produce. This profit stream may not be obvious right away and may take days, weeks, or months to materialize. For example, if a convention and visitors bureau (CVB) sponsors an event outside its jurisdiction with the sole purpose of bringing business to its destination, how can that be seen as having profit potential? Imagine that there is a proviso that the CVB will have an allotted presentation segment at the event that will feature the CVB's president or the city's mayor speaking at the event while showing a video or multimedia presentation featuring its destination. Isn't this opportunity worth underwriting a luncheon or dinner for a ballroom full of meeting or event planners? To justify the cost in dollars and cents, consider how much expense would be involved in locating the name and address of each of those planners and printing and mailing a media kit to each of them. Probably about the same as the cost of the presentation at the event, but the presentation is done in person by a city official, the attendees receive VIP treatment, and the event is memorable. It's a win-win situation for everyone involved.

Nonprofit organizations are not alone in wanting to see a positive return on their investments in event entertainment. "It's not just a party anymore. Your events must contribute to corporate goals. Each event must be integrated into the marketing plan so that it contributes to overall corporate objectives. A corporate event is an occasion that is designed to communicate critical organizational messages and themes in highly personal, entertainment ways that maximize retention" (Doyle, 2002).

Stanley Aaronson, CSEP, project manager for Mark Sonder Productions and ViewPoint International Destination Management Companies USA, shares his thoughts on ROEE:

Only the client can quantify and measure ROEE, since ROEE is either an increase in the services or goods demanded or a decrease in the cost of supplying those goods or services. First, the client needs to see the difference between explicit and implicit costs. An explicit cost requires an outlay of money by the firm. Implicit costs are input costs that do not require an outlay of money by the firm; that is, the opportunity cost (whatever must be given up to obtain some item) of the financial capital (forgone income) that has been invested in the business or, in our case, in paying for the meeting or event. By considering both implicit and explicit costs, we can determine the economic profit as opposed to simply the accounting profit, which takes into consideration only the explicit costs. A short-run economic profit is generally considered to be a positive return on investment.

Next (based on the factors contributing to economic profit or loss), we can run a cost-benefit analysis that compares the costs and benefits or improvements to a firm from the investment in a sales promotion, sales meeting, stakeholders meeting, convention, conference, exhibition, hospitality function, or other in-face event. A positive return on investment occurs when the benefits are perceived to be greater than the costs.

Last, the client needs to see the advantage of taking into consideration the accumulation of investments in people and the firm's relationships with people, such as client orientation, professional development, leadership development, continuing education, and on-the-job training. Generally, accumulating investments in one place, such as in a client or employee, results in a positive return on investment (ROI). Customer relationship management (CRM) practices have demonstrated the intrinsic value and short-run return on investing in alliances that meet corporate and business goals and objectives.

In its *Year 2000 Annual Report,* MicroStrategy claims, "For any business or organization operating in the Internet Age, information is currency. The ability to realize the potential of your information assets—turning data into intelligence—will be vital to the evolution and success of your business."

Tom Carrier, senior meeting planner, IQ Solutions, agrees with the MicroStrategy philosophy: "Management by spreadsheet alone without regard for long-term impact on customer habits, and thus overall asset and/or brand value, is a poorly conceived choice. Perhaps now we can reintroduce hospitality in the hospitality industry."

Evaluations: Surveying Your Attendees

Appallingly sick, with boring chord movement and bad acting.
—JONI MITCHELL, IN A DESCRIPTION OF CONTEMPORARY MUSIC

Some of your attendees will have an emotional answer to a survey; certainly Joni Mitchell has feelings based on her own experiences. What we are looking for is a hard measurement, an evaluation process from which to judge the job that has been done and make the event or meeting stronger in the future.

Organizations understand the important role of events and meetings in establishing positive relationships with customers, clients, and employees. But how do they know that an event has delivered the anticipated results? Although they can certainly tell by how the attendees act and how long they stay and participate in the meeting or event, the things they really want to know about can be answered only by asking the right questions of the attendees. That information is part of the postevent survey and evaluation, the meeting or event's final act. A survey is useful in gaining attendee feedback on the simplest topics, such as "Did you like the event?" as well as answers to specific questions that determine what and how much information was retained from specific presentations at the event or meeting. The survey responses will provide information about many production elements that will be important to you, as the event planner. For your client, they will be important in establishing whether the meeting or event met its goals.

Because the survey is so important, how do you build it so that it asks the right questions and presents valid, statistically significant responses? Stanley Aaronson, recipient of the 2001 Western International Special Events Society Excellence Legacy Award, has done extensive studies with surveys. He offers the following guidelines:

Get help from the experts. A well-drafted survey is key to this process. Never underestimate the value of outsourcing the drafting of a survey. Most of us do not have the background in statistical analysis, sociology, anthropology, or scientific methodology to develop a reliable survey instrument. How does one go about quantifying and measuring goodwill, public relations, or beneficial publicity?

Give your respondents incentives. The survey instrument, in and of itself, is of no value when no one responds to the survey. Therefore, because people respond to incentives, there must be an inducement to complete the survey, in the form of a parting gift or another amenity, handed to them when they present their completed surveys.

Make the survey meaningful to the respondent. In the U.S. market, it is difficult to attract and retain loyalty because a transaction must exceed expectations to result in return business. If meeting the U.S. market's expectations does not induce their loyalty, the survey instrument must provide a variety of responses that allow for a range of expectations of the respondent. This would include responses several degrees beneath the ordinary level of expectation to the level at which the respondent feels that his or her expectations have been exceeded to the point at which he or she is slack jawed in amazement. For example, choices including terms such as "would," "may," "could," "probably," and "might" would be more effective than just two, "definitely would" and "definitely would not." The highest-quality exit surveys are conducted in front of a camera and recorded for future evaluation of body language and the relative coherence of the interviewee.

Getting cooperation is key. Measuring utility—a measure of happiness or satisfaction—is insufficient in determining loyalty or return on investment. Cooperation is difficult to maintain, even when it is mutually beneficial, so getting the attendee to the point of being so wowed that he or she is slack jawed is about the only way we can enlist the cooperation of a potential or existing client.

I've gone to more than 20 teller machines, and not one of them has a single cent. What kind of country is this that there is no money anywhere?

—*Aurora Melgar of Argentina*

At first glance, the reader might think that Aurora Melgar, as quoted here, was simply having a bad day. But perhaps she was looking for the wrong thing. Everyone knows that ATM machines just hand out bills; they do not distribute coins. Was she aware of that? Did she drive around, going to various teller machines looking for coins, and, when she could not get any, assume that ATMs did not have any money? What message would she convey to her friends and family about ATMs in the United States?

This quote is a simple illustration of the importance of surveys to receive feedback from events and meetings. Details that may seem inconsequential to you, as the planner, may be important to your attendees and may make a difference in their perception of the event's results. Using surveys as a measurement tool will give you access to information that will help you assess the results of an event or meeting from several perspectives: event production, client results, and attendee perspective, which can be useful for future events, help your client to maximize the value of the money spent and, it is hoped, add another satisfied client to your client roster.

Calculating ROI is becoming more than an attractive option. For years, industry leaders have urged planners to calculate and verify the return on investment of their meetings. The work of a planner is not focused merely on putting together the right group of talent to successfully produce an event. Now meeting planners have to utilize their marketing and merchandising skills to ensure that, with the client's objectives in mind, they know enough about the organization, the product or service, and the expected ROI to do everything they can to meet and exceed their client's expectations.

The purpose of a survey is to get as much feedback as possible, both good and bad. Although it is always a pleasure to hear good comments, it is the negative comments that are most useful. They point out the areas that need improvement and details that may have been overlooked. Without pointing fingers or blaming anyone, what do you do with negative survey results you obtain after an event? A gap analysis can be worthwhile. A gap analysis is a process whereby the differences between expectations and results are assessed and then used to create positive organizational changes. Eric McNulty, working at Harvard Business School Publishing, explains his version of a gap analysis.

> *We just use the official U.S. Army After Action Review process. It's simple, easy, and we have found that it works well. The first step is to gather everyone and go over the most basic ground rule: No blame is to be assigned to any one individual or group—the goal is learning, not fingerpointing, and credit is to be shared broadly. You learn much more when you focus on* what *went right or wrong than on the* who. *The session takes one hour. There are four 15-minute segments:*
>
> - *What was supposed to happen (lay out your goals in regard to finances, attendance, impact, or any other aspect)*
> - *What actually happened*
> - *What went right, which you would like to replicate at future events*
> - *What went wrong, or what you hope will never happen again*
>
> *Capture all of this knowledge and share it with the team. From there you can develop action plans for incorporating the good and excising the bad going forward.*

Michele C. Wierzgac, MS, CMM, is chief executive officer and president of Michele & Company. Through her Chicago headquarters, her company specializes in "meeting management, incentives, and consulting solutions." She must demonstrate ROI to all of her clientele.

> *There isn't anything magical or mysterious about return on investment—it is quite simply a business measurement and communication skill to measure and justify whatever is important to your organization (not to you!). It takes a major commitment on your part as a professional to undertake the process of measuring and communicating the value of your meetings or what your department produces as a whole. And, yes, to get an agreement on "what" is important to measure requires diplomacy, patience, and a number of other skills as well.*
>
> *ROI is a powerful business tool that many of us, in particular the CMMs [Certification in Meeting Management] and many corporate colleagues, are already working on via experiments, articles, interviews, conversations, studies, white papers, and Meeting Professionals International's Corporate Circle of Excellence, just to name a few. Like all research and experimentation—it takes time!*

Measurement Tools

We have determined that measuring ROEE and ROI is important, but how are they measured? What tools and criteria are recommended by the industry experts and professionals, and how are they utilized? Trace Kuhn of Extreme Meetings!, an interactive audience response company located in Florida, spends his workdays measuring as well as developing clients' attendee responses. He shares his expertise on this subject:

> *This topic of ROEE is not a new one. I believe that it will not be solved in the short or long term. ROI is measured on an event-by-event basis and really cannot be broadened too far. For example, a single measurement tool used for product launches will not be applicable to an incentive or board meeting.*
>
> *Our organization focuses on the meeting objectives and steps backward from there to create measurement opportunities for the client. ROI is not measured by what is put into a meeting, but rather by what the attendees take away. For example, during a recent regional sales meeting with representatives of a large snack food company, we talked with them about their objectives for the meeting. During one particular segment, they had information relating to the product placement and promotion rollouts they considered vital to their immediate sales growth. It was critical to them that the products were set, rotated, and managed correctly. ROI for this session would be defined by the attendees' ability to own information and then transfer that knowledge from the meeting to the field with higher promotional sales and growth.*
>
> *So we created an interactive trivia game for this session. At the check-in desk in the morning, attendees were assigned a wireless keypad. The audience was informed to look for "trivia" slides during the marketing presentation. When one appeared, we would ask five questions about information contained in the presentation. Scores were tallied based on individuals and microregion affiliation. The top individual and team would win a prize at the end of the session (salespeople live for incentives!). Of the 15 questions, 10 had a correct response rate of 90 percent or higher. An interesting finding is that one of the questions was from a previous presentation (before the quiz session), when the percentage of correct responses was only 47 percent.*
>
> *For further evaluation and training, the presenter had an opportunity to immediately address incorrect responses. Better to know the correct information now than after the sales force returns to the field. The client felt this was a critical step and built time into the sessions for further explanations. Immediately after the meeting, all*

*of the information was captured and given to the client in an easy-
to-use CD. The client was then able to determine which microregions
and individuals needed additional training and to provide that information to the field managers later in the day. The client was able to
measure the effectiveness of the presentation and knew exactly what
information was being understood and owned by the attendees. It
also provided some take-away information for immediate follow-up.*

There is information available to help event entertainment industry professionals gain a better understanding of this timely and important subject. In
their book, *Corporate Event Project Management,* William O'Toole and Phyllis Mikolaitis used several tools to measure cost-benefit survey results:

- Actual revenue received
- Media exposure, in both quality and quantity
- Attendance figures and dropouts
- Number of invitations versus number attended ratio
- Time versus money spent ratio
- Recruitment survey
- Post event analysis
- Surveys during the event, including focus groups
- Research awareness
- Male-to-female ratio
- Business generated
- Product awareness
- Increase in tourism
- Sponsorship attracted
- Feedback and evaluation
- Economic injection into community, determined via survey calculations
- Lack of public complaints

Maybe the *BizBash Event Style Reporter* (Winter 2002) has the right idea about
measurement tools when it suggests that the old way was to conduct a follow-
up survey: "Did you get what you need?" It claims that the fresh approach is
a presurvey: "What do you want?" That seems like a simple enough question,
but the response will probably be, in most cases, another question: "What are
you offering or providing?" Depending on the type of organization—private,
corporate, or nonprofit—different goals and objectives will be mentioned during the planning process. Your client will want to know, after the event,
whether those goals and objectives were met. Well-developed surveys are critical to gathering meaningful and statistically significant information, so if it is
important enough to your client, consider having an expert develop your survey. A survey can yield both positive and negative comments; the negative
comments will be the most valuable to you. Collate the data and perform
a gap analysis, with the client, to determine where results did not meet

expectations and what could have been done differently. This is important information for the event planner to keep as part of the production manual and historical files. Finally, how do you determine the best tool to use for this process? Work with your clients so that whatever you use will be meaningful and useful for them.

Scripts for Future Study

Corbin Ball, CMP, highly recommends **SurveyKey** at www.surveykey.com. Its survey questions are easy to set up and configurable for a range of question types. At the time of this writing, there is no charge for the first 50 responses and 30 days are allowed for each survey. If your number exceeds 50, the service will still capture the data, and you can pay per response. Responses are graphed and can be exported into Microsoft Excel and comma-delimited formats (ASCAII).

Exit Stage Right

Now that you know how to save money and create a budget, whom will you subcontract to handle your meetings and events? These are the individuals who will be providing the services and actually doing the work for you, so you want to ensure that you have the best experts and the most skilled and dedicated people for your event. You will be hiring them, for the most part, as independent contractors, and you need to be aware of your legal obligations when working with contractors. These issues are covered in the next chapter, where you will learn about selecting and contracting event production and entertainment vendors.

PART THREE

Coordinating Event Entertainment and Production

CHAPTER 9

Selecting and Contracting Event Production and Entertainment Vendors

This is not something you retire from. It's your life.
Writing songs and playing is like breathing—
you don't stop.

—KEITH RICHARDS, ROLLING STONES LEGENDARY GUITARIST

IN THIS CHAPTER YOU WILL DISCOVER

- Whom you should contact to book entertainment for your event.
- How to conduct auditions to ensure that your entertainment will fit your event, its audience, and your client's expectations.
- How to prepare and agree to a comprehensive contract for your entertainment.
- How to decipher the difference between employees and independent contractors.

This chapter answers the question, "Who ya gonna call?" Entertainment is part of every event, whether it is a speaker, a band, a singer, a dancer, or any of a myriad of other talented people who are ready to help you add value to your event and make it memorable. How do you find them, and once you do, how do you get them booked for your event? You will learn about the availability of expert resources that you can call for your event entertainment and production, who will not only help you find talent, but will also ensure that your talent is center stage at the right time. If you have been asked to produce an incentive program for an organization, there are experienced and specialized incentive management companies that provide events of this type, designed to reward top-performing employees. If your event is to be held out of town, there are destination management companies whose local presence unlocks the resources in a local marketplace. This chapter also covers the audition process, how to develop a network of talent, and tips to ensure that your talent will fit your event, its audience, and your client's expectations. Once you know whom you want as your event's talent, you will have to sign a contract for their services. You protect yourself with a well-written, comprehensive contract that everyone reads, understands, and agrees to. Finding the right vendors is key to the success of your event and you should be aware of your entertainment requirements before making these selections.

Destination Management Companies, Incentive Planners, and Entertainment Management Companies

Entertainment encompasses a huge variety of talent. Jackie Brett, former director of entertainment at the Sahara Hotel and Casino in Las Vegas, Nevada, says, "Broaden your idea of entertainment. Entertainment can involve clowns, musicians, singers, dancers, models, actors, look-alikes, acrobats, specialty acts, headliners, superstars, and even an autograph signer. Don't laugh, but for a company picnic, your entertainment may be the spin paint booth and a dip tank. This is not always a glamorous business."

DESTINATION MANAGEMENT COMPANIES

According to the Association of Destination Management Executives (ADME), a destination management company (DMC) is "a professional management company specializing in the design and delivery of events, activities, tours, staffing, and transportation utilizing local knowledge, expertise, and resources." Event planners can utilize these organizations to deliver an out-of-town event that meets the client's expectations, while coordinating with experienced organizations that have a very specific range of services to help them produce the event. If, for example, a client in New York contracts for an event in Tampa, Florida, a meeting planner would contact a destination management company to produce a package that includes a range of activities, tours, accommodations, and travel. This saves both the client and the planner time and money, because the destination management company has the local contacts and resources to provide cost-effective, innovative, and creative solutions for the event.

Jackie Brett says,

> One advantage to working with DMCs is that they know the talent and the venues in the local area where the event is being held, with strong personal contacts and valuable background history. Even though they take a fee, in the long run, their choices could make or break your events. Also, DMCs tend to specialize in specific areas, just like doctors, attorneys, and other professionals. For instance, one DMC may have a warehouse of sets, another a stable of models; one may have strong catering contacts, and another may specialize in booking talent. Some even have offices in multiple cities and locations.

Carol Krugman, CMP, CMM, president and CEO, Krugman Group International, Inc., comments:

> More often than not, if I needed services such as those provided by different entertainment suppliers, I would find them through whatever DMC I have contracted with to coordinate everything that will be going on at the meeting's location. DMCs may be expanding their offerings, but that just means that they are brokering the services of other companies that are experts in a particular area. I always look for DMCs who have a network of excellent suppliers whose services they can provide at a reasonable price. Sure, they have a markup, but if the final price quote is reasonable and within the client's budget, they will get my business. If I need someone like an entertainment supplier and choose a DMC instead, it is because I have learned after many years that it is ultimately more cost-effective and efficient for everyone to coordinate through a DMC as much as possible, including transportation, production, staging, AV, and special events. Whatever the DMC earns in commission or fee is well worth the services it provides, in the same way that the services and coordination we provide are valued by our clients.

INCENTIVE PLANNERS

Many companies use incentive programs to motivate and reward their top-performing employees. The event may be as simple as a special awards ceremony, on the low end, to an extravagant, all-expense-paid week-long trip to an exotic destination. The costs associated with the more extravagant events are, of course, more significant, but so are the attendees' expectations. The incentive program is often announced at the beginning of the financial year, to encourage higher sales or revenue generation, and employees work hard to meet their performance targets with the hope of being among the top performers and therefore attending the event. It is a win-win situation for the employer, who establishes a competitive environment with the goal of meeting established revenue, sales, or performance objectives, and for the employee, whose hard work will be rewarded by a period of fun and relaxation, as well as being the recipient of company-wide recognition.

Shelli Sutton-Steinberg is director of special events for the destination management company ViewPoint International. She has researched, planned, and coordinated a wide variety of incentive events and offers the following explanation:

> The incentive program is the key motivation tool which an incentive house proposes to a corporation. An incentive is offered to employees, who work toward meeting a target set by the corporation. Originally incentive programs were very basic: Select a destination location, then a property, and create a program surrounding venues offering sightseeing, cultural events, dining, and entertainment. Today's focus is far more elaborate (perhaps a private jet to a private island in the Caribbean, or aboard a private sailing yacht in the Aegean), and the next year's incentive has to be even grander and more elaborate to create a "buzz" and more excitement than the previous year's. Every year has to top the preceding year's choices, as "been there, done that" certainly would not entice.
>
> The execution and production of these corporate incentive programs are generally awarded to corporate incentive houses, whose job it is to meet the expectations and goals of the company. In their bid for the incentive, they must present a program that meets the budget, is extremely creative, and offers a program of events to match the location. In addition, it will offer the participants the cultural and entertainment experiences offered by the destination selected. The corporation will want to see things presented that are unique and specifically designed for its incentive winners. It wants ideas that are not generally available to the general public, but are elite and upscale, thereby making the participants feel special.
>
> Destination management companies (DMCs) are usually called upon to offer assistance to these incentive houses in the destination cities.
>
> A DMC will partner with an incentive house, which will ask for a request for proposal (RFP). It will edit the proposal or ask for addi-

tional information. It will then present these ideas to the client and, if it is accepted, will then return to the DMC to produce the event. Often the DMC will work directly with the corporate client in creating the incentive program without the incentive house. However, the incentive house, at least for incentive works, generally acts as the conduit between their corporate client and the DMC.

According to Sutton-Steinberg,

It is imperative to listen carefully to your clients' expectations and incorporate these into the proposal. It is also the obligation of the DMC to guide clients in the right direction. For example, if a client wants its headline entertainer to mention the company name and its chief producers throughout the incentive program, it should clarify that with the headliner. The headliner may not wish to do this during his or her show, citing that artistic creativity might be compromised. The DMC must act as a mediator between the client and the headliner on this issue, negotiating a successful agreement that both parties are happy with. And the DMC must have enough staff to make things run smoothly or to resolve other risk factors.

Incentive programs have high expectations. After all, these winners have worked diligently throughout the year to achieve this reward. They not only want to see and hear great entertainment, they may often demand to meet the headliner as well. This must be incorporated within your contract with the headliner prior to the event. The availability of this opportunity can then become part of the hype and promotion for the incentive. For example, if Wayne Newton will be performing for the group, the top promoters will be allowed to meet Wayne, up close and personal, for 15 minutes before or after the show.

USING ENTERTAINMENT MANAGEMENT COMPANIES

Jan Davis, president of Jan Davis Entertainment, a 30-year-old event and entertainment company located in Alexandria, Virginia, explains why meeting and event planners should use a professional agency when choosing entertainment for events.

- *You should choose an agency that has a proven track record in the business. Find out what other companies they work with. Check references if you still are not satisfied. Make certain that the agency is licensed and insured, as not all agencies are.*
- *Experience adds value and removes some of the risk elements. Professional agencies know the reputations and track records of the acts they book. What happens if you book an independent*

band for your dinner dance and they disappear a week before your event? In this case, you have no recourse and will not only lose your deposit, you will also have to find another band. If you have booked entertainment with a legitimate agency, they will guarantee that you will have entertainment.

- *Professional agencies know what the fair market price of a band or a national entertainer should be. For example, if you have "surfed the net" and found a band that looks and sounds good, how can you be sure they know the protocol for a special event? Is their price fair, or did they just see dollar signs because you are with a big corporation? Or, just because you recognize the name of a national entertainer, do you know if they have been performing your type of event and what the reports were? Professional agents do this every day, and will know the acts who are well-suited for various types of events, and they will know the reasonable and fair market price.*

- *A professional corporate entertainment agent should be available all day, every day, to answer your questions. You should not spend days trying to catch up with them, as you may experience when working directly with a band, or with someone who works out of their home or has another job during the day. A professional agency should have staff or other agents who can assist you if your agent is not in the office.*

The moral of this story is that while you may have to pay a little extra for an agency's services, the extra expense will be worth the guarantee that you will have professional entertainment at a fair price.

Choosing Your Entertainment

MATCHING THE MUSIC TO THE AUDIENCE

Music is usually a central element of any event, and in addition to providing "white noise" for the background, it is an important factor in setting the tone or mood for an event. Choosing the right music is as important as choosing the right location or venue, as your participants will remember whether they loved (or hated) the music and how it contributed to the event. There are a number of things to consider when selecting the type of music for your audience:

- Establish your organization's goals and objectives for the meeting or event. Is it for the purpose of inspiration, or just to have fun and relax? Would a John Philip Sousa march be appropriate, or Jimmy Buffett?

- Can music make a contribution toward the organization's goals? Is there a theme for the event that can play a significant role in your marketing and promotional efforts, generating interest in the event? Can this music then be carried to the actual meeting or event? For instance, if the organization's goal is employee recognition, some music selections that might be performed are "What a Feeling," "Winners," or "The Way You Do the Things You Do."
- Ask some questions about the event. Will the music be for dancing, just for background, or both? Do you want to encourage networking among attendees? If so, then the music should not be so loud that they have to shout over it. Will the music include vocals or be solely instrumental? Would the attendees like a sing-along activity? If so, a karaoke program would be appropriate.

Establishing how the music fits the event's goals and objectives is important, but then you also have to consider the audience within that context. With the thousands of song titles and many genres available, choosing the music without a good understanding of the audience is fairly risky. There are audience demographics that can provide you with an idea of a range of music styles that may be appropriate, such as the following:

- Age range
- Ethnicity or cultural background
- Educational level

Also consider the desired volume level, according to the purpose of the music (i.e., as background music, central theme, or dance music) and whether the music is themed for an event or a city. Ask your favorite music supplier for suggestions or use the "liberal arts" method, choosing a variety of song titles from the 1940s to the 2000s, which would include music for everyone.

There are a variety of ways to make your musical selections, but if you are inexperienced in this area, always ask some entertainment professionals so that you will be sure to select music that your audience will enjoy.

THE AUDITION PROCESS

Farrington Productions, Inc. is a multiaward-winning full-service entertainment production company, established by Blair and Eunice Farrington. They observe:

> One of the most arduous tasks associated with the entertainment industry is the casting of any entertainment project. Like "branding," developing an intimate knowledge of your product and the desired end result is key to finding the right talent for any artistic endeavor. In addition to knowing your product intimately, it is also important to know where to look for the desired talent that will be able to deliver the anticipated result.

When Farrington Productions was asked to create and develop the Gondola Ride attraction at the Venetian Resort Hotel and Casino, it launched an exhaustive eight-city audition tour to find performers that combined vocal ability and athleticism and who were quick studies. The eight original gondoliers chosen for this project had to learn how to physically row the gondolas, carrying a maximum of four passengers, as they ducked under bridges and sang arias effortlessly. To maintain an aura of authenticity, they had to learn Italian phrases, spoken with an authentic Italian dialect, within a six-week training period.

The tight production schedule demanded that the audition process be well organized so that the candidates' proficiency with the required skills could be ascertained within a few hours. In any audition process, decisions must be made quickly, so audition materials must be prepared in advance with a clear and concise plan for how the auditions will proceed. From vocal, to acting, to dance, to improvisation—the skill sets must be clearly defined from the onset.

The most crucial part of a successful audition process is the audition notice, which is the first thing the actor, or singer, or dancer will see. The notice represents the introduction to the job, so it must clearly define the required skill sets. Not all of the talent that shows up for the audition will be appropriate for the job. In satisfaction of the requirements of the Equal Opportunity Employment Act, however, it is important to see all of the talent that wishes to audition for you. We have found that many times, talent which does not fit the current project is often remembered when the next project, requiring a different set of performing skills, rolls around.

Jackie Brett adds,

We have made the point that when hiring event entertainment, it is best to go to the experts and industry professionals. So what happens when you are actually booking the talent? What do you need to consider and to know? If you have hired a professional, he or she will be able to fill you in on these details. If not, you will learn quickly because there is a lot to consider. You have to hire talent that meets the event's goals, is within the client's budget, and fits the audience demographics. One thing to remember is that there is an extra cost if you bring talent in from out of town, and such costs can include transportation (air and local travel), lodging, food and beverage, per diem, and any other special needs that they may have.

Rather than attend multiple live performances, especially if you are accepting applicants from out of town, you may choose to view tapes of the talent performing. Get assurances from a performer that the tape is current and the talent is still the same. For example, a band made up of six people may now have four new members or a new front person, which may totally change the sound and look.

You may need to hold auditions. This is more common when you are putting on a play or selecting models and look-alikes, but then, you may simply want to increase your talent library and knowledge of the industry. Holding an audition is an event in itself, and your client may even want to be present. You need to pick the place, set a time, provide a proper setting, and either advertise in the newspaper through an ad or column item, or send out invitations to the organizations that performers belong to.

Having adequate lead time helps in booking talent, especially if your event occurs around the holidays. Even with adequate lead time, you should develop a talent roster that you will catalog according to first, second, and third choice in case acts are booked or the act that you have booked has an emergency and cannot perform as planned.

It is always good to ask a number of questions during the audition and booking process, but even more so when it comes to booking superstars and headliners. A lot of headaches can occur at this level. Some major headliners are temperamental, and sometimes it is their management, assistants, or spouses who present the most problems. It helps to know in advance who and what you are dealing with. Some performers may want a limo, special meals, or a dog walker. Some may cause real problems, such as scandals, because of their indiscretions.

Choosing the entertainment and entertainers can be a daunting task, but by understanding the event's goals and eliciting the advice of entertainment professionals, you will find the entertainers that will satisfy your audience.

Contracting: How to Legally Enter into a Binding Agreement

A contract is a legal document that represents the agreements and responsibilities between the parties of your event. Before you sign the contract, however, you have to close the deal. Despite the fact that you have developed a great concept, know that you can provide the best meeting or event ever and "wow" the client, you still have to get the client to accept the proposal, commit the budget, and sign on the dotted line.

When you have closed the deal, you have a signed contract that allows you to begin work on producing the solution (see Figure 9-1). A contract is a legal document that defines performance and other obligations of both parties.

1. Tune your radio to WIFM (What's in It for Me?).
   - This is the only station your client listens to—how they will benefit from what you are selling is the only thing clients want to know.
   - Be sure clients understand what they are buying, and remind them how this deal will help them.
2. Ask for the deal. Sometimes, getting clients to close a deal and to sign a contract can be as simple as asking them for their signatures. In this process, let them know that
   - You have identified their needs and presented a creative, innovative, and practical solution.
   - You have earned the right to ask them to buy your recommended solution—so ask for the deal!
3. Stop selling. When you get to the point where you can ask for the deal, you have to stop talking about the solution so your clients can make their decision.
   - Your clients already know what they want, and you have provided it to them.
   - The more you talk, the more they think you are not finished with the details, so stop talking and let them decide.
4. Close the deal. Get their agreement to your presentation, and sign the contract.
   - Closing means creating confidence on both sides of the table, so if you have confidence in your solution, the client will too.
   - Confidence comes from preparation for that final discussion, so take the time to role-play your final presentation and prepare answers to any objections.

Figure 9-1
The Microsoft Model for Closing the Deal

A contract must contain the following four essential elements to be a legally binding agreement:

1. An identification of the parties competent to enter into an agreement
2. An explanation of the duty of performance
3. An outline of the consideration (payment) being offered
4. Acceptance by the competent parties

Annie Revel, CSEP, president of Revel Productions Inc., is an independent event producer, consultant, and teacher, based in San Diego. Her background as an award-winning entertainer enabled her to develop knowledge and expertise in the technical and artistic components behind the scenes. She offers the following observations:

It is imperative to have clear and precise contracts between all parties—the entertainer, the purchaser, and the ultimate client. Con-

tracts not only secure an artist for a specific event, but also include various legal provisions, which address payment terms, liability, cancellation clauses, forces majeure, indemnification, and breach of contract. A contract will also include any mutually agreed-upon conditions, as well as a production rider that defines various requirements that may include sound, lights, backline equipment, staging, and catering.

In my consulting business, I generate a contract whenever I have confirmed business. When I started my business, I hired an entertainment lawyer to draft the terms and conditions portion of my standard contract, which contains necessary legalese and protects my business from every imaginable scenario that could occur. This standard contract and a letter of agreement are in Appendix 5. For every client, I have the ability to add to the terms and conditions, inasmuch as every piece of business is unique and may include special arrangements that require the addition of clauses to the contract. As long as an addition is mutually agreed upon, initialed, and signed by you and your client, the clause is legally binding.

When I contract entertainment, I always utilize a professional talent and booking agency. I find that this actually saves me time and money, as the agency constantly scouts for new talent, maintains an extensive talent inventory, and carries all necessary licensing, insurance, and contracts. An agency will manage all details with the entertainment, before, during, and after the performance date, and will have an agent on-site to serve as a point of liaison. As I am managing the myriad of on-site details, I appreciate this service, as I know that the agent will oversee the arrival and setup of the entertainers, giving me one less thing to worry about on-site.

In regard to contracts, there may be some question as to whom the entertainer works for. If he or she signs a contract with a planning organization, does the entertainer work for the planner? Does the planner work for the client as an employee for the duration of the event planning and production? How can you tell whether you are an employee or an independent contractor within an organization? These are important distinctions, because they determine liability and compensation issues, as well as establish areas of performance and responsibility.

Blair and Eunice Farrington report,

In the case of long-term entertainment engagements, legally binding contracts are needed. Although most companies will provide a standard contract form, artists will have concerns with various issues that may require individual attention. It is vitally important that both parties enter into the contract with all aspects of their individual performances and specific job requirements mutually agreed upon. Sometimes this can take weeks of discussion to negotiate successfully, but normally takes only a few days. It is always important, however, to instruct the performers to read their contracts carefully, bringing to your attention anything they do not understand. You can then provide appropriate clarification and discuss any other items that are not clear. Many performers have their own lawyers review contracts prior to signing. This is common and should not be misconstrued as a sign of the performer's distrust. In fact, it should always be encouraged, as it usually eliminates any problems that could arise in the future, thus removing a potential risk element.

Contract terms for larger acts and headliner entertainers are usually spelled out by the artist's rider, and negotiations conclude with the issuance of a mutually agreed-upon contract that also includes the entertainment buyer's terms. Such contracts end up being single documents with contractual elements from two or three preexisting contracts, all mutually agreed upon between all parties concerned. A team consisting of the parties' legal representatives usually draws up contracts of this type.

The most important thing to remember about contracts is probably the one thing that is most overlooked by many, and that is to actually read the contract. It is surprising how often a person will sign his or her name to a contract, thinking that there is truth in the cliché, "Contracts are made to be broken." Farrington has had cause on only a few occasions to take contractual agreements into litigation. It has been our experience that in these instances, the courts have upheld the contract terms and agreements that were the subject of mutual agreement by the parties who signed the contract. Of course, there are always exceptions to any rule, but by and large, a good, legally sound, and responsible contract will stand firm in a court of law.

James Goldberg, one of the meeting industry's leading attorneys, is a principal in the Washington, D.C., law firm of Goldberg & Associates, which represents associations and independent meeting planners, and is the author of *The Meeting Planner's Legal Handbook*. He comments specifically on speakers' contracts, but many of the same principles apply for all types of entertainment.

When a meeting planner contracts with a speaker, consider the following tips:

1. Make sure the party to the contract represents the speaker. *Many speakers use agents, or speakers' bureaus, to book their presentations for them. Others work through companies that they own or* *control. A good contract will recite that the party representing the speaker has the authority to do so, and that the individual signing on behalf of the party has the authority to enter into the agreement. In that way, if something goes awry, the planner has a cause of action against the speaker's representative.*

2. Understand when the speaker can cancel. *Some agreements permit cancellation only for reasons such as acts of God, inclement weather, or other unanticipated occurrences. Other agreements permit a speaker to cancel for such things as "overriding professional obligations," or similar reasons; this is especially true for speakers in the entertainment industry. A good agreement will require prompt notice of such cancellation, the specific reasons therefore, an obligation to offer a comparable substitute at the same price, and the ability of the planner to get a prompt refund of any deposit paid in the event the proposed substitute is unacceptable (which always should be within the discretion of the planner).*

3. Understand what expenses are covered. *In order to properly budget for a speaker's expenses, the contract should specify what expenses are covered. Terms like "first-class expenses" should be avoided because they are vague. If a planner expects the speaker to purchase only a coach airline ticket, that should be specified, along with a requirement that the ticket be booked at least 21 days in advance to obtain the lowest possible fare. The number of nights' lodging should also be specified (usually with a requirement to stay in the hotel of the planner's choosing to take advantage of any available complimentary rooms). Ancillary expenses, such as ground transportation and meals, should be specified; any personal expenses should be specifically excluded from reimbursement. Submission of supporting documentation such as receipts should be required where they are available.*

4. Specify the intellectual property "ground rules." *A speaker has a copyright interest in the content of his or her presentation. Therefore, a planner cannot make an audio or video recording of the presentation—especially if the planner plans to sell the tape— without the speaker's explicit written permission. The same holds true for any handouts provided by the speaker. Some speakers also prohibit the taking of photographs during the presentation, or seek to limit distribution of handout material only to those who actually attended the presentation. The contract should also state that the speaker's presentation will not infringe on the copyright or other intellectual property rights of any third party, and that the speaker will indemnify the planner in the event of such infringement.*

5. Agree on the presentation's content. *In many cases, a planner is looking for a speaker to address a particular topic. Any content criteria, such as things to be included or excluded, should be spelled out in the contract; it is always a good idea to get a preview videotape from the speaker, or his/her agent, to understand the speaker's presentation style. Some speakers, especially politicians, simply cannot be held to a specific topic. A planner may wish to preclude a speaker from promoting his/her books or tapes during a presentation. If the speaker is going to discuss a topic for which he/she has been compensated by someone else (especially true in medical meetings), the speaker should be required to make full disclosure to the audience of this outside compensation. As with any contract, the language should be clear and unambiguous. And don't forget the normal legal "boilerplate" about dispute resolution, and indemnification.*

Tyra W. Hilliard, associate professor of tourism at The George Washington University and counsel to associations and meeting professionals, expands on Goldberg's tips on contracting with speakers:

Although having a speaker cancel at the last minute certainly seems beyond your control, the law would say you could have contracted with the speaker to perform or to have to pay damages for not performing. You cannot force a speaker to speak, even with a contract, but you can make that person pay damages if he or she fails to show up. The amount of damages in a contract can be equivalent to the amount the group would have to pay the hotel for canceling at the last minute. This contract should also contain language addressing force majeure, so that a speaker cannot terminate without liability just because, for example, there are tropical storm warnings, but can cancel if a tropical storm actually hits.

A force majeure clause can generally be invoked only when the meeting (or event) is made impossible, illegal, or inadvisable by forces beyond the parties' control. If a tropical storm actually hits an area, stopping air traffic and creating a dangerous situation, this is clearly a force majeure. There are many things that might happen, but to allow individuals or groups to terminate without liability for "mights" would put hotels in a difficult situation.

The law would also look at the fact that your group scheduled the meeting in Miami, a coastal area, during hurricane season. The situation could have been avoided had the meeting been scheduled in St. Louis, for example. I know that does not seem quite fair, but the law would look at decisions that were made and what aspects were under the control of the parties. Some event cancellation insurance covers the cancellation of a major speaker. That might give you the safety net you need should this happen again in the future.

The Difference between Employees and Independent Contractors

Another important element of contracting is to understand whom you are actually hiring. When hiring workers for an event, it is critical to understand the difference between an employee and an independent contractor. The following information was compiled from various IRS documents.

Independent contractors are individuals who contract with a business to perform a specific project or set of projects on an independent basis. Employees provide work in an ongoing, structured order. The Internal Revenue Service (IRS), worker's compensation boards, unemployment compensation boards, federal agencies, and even the courts all have slightly different definitions of what an independent contractor is, though their means of categorizing workers as independent contractors are similar.

Who Qualifies as an Independent Contractor?

One of the most prevalent approaches used to categorize a worker as either an employee or an independent contractor is the analysis created by the IRS. The key issue is how much control the employer has over the worker and the way in which the worker performs his or her job. The IRS considers the following:

- *What instructions the employer gives the worker about when, where, and how to work. The more specific the instructions and the more control exercised, the more likely the worker will be considered an employee.*
- *What training the employer gives the worker. Independent contractors generally do not receive training from an employer.*
- *The extent to which the worker has business expenses that are not reimbursed. Independent contractors are more likely to have unreimbursed expenses.*
- *The extent of the worker's investment in the worker's own business. Independent contractors typically invest their own money in equipment or facilities.*
- *The extent to which the worker makes services available to others. Independent contractors are more likely to make their services available to others.*
- *How the business pays the worker. An employee is generally paid by the hour, week, or month. An independent contractor is usually paid by the job.*
- *The extent to which the worker can make a profit or incur a loss. An independent contractor can make a profit or loss, but an employee does not.*

- *Whether there are written contracts describing the relationship the parties intended to create. Independent contractors generally sign written contracts stating that they are independent contractors and setting forth the terms of their employment.*
- *Whether the business provides the worker with employee-type benefits, such as insurance, a pension plan, vacation pay, or sick pay. Independent contractors generally do not get benefits.*
- *The terms of the working relationship. An employee generally is employed at will (meaning the relationship can be terminated by either party at any time). An independent contractor is usually hired for a set period of time.*
- *Whether the worker's services are a key aspect of the company's regular business. If the services are necessary for regular business activity, it is more likely that the employer has the right to direct and control the worker's activities. The more control an employer exerts over a worker, the more likely it is that the worker will be considered an employee.*

What Can You Do to Avoid Problems?

You can avoid problems by carefully documenting your relationships with your workers and vendors. Although it may not always save you from having to justify your actions, it helps to have a written contract stating the terms of employment. If this is a recurring or significant issue for your business, consult with a qualified attorney.

Note: The foregoing information is provided for informational purposes only and is not meant to constitute legal advice; your specific legal issue may vary from the one described in this section, and you should seek the advice of a qualified lawyer regarding your own situation.

(SOURCE: IRS PUBLICATIONS 1776, 1779, 3518, AND 15-A REVISED INDEPENDENT'S CONTRACTOR OR EMPLOYEE)

In Conclusion

Consider this real-life example of what can happen when contracts are not developed and executed in an effective manner. Rod Stewart, his management company, booking agents, and lawyers were sued by a compendium of concert promoters for allegedly balking on a Latin American tour early in 2002. The suit accuses Stewart and his associates of breach of fiduciary duty, misrepresentation, fraud, contract interference, unfair business practices, and other wrongs. Stewart, his management, and bookers were approached in the final months of 2001 to arrange a nine-city tour of Latin America, in February and March 2002, at venues in Panama, Peru, Chili, Argentina, Brazil, Puerto Rico, and Mexico. The amount of $2.1 million was to be paid in advance and held in escrow by Stewart's talent agency, ICM, pending execution of a written contract.

The lawsuit asserts that payment in two halves was agreed upon, the first in January and the second in February. Promoters claim that as of January 9, $680,000 had been delivered to Stewart's representatives as good faith deposits, though economic troubles in Argentina and Mexico delayed the remaining $370,000. Stewart's attorneys demanded the remainder of the payment, citing breach of terms and conditions. An additional payment of $100,000 was made while venues were already being booked and tickets were sold for the concerts. Stewart's representatives canceled the tour through a letter, claiming no contract existed as of that time. The promoters are now demanding the return of $780,000 in total from Stewart and his associates. The suit seeks approximately $3 million for damages (Morden 2002).

Although finding the perfect entertainment for an event is a difficult task for an inexperienced planner, this chapter has shown that there are a plethora of resources for planners to use in order to find quality entertainment of any type. It is important to consider the goals of the event and the demographic characteristics of your audience when making your selection. It is also critical to write a complete contract and elicit the services of attorneys to ensure that you and your client are protected from liabilities. A sound entertainment selection process followed by a comprehensive contracting process can lead to an excellent entertainment experience for you and your attendees.

Scripts for Future Study

INTERNET RESOURCES

MeetingAdvice, www.meetingadvice.com. Do you have questions about contracts, special events, hotels, meeting logistics, or catering? You can ask seasoned experts at this site.

The Society of Incentive Travel Executives (SITE) is a worldwide organization of business professionals dedicated to the recognition and development of incentive travel, www.site-intl.org

www.incentivemag.com is an on-line magazine, focusing on managing and marketing through motivation.

These sites will help you get started with contracts:

www.findforms.com
www.homebusinessonline.com/a&r/elibrary/legal/index.shtml
www.searchbug.com/legal/forms1.asp

Exit Stage Right

This chapter discussed finding and hiring talent for your event. It also provided the opinions of several experts who all agree that it is important that you treat your event as a business and follow certain legal procedures, such as ensuring that you obtain legal agreements with entertainment providers. In the next chapter you will learn about the roles of various entities in the industry and how you will utilize them to obtain various types of entertainment for your event. Chapter 10 also discusses the important role of entertainment in your events and how finding the right entertainer can make your event memorable.

CHAPTER 10

Entertainment Management Companies, Agents, Managers, and Headline Entertainment

My sole inspiration is a telephone call from a producer.

—COLE PORTER

IN THIS CHAPTER YOU WILL DISCOVER

- How entertainment management companies operate.
- The function of agents and managers.
- How to select and evaluate speakers.
- How to hire and work with headline entertainment.

Cole Porter, the American composer of "Kiss Me, Kate," understood that the promise of a contract from a producer is the greatest incentive to begin work. The American event producer and author, Dr. Joe Goldblatt, CSEP, author of *Special Events: Twenty-First Century Global Event Management,* states that time, finance, people, and technology are the pillars of event management and describes how they work together in the event management industry. In this chapter you will discover the role that each of these entities plays in the industry and how you can use them to obtain various types of entertainment for your event. The chapter also discusses the important role that event entertainment plays in your events and how finding the "right" entertainer can make your event memorable. So if your "fantasy hides in the daylight" and you want to "lose your soul and find your passion,"[1] read on, as numerous industry professionals provide their insight and opinions on the importance of working with professionals and how they can protect your interests and provide the best resources for finding appropriate entertainment for your events.

Entertainment Management Companies

An entertainment management company is an entity/producer/person who makes a match between an event and its entertainment requirements. These professionals can often provide the entire entertainment package for your meeting or event, including locating artists from many different agencies. Other important functions include negotiating and/or realizing the rider and finding the appropriate headline, regional, and local entertainment. They can also provide you with a complete catalog of various entertainment entities, in addition to musicians, in their rosters.

Robert Sivek, CSEP, past president of the International Special Events Society (ISES) and vice president of The Meeting House Companies in Elmhurst, Illinois, has a 32,000 sq ft design center, offering full-service event production. In-house capabilities include set/stage design, theme decor, pipe and drape, floral design, technical production, audiovisual, and entertainment services. Sivek says his prices on the local level "are all-inclusive, so the client does not need to worry about paying band leaders, parking, cartage, or other annoyances." His company, which serves the Chicago metropolitan area, sends out musical groups that range in size from duos to 17-piece orchestras. He also books regional and national name acts, providing his clients with a full spectrum of event entertainment possibilities.

---

[1]Nightlife © Edicoes Intersong Ltda., administered by Intersong USA, Inc. (ASCAP) Music by Tunai; English lyrics by Tracy Mann; arranged by Dori Caymmi and Sergio Mendes; recorded by Sergio Mendes on his 1989 A&M release Arara.

Many corporate entertainment companies provide a wide variety of acts, including variety artists for walk-arounds, caricaturists, jugglers, mimes, stilt-walkers, balloon twisters, and clowns. These are full-time working professionals, not part-timers whose longevity with the agency depends on their reliability and professional delivery.

Because a corporate entertainment company or entertainment management company may be able to procure both headline and local entertainment for your event, they appear to be the logical choice for finding and booking entertainment. Some clients, however, choose to handle the finding and booking of talent themselves. Michael Owen, of All Access Entertainment * Special Events * Marketing Services has some observations on both of these approaches.

> Some clients prefer to deal directly with the entertainment headliner, and anyone can negotiate celebrity appearances on his or her own. Occasionally, you can even work out a better deal this way. But more often than not, you will spend hours, days, and weeks trying to beat down an "un-beat-downable" price quote, and in the end you may have to pursue another avenue. Now you have to start that process all over again.
>
> My question is this: How wise is it for any of us to work so far outside of our core competencies? Not only that, but if the direct-is-always-better model is true in this instance, doesn't it follow that it is true in all areas of planning meetings? Let's see—don't need a caterer, we can make our own breakfast; let's rent equipment and set up our own AV, paint our own fuchsia backdrops; and registration—how hard can that be? I use these examples not to be sarcastic, but to be humorously illustrative. There are occasions when going direct wins the prize. But an experienced professional will close a deal in less time and with far fewer headaches. Sure, it could cost more to work this way—but in many instances it could also cost far less. Regardless, when you factor in time and learning curve, a relationship with a reputable entertainment company is generally competitive in price to doing it alone.

Although booking national acts may present some difficulties, how about local acts, within the client's local area? Michael Owen shares his views on this subject:

> Local acts are market driven just like anything else. Of course, it does not hurt to ask, but be aware that if you are asking for a prime date in prime season, your bargaining position may not be the strongest. If you have found the act you want, you have asked for the best possible price, and it fits your budget, you should secure the act. Number of players, hours played, setup and teardown simply do

not apply when you deal with popular acts. I have seen popular four-member, known locals charge more for one hour than ten-piece acts that are not known charge for four. It's demand that sets prices.

Booking entertainment of any sort for any event is not rocket science, but it is a legitimate business and a significant part of this industry. Common sense goes a long way, but just as you would deal with a professional to set a broken leg, repair your car, or represent you in court, doesn't it make sense that you would seek a professional for such a high-profile segment of your program?

David Williams is the owner of David Patrone Productions in San Diego. He too has his views on the logic behind utilizing professionals to book event entertainment:

In my opinion there are a few good reasons why or when you should use a good entertainment booking service:

- *You don't know much about music or musicians, especially classical or jazz.*
- *You don't have the opportunity to see a band live.*
- *You don't feel like dealing with the process of interviewing and watching bands.*
- *You are booking entertainment for an event that is in another town.*
- *You don't feel like handling the logistics of lighting, stage issues, and prima donna entertainers.*
- *You are hiring a major artist or celebrity.*
- *You feel an obligation to support your local booking agent.*

In conclusion, Williams states,

Basically I am suggesting that you be aware of what is really going on and make your own decisions regarding the way you want to book entertainment. There is no best way across the board. Different methods work more or less effectively in different situations. Establish a relationship with an entertainment booking service you feel you can trust and learn as much about the process as you can.

Dealing with name entertainers requires experienced professional personnel. Do not assume a booking agent is looking out for your concerns. The booking agent is paid by and works for the act, not for you. Bob Cherny, sales manager at Paradise Sound and Light in Orlando, Florida, advises, "You need someone to be your advocate, and that is what a company like Mark Sonder's or Gail & Rice or T. Skorman or a dozen others I could name can do for you. Find a company that has experience working conventions and contract them to negotiate with the performer. The money you save will more than pay their fees."

Cherny goes on to say, "In terms of what you want your entertainment contractor to do, you want it to handle all the contracts and make sure that all the addendums are in your hands and in the hands of your technical support personnel before you sign anything with a performer. You want it to be the liaison between your support personnel and the performer's support personnel, and you want a representative of the contractor to be on-site from the time the performer arrives in town to the time he or she leaves. I have seen it done right, and I have seen it done wrong. Hire professionals!"

Agents and Managers

When working in the event entertainment industry, it is important to know some key terms so that you understand and recognize the channels for hiring entertainment.

Personal or *artist representative* is a term that has no legal definition and is used to loosely describe both managers and agents.

A *manager or personal manager* is responsible for day-to-day career development, personal advice and guidance, and planning the long-range direction of the artist's career. A manager receives a commissions between 15 and 25 percent of the artist's gross earnings, plus reimbursement for travel and other out-of-pocket expenses. He or she is also the negotiator in any kind of business deal that involves the artist, and hires a road manager, equipment crew, and oversees promotional material, including photos. A manager can work through a management office. Either individually or as a company, managers may represent one to five artists.

An *agent* finds or receives offers of employment and usually negotiates the terms of the contract. An agent works on a commission basis, normally 10 to 20 percent of the artist's earnings for a given engagement. An agent can work through an agency. Individually or as a company, agents can represent many artists (Krasilovsky 2000).

A *business manager* handles the artist's investments and taxes and usually earns a commission of 2 to 6 percent of the artist's earnings.

A *promoter* is a financial and publicity organizer, such as for a boxing match or an artistic performance. If your event involves a concert, then you will have to work with a concert promoter in addition to the headliner's agent and manager. Entertainment promoters have very specific functions and can help promote, advertise, and sell your event. Their responsibilities include the following:

- The local buyer, fair or festival planner, public events planner promoter checks on record sales, air play, and the attendance at any previous concerts that a band has given in "the same market."
- Obtain promotional help from the artist's record company, sponsoring newspapers, or radio ads through advertisements for the group's current record and concert.
- Coordinate giveaways, radio interviews and window displays, supply local radio stations and record stores with large quantities of the group's records and record company posters.

- Artists receive a percentage (60 to 90 percent) of the gross receipts of a concert.

Generally, there are two equations promoters can be told to use: A headliner will always receive a guarantee against 60 percent of the gross ticket sales, which is also called "the gate." In the concert business, typical percentages most often mentioned are 85 percent of 60 percent of the gross, or 85 percent of the net. Although the two figures sound radically different, in the end the numbers are quite close. There are some "megastars" who are now demanding 90 percent of 60 percent of gross. This adds a taxing pressure for the promoter to sell out his or her shows to make any money.

Record companies pay for promotional assistance through their tour marketing department by sponsoring newspaper or radio ads and by advertising the artist's current record. They also pay into the Music Performance Trust Funds (MPTF) 0.5 percent of their gross annual profits.

Music publishing companies have three main functions. The first is the collection of royalties paid by the record companies to the publisher, representing mechanical use fees for recordings. Second is the collection of performing rights for radio and TV, which are paid by these entities for permission to use that music. And finally, the actual printing of the music.

Speakers

Event entertainment companies do not only handle musicians. They can also provide you with other entertainment resources, such as speakers and variety acts. Selecting the right speaker for your meeting can be a daunting task, as speakers are available in every fee range and for every specialty topic. Speaker selection is one of the most important elements in a successful meeting, so you should ensure that the speaker's expertise, background, and abilities fit your audience's demographics and expectations. The National Speaker's Association (NSA) suggests following these ten tips in selecting a speaker:

1. *Determine the needs of your audience.*
   Thorough knowledge of the needs of your group is essential in selecting the right speaker. Does your meeting require that the audience leave with specific or technical information? Do you need someone to motivate the group to sell? Are you looking for after-dinner entertainment with a message?
2. *Establish your date, time, and budget.*
   - *Start looking for a speaker as soon as the date for your meeting is set. Many speakers book engagements up to a year in advance and you will want to get on their calendar as soon as possible.*

- *Consider how much time you have to fill and where that time falls in your overall program. If your time slot is flexible, a professional speaker can often tell you the right amount of time for the job. A professional can also make recommendations about the order of topics/speakers if one presentation will follow another. You may not want to follow a humorist with a detailed educational presentation.*
- *Factor in the fee you are willing or able to pay for a speaker. Your search for a speaker can be narrowed or broadened based upon your budget.*

3. *Identify the type of speaker who will best match the needs of your audience.*

A speaker's expertise in a given field may be the big draw, but a well-known name does not guarantee a professional presentation. High prices do not always mean high quality. Will your audience and the overall program benefit most from a celebrity, an expert in the field, a popular sports personality, a best-selling author, or a professional speaker who has a thorough knowledge of the appropriate topic?

4. *Locate your resources.*

- *Personal referrals are a great way to narrow your search. Ask colleagues for recommendations.*
- *Speakers bureaus locate and book speakers according to your specifications and needs. A bureau can locate speakers and quote fees. Many bureaus specialize in particular speakers such as celebrities, authors, or athletes.*

5. *Review your options and interview your speaker candidates.*

- *A professional speaker will be a real partner in this process. Often [speakers] will ask questions about the needs of your audience and what they can accomplish for you. Ask your candidates for references and, if they are speaking in your area, ask if you can attend the program and observe them in action.*
- *Assure that a potential speaker has addressed groups similar to yours. Talk with [speaker] about their experience. Ask for a biography, testimonials, and videos of their presentations, preferably before a live audience.*
- *Find a speaker who will tailor his or her presentation to your group.*
- *Ask [speakers] if they belong to professional associations. Also ask what awards or certifications they have earned. The National Speakers Association's designation is the Certified Speaking Professional (CSP). The CSP is earned for extended speaking experience and client satisfaction.*

6. *Select your speaker.*
   - *Hire a professional and you will hire an ally. Professional speakers understand that your reputation is riding on their performance. Their experience with hundreds of audiences can add to your peace of mind and to the success of the event.*
   - *When selecting your speaker, consider that you are not only paying for the time the speaker is on the platform but also for the hours spent researching, preparing, and customizing the presentation. Some speakers may negotiate their fees when they are doing more than one program for you or when they are allowed to sell their products. Ask about your options.*

7. *Get it in writing.*
   You should have a letter of agreement or contract that clearly outlines the expectations of both you and your speaker. Consider:
   - *Travel arrangements and transportation*
   - *Accommodation and meals*
   - *Fees, reimbursements, and payment terms*
   - *Whether you want the speaker to attend social events*
   - *If the speaker may sell products and if so, how this will be handled*
   - *An agreement on any audio- or videotaping of the presentation*
   - *Cancellation policies*
   - *Audio/visual requirements*
   - *Legal implications, if any, your contract may contain*

8. *Work with your speaker.*
   Share information about your group or company. This will help the speaker become familiar with your organization, while facilitating a customized presentation.
   - *Send the speaker your newsletters or anything which would include the names of key people, buzz words, or insider news and views.*
   - *Give the speaker a clear outline of what you expect.*
   - *Be specific about the size and demographics of your audience.*
   - *Let the speaker know in advance about other speakers on the program. This gives the speaker the opportunity to build on (and not duplicate) what the other speakers say.*

9. *Set the stage.*
   - *Make sure the room is set up for optimum impact. Consider the number of chairs and how they are arranged. Also consider room temperature and lighting.*
   - *Stay on schedule. Although a professional will be able to "make up" time or slow things down if needed, keeping your*

*program on schedule will allow your audience to get the full
impact of the program you have created for them.*

- *Your speaker should be able to provide you with a good introduction of [him- or herself] and [his or her] topic. The introduction should be short, energizing, and create positive
  expectations.*

10. *Evaluate the results.*

    *Have your audience complete evaluations on the speaker and
    his or her presentation. This will allow you to gauge your results
    and plan for future programs. Send copies of the evaluations to
    your speaker.*

    *—Reprinted with permission of the
    National Speakers Association, 2002*

The NSA publishes *Who's Who in Professional Speaking: The Meeting Planner's Guide,* one of the most comprehensive directories of professional speakers. This 496-page directory lists all of the National Speakers Association's
more than 4000 members in 21 countries, alphabetically, with photos, contact
information, and professional descriptions. Speakers are also searchable by
topic or location.

How to Hire and Work
with Headline Entertainment

Entertainment comes in all varieties, in all languages, transcending all bor-
ders, so booking headline entertainment means making choices from among a
vast number of options. For the uninitiated, it can be a crazy process. You
must first determine what fits your client's needs and expectations, based on
the event's goals and objectives, so that you will be able to provide the entertainment management company with an audience profile that will help it to
find the most appropriate performer. The following is a step-by-step guide to
this process:

1. Research the needs of the audience and identify the appropriate resources to fill these needs.
2. Select an artist. This works best if you or your client either select five
   headliners you would like to have perform at your event, or prepare an
   approximate budget and category of music/entertainment/speaker in
   order to narrow the list of options.
3. Have your agent or corporate entertainment company make a written
   offer to the artist. Remember, an agent can offer you only the artists that

are on the agency's roster. If the artists you are looking for are represented by more than one agency, you will need to contact more than one agent or just one corporate entertainment company. Are you prepared and empowered to make a reasonably quick decision? It is common to lose headliners when clients are not able to act quickly enough to secure them.

4. If the offer is accepted, sign a contract with the artist. Once your written offer is accepted, it is very difficult to turn back. Are you prepared to make a 50 percent deposit when and if a headline entertainer accepts your offer?

5. Secure production for the show or have your corporate entertainment company provide the products and services.

6. Monitor the production process and evaluate the outcomes.

THE SELECTION PROCESS

In your selection process, your entertainment company should provide you with not only a list of headliners, but also their pictures, biographies, and possibly their routing information, availability, and cost. Your entertainment company can supply you with the headliner's tour history, venues where they have worked, and the typical sizes of their audiences, if applicable. Ticket prices are also available. Figure 10-1 shows a list of categories to assist in starting to choose the genre of music that might be good for a particular meeting or event.

HOW TO MAKE AN OFFER

An offer is a blueprint for the pending contract. If it is accepted, you will be obligated to move forward towards going to contract. If the offer is declined, there is no further obligation for either party. If you still want to procure the selected artist, you can make an alternative offer in writing. Remember that everything must be in writing in order for it to form a binding agreement.

THE CONTRACT

If your offer is accepted, the next step is to draw up the contract. This is where a professional can provide invaluable assistance. There are two parts to receiving a contract. The first is receiving the actual contract: the who, what, where, when, and how much is described in detail. The second part includes receiving the riders or addendums to the contract. These can be in the form of one large rider or separate components, broken down into a sound rider, a light rider, and a food and beverage rider. These riders are made part of and attached to the contract. The contract may be only 1 to 3 pages, with the rider(s) adding another 50 pages.

Musical Categories

Adult Contemporary	Rock
Alternative	Techno
Blues	Urban Contemporary
Children's Entertainment	Variety
Christian	World Music
Classical	20s
Classic Rock	30s
Comedy	40s
Country	50s
Dance	60s
Folk	70s
Holiday	80s
Jazz	90s
Rap	00s
Reggae	

Other Types of Music or Entertainment

Acappella	Cajun
Accordion	Cajun/Zydeco
Acid Jazz	Calypso
Acoustic	Caricaturist
Acrobatics	Cartoonist
Adult Alternative	Casino Nights
African	Celtic
African Pop	Children's Music
All Female Review	Christian Alternative
All Male Review	Christian Pop
Alternative Country	Christian Rock
Alternative Country-Rock	Circus
American	Classic R&B
American Indian Dance	Clown
Americana	Comedian
Animal Act	Comedy Hypnotist
Art Rock	Contemporary Country
Big Band/Swing	Contemporary Christian
Black Alternative	Contemporary Folk
Bluegrass	Contemporary Instrumental
Blues-Rock	Contemporary Jazz
Brass Hop	Country Rock
Brazilian	Country Swing
Brazilian Pop	Cover Band
Broadway	Cuban
Cabaret	Dance & Party

Figure 10-1
A List of Musical Categories and Music Genres

Dance & Track
Disc Jockey/DJ
Dixieland
Easy Listening
Electronics
Emo
Environmental Music
Escape Artistry
Family Entertainment
Foreign
Funk
Fusion
Game Show
Gospel
Gothic Rock
Hard Rock
Hardcore Punk
Hardcore Techno
Headliner
Heavy Metal
Heavy Rock
Hip Hop
Hypnotist
Ice Ballet
Ice Show
Illusionist
Impersonator
Impressionist
India
Indie Rock
Industrial Rock
Internet
Irish
Israeli
Jam Band
Jazz Rock
Jewish
Jugglers
Klezmer
Latin
Latin Pop
Magician
March
Marketing
Mbube
Mentalist

Metal Rock
Mexican
Military
Mimi
Modern Rock
Motown
Musical
New Age
New Orleans Jazz
Novelty Act
Off Broadway
Oldies
Percussion
Piano Players
Play
Polka
Pop
Progressive Electronic
Psychedelic
Psychic
Punk
Puppetry/Marionettes
R&B
Rap
Rave
Roadhouse
Rock Opera
Rockabilly
Roots-Rock
Sahelian
Salsa
Samba
Seasonal
Senegal
Show Tunes
Ska
Society
Soul
Soundtracks
South African
Southern Rock
Spanish
Special Celebrity & Attractions
Spectator Events & Sports
Surf
Swing

Figure 10-1
(Continued)

186

Tangos	Trip-Hop
Techno	Ventriloquist
Tejano	Wedding
Tex/Mex	World Music
Theatrical Productions	World Music & Dance
Tibetan	Wrestling
Tribute Show	Zydec

Figure 10-1
(Continued)

ADVANTAGES OF WORKING WITH AN ENTERTAINMENT MANAGEMENT COMPANY

You probably will never meet with an agent in person. After an initial conversation with an agent, future conversations will be with his or her assistant. The agent is interested in completing the paperwork and collecting the money. Once that is done, the agent's job is complete. An agent would rarely go to the job site to oversee the artist's performance. This is where the corporate entertainment company takes over. In addition to handling the paperwork and financials, these companies will control communication and will have one of their representatives present on-site. They can also act as the show's producer and handle the rider requirements if the planner transfers that responsibility to them, inasmuch as the entire obligation to fulfill the rider requirements lies solely with the purchaser.

Chris Burke, of William Morris in Los Angeles, says that meeting planners should call the corporate entertainment companies. He says that "90 percent of his bookings are with the "sophisticated producers" from the entertainment companies. These producers, of course, are open to dealing with buyers directly from the corporations, but stress that unsophisticated planners should have some experience before attempting to work with them. Richard Aaron, CMP, CSEP, of bizbash.com in New York City, reveals, "Planning for star shows can often prove to be a complex maze of hidden costs that an experienced producer must carefully probe." Agencies such as William Morris want to know that you are a serious buyer, have bought before, and have the capability to produce the show.

If a meeting planner goes directly to the exclusive agent of a particular artist, cutting out the so-called middleman, that planner will face some challenges. First, how do you find out who is the exclusive agent, especially when artists change agents so frequently? Second, if an agent knows you are from a Fortune 1000 company, be prepared to pay a higher price. Third, are you adept at handling a multipage rider with all its technicalities, both from a planning and a stage/sound/lighting perspective? A corporate entertainment company can provide significant cost savings with the technical side of your event because of the amount of work it provides to its subcontractors.

According to The Celebrity Source's president, Rita Tateel, that is why corporate entertainment companies exist. Tateel's firm is located in Los Angeles and maintains a computer database of celebrity talent. "This information allows us to play a role more like that of a matchmaker, rather than simply a booking agent—matching the right celebrity to the specific corporate, civic, and charity need," says Tateel.

Yes, the artist gets paid, but sometimes even more important, he or she now profits by greater exposure to a different audience. And no, a musical act or headliner does not have to perform its music. An artist (or group) may be called in for a meeting to perform a meet-and-greet, play golf or tennis, ski, run, sail, or participate in an auto race, among other sports. Moreover, other activities may be requested, such as product endorsements, spokesperson campaigns, and corporate cause-related marketing activities. How can an event management company help you find the big-name talent that will help you in this area? "Our success comes in large part from the relationships we have established over the years with the celebrities, and we make it our business to know what, beyond money, may motivate these people to say yes," notes Paula Greenfield, vice president of The Celebrity Source.

Commenting on the increased interest in using entertainment at corporate functions, Tateel points to a variety of roles and activities in which your headline act may be utilized:

- Public relations, advertising, and marketing campaigns
- Satellite media tours
- Press conferences
- Celebrity answers to survey questions
- Appearing or performing at a corporate function, festival, trade show, expo, or convention
- Appearing or performing in a telethon or at a charity fund-raising event
- Product endorsements
- Television, radio, and print ads
- Point-of-purchase promotions
- Internet Web site or e-commerce business spokesperson
- Television specials
- Participating in a sporting event/tournament/race
- Testifying on legislative issues
- Motivational/keynote speakers
- Cruise line promotions and launches
- Resort/hotel openings or promotions

- Corporate, client social events
- Meeting and greeting guests
- Attending a fashion show, opening, or launch
- Ribbon cutting ceremonies
- Voice talent for films or videos
- Poster/print campaigns
- Being honored with an award
- Being a presenter of an award
- Emcee/host
- Appearing in a public service announcement
- Spokesperson for a charity, cause, or service
- Guest instructor or lecturer
- Infomercials
- Documentary/instructional films/videos
- Video greetings
- Signature on fund-raising letters
- Posing for photos and signing autographs
- Appearing in celebrity calendars
- Riding in a parade
- Judging a contest
- Celebrity fashion models
- Celebrity artists/decorators
- Serving as a guest chef
- Providing celebrity recipes

Before Booking Entertainment

Beyond creating an air of cooperation between the headliners and the buyers, an event manager must address several factors involved in booking music for a meeting:

- *The age of the audience.* According to Ben Bernstein of William Morris in Los Angeles, "Business has not only increased significantly, but we find ourselves dealing with the changing demographics in the corporate world. We are dealing with a younger corporate executive, and therefore acts such as The Pointer Sisters and Natalie Cole have become favorites in the corporate arena." Also, in recent years, younger musicians have been emulating songs and the sounds of the big band era, such as Linda Ronstadt, Melissa Manchester, Carly Simon, and, most recently Harry Connick Jr.
- *The theme of the meeting or event.* For a country western theme you might choose Mel Tillis, (not Mel Torme). For a strong female image you might choose Bette Midler.

- *The surroundings.* Where is the meeting being held? In a hotel, a theater, a convention center, an exhibition hall, a tent? What are the logistics of the venue both sound-wise and visually?
- *What food is being served?* Which meal is being served—breakfast, brunch, lunch, dinner? How is it being served—buffet, sit-down banquet, barbeque?
- *Will there be any speeches?*
- *What is the budget?* The agent must make sure the buyers know what they can get for their money. A person who says he or she doesn't have enough money to spend might actually have $1000. Someone else will say the same thing, but mean $100,000.
- *Will the artist accept a corporate date?* Purchasers may want to hire someone like Bruce Springsteen for their corporate reception without realizing that "the Boss" doesn't do corporate or association engagements. Barry Bell of Barry Bell Consultants says, regarding his artists, "We do mostly concerts." Chris Burke of William Morris in Los Angeles explains that one of the major reasons for his agency's position is that "audiences have not purchased tickets for the artists, but are 'forced' to be there for the meeting or convention." Artists enjoy performing for their fans—an appreciative, enthusiastic audience. Furthermore, the news of an artist playing a corporate date will only reach the corporation's or association's community. In a public event, even if you do not hold tickets, you are seeing and hearing television ads, radio spots, and print advertising, so the reach, depending on the marketplace, could be millions!
- *The negotiation.* "It gets tough when you've got an act that charges $20,000 and the buyer has $15,000, and the act is not budging and the buyer is not budging," says Ted Schmidt of Ted Schmidt & Associates, Inc., in Fort Lauderdale, Florida. "If a deal is going to fall through, it will not depend on whether the band gets picked up from the airport in a limo; you are going to lose it on the money issue." "Remember when you ask for the contract to be sure that you also get the speaker's riders and addendums. These added cost items need to be calculated into the budget from the beginning," says Bob Cherny, of Paradise Sound and Light, located in Florida.

When a corporate entertainment company books an act, it is acting as an agent. The company initiates and negotiates a deal between the artist and the buyer. The price can change if the headliners get a new hit or are in a TV commercial or show. Other considerations that may vary the price include scheduling, time of the year, or how far in advance you book. The acts that agents represent and the buyers who book these acts have differing objectives.

Ted Schmidt explains, "On the one hand, the people putting on the event have to worry about getting the best entertainment—say, a band—for their money. They sometimes forget that essentials such as sound equipment and hotel rooms are part of the required expenses of hiring a band."

Joshua Jones, director of sales at Painted Desert Golf Club, agrees that utilizing a corporate entertainment company is beneficial, especially if you are new to booking name entertainment and have not had the experience of negotiating a rider. An entertainment company can often negotiate more out of a rider than the fee they charge. In addition, you must consider that an entertainment booking agency has worked with many celebrities on a regular basis and has more leverage than the meeting planner that may book one of them for a single event. The celebrities' agents have more riding on the deal with an entertainment company that may bring them two, three, or ten engagements a year and are going to be more flexible in their negotiations with that company.

Entertainment companies can also come to the rescue in the event that a celebrity cannot fulfill his or her contract and has to cancel the event. "I have seen firsthand a celebrity back out of an engagement at the last minute, and it seems that the entertainment company is usually the one that comes to the rescue. The reason is the relationship and volume of business that such a company has with the agent, and when situations like this arise, that 20 percent, or whatever the fee may be, is very well worth it. Of course, there is no substitute for experience, but if you are new to this side of the business, I never recommend pretending to be an expert, especially when it comes to the rider."

A professional entertainment company is your best resource when you need to book a celebrity for an event. It has experience in dealing with agents and representatives and knows what to look for, especially with the hidden costs associated with hiring headliners. The entertainer's booking fee may be one amount, but it may cost you a significant amount over that to satisfy the rider requirements for that entertainer, which may put that act over your budget limits. Although individuals can contact large booking agencies for their talent bookings, these agencies generally do not like to work with individuals and prefer working with a professional entertainment company. A professional entertainment company also has buying power, and it may be able to negotiate a better price for you by booking the act for several productions. It may also know the artist, and may have hired the artist for other events, and it will be able to provide assistance before, during, and after production. Yes, there is a cost associated with using a professional entertainment company, which is generally between 10 and 20 percent of the artist's fee. But how much would it cost an individual, in terms of time and effort, to spend hours researching the available talent pool, find a suitable entertainer, know whom to call to get the booking, and then get through the process of agreeing to the terms of the rider, signing the contract, and paying the deposit? Furthermore, a large booking agency can recommend and book only its exclusive artists, whereas a professional entertainment company can sell artists from various agencies. Hiring celebrities for corporate and association events will provide an experience that your audience will remember for a long time. Relying on the experience, information, and results that a professional entertainment company can deliver will ensure that your event is as successful as you and your client want it to be.

A musical act, whether national, regional, or local talent, is the promotional vehicle of this millennium. Having a musical act at your convention or meeting can boost attendance, although that should not be your primary goal. The combination of a corporate meeting and a musical act almost automatically increases visibility, thereby increasing sales, retail sales support, general awareness, image enhancement, and publicity. The entertainment must fit the company's marketing objectives and its consumers. In short, the musical entertainment must share your company's goals.

In *ConventionSouth,* executive editor Kristen S. McIntosh asked, "How do you 'wow' your top clients and/or your company's VIPs?" In response to this question, Carolyn Luscombe, CSEM, CSEP, CMP, president of Eclectic Events International in Toronto, Canada, answered, "Sometimes we add special VIP or client receptions or hospitality suites with private food and beverage and entertainment." Linda Hamburger, marketing communications specialist at ME Productions, responded, "Another way to make them feel special is to bring top-name entertainers to the event." Eric McNulty, managing director of conferences at Harvard Business School Publishing, counters, "We wow them with content, eschewing big-name entertainment" (April 2002).

There are varying opinions on the types of entertainment that make an event memorable and differing ideas as to what types of entertainment will be appropriate for your event. The key to getting the right type of entertainment is to find out what your client wants and what the audience expects. Can hiring headline entertainment make a difference for your event? The experts say that it can not only boost attendance, but can provide lasting memories for your guests.

THE IMPACT OF HIRING HEADLINE ENTERTAINMENT

Hiring headline entertainment is usually a huge investment for an organization, and event planners often wonder whether it is worth the cost and effort. The stories in this section illustrate the impact that celebrities have had on events, which shows the value of taking that extra step of hiring headline entertainment for your events.

GOLF ANYONE?

At the U.S. Open (Pebble Beach), we were brought in to assist our partner with on-site management for a number of clients, including a world-renowned software developer. The CEO of the software company was getting ready to present a post-dinner talk to 150 of his major investors. Earlier that day on the golf course he mentioned to my associate and me that he was lacking a special "punch" to his presentation. All of the technology bells and whistles were there, but he just wished he had a little something extra. Later that evening, as we were preparing things for the group's dinner, we happened to bump into Mr. Jack Nicklaus enjoying a beer at the bar. My associate approached Mr. Nicklaus and introduced us, explained who our client was, and asked if he had a minute or two to come into the dinner to say a quick "hello." Mr. Nicklaus (and I continue to refer to him as "Mr." because of my sincere respect for him) was very open to our approaching and chatting "golf" with him. Surprisingly enough, he was also happy to come with us to say hello to our client and his guests. It was perfect! Just as our client finished his presentation and special thanks to his guests, Mr. Nicklaus walked up to the stage, shook our clients' hand (to his complete surprise) and welcomed all to the Open. He proceeded to give a couple of witty remarks before thanking them again. The guests were ecstatic, and our client was glowing with pride.

Thanks to the enthusiasm, personality, and "guts" of my associate, not only did I have the opportunity to meet one of my all-time idols, but our client ended his presentation with more than just a little "extra punch." I will never forget how friendly and open, (not to mention well-dressed) Mr. Nicklaus was on that fateful day in June 2000. I guess my point is that you will never know what may happen if you don't try.

—Martin Boyle, president, Dimension Four Event Management,
www.dimensionfour.ca

JANET JACKSON

The best celebrity encounter I have experienced was actually watching two celebrities "freak out" over each other. A few years ago, my husband and I brought a group of our friends to the Janet Jackson concert in San Jose. He's good friends with Janet and arranged for all of us to go backstage prior to the concert. One of our guests was Jerry Rice of the San Francisco Forty-Niners. Well, we got backstage, and right when we went to start the introductions, Jerry realized that he forgot his camera. He literally begged Janet to allow him to run and get it. And run he did. All the way back to the suite and back down again. You should have seen the heads turning in the audience. It seems that Janet was as big a fan of Jerry as he was of her. Both of them were quite nervous about meeting each other—took pictures, exchanged autographs, the whole deal. It was kind of fun seeing the two superstars staring at each other with starstruck looks on their faces and stumbling over their words!

—Gael Sandoval, International Meeting Managers, Inc.

BEAM ME UP, SCOTTIE!

C.B. Park, CAE of Able Management Solutions, shares the following story:

I was working for the local NPR station at the time, and one of the popular shows was a call-in talk show called Open Line. *Well, there was a Star Trek convention in town at the time, and it had arranged to have James Doohan (Scottie) come to town. I berated the host of* Open Line *because "a big star" was in town and he did not have him on the show. The next day, Tom told me that they had found Doohan's agent and booked him on the show. Of course, they needed someone to pick up Mr. Doohan and bring him to the station from his hotel. Guess who got to drive! I had a great time talking with him—we did not talk about the show at all. Then we got to the station, and Tom asked me to do the show with them. Afterward, I drove Doohan back to the hotel. It's funny, I didn't get autographs until that night when I stood in line with all the other Trekkie-types at the convention. What a memory!*

Celebrities can create the memories that last a lifetime for your meeting or event. Some headline entertainment is very affordable, and with the assistance of a professional event management company, you can begin to investigate the option of obtaining headline entertainment for your next event. Although the experts admit that booking your own entertainment is certainly possible, it is much easier to let the professionals handle the task of finding the talent and then negotiating what could be a very complex contracting process. Headline entertainment that fits your event's theme and goals will make an impact that your attendees will continue to talk about for months or years after the event.

Scripts for Future Study

See Appendix 5 for an actual contract rider.

INTERNET RESOURCES

The American Federation of Musicians of the United States and Canada (AFM), www.afm.org. With more than 250 local unions throughout the United States and Canada, this is the largest union in the world representing the interests of the professional musician.

Association of Performing Arts Presenters (APAP), www.artspresenters. org. If there is one consistent aspect of the business of presenting performing arts, it is the face-to-face experiences needed for success. Presenters work with managers, artists perform for audiences, and Arts Presenters brings the field together. For more than 40 years, the Association of Performing Arts Presenters has been bringing the performing arts community together, whether face-to-face at the Annual Members Conference and continuing education courses or through the many connections found in the largest network of arts professionals in the industry.

International Association of Speakers Bureaus (IASB), www.iasbweb.org. Member bureaus are in direct contact with meeting professionals to assist them in securing the right speakers and/or trainers for their events. Speaker agencies and bureaus, in many cases, hold the key to a successful event.

The International Managers' Forum (IMF), www.u-net.com/imf/home. html. IMF was founded in the United Kingdom in 1992 by Simply Red managers Elliot Rashman and Andy Dodd, together with Dire Straits manager Ed Bicknell, as a forum for discussion and action among managers of popular music artists and record producers. Until its inception, managers were the only people in the music industry who did not have their own association. There was no easy means of sharing and learning from the experience of other managers and no avenue through which they could discuss common problems and areas of concern. The formation of the IMF has given managers a much-needed voice within the industry. The IMF is already a major force in the music industry and has established meaningful dialogues with other industry organizations.

The Musicians' Union of the United Kingdom (MU), www.musicians-union.org.uk. The MU was founded more than 100 years ago, in 1893, and has a proud history of service to musicians of all types. The music profession and the music industry have seen constant evolution and change over the years. The Musicians' Union has evolved and changed with them, with one aim to offer the musician better service and a democratic organization.

North American Performing Arts Managers and Agents (NAPAMA), www.napama.org. NAPAMA promotes the mutual advancement and the best interests of performing arts managers and agents; promotes open discourse among members and within the larger field; gives active consideration and expression of opinion on questions affecting the industry; disseminates and exchanges information through forums, meetings, publications, workshops, electronic media, and new technologies; and develops and encourages ethical and sound business practices. In all ways, NAPAMA acts as a resource for its members and creates an environment of regional, national, and international alliances on behalf of the vitality of the performing arts.

The National Speakers Association (NSA), www.nsaspeaker.org. NSA is an international association of more than 4000 members dedicated to advancing the art and value of experts who speak professionally. For more than 25 years, NSA has provided resources and education designed to enhance the business acumen and platform performance of professional speakers.

Recording Industry Association of America (RIAA), www.riaa.com. RIAA members are record labels (companies) that pay membership dues to have the

RIAA represent them on different issues. This includes everything from speaking out in support of free speech and against attempts to pass legislation to censor music, to traveling the world in support of free trade, to defending artists and record labels from pirates who sell and distribute fake copies of their music. RIAA also works with its members on issues of new technology and how that technology can best bring artists together with music fans.

Bienstock, Ronald S. (2000). Tips on making it in the biz. www.getsigned.com.

Miller, Gerri (2001). Interview with Danny Goodwin. www.getsigned.com.

Scoppa, Bud (2001). Interview with Matt Aberle, Jim Barber, Liz Brooks, and Geoffrey Weiss. Zen and the art of A&R. www.ascap.com.

Exit Stage Right

Now that you have hired that headline entertainment, next on the agenda is how to work it into your meeting or event. Read on to Chapter 11 to find out how to "run the show."

Chapter 11 also investigates how to monitor sound and lights for your entertainment stage area.

Monitoring Entertainment and Production to Ensure Continuous Quality

My Aunt Minnie would always be punctual and never hold up production, but who would pay to see my Aunt Minnie?

—BILLY WILDER (1906–2002) ON MARILYN MONROE'S UNPUNCTUALITY, IN HOLLYWOOD ANECDOTES (1988) BY P. F. BOILER AND R. L. DAVIS

IN THIS CHAPTER YOU WILL DISCOVER

- How to monitor sound and lights.
- Who operates the technical elements of an event and what may be needed.
- How to manage the technical side of your production to create one cohesive event.
- How timing is an important aspect in managing events.

The Hollywood director Billy Wilder knew that when directing stars such as Marilyn Monroe in the film "Some Like It Hot," waiting for the star to arrive was worth it at the box office. However, in event production, timing is everything. If the headliner is late or does not appear on cue, the lights and sound are not in sync, or the event does not flow properly, the results will be a disjointed series of elements instead of a smoothly flowing production. To understand how to time production elements, it is important to understand what they are and how they work together. This chapter discusses how to monitor sound and lights, with a description of sound reinforcement and lighting, including setup and breakdown, supervision of the production, and what may be needed for your event. Because mastering the timing factor is as much art as science, this chapter also investigates how to manage the technical side of your production to produce a cohesive meeting or event.

Monitoring Sound and Lights

Hear me, see me
—*Lyrics from* Tommy—The Rock Opera *by The Who*

Engaging as many of an audience's senses as possible makes the difference between a great event and one that has a "wow" factor. The natural association between sight and sound plays an important role in how you will set the mood and tone of an event. Playing the right music to accompany various aspects of the event will determine how the audience perceives those elements and what people will remember about them. Sound is an important component of event production. How that sound reaches the audience, whether it is simple background music, the voice of a headline speaker, or of a singer on stage, depends on two factors: the quality of the audio system and the venue's acoustics.

Jan Moxley is a tour and production manager specializing in advance coordination for events produced internationally. Moxley has worked as an independent contractor and consultant for production and management companies to produce music festivals and tour productions, stage plays, industrial events, conventions, trade shows, and sporting events and is a veteran of more than 1000 live event productions. The following excerpt from his book *Advance Coordination Manual* (1996) will help you to understand some of the basic principles of sound and lighting coordination.

> *Venue acoustics can range from outstanding to awful, depending on what's inside the venue. The facility's décor can be a significant factor. If the venue is large and its walls have hard, flat surfaces, the sound will reverberate. This makes sound check for concerts and*

other events especially difficult because the sound will change as soon as the audience arrives, which means you must then fine-tune the sound during the first few minutes of the show.

The Front of House (FOH) mixing console should always be directly in front of the main speakers, either in the center or just off the center. You do not want to be under a balcony or in a booth; the sound coming from the speakers should have no obstructions from overhead or in front. This will assure a clear, unobstructed sound to mix. Remember that in any venue the best sounding mix will be at the FOH console. Sound engineers should walk to other areas of the auditorium during sound check to listen to the mix and adjust it accordingly to get a good balance of sound everywhere. Any mix platform you construct may be shared by the lighting operator and FOH lighting equipment.

[At the stage,] stage monitor systems are necessary for a good show. If artists cannot hear themselves or each other, chances are they will not deliver their best performance. [Sound wings are] in front of the stage wings. Or, in a proscenium theater, they are downstage of the proscenium. The sound wings are where the main speakers, amplifiers and crossovers are located. If you are bringing sound into the venue, you will have to know the location and dimensions of the access to the wings, as well as any weight restrictions. This is important, especially if you happen to be loading in heavy speaker cabinets. The sound wings will have to be reinforced if they cannot hold the weight. Be sure that lighting has been installed in the sound wings. Available light can be blocked by stacked speaker cabinets, and working in the dark is dangerous.

The backstage area is defined by the staging area location. In a theater or arena end stage configuration, this is the area off-stage behind the main curtain line. Its location is within the production staging area but is not always adjacent to the staging area. During some stage productions it may be located a short distance away. If you are producing a show in a theater-in-the-round or in an arena with a center stage, consider backstage to be the area surrounding the dressing room or locker room that is off-limits to the public, and where the production office, artist, and crew entrances and catering are located. (Source: Advance Coordination Manual *by Jan Moxley).*

Jose Campos (2000) suggests "getting the light right. Have you ever sat in a white room with white fluorescent lighting for eight hours? How about a banquet hall with multitiered crystal chandeliers 20 feet above your head and wall sconces with pale-yellow glass shades? In the former, after about four hours you begin to suffer from what feels like 'white-out' blindness. It is physically draining. When evaluating your next meeting space, pay attention to how the lighting makes you feel, and how it will affect attendees' concentration and mood." It's akin to being on top of a mountain in winter; it is important to break up the whiteness. "When we are handling the rider requirements for a headline entertainer, even if not called for on the lighting plot, we will always bring in uplights to place behind the drummer or by the columns or just plain in front of the black or burgundy curtain used as a backdrop on the stage," says an employee of Mark Sonder Productions.

John K. Mackenzie, owner of and writing in www.thewritingworks.com, observes the following about event lighting:

> *It's been said that good sound is the most neglected component of meetings and events. Well, maybe. But lighting use (and abuse) is right up there as a major contender for first place. Simply put, lighting should draw the aggregate audience-eye toward what you feel should be the focus of attention at any given time. Perhaps the best way to start planning your event entertainment lighting is to assume your meeting room does not have any; or, at least, nothing other than standard ceiling fixtures, which are notoriously inadequate for accommodating multiple presentation situations.*
>
> *Preparation: Apologies if we patronize, but meeting planners have been known to check on lighting without being sure what they were going to light. Lecterns? Panel discussions? Performers? Tables? Award presentations? Aisles? High-school marching band? Enough said. Hotels and conference centers do not worry about this. You should.*
>
> *Site Survey: So you're no electrician or lighting designer, but a little observation, plus a few questions, should give you a pretty good idea of the status. Rule number one: If you don't see any lights, ask! Many venues have basic lights that may do a credible job, and the cost should be less than retaining an outside contractor. Here are some questions to consider if you're going to use an "in-house" system.*
>
> - *Can lights be focused (pointed and adjusted) for your particular setup? Some meetings have the lectern center stage, some at the left or right, others on both sides at once.*
> - *Can lights be controlled so they don't wash out projected images?*
> - *Where are the lighting controls?*
> - *Can room and stage lights be turned down quickly and easily, on cue, for video projections? If so, who's going to do it?*
> - *If darkness is important to a presentation, are there windows or skylights that need to be masked or shaded?*
> - *Who's going to install and operate your lights? Will the same technicians be with you for rehearsals and the show? Will you have to use union electricians?*

- *Does your present room reservation schedule have installation time?*
- *What's the cost for rental, installation, and operation?*

The Walk-In: As guests enter your meeting room what do you want them to concentrate on? Décor? Stage set? Wall-mounted graphics? Table numbers? Product displays? Posters? Easels? And after your rose-wash lighting has transformed the environment is there enough light left for people to find their seats? When the meeting starts, will there be enough light for people to take notes?

Speakers: Where there is a meeting, there will be speeches. Some speakers use a lectern, others roam the stage with a wireless microphone, and some may appear on videotape. A built-in lectern light may be enough for a speaker to see his or her notes, but not enough for an audience to see the speaker—or for a TV camera to get a decent picture. Think about pre-lighting your lecterns with a pair of focused spotlights. Your strolling wireless may need a follow-spot operated by someone with experience. It is not as easy as it looks to track someone around a stage, while keeping the light from spilling over onto the screens and washing out graphic projections or video walls.

Entertainers: If actors, singers, or dancers play a role in your meeting you may need a lighting contractor and outside equipment. If you do, remember that additional lighting means additional setup and rehearsal time going in, and additional removal and packing time going out.

Dinners: As if lighting for lecterns and videos was not enough, now you've got this sales award dinner combined with a corporate anniversary and live entertainment. Later, the retiring CEO and spouse will dance by themselves as Barbara Streisand sings "Memories." Some dinner designs to think about:

Dance floor lighting: Everything from a gentle color wash to swirling beams and projected patterns can be used here. The approach depends on the guests and the budget.

Decorative lighting: This includes projected images or patterns, illumination of architectural details, lighting of specific décor items such as foliage, centerpieces, podia, or props. Deep, saturated colors are frequently used to enhance the décor and create a mood.

Entertainment/performance lighting: Automated moving lights, intense color beams, and vibrant special effects including black light, strobes, and lasers can be part of this system.

Ambient lighting: Lighting for environmental manipulation. Blue and lavender will give a cool night feel; amber and yellow are hot and up-tempo.

Rental equipment to light major events is not usually found ready and waiting for your meeting. To compare the merits of several lighting suppliers, you should describe the look, feeling, and effects you wish to get across at your event. Van Allen Rice of Bestek Lighting recommends the following three W's be a part of your request for proposal (RFP):

1. *What kind of event will it be? A fund-raising gala is very different from a product launch, although they may share common features. The approach taken by your lighting contractor will depend on accepted practices for the particular style of event, as well as knowledge of the following: Is it important to get a specific message across? Or are the guests invited just to enjoy themselves?*

   Will lighting be used to accent the décor, or will it function as the main decorative element? Will the event be videotaped? This is especially important because of the different light levels and color requirements needed to satisfy video cameras.

2. *Where will the event take place? Every location, from ballroom to tent, has its own strengths and liabilities: Will the loading dock and freight elevator be open and running when your equipment arrives? Will there be enough electrical power? If you cannot determine this, make sure your lighting contractor can. How high (or low) is the ceiling? Are there any large windows or skylights that you will need to cover? This can be a significant "hidden" cost: Beware! Is your location a union house? There can be charges here you had better know about in advance. If the venue has multiple-function rooms or ballrooms, specify exactly which rooms will be used. Different rooms in the same hotel can have vastly different requirements and capabilities.*

3. *When will the event take place? Many RFPs are written without specifying exact starting and ending times—crucial information for estimating costs. Include the time the lighting contractor can have access to the site in advance of the event. Lights take time to set up. Include a schedule that lists rehearsal times, periods when work must cease (for meetings, lunch, or other reasons), and when all work must be finished and "show ready." Always make sure your contractor has proper liability and workers' compensation insurance.*

Mark Butts, a leading lighting designer and automated lighting programmer, shares his vast experience through two case studies.

As more and more artists realize the profit potential of performing at special events, they have chosen to create special show formats geared to a special event setting. Likewise, many lighting directors have created a "corporate plot." This is usually included in the technical rider and includes the standard lighting requirements for artists when they play festivals, fairs, special events, and corporate functions.

A typical corporate plot will usually ask for 120 1000 W par 64 fixtures, a handful of lekos, two to four spotlights and, sometimes six to twelve moving lights, as seen in Figure 11-1. Even though in many cases this will be a huge simplification of the artist's touring system, there still can be major challenges in the execution of this design.

Many venues that host special events were never built to house such complex entertainment systems. There are a few problems you might face:

- *Insufficient or nonexistent rigging*
- *Insufficient power to operate a large lighting system*

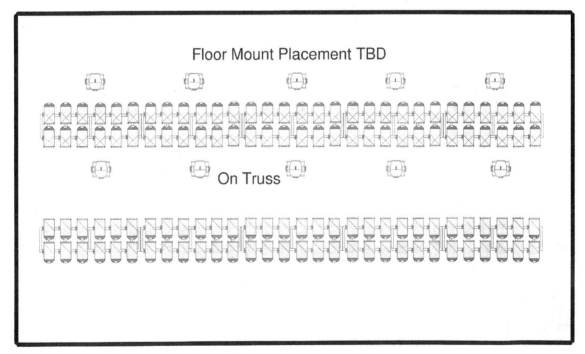

Figure 11-1
The Lighting Setup for a Typical Corporate Event

- *Ceiling too low. Most artists' corporate plots assume a minimum of 25 ft to the bottom of the lighting truss. When you include truss height, rigging, and hoists, you need 35 ft of vertical clearance to achieve a trim height of 25 ft.*
- *Logistical problems; loading docks too small, or too far away, freight elevators that can't handle the weight or are too small.*

How do you overcome these obstacles and still have a first-rate show? Your best bet is to talk directly to the artist's production manager. Explain the logistical challenges you are facing at the venue and ask what kind of compromise can be reached. It is also a good idea to have the event's lighting designer or director talk directly with the artist's lighting director. They can usually iron out any differences and reach a compromise both parties can be happy with.

Make sure the artist's lighting director is kept abreast of any changes in the design and/or any substitutions you are planning. If I am working as the event lighting designer, I usually send a copy of the overall lighting plot to the artist's lighting designer (LD). I then call him or her and go over it, making sure the artist's LD knows what is designated for his or her use and what is reserved for the event. Décor, scenic, and general ambient lighting is usually kept off-limits to the artist's LD.

CASE STUDY 1

A well-known country artist was hired to perform a private outdoor party on a small stage. There were a few problems with initial lighting rider. The original rider had more than 165 pars and lekos hung on a truss more than twice as wide as the stage at a trim height of 25 ft. The system exceeded the weight limit on the roof by 1000 lb, and the roof was able to accommodate only an 18 ft trim height. Moreover, because the show was in an outdoor location that was difficult to get to, truck access was limited.

SOLUTION

The event management and design teams went to the artist's people with the problems. We showed them our site plan and stage drawings and honestly explained the issues we were facing. The system everyone agreed upon shortened the truss so it fit on the stage, and reduced the conventional system to 75 per cans. The artist agreed to accept a small conventional system but required the addition of 12 moving lights to supplement the downsized rig.

RESULT

We provided a system the artist was happy with, and one that took into account the logistical challenges of this event. The audience had a great time, and the event went off on time and on budget.

CASE STUDY 2

A well-known pop star was hired to perform at a one-night private party. The lighting rider called for an all-moving-light system of more than 80 fixtures. The event was scheduled to load in the day of the event, allowing practically no time to program the system.

SOLUTION

Utilizing the most recent pre-visualization lighting software, the lighting plot was drawn in 3-D. A lighting controller was connected to an interface that allowed the user to program the lighting looks on the computer, as opposed to in the venue. This enabled a majority of the cues to be preprogrammed off-site a few days before the event began loading in.

RESULT

The production saved thousands of dollars by not having to hire the venue for a second or third day so that lighting programming could be done. It also saved on other related costs, equipment rental, labor, and per diems (an allowance for daily expenses). The production and the audience got a well-planned and professionally executed show.

Quality Control for the Technical Side of Your Events

You are an event manager, not a lighting technician or designer. So how do you ensure a quality visual effect and, for that matter, aural effect for your meeting or event? Use the Cherny Model.

Bob Cherny offers three considerations to keep in mind to ensure a quality performance for your event:

1. Choose experienced vendors with proven track records in the specialized functions you need.
2. Choose vendors who routinely work well together.
3. Don't be too demanding about the price. Remember the Cherny Quality Triangle: You can have good or fast or cheap. Pick any two. However, if the vendors do not have adequate information, you will get none of the points on the quality triangle.

How do you guarantee the technical quality of your events? If you wait until the gear is rolling off the truck, it is too late. Other than standing next to the audio technician and berating him or her every time the system goes into feedback, there is not a lot you can do during a performance. The key is to check out your vendors and their technicians in advance. The best way to do this is at an event they are working on for someone else. Otherwise, check to make sure that they carry liability insurance and are members of their professional trade associations, including their local convention and visitor's bureau (CVB).

In evaluating a vendor, what do you look for? The most obvious thing is the condition of the equipment. How old is it? How well is it maintained? Cases get beat up pretty quickly, so a few battered cases means little, but if all the cases are battered and all the latches are gone, that's not a good sign.

When you are watching the load-in for an event, what can you do to check out a potential vendor? There are several specific things to look for. How good is the vendor's documentation? Does the vendor know the room? Is someone in charge? Is the crew working at a steady pace? Is there lots of "standing around" time? Is the amount of labor appropriate for the size of the event? Are the crew members fighting among themselves, or are the various subgroups working well together? Remember that if you see problems during your own load-in, it is too late.

One of the best ways to ensure quality is to review the vendor's documentation in advance of your event. This means different things in regard to different crews. For the video projection and audio crews, the documentation is little more than an equipment list and a few boxes on the floor plan where their gear goes. The scenic crew will have renderings and detailed floor plans. Lighting will likely have a plot, an equipment list, and a patch list. It is not as important that you be able to understand the documentation when it is presented as it is for you to ask that the documentation exists and that the planning has been done. The more planning the vendors do in advance of your event, the more smoothly it will go.

There are some limits, however. If the lighting for your event consists of just a front and rear truss with 18 pars on the front, 12 on the back, and a half dozen or so specials here and there, most reasonably experienced lighting designers figure that out in their heads, with a few notes scribbled on a yellow pad. The bigger the event and the more demanding its needs, the more important the documentation.

There are some basic technical concepts that many people in the meetings and events industry seem to have forgotten. The proper angle for lighting is 45 degrees up, 45 degrees left, and 45 degrees right. Lighting a stage with two units on a 12 ft boom stand from 80 ft away is not good lighting. It is cheap lighting. The height of the unit above the speaker is as important as the angle from the side. This almost always means attaching lights to the ceiling or to a truss hung from the ceiling. This is expensive, but it is the right way. Furthermore, unless you are lighting for video, white light is ugly. Pale pinks and pale blues make speakers look much healthier.

In regard to audio, the two big questions are volume and intelligibility. Can you hear the speaker and do you understand what is being said? How the sound gets there is not really your issue. The intelligible sound either works or it doesn't. In that regard, ringing and feedback in the system are totally unacceptable. Once rehearsals are over, there is no excuse for feedback unless a person with a microphone walks directly in front of the main speakers. Even then, with the new digital processing equipment now coming on the market, that problem can be mitigated as well. Given a proper rehearsal, feedback means only one of three things: the speaker is so far from the microphone and so quiet that the situation is beyond help, the wrong equipment is being used for the job in the wrong places, or the operator is incompetent.

When evaluating the video, first check out the projectors with the room light on. If the projectors are properly matched to the screens, the image should be visible with the room lights on. As with lights and sound, look at the quality of the equipment and the attitudes of the crew members. Unless you are a video specialist, you are not going to know the specifics of the equipment they will be using. There are a couple of things to look for, though. How smoothly did the load-in go? How quickly was the equipment set up? Did all the equipment work when it was first turned on?

The answers to these questions and the general body language of the crews will give an indication of what is to come. Problems and complexities may be

---

PINK *THE PARTY TOUR* 2002

Lighting Equipment

111	PAR-64s
22	High End Systems Studio Spots
23	High End Systems Studio Colors
12	ETC Source Four ellipsoidals
2	ETC Source Four PARs
3	LSD Molefays
1	Lycian 1.2kW HMI truss spot
16	Diversitronics D3000 strobes
1	Nook light
2	Reel EFX DF-50 hazers
1	High End Systems F-100 fogger
2	Wildfire UV fixtures
14	LSD D3 8′ truss sections
4	LSD D3 truss corners
14	Columbus McKinnon chain hoists
1	Avolites Diamond 3 console
1	Clear-Com intercom system
2	traveler tracks
16	LSD kabuki solenoids
1	24′ × 50′ black backdrop

Figure 11-2
The Lighting Equipment for Pink's 2002 *Party Tour*

Event Name: _____
Client: _____
Dates of Show: _____ Through _____
Location of Show: Venue _____ Room _____
Load in Date: _____ Time: _____
Show Ready Date: _____ Time: _____
Load out date: _____ Time: _____
Show schedules attached: Y _____ N _____ Projected Audience: _____ppl.
Elements of show:
Speech reinforcement: Y _____ N _____ Video Presentations: Y _____ N _____
Wireless mics: Y _____ N _____ Type and number: Lavalier _____ HandHeld ____
Q & A Sessions: Y _____ N _____ Voiceovers: Y _____ N _____
Teleprompting: Y _____ N _____ Satellite or Recording truck: Y _____ N _____
Entertainment: Y _____ N _____
Stage Plot, Input List and Rider Attached: Y _____ N _____
Production contact number: _____
Production Contact Name: _____ Position: _____
Room dimensions: _____ wide _____ long
Back of room to downstage edge dimensions: _____ deep
Average height to ceiling tile: _____
Height to lowest soffit _____
Mains system:
Rigging specifications attached: Y _____ N _____
Mains Flown: Y _____ N _____
Main Speakers Type and quantities: _____
Subwoofers: _____
Center Cluster: Y _____ N _____ Type and quantities: _____ X _____
Delay lines: Y _____ N _____ Number of discrete delay lines: _____
Delays Flown: Y _____ N _____
Design by Audio department attached: Y _____ N _____
Power requirements:
Any large system shall require a minimum of 100 Amps 3 phase camlok ends terminated where needed.
Any other elements other than sound on a service shall require use of an isolation transformer with earth ground supplied.
Power requirements confirmed: Y _____ N _____
Notes: _____
_____

Edison only: Y _____ N _____ _____ circuits @ 20 amps.
Clearcom: Base channels: _____ Stations: _____
Biscuits: _____ Wireless com: _____
Telephone handsets: _____ IFB: _____
Additional Notes: _____
List by: _____ Date: _____

Figure 11-3
Audio Show List Form

part of all events, but problem solving is a service of the professional vendors you hire to make your event look and sound great.

When you want to see sound or lighting that is on the cutting edge, check on the ultimate road show, the quintessential single engagement: a rock concert. Figure 11-2 shows the lighting and sound equipment responsible for making the Party Tour 2002 show of Pink a success. Figure 11-3 shows a form to help organize an audio show's technical requirements.

Timing

One of the most important elements in show production is the proper timing of the show; that is, having the curtain go up and come down at predetermined times, with the entertainment flowing effortlessly within that time frame. Sometimes this can be a daunting task.

Nobody knows that better then Blair Farrington, CEO of Farrington Productions. Farrington has 25 years of experience as producer, choreographer, director, writer, and conceptual designer and developer for award-winning live production shows, multimedia presentations, television production commercials, industrial shows, film, and, most recently, themed attractions and multiuse venues. He comments,

> Here in Las Vegas, shows are usually kept to approximately 70 minutes, with large productions sometimes running 90 minutes in length. It is imperative that the pacing of the staged entertainment be lively and brisk, in order to allow the audience time in the casino, as well as the restaurants. Because of this, intermissions are the kiss of death for Las Vegas performances, as an audience member who sits down at a slot machine during intermission and hits a few small jackpots will most likely not return to the theater for the second act. Las Vegas is not Broadway and Broadway is not Las Vegas, and because of this, both endeavors require vastly different timing concepts.

The Las Vegas production show is an entity well understood by those who call Las Vegas home. Typically, the show that does well in Las Vegas is one that has a team of Vegas professionals behind it, industry insiders who understand the quirky nature of the Las Vegas audience. Tourists come to Las Vegas to gamble, to be entertained, and, basically, to do things they would never do at home. The shows that have appeal are those that offer spectacular visuals, great music, and a running length that does not allow time to fidget.

Production numbers that excite and hold the audience captive are numbers in which something changes every 30 seconds or so, be it a costume, a song, a set piece, or even the performers themselves. Constant movement is what counts in Las Vegas. As bombastic as this may sound, the shows that traditionally stick to this school of thought are the shows still enjoying audiences 20 years or more later.

Many people are responsible for the smooth operation of a production show; however, how the show was put together in the first place largely determines how "effortlessly" it will run in operation. Stage crews need rehearsals just as the performers do. The timing involved in the lift of a curtain, or the drop of a flat, often becomes the most crucial element in a show. Combined with rehearsing quick costume change, again and again, timing now becomes the most difficult aspect of putting on the show.

The smooth operation of any show relies on the stage manager and his or her knowledge of the show. The stage manager calls the cues and, basically, is responsible for anything and everything that happens on stage. In the case of special events and one-time entertainment, the job of the stage manager becomes even more stressful, because there is only one chance to get it right. For this reason, it is imperative that the person calling the show be not only an industry professional, but also well versed in the material at hand.

For example, Farrington produced a toga party spectacular for Caesar's Palace that involved the proper timing of the food courses and their serving, as well as the processions that brought out the food and a cast of more than 100 performers featured with aerial acts, gladiator fights, pyrotechnics, horses and chariots, camels, a white tiger, an elephant, birds of prey, and a boa constrictor. All of these elements had to use the freight elevators for their entrances and exits, as the party was held in Caesar's Tower. The dressing rooms were a flight below, and the animals had to remain penned in a corral on the ground level. Farrington had only the day of the event to rehearse the timing of the entire production, catering staff included. Therefore, the only person capable of calling the show was Blair Farrington himself, the individual who created the event. As the creator, he knew exactly how it was to operate. Farrington hired a team of respected professionals, each with highly organized tasks to accomplish. If one person dropped the ball, the entire event could come to a grinding halt. Fortunately, as every detail of the party had been carefully thought out prior to its one rehearsal, all elements of the production slowly came together, with the result being a cohesive, seamless entertainment production for Caesar's high rollers.

Complete and intimate knowledge of your event or show is crucial to its smooth operation. Everyone is involved, from the stage manager, to the flymen, to the deckhands, to the lighting and sound technicians, to the riggers and the prop and wardrobe assistants. Productions run seamlessly only when all the elements are carefully and thoughtfully planned, adequately rehearsed, and eventually handed over to a team of industry professionals.

Lighting designer Mark Butts offers his thoughts on the timing of the show:

Timing is crucial to an event. It can be as simple as the podium lights coming on when someone is speaking to complex control systems driving multiple devices. Because lighting can be used to draw the audience's attention toward something, a well planned, scripted, and executed show is essential to keep the audience's attention.

A good example is the product reveal. Some product launches keep the featured item out of sight until the big moment. If a video is shown, the lighting director usually lowers the ambient light level in the room, drawing attention to the video screens. Afterward, there might be high-energy music, coupled with lighting effects or movement; both add energy and create anticipation. The final product reveal might include more special effects, pyro, video, and audio. A lighting director typically makes use of a combination of manually operated spotlights, fixed focus conventional and automated lighting to highlight the product and draw the audience's attention to it.

In this example, there are many things happening simultaneously. All of them have to be executed at the exact time, or things are going to look sloppy. Timing is clearly crucial, but it is not something that just happens. Producers and directors must have a clear understanding of the show flow. The talent onstage must also understand what is happening. When the stage goes dark, when the pyro goes off—where they need to be and when. The technicians must have a clearly written script and cue sheet. And most important: rehearse, rehearse, rehearse.

If there is a secret to share here, it "is to get a flow established," says Doug Matthews, managing director of Pacific Show Productions in Vancouver, B.C., Canada. Matthews gives a sample of calling a show, warning each person ahead of time when it is his or her turn to do something:

"Doug for John."

"Go for John"

"Stand by with Mr. Smith at stage right and put him onstage right after this speaker finishes."

"10-4."

"John from Doug—OK, go with Mr. Smith onstage."

"Mr. Smith is onstage."

"Light—Change to a blue wash for Mr. Smith."

"Video—are you ready with the next clip after Mr. Smith? It's the clip for the new sales program."

"Ready with video clip of new program."

From which location do you call a show? Again, Matthews: "I prefer to call a complex show from the rear of the room from a central communication station that is connected to all the technical people involved, and from where I can see the whole picture."

"To monitor the entire show," Cherny says, "one must get a view of the entire show. To technically call the show, which involves a lot of entertainment that might be entering and leaving from different parts of the venue, I work better calling the show from a wireless station that gives me the flexibility to move around and change the way the show flows if I see it needs it, or to talk directly to an entertainer or presenter."

Running the Show

"We see potential. It doesn't matter who you are. It doesn't matter where you live or what you do. When your potential is pointed in the right direction, it can lead you anywhere. At Microsoft, we see no limits to the potential we all might reach because we see no limits to human imagination. That is what inspires us.
— *MICROSOFT 2002 ANNUAL REPORT*

Microsoft, the world leader in product reveals, has produced many high profile product revelation events. These events involve celebrities and VIPs such as founder Bill Gates. Often these inspiring events may inadvertently create a number of risks that may result in despair. Brad Stevens, a detective with the Fresno Police Department, gives his thoughts on safety for public entertainment events:

In today's society, many people attend entertainment events for many different reasons. The demographics of the type of people that come to your event may vary greatly, based on the type of event you are holding, the type of entertainment, and where the event is held. In recent history we have seen an increase in the number of events that have had security problems. People who attend these events feel that, as attendees, or fans, it is their right to cause disturbances and that if they don't participate in such actions, they are deemed to be nonsupportive fans.

When dealing with incidents at these events, it is very important that a good relationship has been built with the local law enforcement agency, so that these problems can be foreseen and dealt with before your event's reputation is destroyed. At any event, law enforcement looks for several different flash points that can trigger an event to turn bad. Those flash points can be the amount of alcohol consumed by a crowd, the lack of adequate crowd control, leading to excessive hooliganism, the presence of the media, with their bright lights causing exhibitionism, the starting of bonfires, and exhibitionism by people who want to attract attention to themselves through their actions of excessive rowdiness. These all lead to the degeneration of events.

To ensure that an event is successful, managers and planners need to have a set plan to deal with excessive crowds, as well as a single liaison who has the ability to make decisions in law enforcement. Being able to go to the person at the top, who can make decisions without having to justify his or her actions to a higher authority, is the key to ensuring the proper response by law enforcement when events do become uncontrollable. It is important to start working early with your law enforcement representative, months before your event, and to allow that person to be a part of your team, not to make decisions, but to offer helpful suggestions. If you follow these rules, you will have a greater chance of having a successful entertainment event that people will want to return to year after year.

Producing an event at a large facility involves the coordinated efforts of many people, from both the production company and the venue. Because these events draw crowds that can number in the tens of thousands, there is little margin for error on production and safety issues. From the outset, responsibilities must be clearly defined and understood by all parties to the production so as to eliminate confusion and delay when problems do occur. Stan Aaronson, CSEP, of ViewPoint International Destination Management Companies USA and Mark Sonder Productions, Los Angeles office, contributes on this subject. "Learn firsthand from those who make it happen at facilities capable of serving thousands at a time, just what *they* mean by full production. The brand identity of a high-profile facility may draw more attendees. Be sure to know what capabilities are in-house and what are subcontracted out and what planners seek in a supplier."

On the subject of understanding individual responsibilities and the major importance of minor details during an event, Mariana Paolini, CMP and meeting planner at the Navigant Corporation in Connecticut, provides a case study of an event she produced for a client, for which last-minute decisions were required in response to situations involving the venue that nearly derailed the event.

Direction, control, supervision; these are the three concepts the author subscribes to when on-site at "command central." Three words for three teams: your client, your client's attendees, and your own staff. The vibe in the room must always be "read" for what is working, and, perhaps more important, for what is not working. Your client must trust you to monitor and make decisions, as many corrections may be necessary. The author believes this approach to managing events has a proven track record for consistent customer satisfaction.

CASE STUDY

Venue: House of Blues, Orlando, Florida

Client: Boehringer Ingelheim

Event: Entertain 1600 guests with a show consisting of the Cornell Gunter Coasters, the Marvelettes, the Elsbeary Hobbs Drifters, Blood, Sweat and Tears, featuring David Clayton-Thomas, and Joan Jett and the Blackhearts.

Delivery of Services:

- *Meet and greet*
- *Encores*
- *Timing of individual sets, both at the show and in the sound checks*
- *Monitoring the sound reinforcement, lighting, staging, and security for both artists and attendees*
- *Making air, local, ground, and hotel reservations and backline (orchestral instrument rental requirement), with everyone's special quirks adhered to*
- *Handling contract negotiations, not only between artists and source client, but also with the House of Blues regarding live video and photo shoots*

Direction, control, and supervision were essential throughout the entire event. Planning for this event commenced eight months prior to the four-hour show and finished the day after during the post-con meeting.

This was handled by Mark Sonder Productions (MSP). Everyone had his or her own three-ring loose-leaf binder, with tabs on varying subjects,

and specific responsibilities. On-site meetings were scheduled with the artists, the site, and the client. Communication when all of MSP's 59 employees were in town was imperative.

CHALLENGES

1. *The venue was very protective of its artwork around the theater and backstage. Its corporate headquarters was not going to allow any still or video cameras for any type of use whatsoever, even if there was written permission granted by my company on behalf of all the individual artists. MSP got the venue representative, client, and the client's acting attorneys together to have an open discussion to make sure that no one's rights would be infringed upon. An agreement was made, where the video cameras were allowed to record the first 60 sec of the first two tunes for BST; three minutes each or nine minutes total for the EH Drifters, CG Coasters & the Marvelettes, and no live video for Joan Jett and papers were drawn up, the language double-checked, and the parties physically found to sign this agreement. I put my signature on all the papers within minutes of emceeing the start of the show.*

2. *Sale of merchandise: As the venue wanted a hefty cut of the proceeds from merchandise sold, I made a unilateral decision. It seemed best to eliminate the option of selling merchandise inasmuch as little profit would be earned.*

In Conclusion

Quality control in event production includes every aspect of the event, from sound and lights to making sure the headliner is happy and the venue is cleared before you go home after it is all over. How do you do it all?

This chapter discussed sound, lights, coordination, quality control and how the many elements have to work together to produce an event that flows smoothly. Three critical elements in the production of any event, large or small, are the team members' expertise, their experience, and communication between all involved with the event, whether they work for the production company or the venue. The many experts who provided input to this chapter agree on the importance of establishing good communication and that knowing who is responsible for each element can eliminate problems in the future. Here are some tips to help you produce an event that meets your clients' needs:

1. If you accept a job, no matter what the pay, *do it right!*
2. *Always* be honest, first with yourself, then with everyone else.
3. *Just say no,* if you are not the right person to handle an event.
4. *Trust and delegate.* One person's arms are available only so long!
5. Maintain a hierarchy of authority, as well as specific job responsibilities for your staff.
6. You know what *should* happen. Make a list, disperse it to the relevant parties, and discuss what *could* happen.
7. Get paid in full *before* the event.
8. Make sure your team is happy throughout. Good working conditions include the team's ability to work with other professionals, that all equipment is in good, clean working condition, and that food and beverages are available at all times. Publicly express your appreciation for the team, and write thank-you letters.

Scripts for Future Study

PLASA is a diverse organization operating within the entertainment technology industry. It's web site aims to be the prime source of information for entertainment, presentation, and event technology professionals worldwide. www.plasa.org.

INTERNET RESOURCES

Production Services Association, Ltd (in the United Kingdom) (PSA), www.psa.org.uk, founded in 1995, is an active organization representing the professional interests of both freelance technical production personnel and service companies. PSA is the industry voice for the live entertainment and events technical production sector of the wider entertainment industry. It seeks to represent members' professional interests at local, national, and international levels.

Pro Lights and Staging News, www.plsn.com.

The Pro Production Show, www.plsn.com/pp/home.html.

Entertainment Services and Technology Association, (ESTA) is a non-profit trade association representing the North American entertainment technology industry. Members include dealers, manufacturers, service and production companies, scenic houses, designers, and consultants. www.esta.org/index.html

Technical Production Services Association of South Africa, www.tpsa.co.za.
Entertainment Technology On-Line, www.etnow.com.

BOOKS

Fitt, Brian, and Joe Thornley (1997). *Lighting Technology: A Guide for the Entertainment Industry.* St. Louis, MO: Industry Focal Press.

Moody, James L. (1997). *Concert Lighting: Techniques, Art, and Business,* 2d ed. St. Louis, MO: Focal Press.

Vasey, John (1997). *Concert Tour Production Management: How to Take Your Show on the Road.* St. Louis, MO: Focal Press.

Exit Stage Right

Now that you have the correct sound reinforcement and lighting for your meeting and event, you need to take care of what could go wrong. Chapter 12 discusses how to assess and reduce risk.

CHAPTER 72

Reducing Risk: Assessment, Intervention, and Control

This was a very large corporation. It would be impossible to know everything going on.

—JEFFREY K. SKILLING, ENRON'S FORMER CHIEF EXECUTIVE

IN THIS CHAPTER YOU WILL DISCOVER

- The various types of risk in the event entertainment industry.
- How you can manage risk through the use of various tools and techniques.
- How to handle a situation that arises from the manifestation of a risk element at an event.

As preceding quotation from Jeffrey Skilling implies, risk is an inherent part of nearly every business activity, but certainly in the event entertainment and production industry. The coordination and timing involved in the delivery of an event takes months of planning, and every detail has its own risk factors.

Whether an event has an audience of 20 or 20,000, every person adds an element of risk to that event. There is always the risk that something will happen to the venue, the sound system, the food, or the audience, or that Mother Nature will be at her uncooperative worst. Although it is impossible to avoid risk entirely, it is possible to define risks, to plan and prepare for them, and to mitigate their effects.

Managing Risk for Entertainment Events

Risk is *any* condition or occurrence that *might* affect the outcome of an event. It is inherent in *everything* that can happen financially, legally and ethically. Imagine two planners speaking about an event. One asks the other, "How did everything go today?" The other responds, "Really well. You know, the real work happened in the weeks and months leading up to this event." This is so true. In this industry, all of the hard work is done before the event, which then becomes almost anticlimactic. All of the worry, the planning, and preparation have already occurred, and, if done properly, everything that could go wrong has a contingency plan ready for it. Managing risk is an important component of a well-defined planning strategy, and it is completed well in advance of the meeting or event. As the planner, whether you are in charge of the entire event or merely controlling certain of its elements, risk management is your responsibility.

There are four ways to handle risk responsibility for an entertainment event:

1. *Avoidance.* By avoiding all risk, you would not be putting anybody or any property at risk, but then you could not hold any meetings or events. This is obviously a strategy that will not work.
3. *Acceptance.* As you cannot avoid all risk, because by doing so you would not be able to perform your job responsibilities, an alternative is to accept all risk. This is the opposite of the first approach and one that will also not work unless you really enjoy a challenge.
3. *Reduction.* This is a balancing act. You are not totally avoiding risk, nor are you accepting it all. With this option you are able to choose the risks that you will undertake and will therefore have more control over your potential losses.
4. *Transference.* Although you may have to accept some of the risk, there may be others to whom you can legally transfer or assign a significant portion of the risk. These may include other parties or entities such as insurance companies. The risk is still there, as it will be for all events, but it is now a liability that you share with others. Within this indus-

try, you will find that transference of risk will occur during the planning process. This means obtaining the proper licenses, permissions, and approvals, as well as obtaining insurance and other methods of protecting the event from financial losses. A risk transference strategy even includes hiring experienced professionals to work with you on the event.

In this industry we do the same thing over and over again, because we know that it works and that the outcome will be the same. Or, at least, it will be predictable within a certain range of tolerance. We are not totally risk averse, or we would not be in this business. We have learned, through experience, what to watch out for and how to plan for risk, following a process developed through the production of many events.

Chapter 7 introduced "the bible," the Production Book or Operations Manual that is developed for each event, containing all of the information about that event. This manual not only helps you to track the event's production, but once the event is over, it becomes a valuable reference tool for future event and entertainment production. By referring to it, you will be able to figure out what went wrong, what fell through the cracks, and determine where you need to plan more carefully for the next event.

The following process shows how to define the risk elements in an event and create a risk management strategy. This process has been fine-tuned through many years of use and continues to be an integral part of the event entertainment planning process.

- Data collection and research are the first steps of the risk assessment process. The data is compiled through research, which includes reviewing historical accounts of your past entertainment events or other similar events to identify risk elements that could have a negative impact on your event or program.
- Risk analysis is the second step. Here you find out what all of your data means. What should happen at this event? What could happen to adversely affect the event? What are the probabilities of something happening? Bring the team together; "two heads (or more) are better than one" applies to this situation. This is also a good time to engage in some creative brainstorming, as discussed in Chapter 6. Examine the data to identify any existing gaps. Get your insurance carrier involved. It will be able to tell you the specific amount of existing risk for your event.
- Risk planning is the third step of the process. After analyzing the potential risks, you must determine how to address them. This step includes planning for the identified threats, understanding their impact and probability, designing processes to mitigate them, and looking for positive opportunities within the threats. There are several reasons for such planning, the most important of which is to eliminate the need for

improvisational measures to deal with any problems while they are occurring at an event. Thus, if a problem arises at an event, there will be a solution in place to address it, with assigned responsibilities, a dedicated budget, and a rehearsed action plan. This can eliminate, or at least reduce, the probability of threat and its impact. Establish trigger points, specifying that when "X" happens the team will do "Y."

■ Risk control occurs once the risk plan has been developed, and a process called the Shewart Cycle is used to implement it. According to this cycle, control is a five-step process: plan, do, check, act, and, of course, repeat as necessary. Document every aspect of the planning process, including who attends meetings, who misses them, and any incidents that occur at any time during planning or production. The Shewart Cycle is shown in Figure 12-1 minus the "repeat as necessary" step.

Do it/control it: You are in charge, so you must also be in control. Being in control requires your taking proactive measures to stay on top of everything. Do you know what is going on? Own your responsibilities by doing the things required to maintain control of the processes involved.

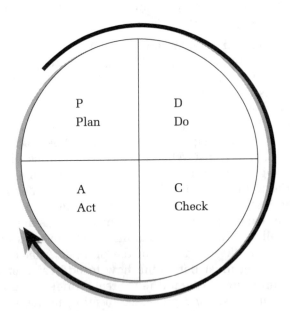

Figure 12-1
The Shewart Cycle

Observe/monitor: Observe the people, places, and things that are occurring around you. Monitor them to learn more about them. What you know and understand you can take control of.

Correct/make decisions: Correct any errors, misunderstandings, or gaps in the processes as soon as they become apparent. Make decisions based on what you know or learn from your research and analysis.

Repeat as necessary: The area of risk management is not always a level playing field, especially because events are usually planned at least six months in advance. A lot can happen in that time period, so repeat this process to ensure that you are prepared for any changes in the landscape since the previous risk planning session.

- The evaluation process is the final step, but one that some planners may omit. It will, however, provide you with an invaluable source of information concerning the event and everything surrounding it, which will help you plan for your next event.

Licenses and Permits

A critical part of planning is to ensure that you have obtained all the required licenses and permits for your events. First and foremost, *all* businesses require a license, and service businesses are *not* exempt from this requirement. These licenses are obtained from the local and/or state agencies. Not having proper licensing can result in fines, legal proceedings, and your event's being shut down or canceled. There may be other licenses or permits or compliance issues that may affect your event entertainment, such as the following:

Licenses/Permits
- Entertainment brokerage
- Liquor, food, waste, public property use
- Police, fire, medical emergency, health and safety, and traffic permits

Other Compliance Issues
- Federal: Fair Employment and Housing Act (FEHA), Americans with Disabilities Act (ADA), Occupational Safety and Health Administration (OSHA), Federal Aviation Administration (FAA), and Bureau of Land Management (BLM) requirements; Federal Communications Commission (FCC), government contracting, other federal land use, patent, trademark, and software infringement laws; and environmental regulations
- State: California Occupational Safety and Health Administration (CAL-OSHA), and public or state park property use requirements; health and safety code, and minimum wage/hiring requirements; Alcoholic Beverage Control Commission (ABC), and public safety regulations

Licenses and Permits: Real Life

What happens when you do not have a license? The following story shows that the consequences can be severe.

The Carling Leeds Festival was refused a license, having failed to make improvements in the management and control of the event. Local residents, as well as the environmental department, had complained of overflowing toilets and urinals at the previous year's festival. The licensing counsel was concerned that improvements to the action plan would not be met, thus causing a multitude of problems for the community, and did not give the needed licenses for the event; therefore the festival was cancelled.

Contracting for Event Entertainment and Production

When the deal is closed between planner and supplier, the parties go to contract. There are many different types of entities with which you will contract, all of which will play a role in the event's production. The various types of contracts, contracting agencies, or agents include the following:

- Artist contracts, contract addendums or riders, and modifications to them
- Certificates of Insurance, riders, endorsements
- Labor work rules, employment, venue rules
- Hotel, speakers, audiovisual equipment
- Vendors, caterers, suppliers, rentals, entertainment, music licensing
- Lighting, power, fireworks, security, waste
- Ambulance, municipal services, ticket sales
- Event or production specifications, work orders
- Memorandums of Understanding, Letters of Intent, confirming letters
- E-mail agreements and exchanges

Everyone should be given the benefit of the doubt in professional situations and assumed to have good intentions. However, in negotiating for products or services, these intentions may be vague and often unenforceable if they are not in writing. A written contract is the best and safest legal mechanism for assurance and enforcement of performance by the contracting parties. This mechanism will increase the probability of the desired outcomes, as the two sides have mutual obligations to fulfill to which they have agreed, in writing, committing those obligations to a document that is enforceable in a court of law.

A contract for entertainment or production requires four items to make it legal and binding:

1. Identification of *parties* competent to make the agreement (a person must be at least 18 years of age to sign a contract)
2. *Duty* to perform and the specific obligations of the contract (who, what, where, when, how)
3. *Consideration* for the agreement and the payment or exchange of goods and services
4. *Acceptance* by contracting parties through signing and dating the contract

Although only four items are required, it is to everyone's benefit to have additional items in a contract, such as the following:

- Cancellation process, liquidated damages, forfeiture/deposit clauses
- Default/waiver provisions
- *Force majeure* provision
- Hold harmless provision
- Applicable insurance obligations
- Waiver of indemnity where applicable
- Arbitration/ Alternative Dispute Resolution (ADR) provision
- Attorney fees provision

It is important to contract for the services of everyone who is contributing to the event; it is also important to manage the contracts as well. Copies of contracts should be kept in the Production Book and the originals in a safe place. There are other steps you can take to manage the necessary contracts that will keep them organized and protect you in the event of a problem. Remember that if there is a disagreement or dispute, your immediate access to a copy of a contract, along with any riders and modifications, may save time, money, and the event.

- Keep each contract in a separate file for easy reference. You can cross-reference contracts by vendor or service in the Production Manual.
- All exchanges and/or modifications should be in writing. No matter how well intended they may be, get all promises in writing and keep copies in the contract folder and Production Book.
- Have deadlines for returning all legal paperwork. Missing or delayed legal paperwork can create serious problems, presenting another element of risk. You can mitigate that risk by being in control of this important part of your event entertainment planning process. Also make sure that you are aware of any deadlines for legal paperwork for which you are responsible.
- Proactively manage the legal paperwork process by knowing the due dates and following up on any missed deadlines. This means making

telephone calls, sending e-mail, faxes, and whatever else it takes to have all paperwork completed.

Good contract management demonstrates control of the event to the client. Maintain zero tolerance. All of the rules should apply to everyone, all the time. Proactively manage this process, and you will remove an element of risk from your event.

Assessing risk is the process that identifies the risks. Once risks have been identified, the next step is to determine what will happen if a crisis occurs and who is responsible. This next step is called *crisis mitigation*.

Crisis Mitigation

With the assistance of Clint Van Zandt, former FBI agent and president of Van Zandt Associates, and Detective Brad Stevens of the Fresno, California, Police Department, this section discusses the following elements of crisis mitigation:

- The components of a crisis mitigation and management plan
- The nature of threats to events
- Building a crisis mitigation and management team
- How that team works together
- Working with public safety organizations
- Command, control, communication, and information systems
- Public and media relations requirements

COMPONENTS OF A CRISIS MITIGATION AND MANAGEMENT PLAN

"The greatest risk is not taking one." It takes courage to do something that has never been done before. To attempt a feat that goes beyond conventional thinking. But it also takes planning and a complete understanding of all the problems that may arise.
—As seen in the 2002 campaign print ad for AIG Insurance

According to the American Heritage Dictionary, 4th ed., *to mitigate* means "to moderate a quality or condition in force or intensity; to alleviate, relieve, or cause to become milder; to act in such a way as to cause an offense to seem less serious." In assessing the risk elements of an event or meeting, decide whether a particular risk is a threat to your program. If the electrical power went out, would that be a risk or threat to the event or meeting? If that same power went out in a tent in the middle of a cold winter, would that change the situation, making it a threat? How will you mitigate that crisis or threat? In the first situation, backup generators may be a way to mitigate the threat.

Along with a plan for mitigating a crisis, there must be a crisis management team whose members will make the tough decisions. They will decide when to use the backup generator, where it can be found, and how it will get to where it is needed. The plan should be in place in advance to mitigate the likelihood and impact of a crisis; it should include an integrated command, control, communication, and information system for internal management and communications. There should also be a public and media relations plan for managing external communications.

TYPES OF THREATS TO EVENTS AND MEETINGS

> *I wasn't invited. Then again, the traffic is so bad I don't want to go anywhere.*
> —GEORGE SOROS, ON A PARTY DURING THE WORLD ECONOMIC FORUM
> FEATURING ELTON JOHN

There are always innumerable threats that can occur at any meeting or event, such as the traffic jams referenced in the preceding quotation. However, meeting and event planners can reduce the risk associated with these threats by recognizing them and forming contingency plans. The following is a list of potential planned and unplanned threats of which you should be aware.

Unplanned Threats
- *Weather.* This threat is out of your control. It is fairly easy to discover the likelihood of your date being within blizzard or hurricane season. Be sensitive to Mother Nature and respect her power. Your crisis mitigation plan should deal with "the elements."
- *Traffic jams.* This threat is out of your control as well. The key to avoiding such situations is to make sure that the limousine driver who is bringing in the headline entertainment from the airport, or the motor coach driver who is bringing your guests to the show, knows many different routes to the destination. Drivers should be connected to a central dispatcher who has an eye on the traffic reports. Your ground transportation company will be of immeasurable assistance here.
- *Utility failures.* If the power goes out or the water stops flowing, what then? The musical entertainment may need electricity, the caterer requires water. Again, this threat is out of your control.

Because these conditions would all be out of your control, they should be included in your plan. They are basic elements of risk in any event entertainment plan. It is important to be aware of these risks and plan for backups if any of them would be a threat to your meeting or event.

Planned Threats
- *Protests.* Unless they act at the spur of the moment, which would then include a strong emotional component, protesters require a permit to make their feelings known. Reviewing their permit will help you determine which areas will be set aside for the protesters. Now you can

easily plan for any disruptions that their activities may cause. Your local police department should be aware of the history of the groups that
are protesting, as well as a history of any violence that occurred during
past protests.

- *Threats of violence or acts of violence.* A short while ago the author had
  a client who was interested in knowing whether Sir Paul McCartney was
  going to be performing at a certain conference. A call was made to Sir
  Paul's manager, but the answer was a vague, indeterminate reply, which
  was his way of protecting his client and shielding him from any potential threats. In today's world, any place you hold an event may be subject to a threat or act of violence. The history of an event can be important in the creation of a crisis mitigation plan for the upcoming program.
- *Digital threats.* Is your data protected? Is your Web site safe? What happens in the event of loss of service? According to the American Hotel
  and Lodging Association (AH&LA), e-business has proven to be the savior for many hotel companies in the aftermath of the September 11
  tragedy, by providing the most efficient and cost-effective channel for
  quickly getting critical information in the hands of important customers
  and generating new business. Will it be possible for your live Internet
  show to be aired to people not physically at your venue? There are
  security companies whose specialty is to address and resolve these
  questions.

Now that you have considered all of the things that *could* happen, you and
your team should be asking what is *likely* to occur at your event instead. A
threat assessment will help to determine that. Conducting a threat assessment
means surveying all aspects of the event to determine the areas of risk where
an incident could significantly harm your meeting or event, your organization,
or your attendees, with an effort to assess the physical safety and other issues
(protest, terrorism, loss of service, power failure, and digital security issues
such as a Web site attack where a hacker may gain access to your registrants'
credit card numbers, Social Security numbers, etc., or may shut down the
site). Once you have analyzed the impact of all threats to your event with your
entire team, you have to establish priorities. Determine which items represent
acceptable risks and which are unacceptable risks. Music, entertainment, and
production constitute a major part of all three of the survey points. How will
a threat against any or all of these elements impact your meeting or event?

We cannot entirely eliminate risk from the art and science of meeting and
event planning, but we can intelligently manage the risks we take, which
means a sharpening of perceptions to bring greater awareness, and thus safety,
to our experiences both indoors and out. The potential for risk can be mitigated through training, experience, and good judgment. That is the message to
convey to your entire team.

How do you build a crisis mitigation and management team? A crisis mitigation and management team should be composed of individuals with open minds, who are quick studies, planners, and executors. They will need the authority to act quickly and decisively. Many decisions are put in action in a split second in a crisis. Your crisis management team, as well as everyone else on your production team, must know who is responsible for these decisions. The schedules that you developed in the production phase (in Chapter 7) will show that they have the power and the authority to act within the scope of their responsibilities. Along with the authority to act comes the need for a budget to underwrite their decisions. Funds should be committed to the budget during the planning process. The crisis management team, or one of its members, should also be given authority to speak on behalf of the organization, the artists, and anyone else connected with the event and the team.

A typical crisis management team may include the vice president of the corporation or association, the meeting or event planner, the public relations director, the security director, the facility's convention services manager, the facility's security director, the general manager, and local public safety officials.

How will you execute your crisis mitigation plan? How will you put it in action? Here are some things to consider:

- Additional security and/or police may be needed, whether in the form of personnel, dogs, or metal detectors.
- Fire exits should be indicated on your floor plan although they are generally clearly marked, even in the event of a power outage, by a facility backup generator. Everyone on the management team should know where the facility's access and egress controls are.
- What is your evacuation plan? Should everyone go out the same way, or do you want to whisk your celebrity act away through a back door into a waiting vehicle?
- Will you need police escorts for buses? If you never thought of that, consider what happens at many soccer matches in Europe.

Another element that should be part of your action plan is a public relations (PR)/media plan. What happens if there really is a fire, a shooting, or a protest? Someone must take care of the attention that the media will be giving to your event. If this "problem" concerns a celebrity, you must inform the artist's management. No doubt, such managers will put their own spin on any issues arising from problems, as they already have a PR/media plan in place. Someone from your organization needs to know what to say, whom to say it to, and how to divert attention away from the problem area. The best way to handle this diversion is to create a hero. If there has been a fire that destroyed everything, simply speak about one of your staff who helped to lead the guests to safety. You are looking to create a balance. If the press is coming to you, it is probably looking for bad news. By limiting yourself (or your PR/media person) to focus the discussion on the hero, a balance has been created.

Here is a list of action plan tips.

- In your action plan you must have a designated protest area if this threat exists for your event. If you are not proactive in this matter, the local authorities will assign the area, one that may be too close to your event, interfere with the evacuation plan, or be inconvenient in some other way.
- You should also have a communication system plan and arrange to have separate radio channels for music, production, and crisis management. What happens if the lights go out? What is your plan? Does the venue have backup power, or do you need to bring in generators?
- Two other items should be in your action plan, and both have to do with health. The first is the health of your backup data systems, including a hard copy of your point-of-contact data. Second is the health of your attendees. Your attendees' health can be attended to as soon as possible with on-site emergency medical technicians (EMTs) present. Their presence can also assist in lowering your insurance premiums in a per-project or annual agreement.

Protect yourself by having a crisis management plan in place to ensure that you can proactively manage disruptions to your event should they occur. Make sure to purchase event insurance to mitigate the risk of financial loss. This, in effect, is selling risk to the insurance carrier or underwriter. Obtain bids from a few insurance sources, as insurance rates can vary, especially in dealing with entertainment. There are many kinds of event insurance, dealing with a host of event types and issues.

John Foster, CHME (Certified Hospitality Marketing Executive), attorney and counselor at law, reports:

> The term event insurance *covers a lot of territory. It includes Commercial General Liability (CGL) coverage that covers anything that may happen at the event for which you, as the planner, may be held liable. This can include injuries to guests and staff at the event. Broad Form Property coverage will handle damage to the venue at the event. Convention Cancellation coverage will cover your costs should the convention that you are producing be canceled for any number of reasons. There are other types of coverage available; you should discuss your needs with your insurance agent. All of the aforementioned types of insurance are recommended because they cover different perils.*

Your action plan will ensure that you know what to do in the event that one of the risk factors turns into a real issue. Then, the insurance coverage that you have provided will cover the risk of liability and loss. To guarantee that your insurance coverage is adequate for the event, you can create a checklist template for every event as part of the event's Production Manual. Review the checklist annually, adding any items that may have been known issues in that year's events. Creating a template ensures that you have a standard format that addresses every known risk factor; you will thereby protect yourself, and your client, from liability and loss.

Everyone who is responsible for or has a role in event production is concerned about the issue of liability. An event's risk potential can include everything from weather problems to attendee injuries to property damage. The larger and more well-attended the event, the greater the risk of liability to the event producer and the client. Your checklist will provide your insurance agent with the range of factors that the event's policy should cover.

The first entry on your checklist should be the name, date, and purpose of the event, as well as a general description of the event, including the names and types of vendors and suppliers. Be sure to identify any unusual or unique components of the event, such as pyrotechnics, water elements, special sound or lighting, and any potential risk factors.

The event's location is the second entry on your checklist; in addition to the address, location includes the venue to be used during production and any ancillary facilities, as well as staging areas and facilities for staff, performers, participants and the audience.

Your checklist should also contain a section that addresses security and attendee management. Are there enough entrances and exits for spectators, participants, guests, or attendees? Have you coordinated with local law enforcement and emergency medical personnel? Are there adequate security personnel on-site? Are they trained professionals? What arrangements have you made for parking and traffic flow into and out of the venue? Are the restroom facilities accessible and adequate? Does the seating arrangement allow for easy access, movement, and exit in the case of an emergency? Remember that all public events should comply with the Americans with Disabilities Act (ADA), and special accommodations for disabled attendees must be available at your event.

As you develop your risk management plan for an event, you identify known and potential risk factors. These potential risk factors become the basis for the individual items that you will identify in an insurance rider as possible sources of claim. They include factors out of your control, such as acts of nature, in others' control, such as acts committed by venue management and staff, simple individual mistakes on the part of anyone that can pose problems for the event, and attendee issues, such as behavior problems, slips, falls, and unsafe activities. Remember that every person at the event represents a potential risk factor.

Your checklist and your action plan should identify the sources and causes of these risks as thoroughly as possible. Your insurance agent will know which ones should be covered, which can be transferred to the insurance company, and which should be covered by your company's other insurance policies. The burden of risk is shared among the sponsors, the performers, and the venue, so all of these entities should be aware of their risk levels and have their own active insurance policies. Managing attendees may be the most significant risk factor for the event, and this process should be well documented in your action plan.

Every event should be covered by a comprehensive general liability insurance policy that provides protection for all of the event's participants. Some venues may not allow an event to occur unless this coverage is in place. An insurance policy protects you, the event entertainment planner, as well as your client, the sponsor, and the attendees. Some insurance companies specialize in event insurance and are therefore more knowledgeable about the specialized needs of event planners. Always choose an insurance company that is rated and licensed in your state.

Because insurance needs are comprehensive and are an integral component of the event planning and production process, the discussion of insurance needs should begin in conjunction with early event planning, so that the insurance agent has adequate time to prepare the policy and riders. In addition to the checklist items noted earlier, there are many details that your insurance agent will need to know, such as whether the vendors and suppliers have insurance, whether there were any losses in prior events, the vehicles to be used in the event, the event and venue staff and volunteers, and any current and prior insurance coverage.

How much will insurance cost? That depends on many factors, including how much money the event is projected to earn, the deductible amount, the type of food that will be served, the anticipated attendance, the location, and the number of years of experience that you, the planner, bring to the event. Is there anyone else who should be included in your event's policy? Your insurance agent will need to know that as well. Include insurance coverage as a discussion item with all of your event's participants, including vendors, representatives of the venue, and any performers you hire. Remember that price is not always a decision point in obtaining insurance for your event. If you have a good relationship with your insurance provider and are happy with the coverage it provides, you should maintain your relationship with that company.

What kind of insurance coverage should you obtain for the event? Start with general comprehensive liability for the event, including provisions for acts of nature, cancellation and medical liability, bodily injury and property damage. Everyone associated with the event should be covered, including your staff, the venue's staff, volunteers, performers, attendees, and security and emergency personnel. Event insurance providing coverage for cancellation may cover related expenses and unrealized profit. Any property associated with the event should be included in the policy, whether you own it, lease it, or borrow it. The event's directors and officers can be covered under the policy, and it should include some type of umbrella liability rider as well as a workers' compensation component. In the meeting and event industry many items may not be covered, which need to be underwritten. An errors and omissions (E & O) Insurance policy should cover most damages that would lead to a claim.

To start the process, ask your insurance agent to prepare a sample certificate for your use as you begin to plan the event. Maintain a running discourse with your insurance agent during this process, and provide the agent with copies of all relevant insurance policies, permits, and licenses for the event. If you are unsure of any requirements, ask the agent to help you. This is his or her area of expertise, so regard the agent as a valuable resource that is part of your event planning team.

WORKING WITH PUBLIC SAFETY ORGANIZATIONS (PSO)

It is very important to know the individuals serving as the initial Points of Contact (POC) for local public safety organizations (PSOs) and at what stage of the meeting or event planning process the POC goes into action. Be aware of the types of services and support that are available, who will pay for them, and how they will be paid for. Are there regulatory compliance or mandated security measures required for your event? If the event is a county fair or an urban block party, there will most certainly be regulations to be adhered to. Your greatest internal responsibility is to assign a media crisis spokesperson to deal with the PSOs.

A COMMAND, CONTROL, COMMUNICATION, AND BUSINESS INFORMATION SYSTEM

A command, control, communication, and business information system is the central nervous system of your plan, which requires identified decision-making authorities. To communicate with these individuals, you will need certain technical devices, such as pagers, cell phones, and radios. Your business information system is your phone book to outside support, which should include the following:

- Your vendors (and backups)
- Radio frequencies and/or channels
- Emergency numbers
- Cell phones (make sure they are in service)
- 800 numbers
- Web sites, broadcast e-mail (utilizing dial-up modems)
- Any other numbers or information relevant to your event

PUBLIC AND MEDIA RELATIONS

Identify and empower a single POC for public/media relations and direct all inquiries to that person. As rumor and innuendo can be devastating to public companies, in a post-Internet investing environment you should ensure that outbound information is both accurate and timely. The POC should undergo media training, as making mistakes in front of the media is easy, but recovery is not.

Your approach should be to address the components of a crisis management plan in relation to the possible threats to the event or meeting, giving suggestions on building a crisis mitigation and management team. This should include working with public safety organizations and the press while putting in place a command, control, communication, and information system. It is with these steps that you can better ensure that your attendees, the organization, VIPs, and headline entertainers will continue to be safe while working with and for you.

REAL-LIFE CRISES AT EVENTS

No matter how many precautions are taken by an event manager, there are always risks involved in conducting an event. The following are examples of situations of crises at events and how they were handled.

More than two dozen people were injured in a stampede while rapper Eminem was performing at RFK Stadium in Washington, D.C. One man suffered a heart attack during the melee and was taken to a local hospital. Four others were taken to area hospitals with injuries not considered to be life-threatening. The rest were treated at the scene for less serious injuries. The two-day concert, sponsored by a Maryland radio station, included a number of acts on several stages. Eminem resumed his performance after a brief delay while police calmed the crowd, and the concert continued on Sunday as planned.

A fire broke out at Royal Albert Hall in London, forcing performer Tony Bennett to stop his concert and the sellout crowd to evacuate the building, though no injuries were reported. The 75-year-old singer was halfway through his signature tune, "I Left My Heart in San Francisco," when smoke began to fill the auditorium. As the evacuation started, Bennett tried to calm the crowd, joking, "I knew I was hot, but not that hot." The smoke had come from a burned-out motor, and although the public was never at risk, the event managers did not want to take any chances and therefore evacuated the hall.

In Conclusion

Consider the words of Patrick W. Tuttle, a 20-year U.S. Air Force veteran in various positions in information and domestic protocol, about risk management:

By myself, I truly cannot eliminate crisis from the meetings and events you plan. At best, I could ease the burden a crisis causes. Any attempt on my part would be useless without your commitment and involvement in the process. It is up to you to conduct research, and open your mind to past experiences. You personally will develop the skills and learn the right details to question, and then employ the answers—the details so vital to our profession. Every meeting and event planner faces change. The impact change has on a planner's details, and how the end result is effected determines if the change happened for the good of the plan or if it created a crisis. Change comes in many forms at any phase of planning and each requires different handling.

Scripts for Future Study

BOOKS

Berlonghi, Alexander. (1990). *The Special Event Risk Management Manual.* Dana Point, CA: Alexander Berlonghi.

Crisis—Disaster—Emergency Planning Notebook. (1996). Waco, TX: Texas Association of Convention and Visitor Bureaus.

Delpy-Neirotti, Lisa, Joe Jeff Goldblatt, and Stedman Graham. (2001). *The Ultimate Guide to Sports Marketing.* New York: McGraw Hill.

Goldblatt, Joe. (1999). *Government, Civic, and Political Event Management.* Washington, DC: George Washington University.

Tarlow, Peter E. (2002). *Event Risk Management and Safety.* New York: John Wiley & Sons.

Tarlow, Peter E. (2001). *Safety and Security for Tourism Destinations.* Washington, DC: George Washington University.

OTHER PUBLICATIONS

Mann, Nancy. "The Calm during the Storm: Hurricane Floyd Forces AAFP into Crisis Management Mode." *Convene Magazine* (April 2000): 34–41.

Obertots, Richard. "Why We Need to Prepare for Medical Emergencies." *Convene Magazine* (December 1999): 89–95.

Potter, Blair, and Funmi Okunbolade. "Sudden Impact." *Meeting Professional* (digital ed.) 21, no. 11 (November 2001): 1–11.

Simpson, Cara, and Matt O'Connor. "Chicago prosecutor slain, another wounded in South Carolina robbery." *Chicago Tribune,* 21 August 2001 (Internet ed.)

Smith, Ginger. "Toward a United States Policy on Traveler Safety and Security." *Journal of Travel Research* 38 (August 1999): 62–65.

Tuttle, Patrick W. (2002). *Eliminating Crisis from Meeting and Event Planning.* Joplin, MO: Tuttle Executive Services.

"Terrorism Effects on Tourism Forum Packs House." *SBPM News* (on-line), George Washington University, 15 November 2001.

Torrence, Sara. "Is Your Conference Ready for Risks?" *Convene Magazine* (December 1999): 27–29.

Exit Stage Right

There is one aspect of risk management for event entertainment that was not covered in this chapter, namely, music licensing. Proceed to Chapter 13, which discusses the licensing of music for meetings and events, as well as copyrights, intellectual property, and their relevance for your events.

CHAPTER 13

Music Licensing

If you need to pay the rent, you've got to be commercial, and there's nothing shameful about that.[1]

—WILLIE NELSON, SONGWRITER/ARTIST

IN THIS CHAPTER YOU WILL DISCOVER

- The songwriters' three basic rights to their music.
- How you can legally respect those rights through the proper licensing of the music you will use for meetings, conventions, trade shows, expositions, special events, and business.
- The current laws and information regarding music licenses and how they apply specifically to the event entertainment industry.

No event is complete without music, whether it is background music, live entertainment, or a recorded sound track that accompanies a presentation. In addition to being a form of entertainment, music is also a business, as Willie Nelson makes clear in the preceding quotation. As an event planner who will constantly use all types of music as part of your events, you need to be aware of music licensing laws, of your compliance obligations under those laws, and

[1]Copyright 1999, *American Songwriter*. Used with permission, courtesy of BMI.

the rights of musicians to payment for the use of their music. Music is a constant presence in our lives today. Nearly everywhere—at the mall, in the grocery store, in our cars, and in our homes, at the movies, on television, at events, in elevators, and sometimes in our offices, some type of music is being played. It is often such a constant presence that we do not even pay attention to it most of the time. Because music is everywhere, we may assume that it belongs to everyone.

This belief was carried to the extreme by Napster, the Internet Web site that allowed free music downloads. Users could access Napster's Web site to get free copies of their favorite songs, which they could save to their computer's hard drive and listen to at their convenience. During its heyday, Napster was one of the Internet's most popular Web sites, with millions of users downloading thousands of songs every day. Napster was sued for its activities and was eventually shut down. Its crime was its failure to pay royalties and licensing fees to the thousands of songwriters and performers who owned the rights to the music Napster was distributing. Napster's activities were illegal because music, in addition to being a form of entertainment, is also a business. Musicians earn their living through their music. They are entitled to receive payment, in the form of royalties, whenever their music is performed.

Songwriters have three rights to their music:

1. Performance rights, governing the performance of their music either by them or by others
2. Mechanical rights, covering the reproduction of songs on tape, such as in a recorded cassette or on a CD
3. "Synch" rights, covering the synchronizing of music with images on video or film, such as in a sales training tape containing video and music

Songwriters have legal rights; they essentially own their music, and through the purchase of a CD, tape, or a license, we pay for the individual and personal use of that music. Different laws apply to the use of music in a public setting or gathering. As an event entertainment planner who will use music in many of your events, you need to be aware of your legal obligations, to the songwriters and to your clients, under these laws.

Your Meetings and Events Are Alive, with the Sound of Music

Music sets the mood and helps emphasize a corporation's message at company events such as management conferences, sales meetings, training seminars, and gala banquets. Imagine a company picnic, holiday celebration, or retirement party without music. Imagine trying to motivate employees at a meeting or seminar without the benefit of some hard-driving music to set the tone. Imagine trying to hold a gala or a large event without music to dance to or to entertain the attendees. Music will be a central part of many, if not all of your events, and there are certain costs and obligations involved.

Here is an excerpt from a press release, sent out to meeting and event planners, dated February 25, 2003, and distributed by Broadcast Music Inc. (BMI) from Nashville, Tennessee, entitled "Music Adds Excitement to Meetings and Trade Shows, But Don't Forget to Pay the Songwriters."

Pssssst. Wanna know the secret ingredient of lively meetings and trade shows? It's music! Music can bring vitality to any gathering. When properly used, music can focus attention, attract customers, and increase the energy level at any meeting, trade show, convention or exposition.

—COURTESY OF BMI

There is so much clutter between the dot-coms and car makers and computer makers that you need a way to connect to people. One of the ways you can do that is through music.[2]
—*Rob Schwartz, creative director, Nissan Motor Company account,*
TBWA/CHIAT/DAY

The power of music in selling a product or service has been recognized by national advertisers for many years. It is difficult to watch television or listen to radio for more than a few minutes today without hearing Shania Twain singing for Revlon, Faith Hill crooning for Pepsi, David Bowie and the Rolling Stones backing Microsoft, Sheryl Crow touting Oldsmobile, or Alan Jackson pushing Ford trucks. Advertisers pay amounts in the five or six figures to use even little-known songs, and they are willing to pay even more for a signature song by a superstar.

Although using music in exhibits and conventions isn't free, it is inexpensive in comparison with what advertisers pay for songs in national TV and radio commercials. For example, BMI can grant a trade show organizer legal access for each exhibitor to perform 4.5 million live or recorded songs of approximately 300,000 copyright owners at a cost of just $0.5 per show attendee. That's just $500 for a show attended by 10,000 persons. In the case of a trade show or convention where live or recorded music is performed on the exhibit floor, the number of attendees equals the number of persons registered at the show or convention. BMI's minimum fee is $110 for the year 2003. The fee is the same whether you play one song or a hundred songs.

Great songs are very precious when you come across them. When you can emotionally connect an artist's ability with what the lyrics

[2]Copyright 1999, *Orlando Sun-Sentinel.* Used with permission, courtesy of BMI.

> *are trying to convey, an audience really feels that. It's a magic combination.*[3]
>
> —RANDY SCRUGGS, SONGWRITER, ARTIST, MUSICIAN, PRODUCER

The organizers or presenters of a meeting, convention, or trade show are responsible for licensing all music used at their event. At the request of trade show organizers, BMI recently expanded its licensing agreement so that management companies may cover fees for their clients. "Having a management company handle music licensing will expedite administration for many organizations," said Tom Annastas, BMI vice president, General Licensing. "We're happy we can accommodate them."

U.S. copyright law recognizes musical compositions as intellectual property, much the same as books, computer software, movies, poetry, and television programs. Songs cannot be used in public without the permission of the copyright owner. The Copyright Act defines as "public" any meeting "where a substantial number of persons outside a normal circle of a family and its social acquaintances is gathered." Because the expense and time required to negotiate with multiple copyright owners would be overwhelming for a typical business playing popular music, most songwriters select a performing rights organization (PRO) to represent them. The United States has three PROs—Broadcast Music Inc. (BMI), American Society of Composers, Authors and Publishers (ASCAP), and the Society of European Songwriters, Authors and Composers (SESAC)—each representing different songs, composers, and music publishers.

Most of the writers of hit songs are not the stars who sing them. Although a few songwriters become recording artists, most are unknown highly creative people who earn modest incomes. According to BMI, the average songwriter earns less than $5000 annually from the public performance of his or her songs. "The revenue from businesses using music to enhance their profit and image is an important part of a songwriter's income," said Annastas. BMI is a non-profit-making organization and all of the money it collects beyond administrative costs is passed on to the copyright owners. Annastas said BMI currently returns more than 82 cents of each dollar collected to the songwriters. "We operate efficiently so that our business customers can more easily afford the music and songwriters receive more compensation for their work," he said. "Songwriters give American business one of its best bargains."

Imagine the following setting at an event that you have planned. The opening session of your event welcomes the crowd with the band playing "Welcome to the Jungle," a Guns N' Roses hit, and Kenny G. jazz tunes frame the background tone during breaks. Your guests love it, so it is a success. Now consider this scenario from a copyright perspective. Unless you, as the planner, have secured a minimum of two different licenses to perform the music,

---

[3]Copyright 1999, *American Songwriter.* Used with permission, courtesy of BMI.

whether live or mechanical, you are infringing on copyright law. And you could be subject to legal action that requires paying fines and damages.

Is this fair? The law does not look at issues from the point of "fairness," but from a position of liability. In this case, you may be guilty of vicarious liability. George Washington University defines vicarious liability as a charge, "imposed on persons *other* than the person who performed the wrongful act." Such other persons include the person or entity who played the music, read the book passage aloud, sang the song, used the software, displayed the picture, and so on.

For some who play without paying, ignorance is to blame. A Massachusetts-based planner told *Meetings and Conventions* (M&C) that when organizing his first convention, he gave absolutely no thought to music licensing. "It simply did not occur to me. I was horrified when I learned that my show was not properly licensed." In the words of ASCAP, "Music is a vital part of the total service businesses offer to customers. ASCAP's licensees recognize that using music benefits their businesses because music, like other amenities or products, pays off in heightened customer satisfaction, increased profits, and improved employee morale and productivity."

The music licensing issue has always been a consideration for many industries, including major television networks, local television and radio stations, cable and satellite networks and systems, public broadcasters, Internet Web sites, colleges and universities, night clubs, taverns and restaurants, background music services, fitness and health clubs, private clubs, concert presenters, dance halls, shopping centers and malls, theme and amusement parks, airlines, skating rinks, and retail stores. It is now a part of the general hospitality sector because of organizations such as ASCAP, BMI, and SESAC. Their intention is to license live and mechanical music that is used for meetings, conventions, trade shows, and expositions.

In the past, music licensing was a private issue between producers, building managers, hoteliers, and the licensing agencies. Now these licensing agencies, starting in the late 1980s, have decided to enforce their contracts through the end user. Who is the end user? The audience. Who represents the audience? The person, association, corporation, or organization that causes the music to be played. One may think that the "band" causes the music to be played. Although musically correct, legally, the "band" is playing only because of the entity that has asked or paid it to play. Thus, it is the contracting entity that constitutes the legal user or the infringer. The law was written with the burden of compliance on the larger organization to aid enforcement. There may be many "fly-by-night" musicians playing unlicensed music to smaller audiences, but corporations, associations, and event-planning entities target larger markets and broadly advertise and market their events, which makes them easier to locate. They also tend to have a physical address, are listed in their local phone and business directories, and are on the Internet.

The point is that if you use music at your meeting, convention, or events, you have financial and legal obligations to reimburse the composers, authors, and publishers through their licensing agencies. If you do not volunteer the reimbursement for the right to use that music, then you are subject to criminal penalties under the copyright laws in the United States. This whole area of copyright is very important with respect to meetings, conventions, and events because it pertains not only to music, but also to artwork, logos, images, and costume characters that are often used or represented.

Joe Goldblatt, CSEP, author of scores of books for the events industry and formerly dean of the Alan Shawn Feinstein Graduate School at Johnson and Wales University, stated,

> When somebody works very hard to create an original work, music, art, what have you, his or her only protection against the unauthorized use of that work is through the copyright laws. So the artist gets it copyrighted, trademarked, and then if you wish to use it, you have to purchase the right for that usage, whether it is a one-day, one-time use, yearly use, or a buyout, which means you buy it for perpetual use in a certain market. I applaud BMI and ASCAP for coming forward, because what they are doing is making all of us more sensitive to the fact that the works of artists have value. They must be compensated for that value, and I think that what it will do is make the average audience member, when he or she listens to music, appreciate it more, because people always appreciate more when they invest in what they pay for.

Although there are three licensing agencies in the United States, there are others that operate internationally. A list is provided in the "Scripts for Future Study" section at the end of this chapter. The U.S. event manager generally deals with two of these agencies, ASCAP and BMI. SESAC is the smallest of the three United States performing rights organizations, and its licenses cover the venue, where the music will be played, as opposed to the event, so meeting or event planners generally do not have to obtain a license from this organization. Bill Lee of SESAC explains:

> A SESAC license is required for meetings, trade shows, and expositions. A key difference between SESAC and the other performing rights organizations is that SESAC licenses the premises where the event is taking place. If the premise does not have a SESAC license, the event coordinator would need to obtain one. The license would be determined by the type and location of the event. I suggest that meeting and event planners contact SESAC to confirm that the premise has a SESAC license, and if it is not licensed, we would arrange a license at that time.

Quick Facts About Music Licensing

Many event and meeting planners are not familiar with the laws of music licensing. Here are some basic facts that you will need to know when licensing your music, a guide to what and when to license music, and some frequently asked questions about the topic.

- Licenses are issued on a blanket basis for meetings or events.
- Neither agency (BMI or ASCAP) can deny a request for a license.
- Terms and conditions can be negotiated separately. You are not required to use a blanket license agreement.
- You would be wise to negotiate a separate and individual license for mega-events, such as an inaugural event.
- Besides the three PROs, there are other licensing companies that are privately owned. For example, both Andrew Lloyd Weber and Billy Joel privately license their own music.
- For films, you must seek a synchronization right from the composers, then license the combined product of audio & video to show the film.
- Jukeboxes must be licensed as well. You will notice a sticker on the side of a jukebox if it has been licensed.
- Music playing on your business phone when a client is put on hold is subject to licensing.
- You do not need to record the tunes the band or deejay is performing in a day.
- A licensing fee is based on the total number of people who come in contact with your music, except for ASCAP and BMI Special Events Licenses.
- The licenses include mechanical music.
- A set fee will cover an entire event (up to 14 days maximum) and reflects a per-person charge.
- You make payments by self-reporting your guest list. ASCAP, BMI, and SESAC, however, reserve the right to audit at their discretion.
- Licenses are tax deductible.

See Figure 13-1 for an easy reference guide as to when and what to license for music performances.

- What does ASCAP actually do?

    ASCAP licenses the right to perform songs and musical works created and owned by songwriters, composers, lyricists, and music publishers who are ASCAP members and members of foreign performing rights organizations who are represented by ASCAP in the United States.

Using Audio (mechanical) Music Only
- Pay BMI and ASCAP.

Using Live Music
- Pay BMI and ASCAP only.

Using Music with Visuals
- Obtain permission (synchronization licenses) from music publishers and record company (if using a record).
- Pay BMI and ASCAP.

Convention, Trade Show, and Exposition Fees
- Convention sponsor (not exhibitor) pays BMI and ASCAP.
- Exhibitor pays synch licenses if using music with visuals.
- Exhibitor pays nothing for audio music.

Figure 13-1
Guide to When and What to License for Music Performances

According to ASCAP,

It is impossible for individual composers and publishers to monitor the hundreds of thousands of businesses that use music. It would be equally difficult, time-consuming, and expensive for business owners to locate and negotiate with all the owners of the music that might be used. There is a simple, fast, and reasonably priced alternative. Through ASCAP, in one simple transaction, businesses can obtain the right to perform the millions of songs created or owned by over 140,000 of America's and hundreds of thousands of the world's best songwriters, composers, lyricists, and publishers. Founded in 1914, and still owned by and managed for its writer and publisher members, ASCAP grants businesses the permission they need to perform music publicly. The money collected is distributed, after deducting operating costs, directly to ASCAP members and to affiliated foreign performing rights organizations for their members.

- What is BMI?

  BMI is a nonprofit performing rights organization recognized under the U.S. copyright law to license businesses and other organizations to publicly perform intellectual property in the form of copyrighted music. BMI grants this permission on behalf of its more than 300,000 affiliated songwriters, composers, and music publishers through music performance agreements. It offers businesses legal access to approximately 4.5

million musical works through just one agreement. That saves you the time and expense of contacting each and every songwriter, composer, or music publisher for permission to use their work.

- What doesn't ASCAP, BMI, or SESAC license?

    The three major licensing agencies are collectively called performing rights society, or PROs.

    - *They do not license "dramatic" rights, sometimes called "grand" rights. Their members who write musical plays, operas, or ballet scores deal directly with those who want to perform their works "dramatically." The PROs license does authorize nondramatic performances of songs from dramatic productions. For example, their respective bar/nightclub license authorizes a piano bar performance of an individual song from a Broadway show.*
    - *The public rights organizations do not license the right to record music on a CD or tape or as part of a multimedia or audiovisual work such as a motion picture, video, or television program. Writers or publishers license those rights, known in the music industry as mechanical and synchronization (or "synch" rights).*
    - *The PROs do not license the right to print copies of musical works, nor do they license rights to make adaptations or arrangements.*
    - *They do not license rights for recording artists, musicians, singers, or record labels. However, artists or musicians who are songwriters can become members. The PROs license the performance rights for the music of their members.*

- How much money is generated by ASCAP and BMI?

    In 1998, ASCAP had more than 40,242 writers and 18,727 publishers and collected $508 million on behalf of its members, 25 percent of which was from foreign sources. BMI, on the other hand, which represents about 140,000 writers and 60,000 publishers, collected $455 million in the same year, with approximately 23 percent of total receipts from foreign sources.

- Our event is not open to the general public. Are we exempt?

    No. Even though your event is open only to select individuals, you must secure both an ASCAP and a BMI music performance agreement. The United States copyright law defines a public place as any place where persons outside "a normal circle of family and friends" are gathered. In other words, even though your event is closed to the general public, your attendees do form a public. Therefore, music for exhibitor booths, general stage presentations, cocktail parties, and banquets, as well as other ambient music use, requires the appropriate music licensing.

- Is the band or deejay we hire for company events responsible for licensing?

  No. It is the corporation's responsibility to secure music licensing inasmuch as it is the company itself that is authorizing the performance. Deejays and bands do not license directly with any of the PROs.

- Is permission to play music publicly included in the cost when I purchase a tape or CD?

  No. Although most people buy tapes and CDs thinking they are now their property to use as they wish, there is a distinction in the law between owning a copy of the CD and owning the songs on the CD. There is also a difference between a private performance of copyrighted music and a public performance of that music. Most people recognize that purchasing a CD does not give them the right to make copies of it to give or to sell to others. The record company and music publishers retain those rights. Similarly, the *music* on the CDs and tapes still belongs to the songwriter, composer, or music publisher of the work. When you buy a tape or CD, the purchase price covers only your private listening use, similar to the home use of videos. Once you decide to play these tapes or CDs in your business, it becomes a public performance. Songwriters, composers, and music publishers have the exclusive right of public performance for their musical works under the U.S. copyright law. Therefore, any public performance requires permission from the copyright owner, or ASCAP or BMI if it is ASCAP- or BMI-affiliated music that is used. Because in many instances the songwriter or composer is different from the artist performing the work, approximately 50 percent, and in some cases as much as 75 percent, of a songwriter's income comes from the public performance of his or her work. This makes it a critical component of the songwriter's income and is what enables the artist to continue to create music for use in your business. With an ASCAP and BMI music performance agreement, you can publicly perform all ASCAP- and BMI-affiliated music.

- What happens to the fees I pay under my music performance agreement?

  Because BMI operates on a nonprofit basis, all music licensing fees, less BMI's operating expenses, go directly to the BMI songwriters, composers, and music publishers whose music you are performing. Currently, 83 cents of every dollar of your licensing fee goes to BMI's affiliated copyright owners.

- Our event is in a facility that has an ASCAP, BMI, and SESAC music performance agreement. Is the event covered under the facility's agreement?

  No, no, and yes. When a facility such as a hotel or convention center leases space to an outside organization for any of its meetings, conventions, trade shows, or expositions, the facility's music performance agreement does not cover music used at those events, except in the case of SESAC. More specifically, the ASCAP and BMI hotel agreement does not include leased areas of the hotel where meetings, conventions, or trade shows take place. Even though the hotel may supply the music to any of the meeting or convention areas, the presenter of the event is still responsible for licensing the music, whether performed live or recorded.

- What are synchronization rights, and how are they different from mechanical rights and performing rights?

    A "synch" license is the form of permission that authorizes the mechanical reproduction of a musical composition, accompanied by a motion picture or other audiovisual work, for use in connection with a motion picture theatrical performance and television broadcast (Kohn 1996). Synchronization rights are rights granted by copyright owners to those wishing to synchronize their musical compositions with visual images on film or tape. This type of musical performance is often employed by trade show vendors to enhance the presentation of their products. If a trade show vendor employs synchronization, for example, by presenting a video, he or she must also obtain performance rights to perform that synchronized music for the public (meeting, convention, trade show, or exposition attendees). Synchronization rights should not be confused with mechanical rights. Mechanical rights are granted by a music publisher, usually to a record company, to record and release a specific composition at an agreed-upon fee for each unit manufactured and sold.

- Does someone actually own a musical composition?

    Yes. Unless the age of a composition has allowed it to enter the public domain, musical compositions, like other copyrighted material, are the legal property of their creators. When your meeting or trade show plans to use music—either from tapes, records, CDs, audiovisual presentations, live entertainment, or even radio—you must first obtain permission from the copyright owners. But the time and expense of negotiating for the use of each of the songs you or your exhibitors might play, which could easily amount to thousands of songs over the course of a year, would be an unaffordable burden.

- If I buy the record or sheet music, why do I need permission to perform the music?

    Copyright owners enjoy a number of different rights, including performance rights, print rights, and recording rights. Rental or purchase of sheet music or the purchase of a record does not authorize its public performance.

- I want to record or videotape a song or record. Do I need permission, and how do I obtain it?

    If you want to make copies of, or re-record an existing record, tape, or CD, you will probably need the permission of both the music publisher and the record label. A music publisher owns the song, that is, the words and music, and a record company owns the "sound recording," that is, what you hear, the artist singing, the musicians playing, the

entire production. If you plan to hire your own musicians and singers
and create an original recording of a copyrighted song, then you need
the permission of only the music publisher.

- How can I find out more about the musical works in the ASCAP and
  BMI catalogs?

    For ASCAP visit: www.ascap.com; for BMI, visit: http://reper-
toire.bmi.com.

    The best advice is to do the right thing and protect yourself and your
event. When providing music for your guests, you should sign a license
with the PROs and pay their respective rates. Information is available at
their Web sites.

Music Licenses That Affect the Meeting and Event Industry

This section provides excerpts of the three different licenses that will affect
you, as an event entertainment planner, from each of the two performing rights
organizations you will most likely be dealing with. The full text of the agreements can be found in Appendix 6.

THE ASCAP BLANKET LICENSE FOR CONVENTIONS, EXPOSITIONS, INDUSTRIAL SHOWS, MEETINGS, AND TRADE SHOWS

*According to ASCAP, the term "event" as used in this Agreement
shall mean a conference, congress, convention, exposition, industrial
show, institute, meeting, seminar, teleconference, trade show, or
other similar scheduled activity of LICENSEE of not more than fourteen days duration. The term "function" as used in this Agreement
shall mean any activity conducted, sponsored, endorsed, or approved by, or presented by or under the auspices of LICENSEE as
part of or in conjunction with any LICENSEE event which is open
only to "attendees." The term "attendees," as used in this Agreement, shall mean all individuals who register or pay to attend a
LICENSEE event.*

Fee Schedule for 2002

*For purposes of computing license fees under this Rate Schedule,
the number of Attendees shall include all persons who have registered or paid to attend LICENSEE's event, but shall exclude those
persons required to produce LICENSEE's event, service contract personnel, temporary personnel, accredited members of the media, and
one-half of the number of persons serving as exhibitor personnel.*

- If "mechanical music" is performed, the fee shall be $.064 times the number of Attendees per event.
- If live music is performed in the main meeting room or on any exhibition floor at LICENSEE's event, see Figure 13-2

Using the two equations given in Figure 13.2 for this blanket license agreement, and knowing that an "event" may go on for up to 14 days, the minimum fee payable hereunder shall be $70 per event and the maximum fee payable hereunder shall be $5650 per event, provided, however, that if neither live music nor mechanical music is performed at an event, then no fee shall be payable under this Agreement for such event.

ASCAP MUSIC-IN-BUSINESS BLANKET LICENSE AGREEMENT

(a) SOCIETY grants and LICENSEE accepts a license to perform or cause to be performed publicly at "LICENSEE'S business locations" and at "LICENSEE'S event locations" (each as defined below), and not elsewhere, non-dramatic renditions of the separate musical compositions now or hereafter during the term of this Agreement in the repertory of SOCIETY, and of which SOCIETY shall have the right to license such performing rights.

Number of Attendees	Daily Live Music Fee
250 or fewer	$ 35
251–500	70
501–750	105
751–1,000	140
1,001–1,500	175
1,501–2,000	210
2,001–3,000	285
3,001–4,000	355
4,001–5,000	425
5,001–7,500	495
7,501–10,000	565
10,001 or more	705

Figure 13-2
The ASCAP Blanket License for Conventions, Expositions, Industrial Shows, and Trade Shows Fee Schedule

(b) As used in this Agreement, the following terms shall have the meanings indicated:

> *(i) "LICENSEE'S business locations" means all locations, not generally accessible by the public, at which LICENSEE conducts its day-to-day business operations, annexed hereto and made a part hereof, as said Schedule may be amended as hereinafter provided;*
>
> *(ii) "LICENSEE'S event locations" means all locations, other than LICENSEE'S business locations, at which LICENSEE conducts any "LICENSEE event(s)" (as defined below);*
>
> *(iii) "LICENSEE'S employees" means all employees of LICENSEE including, but not limited to, full-time, part-time and temporary employees and interns; and*
>
> *(iv) "LICENSEE event(s)" means all activities presented or sponsored solely by or under the auspices of LICENSEE, at LICENSEE event location(s), open only to LICENSEE'S employees and their personal guests.*

(c) This license does not authorize any performance as part of any conference, congress, consumer show, convention, exposition, industrial show, institute, meeting, public show, seminar, trade show or other similar activity, unless such activity (i) is presented or sponsored solely by and under the auspices of LICENSEE, is presented entirely at LICENSEE'S business location(s), and is not open to the general public, or (ii) otherwise constitutes a LICENSEE event.

Fee Schedule for 2002

- *$0.381 for each of the first ten thousand (10,000) of LICENSEE'S employees;*
- *$0.306 for each of LICENSEE'S employees from the ten thousand and first (10,001st) to the twenty-five thousandth (25,000th);*
- *$0.248 for each of LICENSEE'S employees from the twenty-five thousand and first (25,001st) to the fifty thousandth (50,000th); and*
- *$0.192 for each additional LICENSEE'S employees above the fifty thousandth (50,000th)*

The minimum annual license fee payable hereunder shall be $189 for calendar year 2002; and for calendar year 2003 and each calendar year thereafter, the minimum annual license fee shall be the license fees for the preceding calendar year, adjusted in accordance with any increase in the Consumer Price Index, All Urban Consumers (CPI-U) between the preceding October and the next preceding October, rounded to the nearest dollar.

THE ASCAP BLANKET LICENSE FOR SPECIAL EVENTS

This is a new license that was introduced in fall 2002. It is clear that ASCAP has its own definition of the special events industry. ASCAP defines special events as "talent and variety shows, air, sea and balloon shows, pageants, parades, and fashion shows." The ASCAP license, to be used only for up to three special events per year, was devised as an intermediary license between its Fairs and Festivals license and its Music in Business (MIB) license. What is interesting and innovative is that the fee for this license (as well as the original BMI Special Events license) is based on the "live music entertainment costs" and makes a distinction between special events that charge an admittance fee and those that do not. These costs are defined as "Payments to booking agents, outside production companies or payments to other parties who provide such services relating to the performance of live music entertainment." Under the terms of this new license, deejays would be considered live music entertainment.

Fee Schedule for 2002

Annual fee:	$100
Mechanical music:	$ 75 per event
Special events that charge admission:	1.75% of the live music costs
Special events that do not charge admission:	1% of the live music costs
Special events benefits up to 5500 guests	$ 10
Special events benefits more than 60,000 guests	$ 255

THE BMI BUSINESS MULTIPLE USE LICENSE

BMI grants you a non-exclusive license to perform or allow to be performed at the licensed locations and off-site locations all musical works of which BMI shall have the right to grant public performance licenses during the term of this Agreement. This grant of rights includes but is not limited to music performed:

1. *over telephones in the form of music-on-hold;*
2. *as live music or recorded background music;*
3. *in fitness and aerobics facilities;*
4. *in audiovisual presentations in business meetings;*
5. *over teleconferencing at the licensed locations;*
6. *in television and radio programming received by LICENSEE on the locations; and*
7. *performances of music by interactive software, whether (a) delivered by media such as CD-ROM, CD-I, diskette or cartridge, or (b) rendered by multimedia hardware, such as computer-driven handheld devices.*

Fee Schedule for 2002

You agree to pay BMI for each employee for the first year of this Agreement fees [as shown in Figure 13-3].

THE BMI BLANKET LICENSE FOR FESTIVALS AND SPECIAL EVENTS

BMI hereby grants to LICENSEE, for the term of this Agreement, a non-exclusive license solely to perform, present, or cause the performance of, as part of festivals or special events, including recorded music performed in conjunction with attractions before, during or after the intermissions thereof, all the musical works as to which BMI shall have the right to grant public performance licenses during the term hereof. Such license shall be restricted to performance of music in the manner described herein, and is granted in consideration of payment of the license fees as set forth herein and is subject to all of the terms and conditions hereof. This license does not include: (i) dramatic rights, the right to perform dramatico-musical works in whole or in substantial part, the right to present individual works in a dramatic setting or the right to use the music licensed hereunder in any context which may constitute an exercise of the "grand rights" therein; or (ii) the right to simultaneously broadcast, telecast, cablecast, or otherwise transmit (including by the Internet or on-line service) the performances licensed hereunder to persons outside of

Number of Employees	Fee per Employee
First 250	62 cents
251–500	49 cents
501–10,000	37 cents
10,001–20,000	32 cents
20,001–75,000	26 cents
75,001 and Over	17 cents

Note: The tiers are successive, not cumulative. For example, 800 employees would be covered by 250 in the first tier, 250 in the second tier, and 300 in the third tier.

Figure 13-3
BMI's Business Multiple-Use License Fee Schedule

the facility in which they originate; (iii) performances of music by means of a coin-operated phonorecord player (jukebox).

Fee Schedule for 2002

Schedule A License Fee Schedule for Each Festival/Special Event

> *The Festival/Special Event License Fee Rate shall be one and one half percent (1½%) of LICENSEE's Total Entertainment Costs for each Festival/Special Event or $150.00 for each Festival/Special Event, whichever is higher.*

Schedule B License Fee Schedule for Each Benefit Event

1. *Schedule B Benefit Event fees shall be $150 per year or total Schedule B fees, whichever is higher.*
2. *If LICENSEE has both Schedule A Festival/Special Event and Schedule B Benefit Event, then Schedule B Benefit Event fees shall be computed in accordance with Schedule B and not subject to a Schedule B minimum fee [as seen in Figure 13-4].*

THE BMI BLANKET LICENSE FOR MEETINGS, CONVENTIONS, TRADE SHOWS AND EXPOSITIONS

> *BMI hereby grants to LICENSEE a non-exclusive license to perform, present, or cause the live and/or recorded performance during Events of all musical works of which BMI shall have the right to grant public performance licenses during the term hereof. This license does not include: (i) dramatic rights, the right to perform dramatico-musical works in whole or in substantial part, the right to present individual works in a dramatic setting or the right to use the music licensed hereunder in any other context which may constitute an exercise of the "grand rights" therein; or (ii) the right to broadcast, telecast or otherwise transmit, including via the Internet or*

Seating Capacity	Fee per Benefit Event	Seating Capacity	Fee per Benefit Event
0 to 250	$15.00	7,501 to 10,000	$125.00
251 to 750	$18.00	10,001 to 15,000	$190.00
751 to 1,500	$28.00	15,001 to 20,000	$260.00
1,501 to 2,500	$45.00	20,001 to 25,000	$315.00
2,501 to 5,000	$67.00	25,001 to 40,000	$345.00
5,001 to 7,500	$90.00	40,001 & over	$480.00

Figure 13-4
BMI's Blanket License for Festivals and Special Events Fee Schedule B

*on-line service, the performances licensed hereunder to persons out-
side of any premises at which an Event occurs.*

Fee Schedule for 2002

*LICENSEE agrees to pay BMI for each one year term of the agree-
ment a license fee based upon the following:*

Calendar Year   Per Attendee Rate
2002 $.05

*(a) For each year after the year 2000, the per attendee rate shall
be an adjustment of the rate for the previous calendar year based
upon the percentage increase or decrease in the United States Consumer Price Index (National, All Items) ("CPI") between September
of the year which is two years before such year and September of the
preceding year, rounded to the nearest penny (for example, the rate
for the year 2001 shall be an adjustment of the rate for the year
2000, based upon the percentage difference in the CPI between September 1999 and September 2000). BMI shall inform you of the adjusted rate by the end of each calendar year.*

*(b) The minimum annual fee billed and payable for 2002 shall
be $110 per year. The minimum annual fee for each year after 2002
shall be an adjustment of the minimum annual fee for the previous
calendar year based upon the percentage increase or decrease in the
CPI between September of the year which is two years before such
year and September of the preceding year, rounded to the nearest
five dollars.*

*(c) You agree to pay to BMI for each calendar year the total fee
due. The minimum annual fee ($110) only is due simultaneously
with your execution and return of this agreement. The remainder of
the actual license fee for each calendar year shall be due within
thirty (30) days from the beginning of the following calendar year,
upon submission of the report required in paragraph 5, along with
the minimum annual fee for the following calendar year.*

*(d) The license fee for each calendar year shall be based upon
LICENSEE's actual total number of Attendees for that calendar year
as set forth on the report required by Paragraph 5. If such report reveals that the actual fee due BMI for that report's calendar year is
greater than the minimum annual fee previously paid, LICENSEE
shall pay the difference at the same time it submits the report and
pays its minimum annual fee for the following calendar year.*

Although there are many circumstances in which meeting and event planners
must pay licensing fees for music, there are several exceptions to these laws.
See Figure 13-5 for this comprehensive list.

1. Music performed in the public domain (PD)
   a. 75 years after date of first publication before 1978
   b. After 1978, life of the composer plus 50 years
2. Any work entirely created and published by a U.S. government agency is PD.
3. Music that has been commissioned by an association or an exhibitor specifically for its use.
4. Music performed for a gathering of friends is not considered a "performance." Therefore, no license is required. In addition, functions of this type are not open to the public. These include weddings, bar/bas mitzvah receptions, and anniversaries. This exemption directly affects the social, wedding, or party planner.
5. Face-to-face teaching by nonprofit educational institutions
6. The transmission of certain performances in the course of a systematic instructional activity by a nonprofit educational institution.
7. The performance of religious music in the course of services at a religious gathering.
8. Certain performances by not-for-profit groups for which the performers, producers, and other suppliers are unpaid and the proceeds are used exclusively for charitable, educational, or religious purposes.
9. Negotiate your own agreement with the copyright owner.
10. Sign an agreement with an organization that produces its own music.
11. Fund-raisers for the VFW or American Legion require a special contract. Notice must be given to the composer, who has the right to negotiate within 30 days or the music can be performed at no charge.
12. "The Star Spangled Banner" and "Taps."

Note: Music licenses are *much* less expensive than a lawsuit!

Figure 13-5
Exemptions from the Model Music Performance Agreement for Meetings, Conventions, Trade Shows, and Expositions

A note of caution to those looking at the legalese of the licenses, both in this chapter and published in their entirety in Appendix 6: Licenses can change, sometimes dramatically, from year to year. The licenses explained in this chapter were in effect at the time of writing in 2002. Please check for updates to all of these licenses.

Using Trademarked Characters in Special Events

Cheryl Rubin, vice president, Licensing and Merchandising for DC Comics, a division of Warner Brothers, has worked in the licensing industry for more than 20 years. She is responsible for the worldwide licensing and merchandising of world-famous superheroes Batman, Superman, and Wonder Woman. She offers this explanation:

> Costumed characters are effective draws for many types of meetings and events. From kids to adults, everyone enjoys seeing his or her favorite characters brought to life and the opportunity to interact with them. Costumed characters are most often booked for malls, fairs, festivals, special events, meetings, zoos, theme parks, fundraisers, parades, trade shows, and retailers. Some of the more famous characters appear in traveling shows, while the majority are available for meet-and-greet appearances.
>
> Because all characters are owned and trademarked by some entity (the licensor), it is critical to obtain permission from the owners or representatives before proceeding any further in planning the meeting or event. If you don't get written permission to use a character in your meeting or event, you and your client could be held liable for unfair use of a trademark, with remedies due as provided by the law.
>
> Allow a minimum of four weeks to obtain permission, ideally six to eight weeks, depending on the popularity of the character. In fact, the more popular a character is, the further in advance you should contact the licensor for permission. Most companies have a very limited number of costumes available, which can be booked up to one year in advance. Be prepared to provide details on the event and your client, as the licensor will factor in the client as much as the event itself in making its decision.
>
> Some characters are simply not available for general usage in public events, as that may not fit into the marketing strategy for the character. For example, Batman, a world-renowned superhero, owned by DC Comics, a division of Warner Brothers, is available for malls, retailers where Batman merchandise is sold, fairs, festivals, zoos, and parades, but only under certain conditions. Batman makes both meet-and-greet appearances (simple appearances where he greets kids and signs autographs) and a staged 20-minute stunt show, with the fees commensurate with the type of booking. Batman would not be available for an appearance related to a company that is not a licensee (a company licensed by DC Comics to create Batman merchandise or use Batman in a promotion), such as a trade show or sales meeting. Nor is Batman available for bar mitzvahs!
>
> Every licensor has different guidelines for booking its costumed character. Some companies have in-house departments that handle these requests; others license character appearances to an authorized licensee. Some companies book their characters only at major

events with marketing support. Others use character appearances as brand builders and are more flexible about how and where the characters appear. You can always call the owner of a character to find out what kind of appearances the character is most likely to be booked at or to learn the name of the authorized licensee.

Trademarked characters can be great attention-getters and audience builders and can help add to a fun environment for a meeting or event. Just start the proposal process far in advance, be patient, have a backup plan in case the character isn't available, and refrain from using unauthorized characters, so as to keep your reputation and that of your client intact.

In Conclusion

This chapter provides information on an often overlooked but very important aspect of event entertainment, the licensing of music and other protected properties for such entertainment. There are those who may interpret these laws differently and take their chances, just as there are also those who consistently drive their cars over the speed limit, willing to risk getting speeding tickets or losing their driver's licenses. Both of these activities are against the law, and engaging in such behavior makes you susceptible to the consequences. If you play unlicensed music, you are breaking the law. You are responsible on behalf of the organization you are working for to get all necessary licenses and permits or to accept the consequences. Those consequences can be translated into a dollar value of as much as $500,000 per infraction. An average tune plays for about four minutes. An average event lasts for four hours. Each tune played without a license is an infraction, and the total amount of the fines can be substantial.

If you do not obtain proper licensing for your event's music, will you get caught? There are several ways for the "music police" to find you: (1) Most local convention and visitors bureaus send out monthly updates on conventions coming into town, specifying the host hotel, the dates, and the expected attendance. (2) It is customary for a hotel to have a "reader board" on its property, especially in the lobby, which can easily be read by inspectors for ASCAP and BMI (also known as the 'music police'). Once outside your meeting space, they can easily detect whether there is live and/or mechanical music being playing for your meeting or event. It is then a simple matter for them to find you and ask for the licenses or to check their records for payment. Be honest; do the right thing. Remember that if you are caught, you can lose the right to play music listed in the BMI and ASCAP catalogs. Imagine being the only event planner in town who cannot provide music at events.

Scripts for Future Study

BOOK

Kohn, Al and Bob. (1996) *Kohn On Music Licensing.* Second Edition, Englewood Cliffs, NJ: Aspen Law & Business.

INTERNET RESOURCES

Major Licensors

    ASCAP, 800-910-7346, www.ascap.com
    BMI, 877-264-2137, www.bmi.com
    SESAC, 800-826-9996, www.sesac.com

Music Rights Societies

    AMCOS (Australia), www.amcos.com.au
    APRA (Australia/New Zealand), www.apra.com.au
    ARTISJUS (Hungary), www.artisjus.hu/en
    ASCAP (U.S.), www.ascap.com
    BMI (U.S.), www.bmi.com
    BIEM (International), www.biem.org
    BUMA (Netherlands), www.buma.nl
    CISAC (International), www.cisac.org
    CMRRA Ltd. (Canada), www.cmrra.ca
    GEMA (Germany), www.gema.de
    IMRO (Ireland), www.imro.ie
    JASRAC (Japan), www.jasrac.or.jp
    KODA (Denmark), www.koda.dk
    MCPS (U.K.), www.mcps.co.uk
    NCB (Denmark), www.ncb.dk
    PRS (U.K.), www.prs.co.uk
    RAO (Russia), www.rao.ru
    SABAM (Belgium), www.sabam.be
    SACEM (France), www.sacem.org
    SESAC (U.S.), www.sesac.com
    SGAE (Spain), www.sgae.es
    SIAE (Italy), www.siae.it
    SOCAN (Canada), www.socan.ca
    STEF (Iceland), www.stef.is
    STEMRA (Netherlands), www.buma.nl
    SUISA (Switzerland), www.suisa.ch
    TEOSTO (Finland), www.teosto.fi
    TONO (Norway), www.tono.no

U.S. Copyright and Licensing

Copyright and Fair Use (Stanford University Library), http://fairuse.stanford.edu

Copyright Society of the USA, www.csusa.org

Friends of Active Copyright Education, www.face-copyright.org

Kohn on Music Licensing, www.kohnmusic.com

Library of Congress, www.lcweb.loc.gov

U.S. Copyright Office, www.lcweb.loc.gov/copyright

General Copyright

Berne Convention (International Copyright Treaty), www.law.cornell.edu/treaties/berne/overview.html

Canadian Copyright Law, http://canada.justice.gc.ca/en/index.html

European Commission Project, www.imprimatur.alcs.co.uk

International Intellectual Property Alliance, www.iipa.com

World Intellectual Property Organization, www.wipo.org

Other Copyright Resources

The Copyright Website, www.benedict.com

Recent copyright decisions (U.S Supreme Court), www.law.cornell.edu/syllabi?copyright+patent+trademark

THOMAS: Legislative Information (U.S. Congress), http://thomas.loc.gov

Universal Copyright Convention (International Copyright Treaty), www.tufts.edu/departments/fletcher/multi/texts/UNTS13444.txt

U.S. Copyright Law, www.law.cornell.edu/uscode/17

U.S. Copyright Office Regulations, www.law.cornell.edu/copyright/regulations/regs.overview.html

U.S. Patent and Trademark Office, www.uspto.gov

Music Rights Clearance Organizations

EMG Music Clearance (U.S.), www.clearance.com

Parker Music Group (U.S.), www.musicclearance.com

Signature Sound, Inc. (U.S.), www.signature-sound.com

Other Music Rights Clearance Organizations, www.kohnmusic.com/articles/clear.html

Music Mechanical Rights Societies and Collection Agencies

AMCOS (Australia), www.amcos.com.au

BIEM (International), www.biem.org

CMRRA Ltd. (Canada), www.cmrra.ca

GEMA (Germany), www.gema.de

Harry Fox Agency, Inc. (U.S.), www.nmpa.org/hfa.html

MCPS (U.K.), www.mcps.co.uk

Nordisk Copyright Bureau (NCB) (Scandinavia), www.ncb.dk
STEMRA (Netherlands), www.buma.nl/uk/home.htm

MUSIC PUBLISHER ORGANIZATIONS

Music Publishers Association of the U.S. (U.S.), www.mpa.org
National Music Publishers Association (U.S.), www.nmpa.org/nmpa.html
Nashville Publishers Network (NPN) (U.S.), www.songnet.com/npn
Swedish Music Publishers Association (Sweden), www.smff.se/sid04.htm

Exit Stage Right

There are many ways to address risk management for meetings and events. This chapter on music licensing introduced one area of event risk management. Next on the agenda is how to utilize best practices in your event entertainment planning. Utilizing best practices is another way to reduce the risk factors and ensure the success of meetings and events, as discussed in Chapter 14.

PART FOUR

Best Practices and Creative Strategies in Event Entertainment and Production

CHAPTER 14

Best Practices in Event Entertainment and Production

A captured moment of spontaneous creativity is worth more than a thousand hours of computerized perfection.

—LINER NOTES FOR THE LED ZEPPELIN CD BBC SESSIONS

IN THIS CHAPTER YOU WILL DISCOVER

- Best practices in event entertainment for associations, corporate events, cause-related fund-raisers, product launches, ceremonies, and incentive events.
- How to perfect your skills in the event entertainment and production industry.
- How to strategically select entertainment that will best meet your client's goals.

Every event planner knows that it takes many hours of detailed planning to make an event appear spontaneous. Part of that spontaneity comes from the flow between the entertainment and the event's other elements. Electronic media guru Marshal McLuhan first stated, "The medium is the message." In other words, how the message is presented is as important as the message itself. The music you use to accompany a meeting or trade show can often influence the thoughts and impressions of listeners as strongly as the verbal message. Music can create very specific states of mind that absorb information in a more positive manner and, in turn, influence behavior. When a listener is motivated by music, he or she is alert and involved and retains more of the specifics of a message. This chapter illustrates how best to utilize and coordinate event entertainment through a series of case studies and personal observations of event professionals. These represent the best practices in the industry and can help you to better understand the overall strategies involved in organizing a successful entertainment experience at your events.

Best Practices in Planning for Entertainment

James C. Monroe, CMP, CSEP, has been a special events professional for more than 28 years; with his team of designers and technicians, he decorates and manages events for corporate, community, and family celebrations. In *The Art of the Event: Complete Guide to Special Event Design and Décor,* he offers the following observations on best practices:

> *Various types of events, including corporate, association, social, and not-for-profit, have different needs regarding entertainment and production, but the same principles and practices apply when planning entertainment and designing the production for each event. The process begins with research to determine the goals and objectives of the event and the needs and expectations of the guests. The production is then designed to meet these needs and objectives. During this phase the script for the event is conceptualized and the appropriate entertainment is selected.*
>
> *The planning phase follows as the script and timeline are developed and production elements are arranged for, always with the goals and objectives of the event in mind. Each production detail is carefully tailored to support the design concept. This assures an effective production and successful event. After the event, the final essential step is evaluation. The history of each event will provide the foundation for future successful events.*

The research phase can be as simple as interviewing the client, but some preliminary investigation into the corporate entity or family can be valuable. If the event is a repetitive affair, past history becomes invaluable. For associations and certain corporate functions there are several different tools that can be applied to research the needs and expectations of the attendees, including questionnaires, surveys, and focus groups. In addition to this motivational research, functional questions regarding space, attendants, site limitations, access, and power are determined at this time.

Creative concepts are developed during the design phase. A good way to begin this phase is to brainstorm with the client, using free association to list all of those elements and all of the entertainment that might be desirable. At this time, there are no bad ideas. Once this list of wild ideas is made, they can be analyzed in light of practical considerations. Now a timeline, financial structure, and budget will be applied to refine the design concept. The design phase is where the critical decisions are made, goals meet budgets, and the production is given direction.

The coordination or planning phase is the actual production. Entertainment is booked, production support services are hired, and the timeline and production bible are refined and detailed. The most common mistake made in entertainment and production is to start this process out of order, becoming committed to certain entertainers or other production details before determining the goals and objectives, developing an event design, or analyzing the resources. A corporate event, for example, may be a product rollout where the main goal is product exposure or brand identification. An outstanding name performer might be selected with the intention of creating a memorable event. If this is done before the event design is developed, the result can be a memorable event where the event is remembered but nobody remembers the product.

A similar problem can happen with social events. A wedding, for example, should focus on the bride, the bridal party, and the life celebration that is taking place. The bride or her family might get the idea to really celebrate by booking name entertainment. This can become a major attraction for the guests, distracting attention from the bride, unless she is a celebrity. Name entertainment can still be used at a wedding if the bride and her parents determine they want it, but it needs to be carefully integrated into the celebration and the family needs to be aware of the effect it is likely to have.

The most overlooked and underappreciated element in event production is the postevent evaluation. Once the party is over, production crews pack up their gear and go home, the guests go to bed, and it is all over except for counting the money. The professional event manager will have scheduled a wrap-up session, or post-con to do an objective analysis of the event. This past history becomes extremely valuable when doing repeat events or similar events in the future. Associations and corporations can get valuable feedback from their attendees through postevent surveys or questionnaires gathered on-site at the end of the event. The basic questions at the evaluation session should determine if the goals and objectives of the event were achieved, and if the needs and expectations of the attendees were fulfilled.

Association Events

Making the simple complicated is commonplace; making the complicated simple, awesomely simple, that's creativity.
—CHARLES MINGUS, JAZZ COMPOSER AND BASSIST, AND LEADER OF THE
MINGUS DYNASTY

Association events are opportunities for members to network and enjoy themselves. They are there to have fun. Making that event fun and exciting, but appear to be simple, is the event planner's role. Association executives have long understood the potency of music at meetings—as opening session rousers, subtle enhancement at mealtime, or final-night blowout entertainment. Nothing can touch good live performances for buoying attendees' moods. A musical act, whether national, regional, or local talent, may well be *the* promotional vehicle of the opening years of the twenty-first century. A top-name headliner at a meeting can boost attendance and enhance the organization's image.

But hiring live talent has its share of challenges and pitfalls. The entertainment group you book, for example, should fit into the association's marketing objectives and its "corporate culture." A talented but inappropriate act, say, 2 Live Crew at a meeting of the National Organization of Women, can be just as disastrous as an untalented one. You must make sure that the entertainer will cooperate willingly with the function, to serve as an enhancement to the meeting, not as its focal point. The entertainer's booking with you is a private date, not a public concert.

Several factors must be considered in booking music for an association event:

- *The age of the audience.* Try to match the entertainer with the approximate age range of the attendees. The big-band sound, once considered exclusively for an elderly audience, is making a comeback with younger attendees, thanks to the efforts of singers such as Carly Simon, Melissa Manchester, Harry Connick Jr., and Linda Ronstadt, and despite the deaths of the great orchestra leaders such as Duke Ellington and Count Basie, many of their bands are still jumping.

- *The surroundings.* Where is the meeting being held? In a hotel, a theater, a convention center, an exhibition hall, a tent? What are the logistics of the venue, both aurally and visually? Your guests must be able to hear and see well. A sophisticated corporate entertainment company can obtain both sound and lighting for you.
- *Will there be any speeches?* If there are going to be speeches, try to keep them short and have the speakers come on before the entertainment commences. If possible, do not interrupt the flow and energy of the music by positioning a speech in the middle of the show.
- *What is the budget?* Let the client's negotiator know what you can afford. Remember that the amount must cover the artist's fee as well as any accommodations and services specified in the rider. A $15,000 act may have a $15,000 rider attached to it. A rider can be as short as one page or longer, as in Shirley Bassey's 21 pages, for instance.
- *The artist's availability.* Hiring Bruce Springsteen for an association's reception may be within your budget, but there is one problem: The Boss does not perform at such engagements. When you and your committee are deciding which act to buy, make a list of at least three to five acts. The act you want may be out of your price range, may have another engagement, or may not do corporate events. On the other hand, many artists now realize they can profit by greater exposure to a different audience. Sometimes musical acts are hired, not to perform their music, but to meet and greet attendees, play golf or tennis, or do product endorsements or association cause-related marketing activities.

Corporate Events

"It is not just a party anymore. Your events must contribute to corporate goals. Each event must be integrated into the marketing plan so that it contributes to overall corporate objectives. A corporate event is an occasion that is designed to communicate critical organizational messages and themes in highly personal, entertaining ways that maximize retention. Events can motivate" (Doyle 2002).

The following is a case study written by Chris Pentz, CMP, president of PENTZ Group Communications, specializing in health care conference management, about the process that she used to plan a successful corporate entertainment event.

CASE STUDY

Location: Philadelphia, Pennsylvania

Background: We were contacted by a multi-national pharmaceutical company headquartered in Europe and asked to organize its main social event held in conjunction with a large medical meeting that was taking place in Philadelphia in early November 2002.

The task: The client's objectives were to host their foreign physician delegates at an unforgettable evening that would include a reception and dinner. Some of the parameters the client provided us included the following:

- The site must be attractive on its own merit.
- Hotels should not be used.
- The evening would have to provide a lot of entertainment and interaction, before and during dinner.
- There should be a theme for the evening.
- The space should accommodate about 200 guests.

The challenge: To find a location in downtown Philadelphia that would be large enough for a reception, fun activities for the guests, and a separate space for a nice, very upscale dinner.

Selecting the site: Keeping in mind that the client specifically wanted hands-on activities during the reception, we recommended using the Franklin Institute Science Museum. The reception would take place in the different galleries, affording the guests an opportunity to visit all the fun and highly interactive exhibits, including the area on bioscience and the heart, and the gallery of electricity and electronics. Dinner would follow in Franklin Hall, the Benjamin Franklin National Memorial. This very imposing octagonal room, modeled after the Pantheon in Rome, houses a larger-than-life statue of Ben Franklin beneath an 80 ft domed ceiling.

The theme for the evening would be "Neighborhoods of Philadelphia," capitalizing on the rich ancestry of this city. At our event, we would see the city's various neighborhoods come to life through food, music, and color. Providing an authentic touch of Philadelphia, a group of Mummers would welcome our guests as they entered the Franklin Institute through its front door on Twentieth Street. Photographers would be on hand to provide souvenirs to our guests, and an actor portraying Ben Franklin himself would be wandering through his electricity exhibit, telling stories of his times. A party is not a party without music, and so we hired a local band to provide us with background music during dinner.

A New Challenge: Though perfectly happy with the plans so far, our client wanted to have additional entertainment during dinner, especially in between meal courses. Mark Sonder Productions, Inc., was called to help decide what type of entertainment we should have.

A headliner act was considered, but, because of budget limitations, promptly eliminated. The client wanted something very animated. So when Mark Sonder Productions suggested hiring a troupe of Chinese acrobats who were making their way from a public performance in North Carolina to their next stop in New York, I knew we had found our entertainment, the Shangri-La Chinese Acrobats! The client was delighted with the idea and gave us the green light to proceed. Mark Sonder Productions then helped to negotiate and finalize the contract and the riders. The acrobats would perform two acts, in between courses, just as our client had envisioned.

Observations: Having been in the meeting planning industry for over 20 years, I have learned to always hire the experts. Whether it is audiovisual support for a meeting or production services for a show, the best move is always to use your network to identify whom to call when you need a specialist. Another lesson to be learned from this study is that if you can procure entertainment en route or, as it is called in the industry, with favorable routing, you may be able to pick up a group at a much reduced rate. In this case, the client saved on round-trip transportation, especially because the troupe was already in the United States, as well as on hotel accommodations. As this was a 16-piece ensemble, the savings were considerable.

Cause Related Fund-Raising and Nonprofit Events

"To impress people who are used to being impressed all the time, I have done everything from fireworks to people jumping out of cakes, to having top performers like Elton John and other headliners."
—DONALD TRUMP, HOTELIER, ENTREPRENEUR

Every dollar I give to you I can't give to curing heart disease.
—SAID IN CONTRACT NEGOTIATIONS FOR HEADLINER ENTERTAINMENT BY THE
PLANNER FOR THE AMERICAN HEART ASSOCIATION

As reflected in the preceding quotations, when planning cause-related events, you must be careful to secure entertainment that will ultimately benefit the cause. According to Michael Owen of All Access Entertainment,

In working with charities, we must be sensitive to the fact that the object of the fund-raising is the passion of those putting together the event. To them, it is the best cause in the world, but is among hundreds of other best-causes-in-the-world—and each of them is asking for a piece of the headliner's time, at a reduced rate. More often than not, a greatly reduced rate is just not going to happen, unless the headliner shares a passion for the subject charity. For the most successful charity events, expect to negotiate a fair rate for the headliner and then secure an underwriter to mitigate the cost.

Wendy Anderson, owner of WOW! Productions (Events & Public Relations), and partner in Events. with a Twist, provides event production and coordination, as well as community outreach and promotion for corporate, nonprofit, and public events. She offers the following observations:

The nonprofit organization understands the need to provide entertainment for promotional purposes and seeks to make its event different or to give it star power. With the vast number of nonprofit and fund-raising events, there is competition to create spectacular and fun events that will draw attendance, but usually on a restrictive or often nonexistent budget, as the organization knows its goal is to raise funds, not spend them. In addition, many nonprofits often lack the finances to secure entertainment or the expertise or understanding of how to develop entertainment or headliners. But, of course, having entertainment often helps to draw attendees to a nonprofit event.

In order for a nonprofit to have a successful event or fund-raiser, work on such event must start early and be thought through in an organized manner. Creating a buzz around your event requires adequate lead time. If part of your buzz will be the entertainment or headliner, allow enough lead time to secure the type of entertainment that will best fulfill both your needs and those of the headliner.

Pro bono entertainment, emcees, and headliners are great for a nonprofit, with one caveat: At any time, including the day of your event, your entertainment, emcee, or headliner may receive an offer of paid work and may drop your event. It is wise to build an honorarium into your budget for your entertainment. Any time musicians or performers are paid, whether it's full scale or an honorarium, the payment ties them to your event. For the emcee or headliner, seek out entertainers who are community minded or who support the cause you are promoting. They are less likely to put you in a bind by canceling or otherwise not appearing. If an emcee or headliner is unsure and cannot give you a firm commitment, take it as a sign that you have not secured that person.

If you find that your organization has zero dollars for entertainment, not even money for an honorarium, the best thing to do is to start planning your event early. Determine the type of entertainment you are seeking and get out into the community to see who may be available. There may be bands, musicians, entertainers, dancers, and singers who would be willing to work pro bono in exchange for promotion at your event. And somehow, include food in what they re-

ceive at the event. Food and beverages for the entertainers can go a long way if you can't pay them, as well as any giveaways that you have planned for your guests. If you promote the entertainment well, and they are able to get referrals or other bookings from your event, they will likely return and work pro bono for your event again.

A piece of advice from someone who has worked with a lot of nonprofit events: The best nonprofit events happen when the staff or committee members truly focus on the purpose of the event and keep sales at the top of their list. If certain types of entertainment will not add to the sales, then they are not worth pursuing. Look at your audience, your attendees, your demographics, and make sure, if you have the budget for entertainment, that it will add to your event and its cause.

Remember, if an emcee is offering his or her services on a pro bono basis, which will be the case for most emcees of nonprofit events, a good script, tight program, and good stage management will likely endear you to that emcee and he or she will help you again in the future. But if you have a bad script, long timeline, and bad stage management, you will likely not receive help from that person again unless he or she truly believes in the cause and wants to help make a difference.

Emcees, headliners, and entertainment who are helping your fund-raising event on a pro bono basis should all be treated like VIPs. Emcees play an important role at your events, as they act as hosts to your guests. They are as essential to an event's successful delivery as the professional planner is to the event's production process. Although emcees appear to deliver their ongoing dialogue effortlessly, they are actually working from carefully developed scripts. The script is developed through a process of writing, and rewriting, until it fits the time requirements and it is a good, concise script that is easy for your emcee to deliver. Ensure that emcees, headliners, and entertainers have good directions to the event, and send each a copy of the invitation. Provide a copy of the script and timeline at least a week prior to the event, and take care of their parking. At the venue, they need to know through which door to enter and where to unload their equipment, if any. Be sure to have volunteers available if they need help in moving equipment or setting up. When they arrive, introduce them to the key people in your organization, and make sure that you have a volunteer or board member who is with them at all times. Go over the timeline and script with them so there is no confusion and so they have an opportunity to ask questions. They are providing talent, headliner status, or emcee work pro bono, and they are the VIPs because they can make or break your event.

Product Launches

In the factories, we manufacture lipstick, on the shelves we sell hope.

—CHARLES REVSON, FOUNDER OF REVLON

At Microsoft, we see no limits to the human imagination. Our goal is to unleash the creativity in every person, every family, and every business.

—MICROSOFT 2001 ANNUAL REPORT

The following is a case study written by Marianna Paolini, CMP, director of operations at Navigant Meetings Services, NE. It addresses a product launch that she planned and shows the significance of this type of an event for the success of corporations.

CASE STUDY

In November 1999, Navigant International's group and meeting service division handled all aspects of Boehringer Ingelheim's sales meetings. There was to be a 1600-person product launch in June 2000 at the Wyndham Palace in Lake Buena Vista, Florida. The overflow hotel for sleeping rooms would be the Hilton at Walt Disney World, which is five minutes away from the headquarters hotel. The project manager decided to have an exciting, off-property, special evening event for the attendees that included big-name entertainment.

EVENT PROBLEMS AND CHALLENGES

1. This request presented a short lead time for contracting headline entertainment. It was imperative to get a venue and availability secured immediately.
2. The off-site venue had to be no more then 5 to 15 minutes from the hotel, inasmuch as the attendees would be in all-day meetings.

3. Ground transfers had to be coordinated.
4. Previously, the client had the B-52's as the name entertainment. This would be a hit with the 25- to 35-year-olds, but not the older age groups. What would be a good match for all age groups?
5. The structure of the meeting: Half of the group had a half-day off on the day of the off-site event. The other half of the group had a half-day off the previous day. "Free time" was the same for both days.
6. Food and beverage had to be served at the event, but it was not dinner.
7. The headline entertainment had specific requirements clearly outlined in its contract rider. It was imperative to adhere to each requirement.

DISCUSSION QUESTIONS

1. What venue matches the function needs/requirements?
2. What and how will transfers be coordinated?

3. What will be an ideal match for attendees between the ages of 25 and 65?

4. What time should the event take place? Consider the needs of the group that has "free time."

5. Does the client want dinner provided to the attendees? When and where? What types of food should be served at the event?

6. How will we make sure all the contracted requirements are adhered to for the headline entertainment?

7. What kind of security measures should be taken?

8. How do we sell the idea to the clients?

9. How do we guide the clients to sell our idea up the chain of command?

RECOMMENDATIONS FOR RESOLUTION

1. Meeting Planning 101 lesson: The first call should be to the hotel convention services manager (CSM). For this meeting, the CSM had a contact name at the House of Blues. The House of Blues was only five minutes from the hotel. Also, the House of Blues could hold 1600 attendees and already had the bar set up and the staging requirements. The preset staging requirements saved the client quite a bit of money on production needs for the event. The best news of all—the House of Blues was available.

2. There were two hotels, and we wanted to provide the guests with flexibility. We found that continuous shuttle loops, stopping at the Wyndham, the Hilton, and the House Of Blues, ran from one hour prior to the event until one hour after the event. Based on the timing of the enter-

tainment, we scheduled more buses during peak hours.

3. Mark Sonder Productions was able to provide a list of options, rates, and availability for entertainment. After numerous discussions with the client, the best option presented to the client was to hire three different bands to target three different age groups, as follows:

   a. The Hall of Fame Show: the Elsbeary Hobbs Drifters, the Cornell Gunter Coasters, and the Marvelettes
   Target: 50–65-year-olds

   b. Blood, Sweat and Tears, featuring David Clayton-Thomas
   Target: 35–50-year-olds

   c. Joan Jett and the Blackhearts
   Target: 20–35-year-olds

4. The client stressed the importance of having the timing of the half-day off the same for each group. The group that was granted a half-day of free time for the previous day had free time from 12:30 to 8:30 P.M. Members of the entire group were on their own for dinner, and then were expected to be at the Cirque du Soleil showing by 8:30 P.M. Therefore, the next night we needed to start the House of Blues event at 8:30 P.M. On average, the older age group preferred to retire earlier than the younger age groups. We presented the bands' performances in the listed order:

7:30 A.M.	Shuttle transfers begin
8:30 P.M.–9:00 P.M.	Arrival and cocktails
9:00 P.M.–10:00 P.M.	The Hall of Fame Show

10:00 P.M.–10:30 P.M.	Break (equipment changeover)
10:30 P.M.–11:30 P.M.	Blood, Sweat and Tears Show
11:30 P.M.–12:00 A.M.	Break (equipment changeover)
12:00 A.M.–1:00 A.M.	Joan Jett and the Blackhearts
2:00 A.M.	Last shuttle transfer

Mark Sonder Productions also scheduled "meet and greet" opportunities with the different headline entertainers prior to their performances.

5. Ironically, dinner was the most debated issue. The attendees were on their own for dinner the previous night. The client's vice presidents wanted a "group activity for dinner" and wanted the attendees granted a half-day of free time in order to have the same allotted time as the previous day's attendees. The solution was to have a simple barbeque buffet at the hotel for all the attendees who had a full day of meetings, and optional for those attendees who were granted a free afternoon. Then we had "light pub fare" served at the House of Blues throughout the event.

6. The headline entertainment contract was very detailed and long. Initially, I scheduled a lengthy call with Mark Sonder Productions to review and have him explain each contract addendum in layman's terms. I created a grid of who was responsible for each requirement. Then I

scheduled a series of conference calls with the client, the hotels, the ground transportation company, and the House of Blues, depending on which contract requirement was being addressed.

7. Security was a twofold approach.
   a. Headline Entertainers: We housed all the headliners at the Hilton. Each headliner act was carefully located in a separate section of the hotel. We had a dedicated hotel staffperson to attend to their needs. Our ground company had dedicated drivers for each of the headliner acts' needs throughout their stay in Orlando. The House of Blues provided security at the back entrance.
   b. The Attendees: Because these employees historically conduct themselves in a professional manner at Boehringer Ingelheim social functions, we agreed to keep the security minimal. The House of Blues provided security at the entrance and scattered throughout the venue. Each guest needed to show his or her Boehringer Ingelheim conference badge to get into the event. Mark Sonder Productions was in charge of the All Access Pass distribution.

8. Selling the idea to my direct client was easy. The project manager and her team were familiar with all of the headliners presented. They were thrilled with each headliner targeting each age group.

9. Selling the idea to the vice presidents was a bit more challenging. The key was

to speak in terms of finances. The B-52's cost $X the previous year. Each of the three acts presented cost one-third of $X each. Initially, it appeared to be the same amount of money. We had to do a cost analysis, comparing the expenses involved for each headliner. Having three acts involved many more musicians and associated crews. The good news was that the previous year's meeting was in the Bahamas, and expenses in Orlando were less. However, the cost minimum at the House of Blues was a food and beverage minimum of $250,000. This cost was much more than the previous year's

with the B-52's, but the total attendance was only 1200, versus this year's attendance of 1600. After reviewing the cost analysis, we were able to justify the added cost by presenting it on a cost-per-person basis, and finally the vice presidents' committee voted yes.

The event was extremely successful. The evening went smoothly, the vendors worked as a team, and there were no glitches. The attendees had a wonderful time, and so did the vice presidents. The client was very happy with the final product.

Ceremonies

Some of the largest and most elaborate events produced around the world are ceremonies. People remember ceremonies because they elicit an emotional response regarding the event that is being celebrated. The following is a case study on the opening and closing ceremonies for the 2002 Paralympic Games, which were produced by Jack Morton Worldwide.

CASE STUDY

Jack Morton Worldwide's co-production of the 2002 Paralympics opening and closing ceremonies in Salt Lake City, Utah, significantly boosted the company's reputation for producing arena-scale public events (see Figure 14-1). When the job was bid out in 2001, Jack Morton's presentation stressed the very diversity of its experience and clients served, its 60 years of experience, and the size and flexibility of its professional workforce. All the members of the core team

that Jack Morton was proposing had already demonstrated their ability in working on other comparable events.

The client's overall goal was to give the Paralympic Games their own identity during a demanding production cycle that coincided with preparations for the Winter Olympic ceremonies. It was the first time in the 26-year Paralympic history that the Games were to be mounted in the same venues as the Olympic ceremonies and under the auspices of the same organizing committee.

Paralympic athletes are world-class athletes who rely on some kind of physical aid, such as a wheelchair, a prosthesis, or a guide dog, to perform their sports. The Salt Lake Olympic Committee (SLOC) wanted to ensure that the Paralympics did not appear to be shortchanged in any way. The fundamental goal of ensuring a unique spotlight for the Paralympic Games affected every aspect of Jack Morton's challenge—budgeting, management of the client relationship, use of resources, volunteers, and entertainment.

The ambitious schedule had Jack Morton Worldwide in Salt Lake City at the beginning of January, to begin working with the SLOC on what would culminate in two shows, staged only 11 days apart, on March 7 and March 16 respectively. Jack Morton managed the ceremonies' production and technical requirements and supervised an on-site production team of more

Figure 14-1
The 2002 Paralympic Ceremonies
(Photo courtesy of Jack Morton Worldwide; Photography: Jason Meugniot)

Figure 14-1
(Continued)

Figure 14-1
(Continued)

than 150 to coordinate the lighting, audio, special effects, fireworks, wardrobe, and staging, as well as 350 volunteers.

From day one, Jack Morton's project team integrated itself with the SLOC, which was by its very definition a complex and comprehensive organization. Public stadium shows and the large organizing committees that run them involve hundreds of different entities. Jack Morton had to interface with every SLOC department, including those responsible for everything from street closings, to bringing the cast in, to food and beverages, to the works department that removes the snow from the set. All of these entities, at the same time, had

the Olympics in mind as the first thing to take place.

Jack Morton Worldwide brought to the table its ability to dovetail with all of the service organizations within SLOC and enlist their support for the Paralympics and Jack Morton's efforts. It was a priority to meet with those departments on a regular basis and to understand what they were going through on the Olympics, while also inspiring them to support the Paralympics. Because the SLOC had its own creative people, Jack Morton initially approached the collaboration with great sensitivity.

The Paralympics inherited the entire stadium facility and stage equipment from the

Winter Olympics. This presented both advantages and disadvantages. The client provided funds to ensure that as much as possible of the scenic and technical package could be kept there (essentially the entire Olympics lighting plot minus 20 percent, which amounted to more than 700 moving lights plus the other auxiliary fixed lighting), as well as what was needed to give the Paralympics show unique scenic aspects.

The Winter Olympics had already auditioned 21,000 local performers in the Salt Lake area and had cast many of them, leaving the Paralympics at a disadvantage for securing available local talent. The SLOC recognized the need for professional-caliber dancers to give the show a finished look and made it possible for Jack Morton to audition professional dancers in Los Angeles and Las Vegas. Forty were hired, in addition to some of the available local performers.

Jack Morton Worldwide devised a creative solution to keep the costume budget very low. Although some of the more intricate costumes were fabricated in Los Angeles, the rest were produced by volunteers on-site in Salt Lake City at a temporary costume shop that Jack Morton ran for a month and a half. Jack Morton hired a professional costumer and costume supervisor, and the results were quite successful.

The "Inspire the Spirit" opening featured Paralympians from 36 countries marching together with their national teams. A breathtaking performance of original staging and choreography on ice and on stage followed, with singers, dancers, headline performers, and pyrotechnics, all preceding the moving finale, the lighting of the Paralympic torch. NBC's broadcast of the opening ceremony highlights reached an estimated 1.1 million U.S. households and had global feeds to viewers in the United Kingdom and Japan. Louis Gossett Jr. delivered a series of stirring monologues, framing elaborate choreography and original music that combined dancers and skaters, evoking winter and nature, as well as performances by the dynamic violinist Vanessa-Mae, 13-year-old country music star Billy Gilman, Wynonna, and Stevie Wonder. Utah's favorite son, Donny Osmond, sang the original "Inspire the Spirit" theme song composed for the event.

The Paralympic Winter Games closing ceremony took place in downtown Salt Lake City at the Olympic Medals Plaza. Jack Morton orchestrated a 90-minute show, featuring the legendary Patti LaBelle, to celebrate the athletes and game volunteers in style, including a video tribute to the Games and a downtown fireworks finale. All told, the events reached a live audience of 55,000 in Salt Lake City.

Sales Promotions and Incentives

Christen P. Heide is a newsletter editor and a contributor to a variety of business magazines. Author of four books on sales force compensation and a respected speaker on sales force management issues, he contributes the following:

> *Everyone loves music, and there is no denying its ability to excite the senses. If you are trying to connect with your customers in an*

exciting way, music just might get them to tune in to your message. More than any other promotional item, it has the ability to connect with consumers on a personal level. That is the main reason marketers like this medium. Whether they choose an exclusive CD compilation, a gift certificate program, or tunes legally downloaded from the Internet, they are trying new ways to cash in on music's appeal. As a result, more and more companies are discovering how they can use music effectively as a promotional tool to recognize employees, increase sales, reward customers, introduce new products, enhance brand image, and promote events.

Here are the chief reasons marketers are incorporating music in incentive programs and other promotions:

- *It's versatile. With so many genres to choose from, including rock, country, dance, hip-hop, and jazz, marketers are always guaranteed to find music to excite their target market. And there are no worries about sizes, fit, or colors, because music fits everyone.*
- *It's a powerful motivator. Just turn on the radio or TV or go to a movie. Music is everywhere. Why? Because it ties into everyday life. Music is the one thing that people want more of.*

There are many other forms of entertainment, as Chris Pentz's case study has shown. Here are two more that can lend themselves quite well to event entertainment. First, there are the people who find things in your facial features that you, your spouse, or your boss may not see right away. These people are the caricaturists. A caricature is a representation, especially pictorial or literary, in which the subject's distinctive features or peculiarities are deliberately exaggerated to produce a comic or grotesque effect. Sherry Lane is a caricaturist extraordinaire based in New York City. She says,

Using a caricaturist at your event will always be new, fresh, and trendy. A caricature is a piece of art created anew with every person who sits before the artist.

Whether it is at a corporate party, trade show, or personal celebration, the caricaturist becomes a focal point. Guests and clients are drawn together to share in the fun and laughter of a true comic likeness. At a trade show, it draws the crowd—allows you to easily collect business cards and ultimately becomes an effective sales tool. At a corporate or association event caricatures can break the ice quickly and effectively.

People always love to see themselves in photos, but when they possess a caricature of themselves, it is displayed as a work of art. Corporate clients will imprint their logos on the artists' drawing paper and then hang the finished drawings on the office walls, making them feel like stars and keeping the corporate name visible.

Figure 14-2
A Caricature of Colin Powell
(Caricature courtesy of Sherry Lane)

Group caricatures can also be a special gift or award. In recognition of outstanding sales teams or exceptional staff, or honoring top executives in the firm, caricatures become a unique gesture of approval. In today's world of computers and technology the pace is fast, but a caricaturist slows the crowd, brings people together and gives them an opportunity to laugh at themselves.

It is the personal touch that counts and is remembered by your guests. When we are touched in a way that stops us for a moment and makes us laugh, or think, or wonder, if only briefly, your event will always be remembered by the "gift of art." Figure 14-2 is a caricature of the famous political figure Colin Powell.

One-Hour Reception

Number of Guests	Number of Strolling Magicians
Up to 200	1
200 to 400	2
400 to 600	3
600 to 800	4
800 to 1000	5

Two-Hour Reception

Number of Guests	Number of Strolling Magicians
Up to 200	1
200 to 400	1
400 to 600	2
600 to 800	2
800 to 1000	3
1000 to 1200	3

Figure 14-3
The Number of Strolling Magicians That Should Be Hired for Events of Varying Sizes

Another popular form of entertainment is magic. Dick Steiner, a magician and mentalist who performs his tricks around the United States, shares some ideas about his trade:

> *For a reception, it is hard to beat a strolling or walk-around magician for great interactive entertainment. A good strolling magician will be adept at mingling with the crowd, performing short sets of close-up magic for small groups of people, usually three to ten at a time, and moving on to another part of the room. Strolling magicians work out of their pockets with a likely emphasis on cards and coins. Some magicians concentrate on impromptu props as well, such as spectators' rings, napkins, rubber bands, or paper money.*
>
> *A strolling mentalist, like a strolling magician, entertains a few people at a time, but with mind-reading effects involving lots of audience participation. Keep in mind that to be enjoyed, the strolling performer will need to be heard and seen. That means soft background music will work in conjunction with strolling magicians and mentalists, but loud music can restrict your performers' audience size to only one or two people at a time. Lights can be low for ambience, but should not be so low that the performers' effects cannot be seen clearly.*

Is there an equation? How many strolling magicians and mentalists are necessary for an event where people are mingling? Steiner says, "A good rule of thumb is one strolling magician or mentalist per hour for every 200 guests, if no other activities are competing for the attention of the guests. See Figure 14-3 to understand how many performers you should hire.

Cultural Preparedness in Entertainment

> *"Cultural awareness is the key to success in planning for minority groups. It is always good to include specialized music and entertainment in any event you are planning for minority groups. Even for a conference or a meeting, you often have social events that include music and entertainment,"*

says Bessie Edwards of Pizzaz Event and Meeting Planning in Franklin Park, New Jersey.

Edwards goes on to say, "When you hire the entertainment, be sensitive to the fact that this is a minority group, so any services you employ should include representation of that minority group." Edwards is talking about ethnic diversity and cultural awareness in music and entertainment. "If the culture of the group dictates a preference for Latino music or Jazz, Barry Manilow just is not going to cut it," writes Tina L. Miller (2001). She believes that the solution is to "work directly with the leaders in the group to select music and entertainment the group can truly enjoy."

Event Entertainment and Production Short Checklist

Figures 14-4 and 14-5 present checklists of items reflecting best practices that should be considered when planning for entertainment at all types of events. The first is a list of questions asked by Heidi Brumbach, CSEP, and owner of Imagine Enterprises International in Las Vegas, Nevada, when she first consults a client about entertainment needs. These questions are good for planners to ask of themselves when booking entertainment. The second is a list of questions to ask on-site in order to prepare for all possible threats to the success of the event.

In Conclusion

Although events may differ as to venue, size, entertainment, and purpose, they all require the application of the same planning and production practices in order to be successful. Even the simplest events require attention to every detail, and it is the experience and knowledge of event and entertainment plan-

---

- What is the theme and purpose of your event?
- What type of entertainment will enhance your concept?
- What is the demographic of the audience?
- Will your sound affect another group, or will another group cause sound bleeding through air walls?
- Are rehearsals required, and when?
- Do you need to provide meals for talent?
- Do entertainers need custom lighting and sound, or do they provide it themselves?

Figure 14-4
Questions to Ask Before an Event Is Planned
(Courtesy of Heidi Brumbach)

- Is everything set up on the stage on time?
- Have all the entertainers arrived on schedule?
- Have the performers been briefed on the company's event policies?
- Are beverages and snacks available for the performers, either in a dressing room or near the stage?
- Have the performers been shown to the dressing room?
- Has the schedule been reviewed before the event begins?
- Is there prerecorded music on tape or CD to play while the band is on break?
- Are the performers in place before the doors open?
- Are the costumes all in good condition?
- Are all cords taped down to avoid tripping?
- Do the sound and light booths look presentable?
- Is the stage skirted and locked in place?
- Is the dance floor secure?
- Are all of the décor lights turned on and working?
- Has the load-out time been confirmed with the vendor?

Figure 14-5
Questions to Ask When You Are On Site at an Event
(Courtesy of Heidi Brumbach)

ners that allow them to create seamless and flawless events that entertain and awe their guests. Entertainment and production constitute an important part of every event; the music will set the tone of the event and the production will bring it to life. The entertainment must be appropriate to the event's theme and the guests' age range and tastes. Headliners or known entertainment may bring more guests to your event, but may also overshadow the event.

Event entertainment planning for nonprofit organizations has its own unique aspects, which often include an expectation of pro bono services and a limited budget or an unwillingness to spend money on entertainment. A planner who is experienced in providing event entertainment services to nonprofit organizations will be familiar with how to obtain appropriate entertainment that retains the event's focus on its purpose.

Music is only one form of event entertainment, which can also include magicians, actors, mimes, acrobats, caricature artists, and a range of other performers whose skills, antics, and artistry can set the mood, break the ice, and entertain guests. In determining the type of entertainment that is appropriate to the event, experts suggest asking simple questions of the event's hosts concerning the theme and purpose of the event, the type of entertainment envisioned, and the audience demographics. The answers to these questions can help the event entertainment planner to develop a strategy that will make the event successful and memorable.

Scripts for Future Study

INTERNET RESOURCES—MUSIC SUPPLIERS

BMG Special Products, www.bmgsp.com.
Network Music, www.privatelabelcd.com.
EMI-Capitol Music Special Products, www.emicapsm.com.
Sony Music Special Products, www.smsp.com.
Universal Music Special Markets, www.umusic.com.

Exit Stage Right

You have now learned about some best practices in event entertainment. In the next chapter you will learn how to include multimedia production in meetings and events. Chapter 15 discusses how to execute basic audiovisual presentations and how to use multimedia technology, including Webcasting.

The Standard Aspects of Multimedia Production

When I had ascertained what amount of current the Dalai Lama's projector would need and how far the projector would have to be from the screen, I declared myself ready to undertake the work.
—Heinrich Harrer, in Seven Years in Tibet, *recalling his duties in 1949*

IN THIS CHAPTER YOU WILL DISCOVER

- How to plan for multimedia needs.
- How to execute basic audiovisual (AV) presentations.
- How to find and hire an AV company.
- How to use and evaluate new multimedia technology, including Webcasting.

So far, the focus of this book has been on entertainment and music in event management, but there are many events, such as Heinrich Harrer's for the Dalai Lama, that do not utilize any music or entertainment, or at least not the type that we have been addressing so far. Some events, such as meetings, conventions, trade shows, and expositions, are forums whose purpose is to deliver a message or to teach or inform audiences about a topic. The focus of these events is on transferring knowledge, information, or education, and this element becomes the entertainment aspect of the event. The production requirements and needs extend beyond those generally found in the event entertainment planning industry and thus often require additional planning and expertise. For these events, multimedia production can play an important part and should therefore be planned with the same attention to detail as required for an entertainment event's "headliner."

How to Execute Basic Audio-Visual Presentations

The days of using a slide or overhead projector and a podium with a goose-neck microphone and high-powered speaker are ancient history. Many of today's presentations and events focus as much on creating an experience as on its content. Without a performer on stage to capture the audience's attention, innovation and technology are needed to "wow" the attendees. Just as the music, motion picture, theater, and television industries have enhanced their presentations, our industry is moving toward highly produced events. But the basic rules for event entertainment still apply, with respect to delivering an event that meets both the client's and the audience's expectations.

When the event entertainment consists of an image projected on a screen, the audience must not be distracted by white space, an inconsistent or wavering image, or worse, an image that is too big or too small to fit the screen. Motion picture theaters know how important this is to capture the audience's attention, and they have the process perfected to a science. The image completely fills the movie screen, with no white space around the edges or any

Lens	Screen Width			
	60"	**70"**	**84"**	**96"**
2.0"	7.4'	8.6'	10.4'	11.9'
3.5"	13.3'	15.6'	18.7'	21.3'
4.0"	14.8'	17.3'	20.7'	23.7'
6.0"	22.2'	25.9'	31.1'	35.6'
8.0"	29.6'	34.6'	41.5'	47.4'
9.0"	37.0'	43.2'	51.9'	59.3'
12.0"	46.6'	54.0'	64.4'	73.3'

Figure 15-1
Slide Projector (35 mm) Throw Distances

Lens	Screen Width			
	60"	**70"**	**84"**	**96"**
10.5"	5.2'	6.1'	7.3'	8.4'
11.0"	5.5'	6.4'	7.7'	8.8'
11.5"	5.8'	6.7'	8.1'	9.2'
12.0"	6.0'	7.0'	8.4'	9.6'
13.0"	6.5'	7.6'	9.1'	10.4'
14.0"	7.0'	8.2'	9.8'	11.2'

Figure 15-2
Overhead Projector Throw Distances

overflow on the sides or the top. Such problems are resolved by the calculation of "throw distances." As Heinrich Harrer discovered, the length of space between the projector and the screen is the throw distance, consisting of a combination of the projector's lens diameter and the screen width. The charts in Figures 15-1 and 15-2 provide throw distances that should allow your projected images to fill the screen entirely. The *2002 Business Travel Buyer's Handbook* provides some important dimensions you should be aware of, as shown in Figure 15-3.

Emily E. Kresser, a meeting planner for Industrial Research Institute, Inc., located in Washington, D.C., attended a presentation by Nancy DeBrosse of Projection Presentation Technology, and from what she learned, recommends the following considerations for utilizing AV equipment.

- *Rear projection needs a minimum of 20 ft behind the screen and gives a more "professional" look than tripod screens for an insignificant cost increase. A normal dress kit is about half the cost*

- Screen height generally should be the distance from the screen to the back wall divided by 8.
- Chairs should be no closer to the screen than 1.5 times the screen's height.
- Ceilings should be at least 10 ft high.
- A square screen format is ideal for 35mm slides, and a rectangular screen is ideal for video.

Figure 15-3
Dimensions to Consider for AV Requirements

of a screen. Do not put a dress kit on a tripod screen if your speaker is a "walker," as he or she can easily trip. The screen should always be at least 4 ft off the ground.

- *Use 1 ft of screen width for every 8 ft your audience sits away from the screen. Ceiling heights dictate screen size as well.*
- *Use 1 in. of television monitor for every person in the audience. Monitors increase in price as they get larger, so you should probably look at video projection for an audience of 50 or more.*
- *Regarding AV labor costs, do the math before hiring an audiovisual company from out of town or out of house for your meeting. When the labor bill is more than the equipment bill, then use local companies. Watch out for "union" cities and the laws that apply to them. Sunday labor in union cities can require double-time pay. If possible, avoid Saturdays and Sundays as setup days.*
- *Offer to feed the audiovisual crew lunch and other meals so they take less time away from the session and fewer breaks. Let them know that you expect this of them.*

Microsoft's PowerPoint application is the presentation platform of choice for most speakers. The PowerPoint presentation is stored on a computer that is connected to the liquid crystal display (LCD) projector. A laptop is connected to the projector via the monitor port. It is important to note that the projector and any auxiliary devices must be in the "on" position, or connected and initialized prior to connecting the laptop. The projector should also have an "input" port so that the laptop can connect to it. Most computers have a function key that will change the monitor display from *monitor only* to *monitor/projector* to *projector only*. As with any event, rehearsal is key, and it is important to do several dry runs before the meeting commences.

Experienced planners will look to an experienced in-house electrician or in-house audiovisual technician for further clarification or assistance. Troubleshooting highly technical equipment is best left to the professionals. Because computers use electricity and even a long-life battery provides only a few hours of power, your speakers should be instructed to bring their own power cords. Different makes and models have different types of power cords, and you cannot be expected to have a "universal" power adapter for all laptops. Although this may seem like a minor detail, it is a significant risk factor—if presenters cannot run their laptops, they may not be able to give their presentations. In addition, be sure that each presenter brings a backup copy of the presentation on a disk in case there is a malfunction with the computer. Remember, managing details mitigates risk.

What determines the appropriate projector to use? Projectors are classified according to brightness, measured in lumens. A lumen is a unit of measure for the flow of light. In determining the right kind of projector to use, the brighter the better. If your audience is more than 40 people, get a projector with at least

850 lumens of brightness or you will have to turn off all the lights to see what is on the screen. If the presentation requires note taking or reading handouts, turning off the lights will make this nearly impossible. These details become distractions for the audience, which take their attention away from the presentation.

When you are presenting to very large audiences or projecting images that must be seen from very far away, you may consider using an Light Emitting Diode (LED) wall. This is a video display (often seen in ballparks and stadiums) that provides a seamless, large-format video screen that can be seen even in strong sunlight. Typically hung in strips, the LED wall has separated sections by up-lit fabric and designed a combination of several media on the stage, creating a multimedia installation around the wall to add excitement to any event. LED walls have become very popular for rock concerts, for example, to provide a view of the images on stage to those seated at the back of the venue.

Determining Your Audiovisual Requirements

Given the many different types of projection options and technology available, it is important to consider the continuing trend of producing meetings and events that "wow" their guests and the movement towards more highly produced events. Approach these new developments with one thing in mind: *danger! warning!* When your client was sitting in the audience of someone else's event, it looked easy. However, unless that client is in the business, he or she has no idea of the time, energy, patience, technology, and behind-the-scenes people involved in the process, nor does that person realize what it costs.

Analyzing audiovisual needs, developing technical specifications, and putting on a show is a specialization in itself. Event managers who want to play with the "toys" that consist of the basic elements of audiovisual production should consider developing multiple skills that include production, theater, physics, engineering, and weightlifting. Learning to use this equipment requires a highly technical, highly specialized skill set that takes time to master. And, as you might guess, the equipment can be very expensive—not something you would want to "play around with" until you figured it out. This equipment is not self-contained; a laptop requires a projector or an LCD device, which requires a screen. If the venue does not provide all of these elements, someone needs to bring them to the site, and they can be cumbersome and heavy.

According to Frank Beach, president/senior producer, and Benoit Flippen, new media manager and senior programmer, at the video production, satellite teleconferencing, Web and CD-ROM design and development, webcasting firm Beach Associates located in Washington, D.C., determining audiovisual requirements is no different from any other aspect of event management. It follows the same process used in selecting the venue, linens, centerpieces, menu, décor, and orchestra. No matter where your project falls on the scale—from simple to complex—success depends on your accurate analysis of the requirements, as well as making skillful decisions. But how do you get from analysis to execution? Ask yourself if you really want or need to know how projectors are made. Or are you better off seeking the advice of professionals and then delegating these tasks? The following case study presents a hypothetical situation (which may be similar to a situation you encounter in the future) in which you are the event manager, working with a speaker. In this exercise, you are presented with a situation that requires you to make some decisions. Having the tools to make these decisions, however, will require that you gather accurate information, conduct research, and collect data. This information must be analyzed as a first step in determining your requirements. Analysis leads to planning, which determines the production needs.

CASE STUDY

Your client forwards a cryptic e-mail that she received from the keynote speaker who has been hired to speak after the luncheon at an event. Its text is as follows:

RE: AV & TRANSPORTATION: I have graphics to support my talk. I will bring the file on a disk—you supply the computer. I will need an Internet connection. The house lights are to be up full so I can see the faces of the participants. I want three bottles of carbonated Ty Nant spring water at the podium—and don't break the seals. My flight arrives at 10:45. I will need a car to pick me up at the airport. On the way to your venue I must stop at the FOX affiliate for a live interview on its noon news show. Instruct the driver to wait while I am at the station. The driver must also

wait and return me to the airport immediately after I leave the stage. I have a 3:10 departure.

What do you do?

1. Analyze the speaker's request in terms of how it integrates with other AV elements.
2. Develop an A, B, and C version of your flow and risk mitigation plan.
3. Be thankful you do not have to facilitate a book signing for this person.
4. Pray that Murphy is having a busy day at your friendly competitors' events (Murphy's law states that anything that can go wrong will go wrong).
5. All of the above.

The correct answer is 5: All of the above. On its face, this seems to be a relatively easy request to fulfill, and it appears that the details are all there. But can you meet all of these requirements? Do you know what they are? This is an excellent time to introduce a needs analysis that will assess the impact of these requests on the event. For example, a 10:45 A.M. arrival and a 3:10 P.M. departure, with a morning interview and a luncheon talk, does not leave any margin for scheduling errors. Is there enough time to get the speaker to and from the air-port, allowing for traffic problems? This is just one of many questions that should arise from the e-mail. Others are referenced in the following discussion of the needs analysis. The important thing to note here is that in the event entertainment planning industry, nothing is as easy as it sounds and everything that is added to the event becomes an additional planning, risk, and production factor.

Conducting a Needs Analysis

The Convention Industry Council (CIC) defines AV production as accommodating an audience's need to see and hear. Sometimes AV production is simple; sometimes it is not. What your speaker or client calls "AV" needs further clarification. You may think that this person wants an LCD projector and a screen to show his PowerPoint presentation. The client may have something else in mind, which could include an indoor fireworks display. Check to verify how your client defines the term, what her expectations are, and if these expectations will work with her budget.

In each live event you have one opportunity to get it right. Your clients may appreciate you for your successes, but they will remember you for your failures. Every detail has to be perfect, for the entertainment and for every other aspect of production. Be very cautious about taking AV-related requests and requirements at face value. At best, assumptions often lead to unexpected costs. At worst, assumptions can result in a disappointed audience and client— or a showstopper, if the fire marshal shuts you down for a code violation or a minor detail stops the presentation.

The event and meeting planner's role here is much more than collecting AV orders and processing them. It requires critical thinking. It requires listening for what is *not* said, as well as listening to what is said and repeating questions to ensure that you understand every detail. Learn to ask questions like "What did you have in mind?" or "What do you want your audience to see or hear?" For example, suppose a client has decided to use a video projector for a meeting. Is this a simple request? To the client, it involves bringing a video projector into the meeting room. But there is more to it than that for the meeting planner. It can mean additional staff (a technician), lighting and acoustics requirements, seating arrangements, sound checks, and a host of other elements that will increase costs, planning, production, and risk. Almost every request has implications that influence other aspects of the event. Develop a system to analyze what an AV request or requirement means to your overall mission. Ask yourself: What *else* does it mean when a video projector is needed? What other equipment may be required? What impact does this have on the production requirements? Where are the ripples, and can they be accommodated in the budget?

The hypothetical speaker in the preceding case study introduced a series of requests in an e-mail that had been forwarded by the client. The e-mail seemed to provide all of the details with respect to the client's schedule and needs, which did not appear to be too difficult to fulfill. But were they? How many questions can you develop, based on a needs analysis and your knowledge of how to determine requirements? Ask questions such as those shown in Figure 15-4.

It is not a good idea to make assumptions about any of the details of a request. It is better to develop a checklist that includes questions, such as those listed in Figure 15-4, and ask for more detailed information. Not fully understanding the minutiae of a request adds to the event's risk factors and will create problems for you, the planner. The client will not blame the problems on the speaker, who may not have provided sufficient information, but on you, for not being aware of the need to ask more questions.

---

1. Is there any indication that the computer needs to have a specific application (including a specific version) in order for the presentation to play?
2. What kind of computer (PC or Mac) and operating system are required?
3. What type of diskette will the speaker bring?
4. Have you ordered the proper bay for that type of diskette?
5. What is the minimum processing speed required?
6. Where will the computer be set up?
7. Who will operate it?
8. Are there sound files in the presentation?
9. Have you ordered speakers to play the sound files, and do you have the right software on the computer?
10. Are the speakers large enough to accommodate the event's expected attendance or the room size?
11. What is the purpose of the Internet connection?
12. Is a specific type of Internet access required—that is, dial-up, DSL, or high speed?
13. What is the type of microphone preferred?
14. Is there to be a question-and-answer period with the audience after the presentation?

Figure 15-4
Questions to Ask Before Ordering Equipment

Developing the Specifications

Your analysis becomes the basis for a set of specifications detailing what is needed to achieve your client's goals. These specifications are the beginning of the development and eventual implementation of the event plan. Your specifications should be detailed and provide a clear picture of your total needs. Exceptions to the plan are not only costly, but can become impossible to incorporate when the equipment needed to fulfill a last-minute request is not easily available.

Specifications give bidders and suppliers essential details, as opposed to vague instructions. You should not just say that you need a projector and a screen. Rather, saying that the projector, and a ground-supported front projection screen, must, at a minimum, meet the viewing needs of 1000 attendees, the most distant being 80 ft from the screen, allows you and your vendor to plan for the type of projector required, the screen size, and the seating arrangement.

If you want to be specific, say that you need a minimum 4000 lumens XGA projector and a 10.5×14 FP screen. If you really want to impress someone with your knowledge, say that you want a specific make and model number. In this case, you might specify a Barco 6300, but be prepared for your supplier to ask for more money if that particular make is not in inventory. Specifications should include more than just the equipment needed. They should include the time and duration of usage and the labor needed to set up, operate, and remove the equipment.

The schedule for your event is more than a planning tool to determine what everyone will be doing and where they will be during the event. For example, your rental costs for equipment will likely be very different if, in your specifications, you leave out the fact that you are setting up and rehearsing the day before the event requiring the projector. This factor will add at least one extra day of rental costs. The cost will be even more if your supplier discovers that there is no opportunity to break down the projector until after the banquet or gala is over, even though the projector is used only during the luncheon. In other words, think of the whole, not the part.

Your client may require the solicitation of competitive bids for AV services. Even worse, your client may be expecting the quoted cost to be an actual dollar amount instead of an estimate. Help bidders to provide realistic quotes by providing them with comprehensive specifications, accompanied by a detailed schedule and description of your event. Divide your specifications into logical categories, such as projection, video system, audio, and lighting. Ask for line item budgets breaking down labor separately from equipment. Labor quotes should include quantity (number of laborers), number of days or hours, and the rates. Equipment quotes should include quantity, number of days, and rate. Require bidders to list equipment makes and model numbers.

According to lighting designer Mark Butts, it is also important to give the supplier basic guidelines as to how you want the equipment prepped and supplied. Do not assume that all rental houses will supply hanging hardware or that it is included in the price. Moreover, because some companies may supply equipment that was previously used in a rain-soaked outdoor festival or concert tour, be sure to state that dirty, damaged, or poorly functioning equipment will be rejected during load-in and may have to be replaced at the supplier's cost. In the event that a supplier does not have the specific brand of equipment you have requested, make it clear that the supplier must notify you of any substitutions.

Unless you want to spend hours coming up with an apples-to-apples comparison, provide a format for the supplier's quote in a formal Request for Proposal (RFP). See Appendix 7 for an example of this document. The suppliers get points for following directions, and lose points for not following them. There are many benefits to using a formal RFP, including the fact that all bidders are provided with the same information. If you are working with government agencies that have set-asides for minority businesses, an RFP can enable you to make sure that you are providing equal opportunities for all potential bidders.

Evaluate bids on both the bottom lines and the individual parts. Cross-reference individual line items to be sure that bidders have followed the specifications. Look for omissions or line item costs that seem too high or too low. If every bidder has made the same error, there is a flaw in your specifications. If only one bidder is out of range, try to analyze why. You may have found a bargain—or you may have found someone who is cutting corners to win the bid. Do not expect to get the very best if you are paying for the mediocre—and that applies to the equipment as well as the service you receive. If you find that the bids you receive are exceeding your budget, review the specifications; if the budget is too low, go back to the client and let him or her know that the budget cannot fulfill the specifications. The options are to either increase the budget or modify the specifications.

Be very careful in how you describe your event. Some people try to second-guess what you really mean when you use certain words and phrases. Too much embellishment can quickly change your project from a $100,000 event to a $250,000 event. If you have a small budget, do not describe an elaborate event. If pipe and drape is what has been used in the past and the client is happy with it, do not use language that suggests an elegant designed-to-build walled set is expected. Give the bidder some guidance; at a minimum, give a specific estimate of your budget for the event. Phrases in Requests for Proposal that are guaranteed to give false impressions and drive bids into the hundreds of thousands of dollars, perhaps higher than you may be able to afford, include:

"Like the Academy Awards"
"Highly entertaining"
"Highest quality"

"An extravaganza!"
"Premier event"

AV Service Providers

If you are managing a very small, simple event, you may be the AV person. More likely, you will find yourself supervising an AV provider or producer. That person, in turn, manages the small army of specialists who operate the gear and make your event happen. Providers range from the very small to the very large. Some offer a limited or specialized service. Some do it all themselves or contract for the job and then hire their own subcontractors. Try to match providers to your needs, at their previous experience in light of the type of event you are producing and their costs. A large international firm will probably cost more than a local provider, but may have a wider range of expertise and equipment.

Many venues have alliances with AV providers. In exchange for an exclusive or preferential relationship, the in-house service is given status and privileges that do not extend to outside suppliers. Typically, the venue's AV provider pays a commission to the venue for this relationship. Many venues also have work rules that specify who can perform certain services on their property. These rules may specify the number of union-represented workers required for specific tasks and the conditions under which you can supply your own labor.

Because there is not yet a board certifying AV competency, trust is a major issue. In the AV industry there is a tendency for higher-level creative specialists and project managers to build stables of specialists and organizations they know, have worked with before, and can trust in critical situations. Reputation and past performance are the best measure of competence, reliability, and integrity. Event managers face a similar challenge. A supplier may look good on paper, but you will never know how that supplier will perform until it is show time.

How do you assemble a network of competent and qualified AV providers? You can start by finding and befriending an experienced colleague who has many contacts in the area. Ask this person to be your mentor and use his or her first-call list to develop your own network. Meet with the key people on the list and get to know them. Ask for their guidance and recommendations, even when there is no opportunity for them on a specific project. But what if the venue requires you to use in-house suppliers? If the risk factors are high, bring in a trusted provider to help you with the analysis and specification phases. When appropriate, delegate the responsibility for supervising the in-house AV group to your trusted provider. This person can be your eyes and ears in this process and will be acting in a supervisory capacity, even though not actually performing the work.

It is important to match the supplier to the task at hand. For instance, it would be inappropriate to allow a supplier to provide services for 2500 attendees if the largest job that supplier has ever handled involved 250 guests. Although your plan may be flawless, it is the execution that counts, and you must know that your service providers have the know-how and experience to deliver and to meet your client's expectations. Overall, events utilizing AV services can be grouped in two basic categories:

1. Simple meetings and ceremonies, receptions, and breakouts can easily utilize AV providers that are either in-house or independent.
2. For complex meetings, galas, highly produced ceremonies, and outdoor events, look to independent producers specializing in events, staging companies with national reputations, and the national events divisions of the major in-house AV providers.

AV Execution

What is your role, as event manager, in regard to AV production on-site? It depends on what is happening in the event, which depends on all of the planning you did prior to the event. If everyone is having a good day and all is going well, you get a break. You will look into the room occasionally to see that everyone is happy and that the food and beverage services have refreshed the crew's snacks. Other than that you will get to spend your time focusing on all of your other responsibilities. If not, your negotiating skills will be tested as you meet the expectations of your client/speakers/entertainment and the needs of your AV providers. You may have little time left for other concerns. Remember the disgruntled AV crew's hard-hitting mantra: *Your failure to prepare is not our emergency.* Pay attention to the advice of experienced professionals: Take the time needed to do your research.

Execution should be the easiest part of the project. What makes the difference is the preplanning. Although it is safe to predict that you will never have an event with zero on-site AV changes, that should always be your goal. This means you are so well prepared that you have both the time and energy to deal with the changes that are truly unanticipated. This applies to both you and your providers. The effort you put into analysis and developing specifications is rewarded when you are on-site. If your analysis is comprehensive and your specification planning is accurate, you can easily manage minor changes. Periodically review your specifications and schedules, rewriting elements that have changed. Share these revisions with your AV suppliers so that they can be aware of the changes and prepare for them. Encourage and empower your providers to work as a team. It is through your collaborative efforts that the event will proceed smoothly and successfully.

Schedule either a face-to-face or an audio-conference meeting with key department leaders at least one week before any critical milestone associated with everyone's moving to the site of the event. Review responsibilities and requirements one final time to ensure that everyone is aware of his or her obligations. Once on-site and before load-in or setup, meet with the key leaders to conduct a final general review and discuss last-minute changes. Keep leaders apprised of all changes as you learn about them. It is to your advantage to warn them of something that may change. It gives them time to think the issue through and develop a contingency plan. Then, if a change must be made, they can implement it immediately.

Take time to observe. Watch how the crew works. Talk to the crew members so you can develop an understanding of the roles they play and how they work together. Be curious about the equipment. Ask what each piece does and how it integrates with other elements. See how the experience unfolds. Listen to what your attendees are saying. A lot can be learned from overheard conversations.

Conduct a thorough postevent evaluation. After the event, review what worked and what did not work. Involve your key leaders in a meeting to discuss these results. They will welcome the opportunity to participate and can also use the information to their benefit. Turn what you learn into best practices for your next event. Success at fulfilling AV needs comes from a continuous process of tweaking your best practices, studying trends in presentation technology, and keeping a file of trusted suppliers.

What was the result of the follow-up the event manager had with the speaker whose requests were discussed earlier in this chapter in the Case Study on p. 290?

1. PowerPoint would be the default assumption. However, the speaker needed the Director application (assume the speaker will want to make a change on-site or will have forgotten to save the presentation as a player file).
2. PC is the default assumption. Even though the speaker created the presentation on a Mac, Director works on both platforms. However, see the next item (3).
3. Most presentations fit on a CD or 3½ in. floppy. However, this presentation had substantial video and audio files. The speaker arrived with a DVD-RW disc.
4. "Whatever is available" is the default assumption. However, the presentation was designed to run on an Apple G4 with a dual processor.
5. Minimum processing speed would depend on the size of the high-powered video clips, and in this case would be quite high.
6. Most speakers want their computers on stage with them. Not in this case. The speaker did not want to "fool with it."

7. Most speakers want total control of their presentations. Not in this case. The speaker wanted a wireless cue to signal a technician when to advance to the next slide.

8. Not only are there sound files, but the speaker will talk over some of them and expects the audio technician to watch for cues for when to bring the sound clips up and then back under.

9. Real Audio and Windows Media Player are the two most common types of sound software.

10. Speaker size and placement: Only you know how many attendees you expect. This must be communicated to the sound reinforcement technician.

11. The default assumption regarding the Internet connection requirement was that the speaker wanted to make a live demonstration on the Web. In reality, the speaker just wanted to check e-mails while waiting to go on.

12. Learning the hidden agenda about the Internet access requirement revealed that a regular dial-up connection was all that was necessary.

13. The default assumption is that most likely the speaker will stay at the podium and use the hardwired podium microphones. Not in this case. The speaker wants to roam, using a wireless lavaliere for the presentation and a wireless handheld when attendees come to the stage.

14. Yes, there is to be a Q&A. And that is when the speaker wants the lights up on the audience, but not until the presentation is completed.

Webcasting

According to Monte Enbysk, there are two different types of multimedia presentations; videoconferencing and Web conferencing. "Videoconferencing is an interactive use of video, computing, and communication technologies to allow people in two or more locations to meet—either one-on-one or in groups of up to a dozen people or so—without being physically together. Video can be streamed over the Internet or broadcast over television monitors. Web conferencing is videoconferencing without the video—or, put another way, teleconferencing with the addition of the Web for interactive presentations, using PowerPoint, Excel, or other documents. Telephone and/or PC microphones can transmit audio" (Enbysk 2002).

The conference community is getting excited about the many opportunities Webcasting can provide—and rightly so. The following discussion considers some of the pros and cons of Webcasting, as well as issues to consider in deciding when and if a Webcast is right for your event.

Webcasting is simply broadcasting over the Internet (or Web). What do you broadcast? The same elements you would broadcast over other media: audio and video signals. Webcasting provides access to potential attendees who cannot physically attend an event. Webcasting can enable worldwide product launches, with individuals watching the Webcast receiving video and/or audio as it is being sent in real time. It is important to think of a Webcast as a regular broadcast to distinguish it from other ways of accessing on-line audiovisual content. Downloading video is analogous to buying a videotape or DVD in order to be able to view your program of choice—it is less convenient if you need immediate access to the information or if you have storage limitations, and, by its nature, precludes access to live, just-in-time information.

The general requirements and process for a Webcast are similar to those of other broadcasting methods. There is a source, the individual or event that people want to see and/or hear, and there is recording equipment to capture the source. There is special equipment to encode the provided signal into the chosen format and other necessary equipment that the end users must have in order to decode that signal back into the audio and video they are interested in receiving. Finally, as with any other type of broadcasting, the actual transmission of the signal requires certain resources. When you think of it this way, Webcasting should not be a daunting new technology, but a familiar process for which you need only to learn some new terminology.

The main difference between Webcasting and more traditional broadcasting lies in the special equipment needed and the mode of transmission. For your potential audience, the main difference is a positive one: the equipment needed by the recipients to decode the video/audio signal is free. They do not need to own expensive satellite dishes or decoders. As long as they have a computer and an Internet connection, they can get the necessary decoding software at no cost. Your subcontractor, who will provide the Webcast recipients with an Internet link or Website to visit to download the application, will take care of the encoding software requirement. The provider will also handle the details of the signal transmission. Each of these will contribute to the cost of the Webcast, based on available options, which are discussed next.

There are two main types of Webcasting: live and video on demand (VOD). Each has its own specific challenges and rewards. Live has a greater "wow factor." It is the only solution for delivery of just-in-time information. As the name implies, the video/audio signal is streamed in real time and remote viewers watch the feed just as they would a satellite or television feed. Live Webcasting is more expensive and requires more extensive setup and forethought than VOD. VOD is archived content. It is far more economical and easier to set up than live Webcasting. Viewers can fast-forward, rewind, pause, and play back. VOD functions more like a videotape than a live broadcast, so it is available anytime, anywhere. There is less pressure and immediacy in coordinating an on-demand Webcast. There is also less stress for end users if they are experiencing problems receiving the Webcast. The only drawback to VOD is that it lacks the punch and feeling of "having been there," which can be achieved only by experiencing live content.

Why would you want to add Webcasting to your meeting or event? This is the main question that will determine how you will answer all the other questions relating to a Webcast. You will need to consider the answer to this question to determine whether it is worthwhile to invest in the extra resources involved. Keep this question in mind as you consider some of the benefits and potential drawbacks of Webcasting. First, though, how popular is Webcasting? Do people really watch events and performances on the Internet? The following discussion gives examples of this new technology's current applications and popularity.

REAL-LIFE APPLICATIONS OF WEBCASTING

"More than a million music fans around the world watched the Internet broadcast of a Bon Jovi concert in London that kicked off the group's tour. The Sept. 18, 2002, concert at the Shepherd's Bush Empire showcased material from their new album, *Bounce,* and previous hits such as "Living on a Prayer," "Keep the Faith," and "It's My Life." A global audience of more than 375,000 viewed a live Webcast of the performance, but hundreds of thousands were able to watch a recording after the event (*Associated Press,* September 4, 2002). Imagine trying to plan an event such as a rock concert for more than a half million people. Now imagine that event being viewed by people all over the world, at their convenience, many of whom would pay a fee to view the Webcast. What a great way to recapture some of the costs of producing the Webcast!

Webcasting also has an important impact in the business world. Members of the International Association of Conference Centers (IACC) are seeing such a dramatic increase in the use of videoconference facilities that IACC has added a home page link on its Web site to enable planners to find conference centers with on-site teleconferencing capabilities quickly.

> 'When company officials at Eliokem want a potential job candidate in Akron to meet someone at headquarters in France, often no airplanes are involved. Instead, the specialty chemicals business sets up a videoconference session. It gives the job candidates an opportunity to see and talk to key people in France without the company spending thousands of dollars to send people there,' said Communications Manager Valerie Slonsky. Eliokem regularly rents time to use the videoconferencing equipment at the John S. Knight Center, which costs $250 an hour" (Lin-Fisher 2002).

Another interesting application of this technology is to bring groups of people together within a virtual environment. Although they are not physically in the same room, the participants are linked via the Internet and can interact with each other as though they were seated face-to-face. Gartner Group, a technology consulting company, used this tool to help position itself as the premier e-commerce strategist and thought leader. It utilized the services of an event production company, Jack Morton Worldwide, who created Gartner Clarity, a daylong e-commerce panel for 200 executives in New York and a simultaneous Webcast with participants worldwide. By leveraging a traditional case study format to generate ideas for instant action, the Webcast offered a revolutionary new paradigm for positioning business events for far-reaching impact. Led by luminaries including Esther Dyson, Stewart Alsop, and CNBC anchor Forrest Sawyer, live and Web audiences engaged in a dynamic exchange on "clicks and mortar" companies and their impact on the economy. The Webcast offered live audio, video grabs, audience response data, and a Gartner analysts' chat room, and engaged more than 1000 participants from 42 countries. Jack Morton created the event strategy, branding, and a Web site that scored more than 5 million hits, and handled all event production both on-site and on-line.

With the increased technological sophistication of clients and meeting attendees and the acceptance of the Internet as a communications medium, Webcasting may soon become a requirement for event entertainment deliverables, rather than an attractive option. As shown in the preceding examples, it has many creative applications for a variety of events and can add significant value to an event. But you will still need to consider the benefits and drawbacks of Webcasting before you include it in any event you plan.

BENEFITS

The principal benefit of Webcasting is that it allows audience members to participate in an event as if they were physically attending it. Viewer participation is relatively easy, as long as a potential viewer has access to a computer with an Internet connection. The software required to view the event on-line can be obtained free if it is not already installed on the computer. This removes a huge barrier to participation. Even if an audience member does not own a computer, he or she can usually access one, at a public library, for instance, with little difficulty.

Do you want your event to be available to attendees and/or the general public after the event is over? Do you want them to have access to the event's content at any time of day or night, no matter where in the world they are, at any point in the future? On-demand Webcasting can create a low-cost archive of your event and provide added value to attendees. Rather than providing costly paper printouts of notes or requiring attendees to buy videotapes of the presentations, both of which are easily lost or damaged, they can come back to your Web site for a refresher or search out a specific quote that stuck in their memory.

Webcasting can also provide a powerful image boost. If you are marketing your event as being on the cutting edge, leading the field in innovation and exciting new solutions, that image can be underlined with a large heading on your brochure: "The full proceedings will be streamed live over the Web" or

"All content will be archived on-line at our Web site." Not only can this boost your marketing efforts, but announcing that the entire event will be Webcast to your attendees can establish an atmosphere of creativity and excitement and provide them with an opportunity to review the event at a later time. It signals that this is an organization focused on original solutions, rather than rehashing the same tired rhetoric year after year.

A further benefit, and for some the most important, is that Webcasting can provide an additional revenue stream. Those who cannot afford the expense of attending in person can view the full proceedings from their homes or offices for a modest fee. Access to archived content can be granted to attendees as part of their attendance package, and nonattendees or the general public can pay to view it. You need only decide what a reasonable cost is, and what you think people will be willing to pay for access to the content. That is truly a return on investment.

DRAWBACKS: ISSUES TO CONSIDER

There are a number of possible drawbacks, or issues to consider, in deciding whether to provide Webcasting for your event. You need to weigh these against the benefits. The first issue is cost. You need to assess the cost of the type of Webcasting you hope to provide and determine whether your reasons for having a Webcast warrant the cost. You may decide that a less ambitious level of Webcasting is in order, or even none at all.

The second issue to consider relates primarily to live Webcasts. How will you get your signal to your Webcast provider? If you are already broadcasting your event live via satellite, this is not a problem. For television remotes using satellite transmission, you will need to find a clear spot unobstructed by buildings or trees with a wide, clear view of the sky to the south. The site will need power and a path from the meeting room to run the cable to the transmitter or receiver truck. This space must not be actively used by other trucks moving in or out and must not be in the flight path of any nearby airports. Your Webcast provider should be set up to downlink and encode live content from any public satellite network. This is often the preferred mode of picking up your signal. It can also be the most reliable. If you do not have satellite capability and do not wish to make that significant investment, there are other options. You will need to discuss what specific opportunities are available with your streaming subcontractor, which can include fiber broadcast or on-site encoding. Each of these methods requires its own equipment, but your event facility may already be wired for one (either fiber or a high-bandwidth dedicated Internet connection).

The final concern requires some honest self-assessment. Will anyone actually watch the Webcast of your event? Is your subject matter of sufficient broad interest that a significant number of people will take time to view it, even though they are not coming to attend your event in person? If you are spending a large sum of money on the highest-quality live Webcasting and only a handful of people are taking time to watch it, bearing that expense may not be worthwhile. In some cases it may be cheaper to pay for the plane ticket and hotel accommodations of each individual viewer and forgo the Webcast. If you would not consider that as a viable option, then you should think long and hard about whether the intangible benefits of a Webcast are worth the price. Will you really receive a positive return on your investment?

QUALITY AND OTHER ISSUES

Once you have decided to have a Webcast, there are more decisions to make before you hire a subcontractor. The most important decision is about quality. Higher-quality video requires more bandwidth (bandwidth is the amount of information going over a network connection at any given time). However, a large number of Internet users have only limited bandwidth access. Those using dial-up connections to the Internet are limited to 28.8Kb/s (kilobits per second—a standard measure of bandwidth on the Internet), 36Kb/s, or 56Kb/s. Even with the latest code (the software used to encode and decode the video signal), the video image is small and fairly low quality at these bandwidths. Video that is more visually appealing requires bandwidth levels of 256Kb/s and greater. End users will need high-speed access to the Internet via cable, DSL, or faster connections in order to receive this higher-bandwidth video. What is your target demographic? Will most of these people be using modems? If so, and if most of the information will be conveyed via audio, then lower bandwidth video will be acceptable. If the majority of your demographic will have higher bandwidth, then you can provide higher-quality video. Alternately, you can provide both. Many Web sites offering streaming video have separate links for high- and low-bandwidth video. This is the optimal solution, providing the best access to the greatest number of users; however, it costs more. You should determine whether the satisfaction of your potential audience is worth this extra cost.

Another issue to consider is whether to follow the guidelines for Section 508 compliance (note that for any U.S. government-related event, this is required and is not optional). Information on Section 508 compliance can be found at www.section508.gov. This is a requirement that live Webcasts be captioned, and archived Webcasts must either be captioned or have a transcript available for download at the same location as the streaming media link. Live captioning represents an extra cost in Webcast production, but should be considered. One day it may be required for many publicly available events in addition to government-sanctioned ones.

In addition, you should consider whether to provide end user support. No organization producing a satellite broadcast would think of doing so without providing a telephone number to assist end users with problems or other issues. The same level of service is not a necessity for Webcasts, but should be kept in mind. Many potential viewers who are less savvy when it comes to computers can often be pointed in the right direction with a little help, which can generate greater participant satisfaction and a generally higher opinion of your event. Satisfied viewers may even be more inclined to attend future events in person because of your level of professional courtesy. If you are providing a Webcast as a fee-based service, you should definitely be providing support, as it would be dishonest to charge people for a service they are unable to utilize without some basic help. Providing support is, again, an extra cost, and this should be weighed against the many benefits of Webcasting.

Finally, you should consider where the links to the Webcast should appear. Where will users go to access the information? If the links will appear on your own Web site, you will have to set up appropriate links and ensure that the links are in a prominent and easily accessible location. If your subcontractor is providing the jumping-off point for your viewers, be sure that the link provided will not pose too much of a problem for your participants. You should consider linking to this page from your home page as well, to prevent any potential confusion. Regardless, you will need to coordinate with your Web site staff as well as your Webcasting subcontractor.

DEALING WITH YOUR SUBCONTRACTOR

This section should provide you with the basics to communicate with your subcontractor more easily and to make sure that both of you can do your jobs as efficiently as possible. Again, the first thing to think about is cost. In order for your subcontractor to provide you with an accurate price estimate, he or she will need a number of particulars from you. The first is the level of quality you want. Do you want high- or low-bandwidth video, or both? It should not cost any more to encode the video to high bandwidth versus low bandwidth, but it will cost more to encode in both. In addition, you should have a fairly good idea of the number of people you expect to access your Webcast. This factor, combined with the quality level you choose for your video, will determine the amount of expected total bandwidth (total bandwidth used is the sum total of all the information sent out over a network). Total bandwidth or information transfer on the Internet can involve significant costs, and this number will be a strong factor in your final cost of services. You will likely get a number based on expected usage and will be told that any additional usage will be charged at a specific kb/s rate, as shown in Figure 15-5. Charges will vary.

Your streaming provider will build the bandwidth part of your quote based on a price per megabyte (MB) of total bandwidth used. The cost for VOD bandwidth is usually less than the cost of live bandwidth. However, with VOD files, there is also a charge for file storage. This is based on the actual size of the file that your subcontractor must store on their server. The size of the file is equivalent to the amount of bandwidth that would be used by one user viewing your file.

If you are having a live Webcast, you should consider whether to have the live file archived for a period of time so that those who miss the live event can view it at a later time. You should also consider how long you want to keep it archived. Many providers include a month of VOD access after a live Webcast. If you find that a large number of people are accessing your Web site throughout the month, you may consider extending the amount of time you will keep the file available.

Be sure to book your subcontractor's services well in advance, especially if you are having the program captioned. Captioning services require several days of lead time to coordinate with your streaming media provider and to make sure the provider has staff on hand for your event. Get any information you have about the event to your subcontractor as early as possible. It is often helpful to provide him or her with an agenda so that the provider has a sense of the order of events and can more easily anticipate issues as they arise. Providing all of the necessary information early also allows this subcontractor to ensure that he or she will be able to pick up your signal with minimal difficulty.

Once you have taken care of these details, find out from your subcontractor when you will be getting program links and decide what you need to do with them. If you will be linking to a page provided by your subcontractor, you will need to get that link to your Web site staff or developer. This also applies if you will be linking directly to the broadcast; in addition, you should provide any supporting information that should appear on the page with the program links.

Finally, find out from your subcontractor what types of reporting options will be available. At a minimum, you will want to know how many people watched your Webcast. This will help you determine the viability and value of providing this service in the future. Your subcontractor may be able to provide you with much more detailed reports, breaking down usage by day, by hour, and more specific demographic information. You may or may not be interested in this additional detail, but it may yield useful statistics that can help you calculate the return on your investment.

One hour @ 56Kb/s	One hour @ 256Kb/s
Number of users	
1 24.61MB	112.5 MB
2 49.22MB	225.0 MB
10 246.9MB	1125.0 MB
100 2460.94MB	11250.0 MB
1000 24609.38MB	112500.0 MB

Figure 15-5
The Beach Comparison Chart
(Courtesy of Beach Associates)

The basic principle in managing your Webcasting subcontractor, as with any other subcontractor, is that communication is key. The subcontractor should be happy to answer any questions you may have and should feel that he or she can ask you any questions related to the program in order to better serve you. Communicating early and often can help head off any potential problems and reduces the likelihood of inappropriate assumptions by either party.

In Conclusion

The world of event entertainment is changing, as new and exciting technologies present planners with an increasing array of options. Among these options is audiovisual technology that can enhance, or even replace, traditional types of entertainment at events. Webcasting is becoming an important trend in the meeting and event industry. When properly utilized, it can significantly reduce the costs associated with disseminating the content of an event. It can lend a "cutting-edge" mystique to your event that will reflect positively on your organization. As long as you keep a few guidelines in mind, you should be able to make an informed decision in balancing the costs and the benefits of using audiovisual technology and Webcasting for an event. Even if you do not think it is a viable solution at this time, keep in mind that higher bandwidth connections to the Internet are becoming ever more ubiquitous. As the trend continues, high-quality Webcasting will become equally popular. Be sure to keep an eye on this trend and reevaluate the situation periodically so that you will be able to make maximum use of the technology as it becomes more popular and are not left out of this exciting new field of content distribution and event services.

PUBLICATIONS

Lin-Fisher, Betty. *Videoconferencing, Teleconferencing and Webcasting Decreasing Corporate Travel.* First published in the Akron Beacon Journal (OH) on 6/10/02 reprinted by Hotel Online.

Scripts for Future Study

The 2002 Business Travel Buyer's Handbook, published by Business Travel News Magazine.

WEBCASTING RESOURCES

a2zClass—Online learning solution, www.a2zclass.com
Activate, www.activate.net

Akamai, www.akamai.com
Desktop Live, www.desktoplive.com
divine Streaming Solutions, www.divine.com
Eloquent, www.eloquent.com
Eventcom, www.marriott.com/eventcom
Events Digital, www.eventsdigital.com
i-Stream Productions, Inc., www.eventsdigital.com
Laser Webmedia, www.laser-webmedia.com
MediaOnDemand.com, www.mediaondemand.com
Meeting Tech Innovations, www.meetingtechinnovations.com
MeetingCast, www.meetingcast.com
Meetings on the Net, www.meetingsonthenet.com
Money Audio—Audio Interviews with Financial Experts, www.moneyaudio.com
PresentPlus, www.presentplus.com
PRWebcast, www.prwebcast.com
Raindance, www.raindance.com
SeminarSource, www.seminarsource.com
SuccessfulOnlineEvents.com, www.successfulonlineevents.com
Webcast Central, www.webcastcentral.com
WingateWeb, www.wingateweb.com
MCI Conferencing, www.e-meetings.wcom.com

WEB CONFERENCING RESOURCES

Berst Anchor Desk—How to Use the Web for Meetings, www.zdnet.com/anchordesk/story/story_3959.html
Activate Home—Webcasting for the World, www.activate.com
Astound, www.astound.com
Caucus Systems, Inc., www.caucus.com
Centra, www.centra.com
Communicast, www.communicast.net
Conferencing Software for the Web, www.thinkofit.com/webconf
E-Conference Web Based Presentations, www.e-conference.com
EShare, www.eshare.com
Genesys Conferencing, www.genesys.com/na/vialog
iMeet.com, www.imeet.com
Latitude—MeetingPlace, www.latitude.com
Meetings on the Net, www.meetingsonthenet.com
Mshow, www.mshow.com
NetMeeting, www.microsoft.com/windows/netmeeting
PIXION, www.pixion.com
PlaceWare, www.placeware.com
Present on the Net, www.presentonthenet.com

Presentations in Cyberspace—Software Reviews—CNET.com, www.cnet.com/software/0-3227891-8-4730302-1.html

Raindance—Web and Phone Conference Solutions—Training, Seminars, Collaboration, www.raindance.com

WebEx, www.webex.com

MCI Conferencing, www.e-meetings.wcom.com

VIDEOCONFERENCING RESOURCES

www.conferenceglobal.com

Eventcom, www.marriott.com/eventcom

PictureTel—Home Page, www.picturetel.com

TANDBERG, www.tandbergusa.com

Videoconference Resource Center, www.videoconference.com

Exit Stage Right

Chapter 16, "The Future of Event Entertainment and Production," is the last chapter in this book. It explores the trends that you should be aware of in event entertainment and production.

CHAPTER 76

The Future of Event Production and Entertainment

It's a new dawn

—Jefferson Airplane's Grace Slick, introducing the tune "Volunteers" at Woodstock, 1969

IN THIS CHAPTER YOU WILL DISCOVER

- Where the production and entertainment industry is leading us.
- The newest delivery systems for production and entertainment.
- How music can create profits for the hotelier.
- How entertainment can enhance a brand's image.

What is the future of event entertainment? Is this a new dawn? According to the experts, the industry lines will blur to encompass various venues, industries, media, and types of entertainment. The end result will be bigger, better, and more exciting, until its next metamorphosis. Like everything else in today's dynamic world, event entertainment is changing, and it will continue to change to meet customer demands. The event entertainment planners who can stay in touch with the changes, and even anticipate them, are those who will find success.

Yet although some things change, many things stay the same. Certifications and licensing for event planners are signs of professional accreditation and are becoming an increasingly important part of the event planner's resume. Some organizations look for specific certifications when they hire planners. A person who began a career in the industry by organizing entertainment for his or her university should consider entering a certification program to be able to present him- or herself as an accredited industry professional. Certification communicates a certain seriousness about investing time and effort into work at the highest possible level of knowledge and competence in one's field.

Music, and how it is used in event entertainment planning and production, is also changing. Music is an important part of most events and can be present in every aspect of an event, from the headliner to the giveaway bags, to marketing and product promotion. Hotels that include music as part of their marketing plans can increase their profitability, keep guests on the premises, and even attract business from the local community. Music has also become a widely used marketing tool, featuring artists and songs from every generation to appeal to new and older generations of consumers.

2004: An Entertainment Odyssey

For the present, and projecting to the future, there is something to be said about the words spoken by Liza Minnelli in the motion picture *Cabaret,* "Not wisdom, darling, instincts." If you can take those words as advice, tempered with what the Coca-Cola Company writes in its *2000 Annual Report,* then you are well on your way to your future odyssey:

> *The magic of Coca-Cola doesn't come simply from our products and brands. It also comes from the relationships, innovative thinking, and diversity of people who contribute to the fun, energy, and success of Coca-Cola every day. Reaching out, extending boundaries and finding common bonds are part of the real magic of Coca-Cola. That's as true today as it ever has been.*

As rapidly as change seems to occur in the world today, predicting trends may appear to be almost impossible. However, we can look at certain trends, starting in the not-too-distant past, to learn what may happen in the future. The following discussion addresses a number of changes that will likely affect the production and entertainment industry: an increase in certifications, credentialing, and licensure; a change in the structure of traditional entertainment companies; an increase in the cost of entertainment; the addition and removal of entertainment venues; a trend of reinventing traditional entertainment ideas, and an increased focus on outsourcing and globalization.

CERTIFICATION

The first gathering of the International Special Events Society (ISES) in New York City was in the fall of 1987 at Lincoln Center. Philadelphia was the first city to be given a charter, followed by the New York Metro area a few weeks later. Since these first gatherings of "special event professionals," the people who have defined the entertainment and production industry have elected to voluntarily raise the bar. Following in the footsteps of many other professional organizations, they created a professional designation. With its first examination in the summer of 1993 in Toronto, Canada, the Certified Special Event Professional (CSEP) certification was established. The CSEP is similar to the CPA or other industry certifications that are used to achieve consistency and high standards among professionals. The first CSEP recipients had a vision for the industry that included establishing enforceable standards, a code of ethics, and a resource for sharing ideas and experiences.

Why is this important? According to Richard Aaron, CMP, CSEP, adjunct professor at New York University and president of BiZBash in New York City,

Certifications are counting more and more as professionals are seeking their place in the credentialed spotlight. Meeting Professionals International's (MPI) successful new Certified Meeting Manager (CMM) outpaces the Certified Meeting Professional (CMP) designation as proof of this trend, as planners seek strategic skills as a key to enhanced recognition in the job arena. Institutions are establishing more positions for credentialed event managers, as witnessed by the increased number of students studying event management in universities and educational institutions across the world. Hospitality and event management programs are also on the increase in cities across the world. They are opening the door to formal event studies programs, which is qualifying the knowledge of young future professionals with a needed base and thirst for knowledge in this area.

Jerry Wayne, Meeting Professionals International's (MPI) 2001–2002 chairman of the board, says, "When you possess a CMM or CMP designation, you are immediately considered an expert—one that can be trusted and depended upon to do the right thing for the right reason" (Wayne 2002). According to Mary Power, president and CEO of the Convention Industry Council (CIC), the certifying body behind the Certified Meeting Professional (CMP) designation: "If you want to apply for a Convention Services Manager position at Mohegan Sun Hotel and Casino or at Conferon, you better not leave home without your CMP, as this is a mandated qualification for seeking a job at these companies.

About 80 percent of the job descriptions in this industry are 'CMP Preferred,' meaning the successful candidate will be looked at more favorably if he or she has a professional designation." Power reports that there are approximately 8000 CMPs globally. That number will rise by at least 1700 in 2003 as the program expands internationally.

Although neither guaranteeing a successful career nor showing your level of proficiency, professional designations can illustrate that you have dedication and experience in the industry. It also indicates that you have recognized areas of core competence and have fulfilled certain requirements of your profession. Figure 16-1 shows some of the designations available in the entertainment and production industry and their corresponding Web site addresses, where more information is available.

Once you have decided to become certified, it is important to understand exactly what your credential means. There are three credential types:

1. A *license* is a legal document you need to practice certain professions or occupations.
2. A *certification* is a document stating that you have met certain competency requirements.
3. *Registration* is the formal act of registering your personal information and professional or occupational qualifications with an agency.

Certifications for entertainment or production event professionals vary by state. Certification is voluntary, but those who are certified have a competitive edge. Why would you want to be licensed or credentialed? Completing a credentialing or licensure program in your field can enhance your professional identity, boosting your credibility and making you more marketable.

THE CHANGING STRUCTURE OF ENTERTAINMENT COMPANIES

Mergers and acquisitions that allow companies in many industries to diversify their business interests are also prevalent in the entertainment and production industry. Maggie Overfelt gives examples of how famous rock stars have started sideline businesses reflecting their interests. She describes how these musician/entrepreneurs have created success in another field based on their famous names. From 2Dre and Big Boi to Ted Nugent and Sammy Hagar, these people love to work and love to play and have the money to follow through and create successful businesses from their passions.

The world's largest music agency, William Morris, acquired Premier Talent Agency in 2001. "Premier is one of the most respected talent agencies in the music industry because of its approach to the business and the success it has achieved," said Peter Grosslight, senior vice president and worldwide head of William Morris Agency's music division. Morris saw this acquisition as a way for it to enter this market and generate immediate results, building on Premier's client base, name, and goodwill.

Acronym	Title	Issuing Organization	Requirements for Certification
CSEP	Certified Special Events Professional	International Special Events Society	Professional experience and academic examinations. Web site: www.ises.com
CMP	Certified Meeting Professional	Convention Industry Council	Professional experience and academic examinations. Web site: www.conventionindustry.org
CMM	Certification in Meeting Management	Meeting Professionals International	After acceptance, candidates must participate in an MPI learning group using technology, attend a 4.5 day residency program with participation in a group case study, take an individual examination, and complete a business project. Web site: www.mpiweb.org/education/cmm/.
CPPM	Certified Planner of Professional Meetings	International Meeting Professionals Association	Applicants must meet these minimum standards: membership in two professional organizations, documented attendance in 12 seminars relevant to meeting planning, and documented attendance in 3 conferences relevant to meeting planning. Applicants must then pass an exam. Web site: www.cimpa.org
CIMP	Certified Internet Meeting Professional	International Meeting Professionals Association	Applicants must have one of the following designations: CCM, Certified Planner of Professional Meetings (CPPM), CMP, CMM, Certified Association Executive (CAE), Certified Exhibition Manager (CEM), CSEP, CPPM, CGMP. These criteria will be waived for planners with at least five years' experience. Web site: www.cimpa.org.
CGMP	Certified Global Meeting Planner	International Meeting Professionals Association	Applicant must have a minimum of two years' experience in meeting management and three international meetings for which he or she was responsible. Web site: www.cimpa.org

Figure 16-1
Industry Certifications

Mergers and acquisitions do not always have positive results or generate goodwill. As a result of a variety of mergers and acquisitions, Clear Channel Entertainment (CCE) continues to be the subject of a low-key probe by the U.S. Department of Justice for possible antitrust violations. On July 9, 2001, Congressman Robert Andrews (D-New Jersey) drafted a letter to U.S. Attorney General John Ashcroft, formally requesting an investigation of Clear Channel. Andrews says, "Some constituents came to me who are in the [concert] business and said they are concerned that one company is cornering the market. They are freezing out the competition. I do not know whether they are right or wrong. But my job is to take credible questions that are raised and ask the proper authorities to answer them."

"The entire business knows there has been this ongoing investigation," said Jesse Morreale, co-owner of Denver-based Nobody in Particular Presents concert promotions. "We have had discussions with Justice along with everyone else." Clear Channel Entertainment spokesperson Rachel Gary said, "Currently, we are not aware of any ongoing investigation." "At first glance, I think they have a pretty compelling argument," Andrews continued. "It appears if you want to do a national tour, you don't have a lot of choices, given the venues that SFX and Clear Channel control. There are some valid questions whether antitrust laws have been violated."

Why is this important to the meetings and events industry? Stanley Aaronson, CSEP, project manager at Mark Sonder Productions in Los Angeles, explains, "We [MSP] wanted to buy Cher for a corporate event. Instead of going through our 'normal' channels, we were at the mercy of CCE to buy the act." The constant shifting of ownership and structure of entertainment and production companies will have a great impact on how business is conducted in the future.

CHANGING VENUES

Entertainment and production professionals constantly seek ways to create new entertainment experiences for their clients. One method of doing this is to use different types of venues to present entertainers, thereby creating new and different experiences for the patrons. The following are a few examples of the changing uses of venues across the United States.

Meanwhile, on the Political Front . . .

Whereas most candidates for major political offices have election night headquarters at hotel ballrooms, New York's Republican mayoral candidate Michael Bloomberg utilized the BB King Blues Club & Grill on West 42nd Street for his festivities.

Rebuilding for the Future

Los Angeles's Wiltern Theatre is about to undergo a $2 million renovation by Clear Channel Entertainment. The 2200 capacity venue will probably look more like San Francisco's Warfield Theatre upon completion, with the orchestra seats yanked out in favor of tables and chairs and a dance floor. The ultimate goal is to attract more private affairs organized by meeting and event professionals.

Ending in Los Angeles

The 1800-seat Shubert Theatre is ending its 30 years in Los Angeles. The theater, along with the ABC Entertainment Center, will be razed to make room for a 15-story office building. As one of L.A.'s premier theaters since 1972, the Shubert was home to many of the longest-running theatricals in the city.

Starting in New York City

The Julie Wilson Room, named after cabaret singer Julie Wilson, is New York's newest cabaret. Located at the Hideaway Restaurant (32 West 37th Street), also the home of the Red Blazer II, the upstairs club will have a Thursday–Friday schedule. Event regular Wilson will probably perform in her namesake room three times a year, including New Year's Eve. Future bookings include Lainie Kazan, Tom Wopat, Amanda McBroom, Wesla Whitfield, Kristin Chenoweth, and Mark Murphy.

New Home

After a four-year absence, the most requested entertainer at Rodeo Houston will return. George Strait headlined the March 3, 2002, concert that marked Rodeo Houston's final performance in the Reliant Astrodome. The full-length concert was the culmination of a farewell party celebrating the 37 years Reliant Astrodome had served as the home of Rodeo Houston.

OUTSOURCING AND GLOBALIZATION

Availability, attrition, consolidation, technology, standardization, outsourcing, and globalization are the seven critical megatrends that will shape the future of the meetings industry. How do these trends affect the entertainment experience? A few years ago, few entertainment superstars were willing to perform at private functions such as corporate, association, and incentive events. Now, in the early 2000s, everyone is jumping on the bandwagon. The same metamorphosis happened in the TV and radio commercial industry years ago. At that time headline entertainers were not interested in performing or in having their music on a commercial advertising soundtrack. Today, the Rolling Stones, Aerosmith, Britney Spears, and Michael Jackson, to name a few superstars, have all found a new distribution channel that translates into a new line item on their income statements. A few million people hearing their music on commercials translates into more CD and concert ticket sales, not to mention the revenues from licensing and distribution royalties.

From an events perspective, this has increased the booking prices for these entertainers. Although the audience at private events is significantly smaller, numbering in the hundreds at a meeting, convention, or trade show, costs can be two to five times the amount of a public date. And there are significant promotional restrictions, which include no public advertising and no release of photographs, even in local newspapers. The entertainer's time and effort will have almost no impact at the retail record stores or at the local Ticketron. Hence, the purchaser of the entertainment experience will be paying more for the entertainer to give a private showing of his or her talent. Of course, the entertainer will not get any percentage of the ticket sales, as this is a private date. Although there will always be entertainers who do not want the word out on the street to their fans that they have sold out, an increasing number of entertainers are moving toward the corporate stadium of performance (*Update Meetings,* 2001).

Delivery Systems for Production and Entertainment Tomorrow

A captured moment of spontaneous creativity is worth more than a thousand hours of computerized perfection.
—*Liner notes for the Led Zeppelin CD BBC Sessions*

A look at what is happening now in the realm of entertainment delivery systems can give an idea of what will be happening tomorrow. As the preceding quotation implies, many involve the use of new technologies in delivering entertainment, while maintaining the creative element of the various art forms.

Composer, big band leader, pianist, and actor Harry Connick Jr. is an inventor as well. This living version of the late Frank Sinatra received a United States patent for a "system and method for coordinating music display among players in an orchestra." Just prior to Connick's departure for Salt Lake City, where he performed "Over the Rainbow" for the closing ceremonies of the Winter Olympics, he commented, "It basically eliminates old-fashioned sheet music." His patented idea came to him one day several years ago when his big band was playing outdoors and the sheet music was blowing around. Why not, he thought, have all 16 band members read their music from computer screens instead? So before he started a long tour in 1999, Connick bought enough blue-and-white G3 Power Macs, each with a rotatable screen, so that everyone—from his trombonists to his drummer—could read from electronic sheet music. For technical advice he turned to his neighbor David Pogue, a former Broadway conductor and computer guru to the stars. Now when the house and stage lighting is dimmed, Pogue says, all the audience sees of the other musicians is "this super-cool bluish glow on their faces from the computer screens" (Riordan 2002).

You have already heard your favorite tunes and artists live again. They are now living under the guise of rap music. Rappers, although having the message clearly defined in their minds and words, are and will continue to look at other music for their groove, their rhythm, their spirituality, their 'tude. This symbiotic relationship between two prerecorded media (the sampled covered music and their hip-hop groove) is helping define the music of our present and our future. Run-D.M.C., L.L. Cool J, and Snoop Doggy Dog have all explored the music of George Benson, Bob James, Mr. T (Stanley Turrentine), and the late Grover Washington Jr. Steely Dan has brought this groove-driven rhythm into their rock idiom, a sort of rock-fusion. Even Fat Boy Slim and the Beastie Boys have used sampling in their brand of music. Tribe 1, from Los Angeles, California, among others, continues to explore mating the future with the past as its trio consists of a female deejay with live percussion and guitar. This is truly the best of all worlds. It has been playing the corporate circuit throughout the country and in Mexico (Considine 2002).

> *Wearable devices are being developed to create music; some are simply electronic versions of traditional instruments, but others include motion-sensing devices that translate gestures into music and sensors that generate sound based on body movement. Such devices could allow the crowd at a disco to shape the beat or let a ballerina's feet create music as well as the dance. One goal of many researchers is moving music-making into new settings. Professional musicians and performance artists are exploring interactive technologies in search of new areas of expression. (Bhattacharjee 2001).*

As meeting planners have already discovered, on-line registration and ticketing has become a popular and convenient way for attendees, individual event ticket purchasers, and concert goers to purchase tickets without leaving home. In some cases they are also given a chance to view the angles from available seats by downloading a photograph from the Web site. Ballena Technologies has gone even further to assist these buyers by developing Seats 3-D, a computer-generated model with a three-dimensional feel for the seats the registrants have purchased.

There are also some companies that are trying to redefine the traditional distributor model for ticketing that is utilized by ticketing giant TicketMaster. For example, the ticketing company Paciolan has developed a system that allows venues to control their ticket distribution. It automates the ticket selling process by allowing transactions to be made on-line and implements a system that rewards repeat customers. With each additional purchase, the customer receives higher preference from the venue, in the form of advance notification and purchasing opportunities and better seats. This increases revenues for the venue and generates customer loyalty. In the future the system may also allow for on-line ticket exchanges and on-line donations to the organization, again rewarding the customer for these transactions. This type of new thinking about the ticketing process and the ways in which the Internet can increase revenues will be a key factor for any organization that derives its revenues from ticket sales (Kleinberger 2002).

"Music Makes the People Come Together" is a tune by Madonna. If we are going to examine delivery systems for hiring headline entertainment, nobody does it better than the Material Girl. Yes, Madonna, in her Drowned World Tour, created a live and multimedia set for her audiences for all live, acoustic, electric, and video hookups, backed up by Webcasting on the Internet.

In her show, Madonna included the following:

- Complex cueing and scripting
- Cartoons
- Nunchucks
- Folk and country music, in addition to the trailblazing music from the last two decades
- Erotica
- A rebroadcast on a major cable network
- Fire and ice
- Multilingual and multicultural elements
- A teleprompter, though it was invisible to the audience
- Wireless everything
- A mixture of orchestral textures
- A mixture of "cirque" performers
- Exaggerated clothing, hair, rings, and wigs
- Hard edge and attitude
- Live music combined with video stage show
- A tight, well-rehearsed performance
- Use of all sides of the venue, including the ceiling
- World music, Asian fusion, and world instruments
- Voice decoders
- Violent acts acted out on stage
- Industrial-sized fans on stage for cooling the temperature and wind-blown hair
- Stage monitors as part of the décor
- Ballet music

This show was performed in her hometown of Detroit. When you want to look carefully at what will wow your attendees, study Madonna.

The Internet broadcasts sounds as well as images. In addition to putting their merchandise for sale on the Internet, retailer Web sites have developed "Web" radio to help set the right tone, atmosphere, and mood for the customer. For example, Polo Radio is available on the Polo Web site for the company's customers' listening and shopping pleasure. Of course, the type of music it plays reflects the Polo brand and is different from the music featured on Old Navy Web radio. This is an attempt by retailers to create a more rounded shopping experience and to alleviate the isolation factor associated with Internet shopping.

David Cerone, president of the Cleveland Institute of Music, writes on the institute's Web site, "Music is frequently a means to convey great joy or sorrow. As its own unique language, it can be the only way to express the emotions which are often thrust upon us." As ambassadors of music, the Cleveland Institute of Music offers a guide to help listeners find solace in the power of music at www.cim.edu. This listening guide has been created to share the music many people turn to for inspiration. In times of stress, we seek something bigger, something to which we can relate in our own way. We turn to music to express what words often cannot.

Music and Profits for the Hotelier

Hotels will play an increasingly important role in the event entertainment industry, and music will be an important component of that process. Hotels feature music at their properties to fulfill a number of goals:

- Provide atmosphere and call attention to the property
- Bring in new and different business than that normally attracted to the property and translate that business into increased food and beverage revenues
- Provide better customer service to their clients.

The following discussion explores these three goals and gives examples of how to use music and other entertainment options to achieve them.

When thoughtfully coordinated with a hotel property's goals and marketing strategies, music can boost guests' contentment level and generate significant food and beverage sales revenues. Like the well-selected carpet, artwork, and staff uniforms, music plays a significant role in a hotel's décor. Music can be used to distinguish a hotel from its competition. It can make guests feel appreciated, cared for, and at home.

Choosing the music style best suited to a property involves some basic marketing research. Start by identifying the target market and evaluating its demographics. Ask questions to discover where its constituents are from, age, gender, and level of education. Then consider the image you want to project—sophisticated and elegant, or trendy and upbeat? Are you trying to create a mood of serenity or excitement? Finally, determine the type of business you are trying to attract. Do you want guests to linger, or are you hoping to quicken the turnover in your restaurant? Once you have established your goals, a local professional music company can provide valuable assistance in selecting the ideal musical accompaniment for the lobby, lounge, and restaurant. It can also provide recommendations regarding the lighting, placement, attire, and speaker systems that will best enhance the desired mood and image.

Hotels located in a metropolitan area will compete with many venues for their guests' leisure time. To compete with these other options, a restaurant or bar must have personality in addition to a pleasant atmosphere. The right musicians can make the lounge an exciting destination in and of itself, not just a place for the guest to have a drink before going out to explore the city.

What can a property do to keep its guests from leaving the premises and investigating what the host city has to offer? It might consider offering entertainment that will be popular with the community, such as a cabaret room or a comfortable bar with live entertainment. With live music, people are more alive, and instead of ordering one drink and leaving, a customer is invited to relax and unwind and, ultimately, to become aware of other people in the room. This generates social or business networking and keeps guests at the bar, buying drinks. Although this strategy may not generate as much income for a hotel as room sales, it will yield significant beverage sales, and the property's bar may become the "go to" place in the community, attracting both guests and local people.

Make the music fit the objectives. Musicians who perform for 40 minutes on the hour and play with a sense of urgency may be the suitable choice for a quick turnover, such as during brunch service. Long and slow ballads may have customers eating more deliberately. When the dining experience is the entertainment for the night, the hotel restaurateur must keep the customers happy throughout the evening. Fine cuisine, fine service, fine linens and cutlery, and fine visual décor are enhanced when accompanied by fine music. This means a selection of music that can be prepared specifically to meet these objectives, with, of course, fewer breaks.

Most hoteliers will agree that it is more effective to increase the productivity and profitability represented by a current guest or client than to try to find a new one. The challenge lies in providing the services that go above and beyond the guest's expectations. The engagement of live music is an often overlooked tool you can use to enhance both service and profitability for rooms, food, and beverage sales.

Hotels, while having the responsibility of attracting guests to their properties, should exceed the service expectations of today's customer. Arrange the optimum sensory perception package! This is essential to a hotel's success. It takes more than just putting musicians in a corner and asking them to play music to set the tone or complement the setting. Assist them with their live aural décor by organizing a package deal. Theatrical lighting plays an important aesthetic role in revealing colors, shading, and ambiance with tracking, pin spots, gobos, fresnels, or lekos. Lighting can immediately focus the audience's attention and can be animated to excite the viewer and listener.

Music is sound. Your equipment and sound quality are important. A person can hear only by listening directly to the music (acoustic sound) or by hearing the music amplified. Speakers, mixing boards, microphones, and amplifiers are prerequisites. Amplitude, tone, style, entertainment, distortion, and background all play a major part in preparation for the specific sound you need. Keep in mind the importance of visual finesse and placement of the equipment. For example, a major downtown New York venue, brought down on 9/11, had the house speakers lodged in palm trees. Today's audiences are accustomed to listening to state-of-the-art audio technology.

In *On-Premise Catering: Hotels, Conventions Conference Centers, and Clubs,* authors Patti Shock and John Stefanelli suggest you should;

> *"Include bands and other musical entertainment as part of your banquet package. When the meeting or event planner is in the mood to sign on the dotted line, sell a package to include food and beverage, music, and entertainment. The "outside" vendors are booked through the property at a commissionable rate to the property, thereby creating a line item on the income statement for that event for the hotel. If the hotels are making a 15 percent margin from outsourcing the entertainment for the clients, it will be good for both the hotel and the planner, who now does not need to be concerned about this element of his or her event (Shock and Stefanelli 2001)."*

Both hotel employees and event planners who use hotels should be aware of such entertainment possibilities for these venues. For hoteliers, this kind of entertainment can significantly increase revenues and make their properties more attractive to large corporate and association group business. For event planners, having built-in entertainment in a hotel is a major benefit, as it keeps the attendees entertained and potentially reduces the actual costs of entertainment.

How Entertainment Can Enhance Your Brand's Image

> *Miramax spends a fortune. And the people over at DreamWorks run a campaign like they've got a candidate in the New Hampshire primary.*
>
> —Tom Ortenberg of Lions Gate Films,
> on campaigning for Oscar nominations

Marketing is a big business, as the preceding quotation implies, and every event planner must thoroughly examine the marketing elements of an event in order for it to be successful. Major marketers and media often stage lavish events to meet consumers face-to-face, but a company of any size can take advantage of face-to-face events if it provides enough reasons for people to attend. In the business-to-business sector, it is possible to reduce costs for travel, selling, and trade shows with regional events that give buyers a reason to show up. Such gimmicks as hiring a well-known retired athlete, holding the event in a desirable dining or entertainment venue, focusing on providing objective information on a subject related to your product or service, or bringing in experts to address critical issues related to your industry, can all help in attracting attendees to the event and therefore building the brand image.

Marketers with an eye for muscular promotions are turning increasingly to the entertainment industry for solutions. There are many promotional options available in the industry, and entertainment is highly effective in reaching consumers of any age, ethnicity, or income level. Entertainment is unique in its ability to transcend lifestyle categories, providing marketers with the ability to saturate a targeted demographic group at work, rest, and play, often over a period of many months. The export strength of American entertainment products often makes them ideal vehicles for building brand identity overseas through tie-ins, and because of the extended life provided by TV reruns, movie video rentals, and concert films, entertainment can be the marketing gift that keeps giving for years to come. There are many promotional opportunities available that use entertainment, and sorting them out is a critical first step in determining which will work best. Among the most important marketing opportunities are the following:

- *Product placements.* Utilizing motion pictures, television, and Broadway to display products in a variety of settings.
- *Event sponsorship.* Corporate tie-ins have become a staple of superstar concert tours, mainly because corporate partnering was the only way to make concert tours profitable. Marketers of products as diverse as soap and salad dressing witnessed sales gains of 52 to 1454 percent as a result of these sponsored events.
- *Co-pack promotions.* There has been an increase in coupons and special offers featured on video movies. They are used in both video sales and rentals, with such companies as Blockbuster Entertainment increasingly using their boxes to sell advertising.
- *Direct-to-consumer promotions.* Top movies and music hits are available to marketers for a number of consumer promotions, including on-pack offers, sweepstakes, and premiums.
- *Customized CDs and tapes.* Given the enormous music catalogs owned by major record labels, marketers have little trouble finding selections with special appeal for a given demographic group. These can be customized music collections on a CD or audiotape that are made available under the sponsor's logo or brand. An example of this strategy is to purchase the headline entertainment's CD prior to an event, have it autographed, and add it to guest gift bags, with the corporate logo on the cover.
- *Gift certificates.* One of the easiest ways to take advantage of entertainment's appeal is through gift certificates, which are widely available for

everything from CDs to movie rentals. Certificates are ideal for incentive awards, contest prizes, and gifts, and they can be used effectively as part of an integrated promotional approach.

- *New media.* There are an increasing number of ways in which marketers can take advantage of new media such as interactive CDs, video games, and even entertainment offerings on the Internet. One way is to advertise on the products themselves. For example, when Creative Multimedia released the interactive CD-ROM *Golf Digest's Best Places to Play,* it interspersed ads from three companies throughout the presentation. The advertisers, one of which was diamond syndicate DeBeers, thus got exposure plus the chance to provide detailed product information to those viewers who chose to click on the appropriate icons in the ad.

The entertainment industry is a maze of fiefdoms interconnected through corporate ties. For example, today's entertainment conglomerates own movie studios, record companies, TV syndicators, and publishing companies, and some have even formed their own multimedia divisions. Each area of the entertainment business has its own distinct culture. Thus, for the uninitiated, negotiating an integrated promotion involving, for example, movies, music, and publishing, can be difficult. Even when dealing with a single company in the United States, there can be numerous parties on both the East and West Coasts who are each responsible for a particular aspect of your promotion. For simple things, like gift certificates, all it may take is a call to a division's special products department. But for cross-media promotions, the services and expertise of a specialized entertainment promotion agency may be required.

TIPS FOR SUCCESS IN USING ENTERTAINMENT PROMOTIONS

Linking a promotion with some sort of entertainment requires special skills and an understanding of which media are best equipped to boost your product or service. Here is some basic advice from Selling Communications, Inc.:

- *Work with professionals.* More than one otherwise savvy marketer has been sold a bill of goods when he or she tried to catch a promotional ride in the entertainment industry. That is why it pays to work with a promotion or advertising agency in conjunction with a corporate entertainment company that knows how to fit your products or services with the right media options. Experienced pros will know how and with whom they should negotiate to get you the best results.
- *Make the right fit.* Entertainment promotions work best when the product fits the demographic profile of the attendees and the creative content of the entertainment product.
- *Get the right kind of exposure.* Always check out the context in which the entertainment product is to be featured. There is often a conflict of interest in the entertainment industry between, on one hand, those

exercising their creative freedom (such as filmmakers or musicians) and, on the other, executives trying to cover the growing cost of production. For marketers looking for product placements and other tie-ins, the rule is: Do not get caught in the middle. For instance, it will not help the sales of your car if the hero cannot start the product during a critical scene in the movie. Beware of any deal in which you do not have satisfactory control over how your product, corporate identity, or reputation is to be represented.

- *Build synergy with an effective cross-media strategy.* Using the right mix of targeted entertainment media options can put added muscle into your campaign.

MUSIC AND ENTERTAINMENT AS MARKETING TOOLS

Music and entertainment have been an integral part of the human experience since the dawn of civilization. Although marketers were quick to inject music and entertainment into TV and radio commercials, it was not until the arrival of the CD that they recognized its potential for sales promotion. In the last few years companies have discovered inventive ways to cash in on the power of this medium. They have learned that music and entertainment may be used effectively as a tool to

- Promote events
- Reward customers
- Increase sales
- Introduce new products
- Recognize employees
- Enhance brand image

There is no denying music's popularity. In the last decade, the overall size of the U.S. sound recording industry has nearly doubled. According to data from the Recording Industry Association of America (RIAA), manufacturers shipped $7.541 billion worth of product, including cassettes, CDs, LPs, and singles, in 1990. By 1999, this figure had climbed to $14.584 billion. The RIAA study shows sales by year, type of music sold, age of purchaser, gender, and where purchased. Its year-end numbers represent data from companies that distribute approximately 90 percent of the prerecorded music in the United States.

Contributing to the growing popularity of music is the proliferation of modern sound systems, such as home theater systems and portable CD players, not to mention the prevalence of CD players in home and office computers. All have made quality music more accessible. Clearly, marketers who overlook music when they plan their promotions are missing a good promotion and income source. Although the tracking firms do not compile statistics on the growth of music as a promotional item, industry sources note that there have been significant sales increases in recent years (Heide 2002).

WHY MUSIC FOR YOUR MEETING OR EVENT?

If you have been trying to connect with your customers or attendees, music just might help you tune them in to your message. Although live music costs more than some traditional promotional items, such as deejays, the ability to connect on a personal level with customers has marketers excited. High perceived value and long shelf life are just two of the reasons that giveaways of music CDs are making them big items in the promotional market. Here are just a few of the reasons music is attractive to marketers:

- *It is versatile.* Live music can be used anywhere a traditional giveaway item such as a baseball cap, mug, pen, or T-shirt can be used.
- *It has a high perceived value.* To hear, to see, to meet a headline entertainer maintains a high perceived value for most attendees.
- *It creates an emotional connection to customers.* People closely identify with music. A certain song, for example, can evoke pleasant memories and helps to create a favorable product tie-in.
- *It is a powerful motivator.* John Penn, vice president of marketing for Sony Music Special Products, says, "Just turn on the radio or TV or go to a movie. You will see that music is everywhere. When you bring music and entertainment into your [event's] promotion plans, you add a unique mix of power and effectiveness for reaching your objectives, whether it is driving traffic, selling more products, rewarding employees and customers, or establishing a bond with your customers."

Promoting Events with Music and Entertainment

There are countless ways that marketers incorporate music and entertainment in their promotional campaigns. Using music to boost attendance at your trade show booth or at special events can be very useful. Here are some tips:

- *Target your audience.* Use live music and entertainment to connect your message, image, or theme to a chosen demographic group.
- *Before the show.* Use mailers, ads, door hangers, and inserts to attract prospects with the promise of a headline entertainment.
- *During the show.* Secure leads, extend booth visits, and generate traffic for future shows by offering a selection of entertainment such as magicians, tarot card readers, jugglers, and clowns.
- *After the show.* Follow up with attendees at a hospitality suite, and include live entertainment. Many suites already house a baby grand piano; do not just use it as a piece of fine furniture; utilize its full musical and

customer-related potential. A less expensive approach is to utilize music CDs. Pepcid AC used a music CD to encourage people to visit its booth at a trade show in New Orleans. The CD, entitled *Music of the Big Easy,* contained such hot-and-spicy numbers as "Basin Street Blues," "When the Saints Go Marching In," and "Louisiana Twilight." Not only did the CD increase booth traffic, but the selections increased awareness of the benefit Pepcid AC promises. Following the success of *Music of the Big Easy,* an additional CD, *Salsa Music,* was created.

MUSIC CDS AS A PROMOTIONAL TOOL IN STRENGTHENING BRAND IMAGE

A gift to valued customers shows you appreciate their business and creates goodwill. For example, Shell Oil has used music premiums successfully for many years. Its line of large-truck lubricants has a strong following with high levels of repeat purchase. A program was designed to reward loyal commercial trucking customers of Shell's Rotella line of lubricants. Three cassette volumes were produced for this program. They featured 30 hit songs (10 per cassette) from such country music superstars as Alan Jackson, Clint Black, Lorrie Morgan, and Martina McBride. The result was that sales increases of more than 20 percent were reported during the promotional period. More than 200,000 cassettes of each volume were distributed.

Offering a free CD with a specified level of purchase can boost sales of most any product. For example, Delia's, a New York City-based retailer catering to trendy female buyers aged 12 to 21 years old, offered a free CD with a purchase of $75 or more. This gave Delia's an opportunity to boost sales as well as introduce new, developing artists to their customers. Sony Music Special Products has produced six volumes (75,000 CDs in each volume) for this ongoing series. The music, selected especially to appeal to Delia's customer base, included such songs as "Rollercoaster" (B*witched), "She's So High" (Tal Bachman), "If I Was a River" (Tina Arena), and "Hey Now" (Cyndi Lauper).

Introductions of new products can be expensive, especially utilizing live headline entertainment. Yet a promotional music CD can help you gain attention—and create impressive sales numbers. For example, the Donna Karan Company created a new perfume, Chaos, to appeal to a fashion-conscious clientele. Pricing, packaging, and limited distribution through department and specialty stores helped to create a mood of exclusivity. The company sought a promotional item that would reward buyers with a gift that evoked a mood similar to that associated with the perfume. It chose the CD album *Pure Calm* as a gift-with-purchase. The album featured ten selections from the Windham Hill label and included such artists as Mark Isham, David Arkenstone, and Uman. Retailers reported strong fragrance sales and credited the CD promotion for the success of the product launch.

In Conclusion

The world of event entertainment is expanding to include opportunities for different types of entertainment, venues, and technologies. Although the notion of delivering a live band as entertainment for an event may not be entirely in the past, today's event may include a headline entertainer or speaker, a strategically planned assortment of themed music, and gift bags that include CDs and promotional items from corporate sponsors. Event entertainment is expanding to incorporate many different types of media and music to provide customers with an increasingly large array of options to entertain, inspire, and "wow." Although experience is still an important factor in choosing an event entertainment planner, those with professional certifications, such as the CSEP and CMP are in demand. Professional certifications afford credibility and stature in the industry and are seen by customers as signs of professionalism.

Music is playing an increasingly important role in marketing, as musicians and entertainers lend their talents and their music to promote a wide array of products. Marketers who do not use music in their promotional activities are missing out on an opportunity to leave a lasting impression on their audiences. Where will all this lead? Time will tell. What is important is that you watch the trends, listen to customers, be creative, and have fun, which is what event entertainment and production is all about.

Scripts for Future Study

BOOK

Lathrop, Tad, and Jim Pettigrew (1999). *This Business of Music Marketing and Promotion.* New York: Billboard Books.

INTERNET RESOURCES

Hospitality Sales and Marketing Association International (HSMAI), wwwl.hsmai.org, provides access to sales and marketing resources, including links to hospitality industry companies and organizations, professional development opportunities and industry research.

OTHER PUBLICATIONS

Update Meetings, *the magazine from Southwest Airlines.*

Finale

This book has provided you with information about event entertainment and production. You have discovered how entertainment is an economy unto itself, how to research, create, plan, coordinate, manage, and monitor event entertainment and production, how to create something that is fresh, and how to anticipate future trends. Many experienced professionals have contributed their knowledge and expertise to give you a broad perspective on the event entertainment and production industry.

A characteristic that has been consistently stressed throughout this book is the aspect of *relationship* in the event entertainment business. Maybe Secretary of State Colin Powell said it best: "There are no secrets to success: don't waste time looking for them. Success is the result of perfection, hard work, learning from failure, loyalty to those for whom you work and persistence." Stan Aaronson, CSEP, of Mark Sonder Productions and ViewPoint International Destination Management Companies, defines success as "the point at which preparation collides with opportunity." Mark Sonder Music was created as a sole proprietorship in June 1985 and incorporated in 1990. At that time, another point where "preparation collided with opportunity" arrived when I attended a seminar about music and entertainment at the special event conference, and exposition. Robert Sivek, CSEP, the speaker, was a pioneer in the event industry and later became president of the International Special Events Society (ISES). After hearing Sivek's speech, I developed a clearer vision of the future of the events industry and the role I could play in it. I realized that I had the knowledge and experience to address the need for event entertainment and production and, with my professional network, to build a business.

Although having career experience in the entertainment industry is helpful to achieving success, it is also important to watch industry trends. In 1997, I acquired New York City's destination management company, ViewPoint International, as I observed that mergers and acquisitions were key to growth—

otherwise a company stands the chance of being bought out or worse, losing it all. It was in this fashion that the two companies were able to share their respective client bases. Combining these services was also a means of maintaining quality control and keeping subcontracting within projects to a minimum. By correctly identifying this industry trend, I was able to capitalize on the opportunity to purchase a DMC, another instance in which "preparation collided with opportunity."

Finally, this book would not be complete without a quotation that summarizes the passion, commitment, and vision that are essential to success in the event entertainment and production industry. It is from a song, "I Hope You Dance" in Lee Ann Womack's twenty-first-century hit album: "And when you get the choice to sit it out or dance, I hope you dance."* Welcome to the world of event entertainment and production.

Organizations and Associations

Joining industry associations is one of the best ways to become involved in the event entertainment and production industry. The following is a list of the major organizations for both the event management and the music and entertainment industries. I encourage you to join associations and use the resources they provide to advance your career.

Academy of Motion Picture Arts and Sciences

After nearly three-quarters of a century of recognizing excellence in filmmaking achievement, the presentation of the Oscars has become the Academy of Motion Picture Arts and Sciences' most famous activity.

8949 Wilshire Boulevard
Beverly Hills, CA 90211-1972
Phone: (310) 247-3000
Fax: (310) 859-9351
www.oscars.org

Acoustical Society of America

Suite 1NO1
2 Huntington Quadrangle
Melville, NY 11747-4502
Phone: (516) 576-2360

Fax: (516) 576-2377
http://asa.aip.org

Actors' Equity Association

Actors' Equity Association is the union of American actors and stage managers in the theater.

165 West 46th Street
New York, NY 10036
Phone: (212) 869-8530
Fax: (212) 719-9815
www.actorsequity.org

American Association of Community Theater (AACT)

The national voice of community theater, representing the interests of its members and more than 7000 theaters across the United States and its territories, as well as theater companies with the armed forces overseas.

8402 Briarwood Crescent
Lago Vista, TX 78645
Phone: (866) 687-2228
Fax: (512) 267-0712
www.aact.org

American Disc Jockey Association (ADJA)

The association of professional disc jockeys, which promotes ethical behavior, industry standards, and continuing education for its members.

1964 Wagner Street
Pasadena, CA 91107
Phone: (626) 844-3204
www.adja.org

American Federation of Musicians (AFM)

The largest union in the world representing the interests of the professional musician. www.afm.org

American Federation of Television and Radio Artists (AFTRA)

AFTRA represents actors and other professional performers, as well as broadcasters in television, radio, sound recordings, nonbroadcast/industrial programming, and new technologies such as interactive programming and CD ROMs.

www.aftra.org

American Society of Composers, Authors and Publishers (ASCAP)

ASCAP is the only American performing rights organization whose board of directors consists solely of member composers, songwriters, and music publishers elected by the membership.

One Lincoln Plaza
New York, NY 10023-7129
Phone: (212) 95-ASCAP
Fax: (212) 595-3276
www.ascap.com

American Society of Music Arrangers and Composers (ASMAC)

PO Box 17840
Encino, CA 91416
Phone:(818) 994-4661
Fax: (818) 994-6181
www.asmac.org

Art Directors Guild

11969 Ventura Boulevard, Suite 200
Studio City, CA 91604
Phone: (818) 762-9995
Fax: (818) 762-9997
www.artdirectors.org

Association of British Theatre Technicians (ABTT)

The U.K. association for all theater professionals.

> 47 Bermondsey Street
> London, SE1 3XT
> Phone: 0207 403 3778
> Fax: 0207 378 6170
> www.abtt.org.uk

Association of Lighting Designers (ALD)

The Association of Lighting Designers is the professional body representing lighting designers in all fields in the United Kingdom and the rest of the world.

> PO Box 89
> Welwyn Garden City, AL7 1ZW
> Phone: 01707 891848
> Fax: 01707 891848
> www.ald.org.uk

Association of Professional Recording Services (APRS)

The APRS promotes the highest standards of professionalism and quality within the audio industry in the U.K. Its members are recording studios, postproduction houses, mastering, replication, pressing, and duplicating facilities, and providers of education and training.

> PO Box 22,
> Totnes, U.K. TQ9 7YZ
> Phone: 01803 868600
> www.aprs.co.uk

Australian Entertainment Industry Association (AEIA)

The AEIA is the chief employer body in the Australian arts and entertainment industry, registered in the Australian Industrial Relations Commission (AIRC) since 1917.

> 8th Floor, West Tower
> 608 St. Kilda Road

Melbourne, Victoria 3004
Phone: +61 3 9521 1900
Fax: +61 3 9521 2285
www.aeia.org.au

British Kinematograph Sound and Television Society

BKSTS (The Moving Image Society) has been hosting the only dedicated special effects conference in the world since 1984 as a biennial event.

Ealing Studios
Ealing Green, London W5 5 EP.
Phone: +44 (0)20 8584 5220
Fax: +44 (0)20 8584 5220
www.bksts.com

Broadcast Music, Inc.

10 Music Square East
Nashville, TN
Phone: (615) 401-2000
www.bmi.com

Club Managers Association of America

The Club Managers Association of America is the only international association representing club management.

1733 King Street
Alexandria, VA 22314
Phone: (703) 739-9500
Fax: (703) 739-0124
www.cmaa.org

Connected International Meeting Professionals Association (CIMPA)

9200 Bayard Place
Fairfax, VA 22032

Phone: (703) 978-6287
Fax: (703) 978-5524
www.cimpa.org

Convention Industry Council

The Convention Industry Council (CIC) is composed of 30 leading national and international organizations representing more than 81,000 individuals and 13,000 firms or properties involved in the meetings, conventions, exhibitions, and travel and tourism industries. It provides an important forum for member organizations to work together to enhance the industry.

801 Greensboro Drive, Suite 30
McLean, VA 22102
Phone: (800) 725-8982
Fax: (703) 610-9005
www.conventionindustry.org

Creative Musicians Coalition

The Creative Musicians Coalition is dedicated to the advancement of new music and the success of independent musicians.

1024 W. Willcox Avenue
Peoria, IL 61604
Phone: (309) 685-4843
Fax: (309) 685-4879
www.aimcmc.com

Entertainment Services and Technology Association (ESTA)

ESTA is a nonprofit trade association representing the North American entertainment technology industry.

875 Sixth Avenue, Suite 1005
New York, NY 10001
Phone: (212) 244-1505
Fax: (212) 244-1502
www.esta.org

Exhibit Designers and Producers Association (EDPA)

EDPA is an internationally recognized national trade association whose members are engaged in the design, manufacture, transport, installation, and service of displays and exhibits primarily for the trade show industry.

5775 G Peachtree-Dunwoody, Suite 500
Atlanta, GA 30342
Phone: (404) 303-7310
www.edpa.com

Exposition Service Contractors Association

The association for firms engaged in providing services and materials for trade shows and exhibitions, conventions and meetings, and sales meetings.

2260 Corporate Circle, Suite 400
Henderson, NV 89074-7701
Phone: (702) 319-9561
Fax: (702) 450-7732
www.esca.org

Institute of Broadcast Sound

Professional association for practitioners in sound for broadcast television and radio, formed in 1977 in the United Kingdom.

27 Old Gloucester Street
London WC1N 3XX
Phone: +44 (0)1483 575450
www.ibs.org.uk

International Association of Amusement Parks and Attractions (IAAPA)

IAAPA exists to foster the highest degree of professionalism within the amusement industry, to promote the market for its goods and services, to gather and disseminate information on the industry, and to represent the interests of the industry before government—all to the end that its member companies grow and profit.

1448 Duke Street
Alexandria, VA 22314
Phone: (703) 836-4800
Fax: (703) 836-9678
www.iaapa.org

International Association of Fairs and Expositions (IAFE)

IAFE is a voluntary, nonprofit corporation, organizing state, district, and county agricultural fairs, expositions, associations, corporations, and individuals into one large association interested in the improvement of fairs and allied fields.

3043 E. Cairo
Springfield, MO 65802
Phone: (800) 516-0313
Fax: (417) 862-0156
www.fairsandexpos.com

International Association of Lighting Designers

The International Association of Lighting Designers provides education, networking, recognition, membership advocacy, and professional practices to promote innovative ideas toward the future direction and growth of the profession.

Merchandise Mart, Suite 9-104
200 World Trade Center
Chicago, IL 60654
Phone: (312) 527-3677
Fax: (312) 527-3680
www.iald.org

International Association of Speakers Bureaus (IASB)

IASB is the worldwide trade association of speaker agencies and bureaus.

6845 Parkdale Place, Suite A
Indianapolis, IN 46254-5605
Phone: (317) 297-0872

Fax: (317) 387-338
www.igab.org

International Events Group (IEG)

A for-profit organization that provides information on sponsorships in sports, arts, entertainment, causes, and events. Its comprehensive services include an industry newsletter, sponsor locator service, books, conferences, workshops, consulting, and nearly 30 boilerplate contracts for a variety of sponsorship situations.
Phone: (312) 944-1727
Fax (312) 789-6488
www.sponsorship.com

International Federation for Choral Music (IFCM)

ChoralNet provides a central portal to on-line resources and communications for the global choral music community.

Phone: (312) 996-8744
Fax: (312) 996-0954
www.choralnet.org

International Jugglers Association (IJA)

Founded in 1947, the International Jugglers Association is a nonprofit organization uniquely dedicated to the advancement and promotion of juggling worldwide. The IJA membership represents an incredibly diverse array of skills, ages, and interests and spans the range from full-time working professionals to hobbyists.

PO Box 218
Montague, MA 01351
Phone: (413) 367-2401
Fax: (413) 367-0259
www.juggle.org

International Special Events Society (ISES)

The International Special Events Society represents special events producers (of events ranging from festivals to trade shows), caterers, decorators, florists, destination management companies, rental companies, special effects experts, tent suppliers, audiovisual technicians, party and convention coordinators, balloon artists, educators, journalists, hotel sales managers, specialty entertainers, convention center managers, and many others.

> 401 N. Michigan Avenue
> Chicago, IL 60611-4267
> Phone: (312) 321-6853
> Fax: (312) 673-6953
> www.ises.com

Meeting Professionals International

MPIWeb is the meeting industry's business exchange forum on the Internet.

> 4455 LBJ Freeway, Suite 1200
> Dallas, TX 75244
> Phone: (972) 702-3000
> www.mpiweb.org

National Association of Broadcasters (NAB)

The National Association of Broadcasters is the premier broadcast association worldwide. NAB serves radio and television broadcasters with representation on Capitol Hill, along with serving all electronic media industries with education and world-class conventions and expositions.

> 1771 N Street NW
> Washington, DC 20036
> Phone: (202) 429-5300
> Fax: (202) 429-4199
> www.nab.org

National Speakers Association (NSA)

As the leading organization for experts who speak professionally, NSA provides resources and education to advance the skills, integrity, and value of its members and the speaking profession.

> 1500 South Priest Drive
> Tempe, AZ 85281
> Phone: (480) 968-2552
> www.nsaspeaker.org

New Zealand Association of Theatre Craft, Design and Technology Inc. (NZATT)

The association was founded in 1981 for amateur and professional technicians of the live theater industry. It offers a forum for the exchange of information and ideas and provides a vehicle for the collective voice of its members.

> The Secretary, NZATT
> PO Box 11-957
> Manners Street
> Wellington 6034.
> www.nzatt.org.nz

Production Services Association (PSA)

An association of personnel and companies working in the production, design, touring, technical, and support services in the live entertainment industry in the U.K.

> 1301 Stratford Road
> Hall Green
> Birmingham, U.K. B28 9HH
> Phone: 0121 693 1424
> Fax: 0121 693 7100
> www.psa.org.uk

Recording Industry Association of America (RIAA)

The RIAA is the trade group that represents the U.S. recording industry. Its mission is to foster a business and legal climate that supports and promotes its members' creative and financial vitality.

> www.riaa.org

SESAC

A performing rights organization.

> 55 Music Square East
> Nashville, TN 37203
> Phone: (615) 320-0055
> Fax: (615) 329-9627
> www.sesac.com

Showmen's League Of America

The Showmen's League of America is an organization of outdoor amusement professionals who operate fairs, festivals, carnivals, and church events throughout the United States.

Phone: (312) 332-6236
Fax: (312) 332-6237
www.showmensleague.org

Songwriters Guild of America (SGA)

The nation's largest, oldest, and most experienced songwriters' association, serving its members with vital information and programs to further their careers and an understanding of the music industry.

1222 16th Avenue South, Suite 25
Nashville, TN 37212
Phone:(615) 329-1782
Fax: (615) 329-2623
www.songwriters.org

United States Institute for Theater Technology, Inc. (USITT)

The mission of USITT is to actively promote the advancement of the knowledge and skills of its members.

6443 Ridings Road
Syracuse, NY 13206-1111
Phone: (315) 463-6463
Fax: (315) 463-6525
www.usitt.org

World Clown Association

PO Box 77236
Corona, CA 92877
Phone: (800) 336-7922
www.worldclownassociation.com

APPENDIX 2

References

There are a plethora of resources for those working in the event entertainment and production industry, many of which are used in this book. I encourage you to consult these books and periodicals in order to advance your own knowledge of the industry.

Books

Allen, Judy (2000). *Event Planning: The Ultimate Guide to Successful Meetings, Corporate Events, Fundraising Galas, Conferences, Conventions, Incentives, and Other Special Events.* Hoboken, NJ: John Wiley & Sons, Inc.

Allen, Sylvia, and C. Scott Amann (1998). *How to Be Successful at Sponsorship Sales.* Holmdel, NJ: Allen Consulting.

Annual Handbook for Group Facilitators (1972). Oceanside, CA: University Associates.

Baskerville, David (1985). *Music Business Handbook and Career Guide.* 4th ed. Los Angeles: Sherwood.

Bekken, Bonnie Bjorguine (1991). *Opportunities in Performing Arts Careers.* Lincolnwood, IL: NTC Publishing Group.

Berlonghi, Alexander (1990). *The Special Event Risk Management Manual.* Dana Point, CA: Alexander Berlonghi.

Cameron, Julia (1999). *Transitions: Prayers and Declarations for a Changing Life.* Los Angeles: J. P. Tarcher.

Campbell, Don (1997). *The Mozart Effect: Tapping the Power of Music to Heal the Body, Strengthen the Mind, and Unlock the Creative Spirit.* New York: Avon Books.

Career Opportunities in Theater and the Performing Arts. (1992) New York: Facts on File.

The Columbia Dictionary of Quotations (1995). New York: Columbia University Press.

Coxson, Mona (1989). *Some Straight Talk about the Music Business.* 2d ed. Toronto, ON: CM Books.

Crisis—Disaster—Emergency Planning Notebook. (1996). Waco, TX: Texas Association of Convention and Visitor Bureaus.

D'Alessandro, David F. (2001). *Brand Warfare: 10 Rules for Building the Killer Brand.* New York: McGraw-Hill.

Danner, Fredric (1991). *Hit Men.* New York: Vintage.

Delpy-Neirotti, Lisa, Joe Jeff Goldblatt, and Stedman Graham (2001). *The Ultimate Guide to Sports Marketing.* New York: McGraw Hill.

Gerardi, Robert (1991). *Opportunities in Music Careers.* Lincolnwood, IL: VGM Career Horizons.

Getz, Donald (1997). *Event Management and Event Tourism.* Elmsford, NY: Cognizant Communication Corporation.

Gibson, James (1987). *Getting Noticed: A Musician's Guide to Publicity and Self-Promotion.* Cincinnati: Writer's Digest Books.

Goldberg, James (1996). *The Meeting Planner's Legal Handbook.* Washington, DC: Goldberg & Associates, PLLC.

Goldblatt, Joe (2002). *Special Events: Twenty-first Century Global Event Management.* 3rd ed. New York: John Wiley & Sons, Inc.

Goldblatt, Joe (1999). *Government, Civic, and Political Event Management.* Washington, DC: George Washington University.

Goldblatt, Joe, and Kathleen S. Nelson, eds. (2001). *The International Dictionary of Event Management.* New York: John Wiley & Sons, Inc.

Goldblatt, Joe Jeff, and Frank Supovitz (1999). *Dollars and Events: How to Succeed in the Special Events Business.* New York: John Wiley & Sons, Inc.

Grout, Donald Jay (2000). *A History of Western Music.* 6th ed. New York: W.W. Norton.

Han, Silvia S., comp. (1988). *Applying to Graduate Music Programs.* Boston: New England Conservatory Office of Career Planning and Alumni Relations.

Hoyle, Leonard H. (2002). *Event Marketing: How to Successfully Promote Events, Festivals, Conventions, and Expositions.* New York: John Wiley & Sons, Inc.

Ismail, Ahmed (1999). *Catering Sales and Convention Services.* Clifton Park, NY: Delmar Learning.

Kohn, Al, and Bob Kohn (1996). *Kohn on Music Licensing.* Englewood Cliffs, NJ: Aspen Law and Business.

Mackoff, Barbara, and Gary Wenet (2001). *The Inner Work of Leaders: Leadership as a Habit of Mind.* New York: Amacom Books.

Malouf, Lena (2002). *Parties and Special Events: Planning and Design.* Weimar, TX: Culinary and Hospitality Industry Publications Services.

McAdams, Jerry L. (1996). *The Reward Plan Advantage: A Manager's Guide to Improving Business Performance through People.* New York: Jossey-Bass.

Monroe, James C., CMP, CSEP (in press). *The Art of the Event: Complete Guide to Special Event Design and Décor.* New York: John Wiley & Sons, Inc.

Morrow, Sandra L. (1997). *The Art of the Show.* Dallas: IAEM Foundation.

Moxley, Jan (1996). *Advance Coordination Manual.* Boulder, CO: Zone Interactive.

O'Toole, William, and Phyllis Mikolaitis (2002). *Corporate Event Project Management.* New York: John Wiley & Sons, Inc.

Papolos, Janice (1984). *The Performing Artists Handbook.* Cincinnati: Writer's Digest Books.

Passman, Donald S. (1994). *All You Need to Know about the Music Business.* New York: Simon & Schuster.

Price, Catherine (1999). *The Complete Guide to Professional Meeting and Event Coordination.* Washington, DC: George Washington University.

Reed, Mary Hutchings (1989) *The Legal Guide to Sponsorship.* Chicago: International Events Group.

Shemel, Sidney, and William Krasilovsky (1994). *More about This Business of Music.* New York: Billboard Books.

Shemel, Sidney, and William Krasilovsky (2000). *This Business of Music.* New York: BPI Communications.

Shock, Patti, and John Stefanelli (2001). *On-Premise Catering: Hotels, Convention and Conference Centers, and Clubs.* New York: John Wiley & Sons, Inc.

Silvers, CSEP, Julia Rutherford (in press). *Professional Event Coordination.* New York: John Wiley & Sons, Inc.

Tarlow, Peter E. (2001). *Safety and Security for Tourism Destinations.* Washington, DC: George Washington University.

Truskot, Joseph, Anita Belofsky, and Karen Kittilstad, eds. (1984). *Principles of Orchestra Management.* Washington, DC: American Symphony Orchestra League.

Ukman, Lesa (1999). *IEG's Complete Guide to Sponsorship.* Chicago: International Events Group.

Uscher, Nancy (1990). *Your Own Way in Music.* New York: St. Martin's.

Wadhams, Wayne (1990). *Sound Advice.* New York: Schirmer/Macmillian Books.

Weisman, Dick (1990). *The Music Business: Career Opportunities and Self-Defense.* New York: Crown Publishers.

Wiersma, Betsy, and Kari Strolberg (2001). *Exceptional Events: Concept to Completion.* Weimar, TX: Culinary and Hospitality Industry Publications Services.

Wolf, Michael (1999). *The Entertainment Economy: How Mega-Media Forces Are Transforming Our Lives.* New York: Times Books.

Zemke, Ron, Claire Raines, and Bob Filipczak. *Generations at Work: Managing the Clash of Veterans, Boomers, Xers, and Nexters in Your Workplace* (2002). New York: AMACOM.

Periodicals

"'N Sync's Joey Fatone to Star in *Rent*" (July 23, 2002). *Encore* newsletter. Boulder, CO: Gen-Den Corporation.

ARTICLES

Bhattacharjee, Yuduit (November 29, 2001). "Making the Music Sway to Your Beat." *New York Times.*

Brickman, Nanci (2002). "Sales Management Resource Overview and Statistics." *InfoNow.*

Campos, Jose (September 2002). "Smart Planning: Content Is King." *Successful Meetings.*

Chatfield-Taylor, Cathy (March 2002). "Technological Support: Benefits of Online Survey Tools." *The Meeting Professional.*

Considine, J. D. (March 31, 2002). "That '70s Jazz (for the Discriminating Rapper)." *New York Times.*

Cooke, Martha (March 2002). "Event Sponsorship." *Meetings and Conventions.*

Doyle, Marie (March 2002). "Off-Site Venues." *Corporate and Incentive Travel.*

Enbysk, Monte (2002) "Virtual Meetings Can Cut Travel Costs." *SmallTech* (www. bcentral.com/articles/enbysk/132.asp).

"Entertainment Tie-Ins" (March 18, 2002). *The Sales and Marketing Network.*

"Event Solutions Magazine 2002 Fact Book: A Statistical Analysis of the Event Industry" (2002). Tempe, AZ: Event Publishing LLC.

Firestone, David (January 29, 2002)."Party On: When Bacchanals Collide." *New York Times.*

Garner, Stacy (April 14, 2002). "Stage Movies May Save Broadway." *New York Times.*

Gesell, Izzy (April 2002)."Energizing Meetings." *Corporate and Incentive Travel.*

Hammock, Shannon (October 7, 2002). "House Approves Web Radio Royalty Deal." *New York Times.*

Hurley, Lisa (January 1, 2002). "Forecast 2002." *Special Events.*

"If You Ask Me"(March 2002). *The Meeting Professional.*

"International" (March 2002). *Convene.*

"Leeds Festival Refused License" (June 18, 2002.). *Encore* newsletter. Boulder, CO: Gen-Den Corporation.

"Music Adds Excitement to Meetings And Trade Shows, But Don't Forget to Pay the Songwriters" (April 28, 2000). Broadcast Music Inc. (BMI) press release.

"Over Million Watch Bon Jovi Webcast" (September 4, 2002). *Encore* newsletter. Boulder, CO: Gen-Den Corporation.

Jacobs, Judy (September 17, 2001). "City's Musical Heritage Keys Meetings Outreach." *Meeting News Magazine.*

Jacobs, Judy (March 2002). "Special Venues: Choosing a Unique Meeting Site Creates Lasting Impressions." *Meetings South Magazine.*

Kleinberger, Jane (April 10, 2002). "e-Trends in College Athletics." Paciolan, Inc. Paciolan is an Irvine-based company that provides software for handling ticketing, fund raising and marketing for live entertainment organizations.

Lin-Fisher, Betty (June 10, 2002). "Videoconferencing, Teleconferencing and Webcasting Decreasing Corporate Travel." *Akron Beacon Journal.*

Mann, Nancy (April 2000). "The Calm during the Storm: Hurricane Floyd Forces AAFP into Crisis Management Mode." *Convene.*

McDonald, Tom (April 1, 2001). "People Skills Needed for Business Results." *Successful Meetings Magazine.*

Miller, Tina (November 2001). "Planning for Minority Groups." *Corporate and Incentive Travel.*

Morden, Darryl (2002) Freelance writer, editor, radio producer and web content providers

National Speakers Association (NSA) (January 2003) "Who's Who in Professional Speaking: The Meeting Planners Guide"

Nelson, Jamie (April 10, 2002). "Microsoft Moves to Movie and Television Distribution." *Yahoo News.*

Obertots, Richard (December 1999). "Why We Need to Prepare for Medical Emergencies." *Convene.*

Overfelt, Maggie (February 2002). "Side Gigs." *Fortune Small Business.*

Potter, Blair, and Funmi Okunbolade (November 2001). "Sudden Impact." *Meeting Professional* (digital ed.).

Riordan, Teresa (March 4, 2002). "Crooner Uses Computers to Replace Sheet Music." *New York Times.*

Rose, Norm (April 2002). "Pyrotechnic Savvy: What You Should Know for a Successful Show." *Event Solutions.*

Rowe, Megan (September 2002). "Alphabet Soup or Seal of Approval?" *Corporate Meetings and Incentives.*

Smith, Ginger (August 1999). "Toward a United States Policy on Traveler Safety and Security." *Journal of Travel Research.*

Sparks, John (September/October 2001). "Wax in Your Ears?" *Symphony Magazine.*

"Terrorism Effects on Tourism Forum Packs House" (November 15, 2001). *SBPM News,* George Washington University.

Tindall, Blair (November/December 2001). "The Virtual Box Office." *Symphony Magazine.*

Torrence, Sara (December 1999). "Is Your Conference Ready for Risks?" *Convene.*

"2002 Business Travel Buyer's Handbook" (2002). *Business Travel News.*

Wayne, Jerry (March 2002). "Professionally Speaking: Proud to Be a Professional." *The Meeting Professional.*

ARTICLES ON-LINE

Bienstock, Ronald S. (2000). "Tips on Making It in the Biz." www.Getsigned.com.

"Closing the Deal" (2002). www.microsoft.com.

"Everyone Loves a Parade: The Authoritative Guide on How to Plan, Start and Improve Your Local Parade" (2003). Victory Corps. www.victorycorps.com/ebook/PARADE.pdf.

"General Mills Case Study" (2003). BMG Special Products. www.bmgsp.com/casestudies/genmills.html

Heide, Chris (June 28, 2002). "Using Music in Sales Promotion." *Info-now.com.*

"IEG's Sponsorship Report" (2002). www.sponsorship.com.

Mackenzie, John K. (2002). "Qualifying Meeting Producers." www.thewritingworks.com.

Miller, Gerri (2001). (Interview with Danny Goodwin). www.getsigned.com.

Scoppa, Bud (2001). "Zen and the Art of A&R" (interview with Matt Aberle, Jim Barber, Liz Brooks, and Geoffrey Weiss). www.ascap.com/muscibiz/zenl.html.

Shirley, Donna (2001). "Managing Creativity" (handout from educational course). www.managingcreativity.com/course.doc.

"Successful Brainstorming" (2002). www.microsoft.com.

PERIODICALS—WEB SITES

Amusement Business, www.amusementbusiness.com.

Arts Journal: The Daily Digest of Arts, Culture and Ideas, www.artsjournal.com.

Backstage Magazine, www.backstage.com.

Bureau of Tourism Research in Australia, www.btr.gov.au.

The Band Register (large database of bands and artists), www.bandreg.com.

Billboard, www.billboard.com.

Box Office, www.boxoff.com.

Business Travel News, www.btnonline.com. Publishers of *The Business Travel Buyer's Handbook.*

The Communique (a publication of the Association of Collegiate Conference and Events Directors-International), http://acced-i.colostate.edu.

Convene Magazine (a publication of the Professional Convention Management Association), www.pcma.org/resources/convene.

ConventionSouth, www.conventionsouth.com.

Corporate and Incentive Travel Magazine, www.corporate-inc-travel.com.

Corporate Meetings and Incentives, www.meetingsnet.com/cmi.

DotMusic, www.DotMusic.com.

E! Entertainment News, www.eonline.com/News.

Entertainment Management Online, (Southwest Missouri State University), www.entertainmentmanagement.com

Entertainment Marketing Letter (published by EPM Communications), www.epmcom.com/html/entertainment.html.

Entertainment Weekly, www.ew.com.

Event and Meeting Security Services, www.eventsecurity.com.

Event Management: An International Journal, www.cognizantcommunication.com.

Event Solutions, www.event-solutions.com.

EventWeb, www.eventweb.com.

Fairs and Expos (a publication of the International Association of Fairs and Exhibitions), www.fairsandexpos.com/resfande.html.

Incentive, www.incentivemag.com.

Incentives & Meetings International, www.i-me.com.

International Congress and Convention Association Survey, www.icca.nl.

Lighting and Sound International, www.plasa.org/media/lsi.

Lighting Dimensions, www.lightingdimensions.com.

Live Sound International, www.livesoundint.com.

Medical Meetings, www.meetingsnet.com/mm.

Meeting News, www.meetingnews.com.

Meetings and Conventions, www.meetings-conventions.com/index.html.

Mid-Atlantic Events Magazine, www.eventsmagazine.com.

Musical Stages Online (UK), www.musicalstages.co.uk.

Opera Magazine, www.opera.co.uk/magazine/diary.htm.

PlayBack (a publication of the American Society of Composers, Authors and Publishers), www.ascap.com/playback.

Playbill, www.playbill.com.

Pollstar—The Concert Industry Hotwire, www.pollstar.com.

Potentials in Marketing, www.potentialsmag.com.

Presentations, www.presentations.com.

Production Weekly, www.productionweekly.com.

Professional Speaker Magazine, (a publication of the National Speakers Association), www.nsaspeaker.org/information/speaker_mag.shtml.

Promo Monthly, www.promomagazine.com.

Religious Conference Manager, www.meetingsnet.com/rcm.

Rolling Stone, www.rollingstone.com.

Sales and Marketing Management, www.salesandmarketing.com.

Sales and Marketing Strategies and News, salesandmarketingmag.com.

Show Music Magazine, www.goodspeed.org/sm/current.htm.

Silverstein, Joseph (May 19, 2001). "Commencement Address to the Cleveland Institute of Music." Published on www.cim.edu.

Small Market Meetings, newspapers, www.smallmarketmeetings.com.

Special Events Magazine, www.specialevents.com.

Spin, www.spin.com.

Stage Directions Magazine, www.stage-directions.com.

Stagebill, www.stagebill.com.

Successful Meetings, www.successmtgs.com.

Technology Meetings, www.meetingsnet.com/tm.

The Meeting Professional, (a publication of Meeting Professional International) www.mpiweb.org/news/tmp.

The Music Trades, www.musictrades.com.

The Musicians Net, www.musicians.net.

Tradeshow Week Magazine, www.tradeshowweek.com.

APPENDIX 3

Internet Sites

This appendix has a number of Web sites that can give you excellent information about the event entertainment and production industry and can point you in the right direction for information you may need when planning your events. Also refer to the association Web sites that were provided in Appendix 1.

Alive Network

Provides a wide variety of artist support services for both musicians and the music industry.
www.alivenetwork.com

Anglo Plugging

Filled with up-to-the minute information on some of the most popular artists in the music industry. Anglo Plugging represents these artists' interests on radio, television, and now the Internet.
www.angloplugging.co.uk

Arts-Info

Arts-Info has information for the professional performing arts community in the United Kingdom and Ireland.
www.arts-info.co.uk

Bandit

A&R (Artists & Repertoire) newsletter; includes regularly updated information on music business companies looking for new talent.
www.banditnewsletter.com

Canyon Cinema

Canyon Cinema is an independent distributor of works by experimental, established, and emerging filmmakers.
www.canyoncinema.com

Center for Exhibition Industry Research

www.ceir.org

Convention Industry's Council (CIC) APEX Terminology Initiative

www.conventionindustry.org/apex

Findspeakersandbureaus.com

An on-line directory to find speakers for any type of event.

Guide to North American Fairs

A guide to county and state fairs throughout North America.
www.fairsnet.org

Hospitality Index

www.hospitality-index.com

Hospitality Net

An excellent site with lots of links.
www.hospitalitynet.org

International Heavy Metal Agency

Promotes heavy metal bands worldwide.
www.nwoghm.com

Jack Morton Worldwide

www.jackmorton.com

MadSearch.com

MadSearch is a global electronic media information source for the hospitality industry, featuring *MADNews,* a weekly e-newsletter, *MADBlast,* a promotional e-flyer, and a premier destination search engine.

MeetingsNet

www.meetingsnet.com

Pro Lighting and Staging News

www.PLSN.com
www.PLSN.com has information about pro lights and staging news.

Serious International Music Producers

Jazz, world, and contemporary music concerts, tours, and special events. Also acts as an artists' representative.
www.serious.org.uk

SpecialEventSite.com

The site's most requested feature is its directory of services, enabling viewers to shop prices for products, services, and music.
www.specialeventsite.com

TAXI

Get your music to the right people with TAXI, the leading independent Artist & Repertoire company, helping unsigned bands, artists, and songwriters to get record deals, publishing deals, and placement in films and TV shows.
www.taxi.com

TSNN.com

The best on-line calendar of international trade shows, events, and suppliers. Searchable by industry, city, state, country, time frame, and key words in the show name.
www.tsnn.com

APPENDIX 4

Software

If you are working in the event entertainment industry, it is important to be aware of the various types of software that either you or your vendors can use. There are many types of software, particularly in the music industry, as seen in the following list. It is important to continue to research new types of software as they become available.

Ceol Mor Software

Offers bagpipe music and drum score-writing software.
www.ceolmor-software.com

Data Becker

Create your own techno music with this software for Windows.
www.databecker.com

Evolution Electronics

The leading name in computer music products.
www.evolution.co.uk

Neuratron PhotoScore

Music scanning and recognition software for Windows and Mac. Offers downloadable demo.
www.neuratron.com

Sibelius Software

Provides various types of music notation software.
www.sibelius.com

SSEYO

Windows music creativity software.
www.sseyo.com

STI—Entertainment Agency Software

If you are a busy theatrical or entertainment agent whose office is constantly bottle-necked by paperwork such as contracts, confirmations, and invoices waiting to be processed, then you will be pleased to know that there is a software package written and designed especially for your business. Agencies save weeks every year in administration time by using STI, and then turn that extra time into creating more business.
www.mainline-computers.co.uk/about_sti.htm

Timesaver Software Company— Room Viewer

Presenting accurate, professional-looking diagrams to your clients is a must in order to stay competitive. The quality diagrams produced with Room Viewer show your clients how their events will look. Once the client approves, pass the diagram along to the people setting up the event.
www.timesaversoftware.com

APPENDIX 5

Sample Contracts

Contracting is discussed at length throughout the book, but one of the best ways to create your own comprehensive contracts is to look at other professionals' contracts. Remember that the contracts in this appendix show only examples of the clauses that you can use. Consult your own attorney before using a contract for your services.

Contract for Event Entertainment Services

TERMS AND CONDITIONS

A) Please endorse all copies of this agreement (initial where requested and sign below) and r eturn t he o riginal to our office by facsimile (619) 582-6250 and by regular mail. Signed FAX copies are considered legal and binding. <u>Please enclose any required payment with your signed contract</u>. Make your check(s) payable to REVEL PRODUCTIONS.

B) A monthly service charge of 5% will be added to all unpaid balances.

C) Unusually late or early set-up, or same night strike of decor will result in additional labor charges.

D) All rental items shall remain the property of REVEL PRODUCTIONS. With respect to equipment, food service, rentals, lighting and sound, it is understood that CLIENT will bear the sole responsibility of any loss, theft or damage to all equipment not caused by any fault of REVEL PRODUCTIONS or the staff and will be billed separately, after the event. Please note that on occasion, conditions may require that we make appropriate substitutions to ensure the highest quality product available.

E) Musicians fees are based upon standard union regulations with standard breaks of 15 minutes every hour. Should continuous music be requested, there will be an additional fee.

F) CLIENT will be responsible for unrestricted access to the venue for installation, rehearsals, shows and equipment removal from the event site.

G) CLIENT will be responsible for all costs that pertain to the use of the venue, including but not limited to: Hook-up, fees and permits, electrical power charges, staging platforms, modification and restoration of existing facility and clean-up charges, adequate storage space for all vendor road boxes and incidental equipment, adequate security of the protection of all vendor equipment.

H) PURCHASER will not permit the recording or broadcast, oral and/or visual, of any performance without the express prior written consent of Producer.

I) CLIENT is responsible for all music fees due to BMI or ASCAP under new music licensing laws.

J) REVEL PRODUCTIONS provides a one million dollar liability policy. Any increments over one million dollars are the responsibility of the CLIENT. If CLIENT wishes to be named additional insured, there will be an additional fee of $125.00. REVEL PRODUCTIONS will verify that all entertainers, artists and production staff (lighting, stage and sound) have worker's compensation coverage for their employees. A nnie Revel will be the only employee of REVEL PRODUCTIONS present at the job site, and as owner she is exempt from worker's compensation coverage.

K)   All items and/or services ordered after this contract has been issued will be considered as extras to this contract, and all fees for extras will be due and payable on or before the date of the original fee due dates.

L)   CLIENT agrees to and shall indemnify and hold REVEL PRODUCTIONS, its employees, officers, agents, vendors, retainees and subcontractors harmless from and against any and all claims losses, damages, causes of actions, suits and liability of every kind, including all expenses of litigation, court costs, and attorney's fees, for injury to or death of any person, or for damage to any property if caused, directly or indirectly, solely or jointly, by the negligence and/or intentional acts of one or more of the following: The CLIENT, its employees, guests, invitees, attendees, or any other person or entity involved in any way with or attending the event not including REVEL PRODUCTIONS.

M)   REVEL PRODUCTIONS agrees to and shall indemnify CLIENT, its employees, employers, officers, agents, vendors, successors, assignees, retainees, contractors, and subcontractors from and against any and all claims, losses, damages, caused of action, suits, and liability of every kind, including all expenses of litigation, court costs, and attorney's fees, for injury to or death of any person, or for damage to any property if caused by the negligence or intentional misconduct of REVEL PRODUCTIONS whether contributed to in whole or part by the negligence of CLIENT.

N)   CLIENT further agrees that REVEL PRODUCTIONS will have no responsibility or liability for the delivery or furnishing of products and services provided by any other persons or entities as provided for in the agreement, or otherwise contracted by the client directly, and REVEL PRODUCTIONS will not be liable for any damages or losses suffered by CLIENT.

O)   All contract changes or amendments must be in writing and signed and dated by both parties to be effective. If the changes reflect a higher price than was quoted for the original project, CLIENT agrees to pay at the time the change order is signed an additional deposit of 50% of the additional price increase.

TERMS OF CANCELLATION

A) Upon receipt of written notice received 30 days prior to the event date, PURCHASER will be entitled to receive a refund of 50% of the cost of the event, pending costs of custom materials ordered.

B)   Upon receipt of written notice received within 8-29 days prior to the event date, PURCHASER will be entitled to a refund of 25% of the cost of the event, pending costs of custom materials ordered.

C)   Upon receipt of written notice received within 0-7 days prior to the event date, PURCHASER agrees to pay the full-stated fee as specified in this contract.

FORCE MAJEURE

In the event of sickness or accident to Artist(s), or if the performance is rendered impossible or infeasible by any act or regulation of any public authority or bureau, civic tumult, strike, epidemic, interruption or delay of transportation services, war conditions or emergencies, or any other cause(s) beyond the control of Artist(s), it is agreed that there should be no claim for damages by either party to this agreement, and Artist(s) obligation as to the performance affected shall be deemed waived. Inclement weather rendering a performance impossible or infeasible shall not be deemed an emergency and payment for the guaranteed compensation herein shall be made notwithstanding, provided that Artist(s) is/are ready, willing and able to perform pursuant to terms.

If these arrangements meet with your approval, please sign and return one of the originals to my attention by_____ . A definite acceptance will occur upon receipt of a signed original, or a facsimile (FAX) transmittal of the signed original. If a FAX is used by either party, then the FAX copy shall serve as an original unless an actual original is executed and received by both parties within 10 days.

Letter of Agreement for Event Entertainment Services

Date

Name
Company
Address

RE: Event Name
       Location
       Date of Event

Dear Name:

Thank you for the opportunity to provide event coordination services for the above-mentioned e vent. W e a re e xcited t o w ork with you and will do everything within our power to ensure smooth orchestration and management of your extraordinary weekend.

REVEL PRODUCTIONS, INC. WILL:

X   Provide the products and services outlined in the attached proposal.
X   Provide (1) operations manager throughout the planning and execution stages of
     the event.

CLIENT WILL:

X   Provide necessary internal correspondence to members.
X   Disburse all monies to all vendors in a timely manner.
X   Ensure attendees arrive at the appropriate terminal on time for boarding.
X   Cover parking expenses at the terminal, and food & beverage.

TERMS AND CONDITIONS:

1)   Payments to Revel Productions shall be as follows:

X   A 50% deposit of $5,500.00 will be due upon signature of Letter of Agreement.
X   A final payment of $5,500.00 (and any other approved expenses) will be due on
     or before Friday, July 5, 2002.

     A final guest count is due (7) days prior to the event, or on Friday, July 12, 2002. If
     final guest count decreases within (7) days of the event, no refunds will be given.

     Revel Productions is a corporation hired by Cardiff Software for the preparation and
     on-site management of the above-mentioned events. Nothing in this Letter of
     Agreement shall be construed as creating an employer/employee relationship or
     guarantee of future employment.

3)   Revel Productions is free to engage in other independent contracting activities,
     provided that Revel Productions does not engage in any such activities which are
     inconsistent with a ny p rovisions h ereof, o r t hat s o o ccupy R evel P roductions=

time as to interfere with the proper and efficient performance of Revel Productions services hereunder.

4)   Revel Productions reserves the right to terminate this contract, with 2-weeks notice, if CLIENT fails to provide the services outlined in this Letter of Agreement.

5)   CLIENT reserves the right to terminate this contract, with 2-weeks notice, if Revel Productions fails to provide the services outlined in this Letter of Agreement, however, Revel Productions will be paid for services rendered up to the point of termination.

6)   Should CLIENT cancel all or any part of the services to be rendered by Revel Productions, CLIENT agrees to immediately notify Revel Productions in writing of such cancellation. In such event, CLIENT agrees to pay Revel Productions the direct costs expended or incurred by Revel Productions, with a cancellation fee for that portion of the projected contract amount which was canceled:

- Services canceled 90-60 days   =   50% cancellation fee
- Services canceled 59-30 days   =   75% cancellation fee
- Services canceled within 29 days   =   100% cancellation fee

7)   Revel Productions shall be excused from performance if performance becomes impossible or commercially impractical because of:
- Federal, state or municipal action, statute, ordinance or regulation.
- Natural disasters or acts of God.
- Strike or any other labor stoppage or trouble.
- Any other cause, contingency or circumstance which materially prevents or hinders the   performance of Revel Productions= obligations under this Letter of Agreement.

8)   In the event any suit, action or proceedings arise from or based upon this Letter of Agreement, the prevailing party shall be entitled to recover reasonable attorney=s fees, costs and disbursements.

9)   This Letter of Agreement shall be governed by the laws of the State of California and Revel Productions consents to jurisdiction and venue in the state and federal courts of San Diego County, California.

10)   Signee agrees to all terms and conditions contained herein.

Agreed to by:

_____ Client
Revel Productions, Inc.

_____ Date
Date

Please Sign and Return

MARK SONDER PRODUCTIONS – Personal Services Agreement

THIS CONTRACT for the personal services of «group» on the engagement described below is made this «number» day of «month», 2004, between the undersigned purchaser of music (herein called "Purchaser") and Mark Sonder Productions (herein called Artist Representative or AR).

1. Name and Address of Place of Engagement:
    «place»
    «paddress»
    Name of Artist, Band or Group: «group» Number of Musicians and Staff: «nom»

2. Date(s), Starting and Finishing Time of Engagement:
    «date»
    «stfi»

3. Type of Engagement: «type»

4. Total Contract Price Agreed Upon: $«money»   NOTE: After «OT» the cost of «group» will be charged at the rate of $X US/per set, or any portion thereof. Contract Price does not include expenses agreed to by the Purchaser in accordance with agreement. Attached Addendum(s)/Rider(s) is (are) a part of this contract.

5. Purchaser Will Make Payments As Follows: Fifty percent (50%) non-refundable deposit due upon receipt and acceptance of contract; Non-refundable balance due four (4) weeks prior to date of performance.

6. The Purchaser shall be legally and financially responsible for all licensing fees with regards to music, live or recorded, in any form. AR, shall assist Purchaser as to fulfilling these responsibilities if requested.

7. Purchaser will hold AR harmless for any and all claims including any and all attorney's fees.

8. AR's obligations hereunder are subject to detention or prevention by sickness, inability to perform, accident, means of transportation, Acts of God, riots, strikes, labor difficulties, epidemics, any act or order of any public authority or any other cause, similar or dissimilar beyond «group»'s control.

9. For a period of one year from the Engagement Date hereof, all dates that result either directly or indirectly from this engagement will be referred solely to AR. Artist and Purchaser will neither negotiate nor consummate any future engagements which are not negotiated and consummated by AR. A commission equivalent to that of the Engagement Date's shall be immediately due and payable to AR for any Engagement performed by Artist for Purchaser, whether directly or indirectly, in violation of this paragraph 9, for which Artist shall be liable. All payment shall be made in full without deductions

10. Anything herein to the contrary notwithstanding, AR assumes no liability or responsibility whatsoever for any act, failure or breach of any provision of the contract or of any other duty or responsibility of Artist or Purchaser to each other or to any other person, and is a party to this contract solely for the purpose of protecting his interest as an AR in connection with the Engagement Date(s) set forth as well as any other Engagement hereinafter described for which a commission may be payable.

11. Artist may cancel this engagement without liability in order for Artist to render services in preparation, performance or other activity relating to a television appearance, motion picture, commercials, writing, recording or stage production agreement, as well as, a performance in Atlantic City or Nevada casino.

12. If any union, international or local, shall require a bond of service, Purchaser will pay cost thereof:

13. The attached Addendum(s)/Rider(s) is (are) hereby incorporated and made a part of this agreement and, with this Contract, must be returned signed with deposit within 14 days from above "made" date, otherwise, Contract will be considered null and void.

14. This contract shall be governed by the laws of The Commonwealth of Virginia.

In Witness Whereof, the parties hereto have hereunto set their names & seals on the day & yr. first above written

«P»   MARK SONDER PRODUCTIONS

_____ _____   _____ _____
                    Date   Date
«add»   4611 Deerwatch Drive
«city», «state» «zip»   Chantilly, VA 20151
«tel»   703-968-8670 ★ Fax: 703-968-4280

NOTES: PURCHASER WILL SEE THAT: «notes»

Sample Rider
Riders can be of any length, almost always longer and even much longer than the actual contractual agreement. Below is a short but actual Rider for a show produced by my office. It has all the elements that larger Riders may have.

The Hall of Fame Show starring:
The Elsbeary Hobbs Drifters & The Cornell Gunter Coasters with The Marvelettes

Produced by: **Mark Sonder Productions**

The following rider is intended to insure that your association, benefit, corporate function or concert becomes a special event. The following provisions shall be deemed incorporated in and part of the agreement to which this rider is annexed. The Purchaser shall furnish at Purchaser's sole cost and expense:

1) **Minimum Stage Requirements:** The magic of *The Hall of Fame Show* is their interaction with your audience. However, our staging is part of our theatrics that sets us apart from your audience. Stage: 20ft deep, 24ft across, a height of 2-4ft with stairs and an 8'x8' drum riser (see stage plot enclosed). Any stage that is constructed must be secured and fastened properly. Another size stage may be acceptable, but must be approved by our office prior to booking.
Furthermore, we require 16 chilled bottled waters with 16 glasses and 15 cloth towels on stage (placed on a table) for the performance.

2) The Purchaser will provide four (4) clean, private dressing facilities within close proximity to the stage and supplied with the following:
   a) At least 1 mirror in each room, adequate lighting & comfortable temperature.
   b) 8 clean towels (hand or bath)
   c) A small hanging rack
   d) Shower and toilet facilities in the dressing area
   e) An assortment of juices, bottled water, hot coffee/tea with condiments, ice and cups, plus a deli tray with several fresh meats, vegetables, cheeses and assorted breads at technical rehearsal and to be replenished before show.

3) **Security:** The Purchaser will provide: Security for equipment left on band stand between tech rehearsal and performance plus Security at the dressing facilities before, during and after performance.

4) **Backline:** The Purchaser will provide the backline as outlined in the Orchestral Equipment List (see enclosed).

5) Musical Director reserves the right for reasonable placement of sound and lighting equipment to insure maximum efficiency.

6) **Lighting Requirements:** Purchaser will provide an electrician to hook-up our power distribution and lights. All dependent upon size of venue however as a minimum: 2 trees with six (6) 1K par lights on each tree, or stage lights with operator, to include: multi-colored gels all on a dimmer, plus four follow-spots with multi-colored gels with operators. All stations must have headphone communications. Other lighting options may be acceptable, but must be approved by our office prior to booking. Plus, two (2) 20 amp circuits made available at back of stage.

7) The Purchaser will assume liability for any damage to equipment or costumes caused by any person, other than the members of *The Hall of Fame Show/Mark Sonder Productions* organization. The Purchaser agrees to indemnify and hold harmless, *The Hall of Fame Show/Mark Sonder Productions*, of any liability of

accidents causing bodily injury or property damage as a result of the concert or their performances including any and all attorney's fees. Purchaser shall obtain liability insurance naming the individual bands and Mark Sonder Productions as insured for a limit no less than One Million Dollars US ($1,000,000.00 US) combined single limit for bodily injury and property damage. Certificates of insurance relating to the coverage listed above shall be furnished by Purchaser to Mark Sonder Productions at least fourteen (14) days prior to the Engagement.

8) In the event that Artist fails to perform for any reason(s), Purchaser agrees to indemnify and hold Mark Sonder Productions harmless from any and all liability resulting therefrom, and shall deliver to Mark Sonder Productions a written release to that effect within ten days of Artist's default. Mark Sonder Productions shall return all of the Purchaser's deposit monies pertaining to this contract within a reasonable time after the receipt of said release. In the event that the Purchaser does not want to furnish a written release, Mark Sonder Productions reserves the right to place the aforementioned deposit monies in a non-interest bearing escrow account, pending a final deposition of the matter by a court of competent jurisdiction.

9) In the event that the engagement, referenced on the Contract is cancelled due to no fault of Mark Sonder Productions and/or the Artist, all deposit monies tendered, by Purchaser, shall be forfeited. In the event that the engagement called for in this Agreement is an engagement where there are a multitude of Artists, whether supplied through Mark Sonder Productions or supplied through another entity, the cancellation by one of the Artists, but not all of the Artists, shall not relieve the obligations of Purchaser as outlined herein and on the Contract, shall not be waived and Purchaser shall remain obligated to all the terms and conditions contained herein. Should Purchaser cancel or default on any of the terms and conditions, as contained herein, Purchaser shall forfeit all deposits tendered, for said engagement.

10a) Indemnification: Purchaser agrees to indemnify and hold harmless Mark Sonder Productions and his employees, contractors and/or agents from and against any claims, costs (including attorney's fees and court costs), expenses, damages, liabilities, losses or judgments arising out of, or in connection with any claim, demand or action made by any third party, if such are sustained as a direct or indirect consequence of the Engagement.

10b) Purchaser shall also indemnify and hold harmless Mark Sonder Productions and his employees, contractors and/or agents from and against any loss, damage and/or destruction occurring to its and/or its employees, contractors, or agents' instruments and equipment at the place of the Engagement, including but not limited to, damage, loss or destruction caused by Act of G-d.

11) **Sound Requirements:** (See Sound Board Input List) Purchaser will provide:
    a) 7 stage monitor wedges with 4 separate monitor mixes
b) Vocal microphones: 6 wireless and as a backup, 6 Shure SM-58s with 50 foot microphone cables on straights with round bases
    c) 4 microphones for the drums (SM-57s/Sennhieser 421s/AKG D112s, 451s)
    d) 1 guitar microphone for amp (Shure SM-57, Sennhieser 504)
    e) 1 Fender Twin Reverb amp or similar _tube_ amp/1 bass amp with min. 150 wts
    f) 3 direct boxes
    g) 1 24 channel mixing board with 4 separate monitor mixes

h) Digital reverb & digital delay / Speakers to be dependent upon size of venue

i) 1 sound technician / 1 monitor technician

j) 6 separate 20a/120v circuits with quad boxes at opposite ends of the stage

12) **Accommodations:** Fifteen (15) non-smoking singles for night of performance plus one (1) one-bedroom non-smoking suite hotel room for the night before and of performance of a standard no less than Hilton, Sheraton, Marriott, etc. quality..(May require 2 singles instead of a suite).

13) **Transportation:** The Purchaser will provide 17 round-trip first class airline tickets from originating city to another destination (generally BUR/DFW/IAD/LAS/LGA) or cash equivalent plus ground transportation to/from airport, hotel, venue, etc.

14) The Purchaser agrees to furnish and reserve parking for 10 spaces for band personnel and one equipment truck as close to the stage as possible (if applicable).

15) The Purchaser will allow up to 20 guests/performance of *The Hall of Fame Show*.

16) **Catering:** Hot dinners (with vegetarian meals) for 2 on night before; breakfast and lunch for 2 on day of; and 17 hot dinners (with vegetarian meals) on night of engagement. Breakfast for 2 on morning after performance.

17) A full technical rehearsal with musicians, sound/light, etc. will take place from TBA.

18) **Communications:** Four (4), Motorola or equivalent, radios with minimum two separate channels with headsets.

19) 1 stage hand for tech rehearsal, before and during performance.

20) Four (4) music stands and four (4) music stand lights.

21) Purchaser shall not have the right to broadcast, televise, photograph or otherwise reproduce the performances or any part thereof. (No motion picture, video or audio tapes made without written permission of the artists representative.

22) On all outdoor engagements, adequate heat/air conditioning must be provided. Should inclement weather conditions, such as rain, sleet, hail or snow prevail, and *The Hall of Fame Show/Mark Sonder Productions*, is expected to perform, the Purchaser must furnish an overhead waterproof stage covering, extending 1 foot beyond the stage in all directions. Stage must be completely dry. In the event of winds in excess of 20mph, side coverings must be installed. Temperature on stage must be at least 50 degrees Fahrenheit. Should inclement weather conditions make it impossible to start or complete the show, *The Hall of Fame Show/Mark Sonder Productions* shall nevertheless be paid in full.

23) *The Hall of Fame Show starring: The Elsbeary Hobbs Drifters / The Cornell Gunter Coasters / The Marvelettes Produced by Mark Sonder Productions* shall receive 100% headline billing unless approved by Artist Representative at signing of contract.

24) Any changes in this rider must be agreed upon at consummation of the contract. The conditions in this rider supersede any other written or verbal commitment on the part of the purchaser, except for the contract.

Agreed Upon By_____Date_____Revised January 2003

Backline/Orchestral Equipment List

Guitar:
Fender Super Reverb or Mesa boogie with graphic eq. or Marshall Combo

Bass:
Gallian Kruger 800 with 1-15 and 1-4x10 speaker enclosures or Ampeg S.V.T. with S.V.T. bottom.

Drums: Preferred brands: Yamaha or Tama
20" or 22" bass drum with bass drum pedal
2 mounted toms on bass drum; 8x12 and 9x13 / 1 floor tom 14x14
1 snare drum 5 1/2"x14"
high hat pedal / 3 cymbal stands with cymbals!
1 drum throne (swivel seat) / 1 6'x6' carpet under complete drum ensemble

Keyboards:
Korg P.C. 88; Korg SG-1 Sample Grand Piano & Korg 01W FD + keyboard amplifier for personal monitor.

Four (4) music stands with music stand lights and Two (2) guitar stands.

Channel	Source	Transducer	Stand
1	Kick	AKG D112	Short boom
2	Snare	Shure SM57 or Sennhieser 421	Claw or boom
3	Hi Hat	Shure SM57 or AKG 451	Straight stand
4	Rack Toms	Shure SM57 or Sennhieser 421	Claw or boom
5	Floor Tom	Shure SM57 or Sennhieser 421	Claw or boom
6	Bass	DI	
7	Keyboard Left	DI	
8	Keyboard Right	DI	
9	Guitar	Shure SM57 or Sennhieser 421	Short boom
10	Vocal Stage right	Wireless plus a backup of Shure SM58 or Beta 58	Straight stand w/round base
11	Vocal Center Stage right	Wireless plus a backup of Shure SM58 or Beta 58	Straight stand w/round base
12	Vocal Center Stage Left	Wireless plus a backup of Shure SM58 or Beta 58	Straight stand w/round base
13	Vocal Stage Left (Lead Vocal)	Wireless plus a backup of Shure SM58 or Beta 58	Straight stand w/round base
14	MC (stage/monitor/hse)	Wireless	
15	Reverb Return		
16	Delay Return		

Channels 17-23 for hand held vocals (wired or wireless) to be used for encore only!

Concert Tour Sponsorship Agreement

This is not necessarily a complete tabulation of items that should be incorporated into this agreement, but a common sense guide.

Agreements presumes the performers are incorporated, i.e., the Corporation owns all rights to their performing services and to their personae.

Sponsor's marketing objectives should be indicated.

Territory
A specific listings of the miles, cities or countries that this agreement encompasses.

Exclusivity and Non-Compete
Will there be only one beverage company for instance, or snake food company? And will offer protection to that company?

Duration of Agreement
An inclusion of the number of concerts in X amount of market places. These market places can be defined by population, which is a measurement of exposure of your sponsor's product and/or services.

Control of Concerts
The Corporation (performer) is to organize a Tour of the highest quality as well as giving due regard to Sponsor's marketing objectives. Artistic control is not handled by Sponsor but by the Corporation!

Advance Concert Information
The Sponsor must be allowed to plan and implement its local promotional programs. The following four steps assist in enabling Sponsor to do its planning.
1. Full disclosure of the schedule of concert dates and locations for the Tour given to Sponsor by Corporation.
2. Names with other pertinent information of each local promoter for each concert date.
3. Hall capacities and ticket sales of each date. This will also be reported in Pollstar Magazine and other trade publications.
4. Date tickets are scheduled to go on sale to the general public.

Concert Advertising and Promotional "Credit"
1. Corporation should prominently include the words "Sponsor Presents (name of band/tour)
2. The "correct" order on the marquis should be, Sponsor's name first then local promoters'
3. Billing responsibility gets transferred to the local promoter as he/she will be placing much of the advertising.
4. Individual and collective personalities and appearances of Performers in TV, print, radio, posters, flyers, concert tickets, programs and similar advertising and promotional media requires credit.

Concert Advertising

Corporation will advertise and promote the Tour and each concert. After X days after each concert, Corporation gives a ticket reconciliation and statement of all advertising including the identity of TV and radio stations, newspapers size of insertions and the length of spots.

Sponsorship Activities

1. The Sponsor has the right to utilize the names, photos, likenesses, and bios info concerning Performers. Included in this right is the name of the band, of the Tour, and any logos of the Tour, without restriction to territory.
2. Sponsor can use above to create and broadcast TV and radio spots and to use brief segments of hit songs and video recordings of hit songs of Performers (provided rights are owned or controlled by Corporation or Performers). This can be prepared at no additional charge during the Term of the Agreement. NOTE: pension and welfare for SAG and/or AFTRA members may still have to be paid.
3. Corporation should have Performers appear in at least one press conference to be held by Sponsor prior to the Tour, location and time chosen by Sponsor. All expenses to be paid by Sponsor additionally. A press conference is the Sponsor's first opportunity to generate some publicity with respect to its sponsorship.
4. Performers agree that they will use Sponsor's products where practical during all public appearances exclusively, and especially while on stage. They will have the road crew wear T-shirts, and other apparel, etc. of the Sponsors'. The Sponsor will pay or supply all of these items.

Tour Merchandise

1. All will include the words "Sponsor Presents".
2. Sponsor will get a full page 4 color advertisement on the back cover of the Tour program at no additional charge. Any monies received from merchandise sold is the property of Corporation and Performers.
3. Sponsor can use any and all Tour Merchandise but cannot sell said merchandise to the public except for contest give-a-ways, radio contests, etc. The Sponsor pays for all production of the Merchandise. If Sponsor wants any merchandise then Sponsor must pay for them, however, royalties are subtracted from the price.

Signage

Signage should be prominently displayed at each concert. If the signage does not interfere with the artistic presentation then there may or may not be signage on-stage.

Sponsor's Tour Coordinator

This person goes "on the road" with the tour, as an employee of Sponsor for purposes and responsibility for implementing Sponsor's sponsorship program.

Concert Tickets (example)

1. Sponsor should receive a minimum of 50 free prime location tickets per concert in receipt 30 days before each event. Free tickets are a benefit of sponsorship. Sponsor should be granted a larger amount of tickets at Sponsor's city headquarters.
2. Sponsor may purchase up to 200 seats for each show to be paid for at full price, prior to them going on sale.
3. Sponsor gets a "reasonable" number of all access laminated Tour passes. These "all access" passes could be used for VIP's or for promotional contest winners, etc.

Meet & Greet / Hospitality / Green Room

As meeting or event planners, you should always negotiate for Meet & Greet before and/or after show for your client's benefit. Sponsor shall always have the right to ask for this item to be paid at Sponsor's expense. The Performers' duty is subject to contractual obligation.

Record Company Activities
The Record Company, if applicable will give X amount of free records to Sponsor for promotional purposes, plus monies not covered by Sponsor.

Death or Disability of Performers/Cancellation
This clause may include many options available to Sponsor. Sponsor should clearly define the circumstances under which the Tour can be cancelled.

Permits and Licenses
This is the responsibility of the Corporation including ASCAP/BMI/SESAC. Any radio or TV uses will need additional permits and/or licenses.

Indemnity and Insurance
This clause may contain many elements. Generally the Corporation holds harmless the Sponsor and the Sponsor holds harmless the Corporation. Insurance will be an issue for the insurance carriers.

Right of First Refusal
The Sponsor should be granted the right of first refusal for future TV and radio broadcasts etc. Sponsor can also buy advertising time on such broadcasts.

Force Majeure
A circumstance not contemplated by either side that makes it illegal or impossible to perform. Both elements must be present: the unexpected circumstance *and* the resultant impossibility. The Agreement should state that in the event this clause takes affect, that one party may or may not still pay a consideration.

Personal Guarantee
This should be given by each of the Performers.

Fees and Payments
1. X shall be paid by Sponsor upon execution of Agreement.
2. Y shall be paid by Sponsor upon the commencement of the Tour.
3. Z shall be paid by Sponsor within 10 days after complete performance of all obligations of Corporation. Or Z could be paid after the completion of each concert. As "the gate" monies and attendance get easier to define, this act gets completed sooner and sooner as computers and programs get to be more accurate and efficient.

Technically, the Performers are employed by the Corporation, which is responsible for any taxes due on the sponsorship fee and for any amounts to be paid to the Performers, including Performers' withholding and social security/FICA (in the United States) obligations.

Assistance for the above Agreement from Mary Hutchings Reed's, <u>International Events Group Legal Guide To Sponsorship</u>.

Scheduling Confirmation Between Client and ABC Seminar Group

This letter outlines the understanding and agreement between Client and ABC Seminar Group (ABC) regarding a presentation to be provided for Client by ABC. It is designed to be a communication tool clearly confirming time, date, title, etc., and defining responsibilities of both parties. Please let us know immediately if your understanding is different than the following.

ABC Seminar Group Will:

- Present a program titled _____ for Client.
- Customize the program, as needed, to fit the needs of this group.
- Provide the materials for the participants' use only. Materials are copyrighted, and unless specified in the materials or in writing, reproduction of any portion i prohibited.
- Abide by the professionalism and ethics guidelines set forth by the National Speakers Association at all times. A copy is attached.
- Jane Doe will personally conduct this session; if, because of physical incapaci-tation, she is unable to do so, Client will have the choice of having another ABC presenter conduct the session or having Jane speak at another session with no cancellation fee. ABC is in no way liable for any expenses relating to this program in the event Jane is unable to appear. (Jane hasn't missed an engagement in her 21 years in business.)

Date and Time of Presentation:

_____2001 ____:____a/pm -____:____a/pm
Jane will be there approximately 1 hour before her program begins. Please make arrangements so she can get in the room to set up.

Location of Presentation:

_____
(Company, Hotel, Convention Center)   Street   City   Phone

Equipment Preferences:

- **NO** lectern
- 1 flip chart with markers
- ½" VCR w/ monitor
- LCD projector —NOT LCD pad (for our Macintosh computer)
- Overhead projector
- Which will sit on 6' table in front with tablecloth
- Freestanding screen (preferred, but fixed screen OK)
- Lavaliere mic (if more than 60 people), wireless preferred
- If corded mic - cord long enough to reach back row
- 1' high riser if more than 100 people
- Stair set in front of riser
- If there is a head table on riser, please set it back 2-3' so Jane can speak in front of it
- 6' table near door for educational materials display

Room Set-up Preferences:

- Rounded U-shape or Chevronned Classroom or Semicircular Theater (see attached diagram)
- Please set the room wide rather than deep

Client will make all arrangements for the location of this program, and for informing the participants.

Please send ABC copies of any announcements to the participants regarding this program.

Honorarium, Terms and Conditions:
Honorarium: $_____

In order to cover advance costs (e.g., air fare) and assure Jane will be available for your program, a deposit in the amount of $_____is required by _____.

The remainder of the honorarium, $_____,is due at the conclusion of the presentation; please present it to Jane.

Jane will provide all workbooks, at a cost of $_____per person. This will be billed after the program.

Early Bird Payment Discount
If **full** honorarium is received by ABC on or before the deposit due date, deduct 5% of payment as Early Bird Payment Discount.

Expenses:
Shall include round-trip coach-plus* air fare from Anywhere,CA to _____; ground transportation; hotel (if not billed to Client 's address); food and gratuities. Balance of travel expenses will be billed after event. Travel expenses will be prorated among all clients served in your area on the same trip.

*Coach-plus air fare is the least expensive air fare available at time of booking (usually Super Saver) plus the cost of upgrade stickers. This enables us to fly first class but only charge you a deep discounted coach rate.

In order to save you money, when available and practical, we book the most cost and time effective flights. Often these flights have penalties if changed so if there is a cancellation or postponement on the part of Client. Client is responsible for reimbursement of the non-refundable part of the air fare.

Overnight Accommodations:
Shall be made by Client,and billed to Client at Client's business address.(A non-smoking room is preferred.) Reservations have been made for Jane:

For:_____,2001   At:_____
　　　　　　(Date/s)　　　　　　　　　　　　　　(Name of Motel, Hotel, etc.)

_____　　　　　　_____
　　　　　(Phone)　　　　　　　　　　　　　　　　　　(Street)

_____　　　　　　_____
　　　(Confirmation #)　　　　　　　　　　　　　　(City, State, Zip)

Contact:
Name, description and phone numbers of persons picking Jane up from the airport:

_____　　_____　　_____
　　　　Name　　　　　　　　　Business phone　　　　　　　Home phone

Description:_____

If before or on the way to the event, an emergency should arise, Jane should contact the following person(s).

| _____ | _____ | _____ |
| Name | Business phone | Home phone |

| _____ | _____ | _____ |
| Name | Business phone | Home phone |

Reinforcement Option:

ABC extends to Client the option to purchase reinforcement materials at special quantity pricing of 10% discount off retail price (in parentheses).

☐ Yes, we wish to exercise this option. Please provide the quantities listed.
_____*Customer Service* book ($12.95)
_____*Success* tape ($9.95)

☐ We regret we cannot exercise this option at this time. You may make reinforcement materials available for individual purchase at the time of your program.

Cancellation/Postponement:

Once a date is set aside and a presentation confirmed, we often incur commitments of time and resources on your behalf, well in advance of the program date. Because a cancellation/postponement initiated by the Client causes losses, either through direct resource expenditure or because of turning down other business for this date, we have found it necessary to include the following cancellation clause, effective in all cases other than acts of God (e.g., major disasters):

> 100% of fee if cancelled in less than 30 days before;
> 50% of fee if cancelled in 31 to 60 days before;
> 25% of fee if cancelled in 61 to 90 days before.

If cancellation/postponement is unavoidable, please verify the cancellation by telephone, followed by a written letter to ABC within five days. If we can sell the time, we will, of course, refund your fee, minus any out-of-pocket expenses we have incurred on your behalf.

Audio & Video Recording:

We encourage professional audio and video taping of our sessions. We ask:
  1) a professional taping technician to do the taping;
  2) we receive the master copy within 30 days of the session;
  3) copies may not be sold, but distributed to your internal staff only.

If this is of interest, we will send an addendum to this agreement, as any taping arrangements must be made in advance of the program.

Agreed:

By: Jane Doe   By:_____
Title: President   Title:_____
Co: ABC Seminar Group   Co: _____
Date: _____   Date:_____

National Speakers Association Code of Professional Ethics

To establish and maintain public confidence in the professionalism, honesty, ability and integrity of the professional speaker is fundamental to the future success of the National Speakers Association, its members, and the profession of speaking.

To this end, members of the Association have adopted and, as a condition of membership, subscribe to this Code of Professional Ethics. By doing so, the members give notice that they recognize the vital need to preserve and encourage fair and equitable practices among all who are engaged in the profession of speaking.

Members of the NSA are dedicated individuals sincerely concerned with the interests of all who come in contact with the profession. To this end, NSA members subscribe to this Professional Pledge:

I **pledge** myself to honesty and integrity; to pursue my profession and education to the end that service to my clients shall always be maintained at the highest possible level.

I **pledge** myself to seek and maintain an equitable, honorable and cooperative association with fellow members of NSA and with all others who may become a part of my business and professional life.

I **pledge** myself to comply with the standards of NSA as set forth in its bylaws and this Code of Professional Ethics.

• The NSA member shall accurately represent qualifications and experience in both oral and written communications.

• The NSA member shall act and speak on a high professional level so as to neither offend nor bring discredit to the speaking profession.

• The NSA member shall exert diligence to understand the client's organization, approaches and goals in advance of the presentation.

• The NSA member shall avoid using materials, titles and thematic creations originated by others, either orally or in writing.

• The NSA member shall limit services to those areas in which the member is qualified to serve, taking into consideration available opportunities for the member to develop new materials or to undertake new fields. When unable or unqualified to fulfill requests for presentations, the NSA member shall make every effort to recommend the services of other qualified speakers or bureaus.

• The NSA member shall maintain the trust of clients, and fidelity concerning the business or personal affairs of a client, agents and other speakers who may reveal confidential information.

• The NSA member shall protect the public against fraud or unfair practices and shall attempt to eliminate from the speaking profession all practices which bring discredit to the profession.

• Violations of the obligations of this Code shall be determined in accordance to the Bylaws, policies and procedures of the National Speakers Association. Disciplinary actions shall be instituted by the National Speakers Association in accordance with Bylaws and Rules and Regulations established by the Association. Any such disciplinary action shall be final and binding upon the NSA member and without recourse to the Association, its officers, members or staff.

APPENDIX 6

Performing Rights Organizations' Licenses

As discussed in Chapter 13, music licensing is a key issue that you must be aware of when you are planning events. If you do not remember to purchase licenses for the music you use at your events, you are making yourself susceptible to additional risk. This appendix contains the full license agreements for the three major performing rights organizations: ASCAP, BMI, and SESAC. The exact license that you apply for will depend on the type of event you are holding and the music you will use. Remember that these licenses are current as of the time that this book is being published in 2004. You should go to the individual Web sites provided in Appendix 1, for the most recent licenses.

ASCAP MUSIC-IN-BUSINESS BLANKET LICENSE AGREEMENT for 2002, ©ASCAP

Agreement between American Society of Composers, Authors and Publishers ("SOCIETY"), located at:

2690 Cumberland Parkway, Suite 490
Atlanta, GA 30339 and

("LICENSEE"), located at:

as follows:

1. Grant and Term of License

(a) SOCIETY grants and LICENSEE accepts a license to perform or cause to be performed publicly at "LICENSEE'S business locations" and at "LICENSEE'S event locations" (each as defined below), and not elsewhere, non-dramatic renditions of the separate musical compositions now or hereafter during the term of this Agreement in the repertory of SOCIETY, and of which SOCIETY shall have the right to license such performing rights.

(b) As used in this Agreement, the following terms shall have the meanings indicated:

   (i) "LICENSEE'S business locations" means all locations, not generally accessible by the public, at which LICENSEE conducts its day-to-day business operations as specified on Schedule "A", annexed hereto and made a part hereof, as said Schedule may be amended as hereinafter provided;

   (ii) "LICENSEE'S event locations" means all locations, other than LICENSEE'S business locations, at which LICENSEE conducts any "LICENSEE event(s)" (as defined below);

   (iii) "LICENSEE'S employees" means all employees of LICENSEE including, but not limited to, full-time, part-time and temporary employees and interns; and

   (iv) "LICENSEE event(s)" means all activities presented or sponsored solely by or under the auspices of LICENSEE, at LICENSEE event location(s), open only to LICENSEE'S employees and their personal guests.

(c) This license shall be for an initial term commencing   , and ending December 31 of the same calendar year, and continuing thereafter for additional terms of one year each unless terminated by either party. Either party may, on or before thirty days prior to the end of the initial term or any renewal term, give notice of termination to the other. If such notice is given, the license granted by this Agreement shall terminate on the last day of the term in which notice is given.

2. Limitations on License

(a) This license is not assignable or transferable by operation of law or otherwise, except upon the express written consent of SOCIETY, and is limited to LICENSEE, LICENSEE'S business locations and to performances presented during and as part of LICENSEE event(s).

(b) This license does not authorize the broadcasting, telecasting or transmission by wire or otherwise, of renditions of musical compositions in SOCIETY'S repertory to persons outside of LICENSEE'S business locations or LICENSEE'S event locations, other than by means of music-on-hold telephone system(s) operated by LICENSEE at LICENSEE'S business locations.

(c) This license does not authorize any performance as part of any conference, congress, consumer show, convention, exposition, industrial show, institute, meeting, public show, seminar, trade show or other similar activity, unless such activity (i) is presented or sponsored solely by and under the auspices of LICENSEE, is presented entirely at LICENSEE'S business location(s), and is not open to the general public, or (ii) otherwise constitutes a LICENSEE event.

(d) This license does not authorize any performance by means of a coin-operated phonorecord player (jukebox) for which a license is otherwise available from the Jukebox License Office.

(e) This license is limited to the United States, its territories and possessions, and the Commonwealth of Puerto Rico.

(f) This license is limited to non-dramatic performances, and does not authorize any dramatic performances. For purposes of this Agreement, a dramatic performance shall include, but not be limited to, the following:

(i)   performance of a "dramatico-musical work" (as defined below) in its entirety;

(ii) performance of one or more musical compositions from a "dramatico-musical work" (as defined below) accompanied by dialogue, pantomime, dance, stage action, or visual representation of the work from which the music is taken;

(iii) performance of one or more musical compositions as part of a story or plot, whether accompanied or unaccompanied by dialogue, pantomime, dance, stage action, or visual representation;

(iv) performance of a concert version of a "dramatico-musical work" (as defined below).

The term "dramatico-musical work" as used in this Agreement, shall include, but not be limited to, a musical comedy, opera, play with music, revue, or ballet.

3. License Fees

In consideration of the license granted herein, LICENSEE agrees to pay SOCIETY the applicable license fees as set forth in the Rate Schedule, attached to and made a part of this Agreement, and based on "LICENSEE'S Operating Policy." The term "LICENSEE'S Operating Policy" means the factors that determine the license fees applicable under the Rate Schedule.

4. Reports

(a) LICENSEE shall furnish reports to SOCIETY upon entering into this Agreement and on or before January 31 of each succeeding year, on forms supplied free of charge by SOCIETY.

(b) The report to be submitted upon entering into this Agreement shall state for LICENSEE'S business locations(s) specified on Schedule "A", the total number of LICENSEE'S employees as of that date; and the license fee due for that year.

(c) The reports to be submitted on or before January 31 of each succeeding year shall state the address of each of LICENSEE'S business locations and the total number of LICENSEE'S employees as of January 1 of such year at all such locations, and Schedule "A" shall be deemed amended accordingly; and the total license fee due for all such locations for that year.

(d) LICENSEE is not required to submit an annual report indicating the total number of LICENSEE'S employees provided that the number of LICENSEE'S employees has not increased or decreased by more than 5% from the previous report submitted by LICENSEE. If LICENSEE does not submit the annual report, LICENSEE'S prior annual report will be used to determine the license fees for the current calendar year.

5. Payment of License Fees

(a) LICENSEE shall pay SOCIETY the license fees due hereunder as follows:

(i)   Upon entering into this Agreement, the license fees due for the first calendar year of this Agreement as shown by the report due at that time; and

(ii) By each succeeding January 31, the license fees for the then current calendar year, and any additional license fees due for the previous calendar year, as shown by the report due on that date.

(b) In the event LICENSEE shall be delinquent in payment of license fees due to SOCIETY by thirty days or more, LICENSEE shall pay a finance charge on the license fees due of 1% per month, or the maximum rate permitted by law, whichever is less, from the date such license fees should have been paid.

6. SOCIETY'S Right to Verify Reports

(a) SOCIETY shall have the right to examine LICENSEE'S books and records to such extent as may be necessary to verify the reports required by this Agreement, provided however, that if the reports submitted by LICENSEE are FICA statements which contain LICENSEE'S number of employees a nd a re c ertified b y a n i ndependent certified public accountant and are submitted in a timely manner, SOCIETY shall forego its right of verification pursuant to this paragraph 6.

(b) SOCIETY shall consider all data and information coming to its attention as the result of the submission of Statements of LICENSEE'S Operating Policy or other documentation submitted by LICENSEE as completely and entirely confidential.

7. Breach or Default

Upon any breach or default by LICENSEE of any term or condition herein contained, SOCIETY may terminate the license granted by this Agreement by giving LICENSEE thirty days written notice to cure such breach or default, and in the event that such breach or default has not been cured within said thirty days, said license shall terminate on the expiration of such thirty-day period without further notice from SOCIETY. In the event of such termination, SOCIETY shall refund to LICENSEE any unearned license fees paid in advance.

8. Interference with SOCIETY'S Operations

In the event of:

(a) any major interference in the operations o f S OCIETY i n t he s tate, t erritory, d ependency, possession or political subdivision in which LICENSEE is located, by reason of any law of such state, territory, dependency, possession, or political subdivision; or

(b) any substantial increase in the cost to SOCIETY of operating in such state, territory, dependency, possession, or political subdivision, by reason of any l aw o f s uch s tate, t erritory, dependency, possession or political subdivision, which is applicable to the licensing of performing rights,

SOCIETY shall have the right to terminate this Agreement forthwith by thirty days written notice. In the event of such termination, SOCIETY shall refund to LICENSEE any unearned license fees paid in advance.

9. Indemnification

SOCIETY agrees to indemnify, save and hold harmless, and to defend LICENSEE from and against all claims, demands and suits that are made or brought against it with respect to the non-dramatic performance under this Agreement of any compositions in SOCIETY'S repertory. LICENSEE agrees to give SOCIETY immediate notice of any such claim, demand or suit and agrees immediately to deliver to SOCIETY all papers pertaining to it. SOCIETY shall have full charge of the defense of any such claim, demand or suit and LICENSEE shall cooperate fully with SOCIETY in such defense. LICENSEE, however, shall have the right to engage counsel of its own, at its own expense, who may participate in the defense of any such action. SOCIETY'S liability under this Paragraph "9" shall be strictly limited to the amount of license fees actually paid by LICENSEE to SOCIETY under this Agreement for the calendar year in which the performance o r p erformances which are the subject of the claim, demand or suit occurred.

10. Notices

All notices required or permitted to be given by either party to the other hereunder shall be duly and properly given if:

(a) mailed to the other party by registered or certified United States Mail; or

(b) sent by electronic transmission (i.e., Mailgram, facsimile or similar transmission); or

(c) sent by generally recognized same-day or overnight delivery service, addressed to the party at the address stated above. Each party agrees to notify the other of any change of address.

IN WITNESS WHEREOF, this Agreement has been duly executed by SOCIETY and LICENSEE, this _____ day of _____, _____.

AMERICAN SOCIETY OF COMPOSERS,   LICENSEE
AUTHORS AND PUBLISHERS

By: _____   By: _____

Title: _____   Title: _____
(Fill in capacity in which signed:
(a) If corporation, state corporate office held;
(b) If partnership, write word "partner" under signature of signing partner;
(c) If individual owner, write "individual owner" under signature.)

2002 MUSIC-IN-BUSINESS
BLANKET LICENSE AGREEMENT

RATE SCHEDULE

FEES FOR PERFORMANCES AT LICENSEE'S BUSINESS LOCATIONS
AND AT LICENSEE'S EVENTS

A. Fees for Calendar Year 2002
The annual fee for calendar year 2002 shall be:

$0.381 for each of the first ten thousand (10,000) of LICENSEE'S employees;

$0.306 for each of LICENSEE'S employees from the ten thousand and first (10,001st) to the twenty-five thousandth (25,000th);

$0.248 for each of LICENSEE'S employees from the twenty-five thousand and first (25,001st) to the fifty thousandth (50,000th); and

$0.192 for each additional LICENSEE'S employees above the fifty thousandth (50,000th)

B. Fees for Subsequent Calendar Years. Subject to the maximum and minimum fee provisions set forth below, for calendar year 2003 and each calendar year thereafter, the license fees under A. above shall be the license fees for the preceding calendar year, adjusted in accordance with any increase in the Consumer Price Index, All Urban Consumers (CPI-U) between the preceding October and the next preceding October. Any such adjustments to the per-employee license fees shall be rounded to the nearest one-half cent.

C. Maximum Fees for Subsequent Calendar Years. The maximum annual license fee payable hereunder shall be $24,500 for calendar year 2002; and the calendar year 2003 and each calendar year thereafter, the maximum annual license fee shall be the license fees for the preceding calendar year, adjusted in accordance with any increase in the Consumer Price Index, All Urban Consumers (CPI-U) between the preceding October and the next preceding October, rounded to the nearest dollar.

D. Minimum Annual Fee. The minimum annual license fee payable hereunder shall be $189 for calendar year 2002; and for calendar year 2003 and each calendar year thereafter, the minimum annual license fee shall be the license fees for the preceding calendar year, adjusted in accordance with any increase in the Consumer Price Index, All Urban Consumers (CPI-U) between the preceding October and the next preceding October, rounded to the nearest dollar.

**ASCAP, 2690 Cumberland Parkway, Suite 490, Atlanta, GA   30339-3913   1.800.505.4052,
1.770.805.3475 (Fax)**

ASCAP LICENSE AGREEMENT – SPECIAL EVENTS for 2002

Agreement between American Society of Composers, Authors and Publishers ("ASCAP"), a New York membership association, located at 2690 Cumberland Parkway, Suite 490, Atlanta, GA 30339 and _____ ("LICENSEE"), located at _____ as follows:

1.   Grant and Term of License

(a)   ASCAP grants and LICENSEE accepts a license to perform publicly or cause to be performed publicly at "Special Events" presented by or under the auspices of LICENSEE, and not elsewhere or otherwise, non-dramatic renditions of the separate musical compositions in the "ASCAP repertory." For purposes of this Agreement,

> (i)   "ASCAP repertory" means all copyrighted musical compositions written or published by ASCAP members or members of affiliated foreign performing rights societies, including compositions written or published prior to or during the term of this Agreement and of which ASCAP has the right to license non-dramatic public performances.

> (ii)   "Special Events" means events and functions which take place on a limited basis, and, in no event, more than three times per year. "Special Events" include, but are not limited to, talent and variety shows, air, sea and balloon shows, pageants, parades, and fashion shows. Special Events do not include, for example, musical performances in restaurants, bars, or similar facilities, circuses, concerts and recitals, "battle of the bands" and similar events.

(b)   This license shall be for an initial term commencing _____ and ending December 31 of the same calendar year, and shall continue thereafter for additional terms of one year each unless either party terminates it by giving the other party notice at least 30 days before the end of the initial or any renewal term. If such notice is given, the license shall terminate on December 31 of the year in which notice is given.

2.   Limits on License

(a)   This license is not assignable or transferable by operation of law or otherwise, except upon the express written consent of the parties, but no assignment shall relieve the parties of their respective obligations as to performances rendered, acts done and obligations incurred prior to the effective date of the assignment.

(b)   This license is strictly limited to the LICENSEE and to the premises. This license does not authorize any other performances other than those given at the premises during the course of the Special Event, nor does it authorize performances given by anyone else at the premises or at any other time.

(c)   This license does not authorize the broadcasting or telecasting or transmission by wire, Internet, webcasting, on-line service or otherwise, of renditions of musical compositions in ASCAP's repertory to persons outside of the premises.

(d)   This license is limited to non-dramatic performances, and does not authorize any dramatic performances. For purposes of this agreement, a dramatic performance shall include, but not be limited to, the following:

> (i)   performance of a "dramatico-musical work" (as hereinafter defined) in its entirety;

(ii)   performance of one or more musical compositions from a "dramatico-musical work" (as hereinafter defined) accompanied by dialogue, pantomime, dance, stage action, or visual representation of the work from which the music is taken;

(iii)   performance of one or more musical compositions as part of a story or plot, whether accompanied or unaccompanied by dialogue, pantomime, dance, stage action, or visual representation;

(iv)   performance of a concert version of a "dramatico-musical work" (as hereinafter defined).

The term "dramatico-musical work" as used in this agreement, shall include, but not be limited to, a musical comedy, opera, play with music, revue, or ballet.

(e)   This license does not authorize any performance by means of a coin-operated phonorecord player (jukebox) for which a license is otherwise available from the Jukebox License Office.

(f)   This license is limited to the United States, its territories and possessions and the Commonwealth of Puerto Rico.

(g)   This license does not extend to performances by LICENSEE or during any Special Event for which ASCAP has issued a license covering the Special Event to a third party.

3.   License Fees

(a)   In consideration of the license granted herein, LICENSEE agrees to pay ASCAP the applicable license fee based on the Rate Schedule, attached to and made a part of this Agreement.

(b)   LICENSEE shall pay a finance charge of 1.5% per month from the date due, on any required payment or report that is not made or submitted within thirty days of its due date. LICENSEE shall pay ASCAP a $25 service charge for each unpaid check, draft or other form of instrument submitted by LICENSEE to ASCAP.

4.   Reports and Payments

(a)   Thirty days after the end of each calendar quarter of this Agreement, LICENSEE shall submit to ASCAP a report in printed or computer readable form stating (i) whether Special Events were presented during the previous quarter; (ii) the type, name, date and location of each Special Event; (iii) the total number of days of each Special Event; (iv) the "Live Music Entertainment Costs" (as defined in the Rate Schedule) of each Special Event; (v) the license fee due for each Special Event and (vi) the total license fees due for the previous quarter.

(b) If the Special Event is a "Benefit Event," the report shall contain the information contained in paragraph 4(a) above and the name and address of the organization for which the benefit is conducted. "Benefit Event" means an event which is not exempt from copyright liability under Section 110(4) of the United States Copyright Law, and which is held to raise money for a specific, bona fide charitable institution or cause to which all the proceeds from the event, after deducting the reasonable costs of producing the event, are donated. LICENSEE, upon ASCAP's request, shall provide documentation of expenses and proof of payment to the institution or cause.

(c)   License fees shall be payable at the time the quarterly report is submitted. The minimum annual fee shall be payable within thirty days of invoicing by ASCAP.

(d) ASCAP shall have the right, by its authorized representatives, at any time during customary business hours, and upon thirty days written notice, to examine the books and records of account of

LICENSEE to such extent as may be necessary to verify any statements of LICENSEE'S Operating Policy rendered pursuant to this Agreement. ASCAP shall consider all data and information coming to its attention as the result of the submission of statements of LICENSEE'S Operating Policy or as the result of any examination of LICENSEE'S books and records hereunder as completely and entirely confidential.

5.   Breach or Default

Upon any breach or default by LICENSEE of any term or condition herein contained, ASCAP may terminate this license by giving LICENSEE thirty days notice to cure such breach or default, and in the event that such breach or default has not been cured within said thirty days, this license shall terminate on the expiration of such thirty-day period without further notice from ASCAP. In the event of such termination, ASCAP shall refund to LICENSEE any unearned license fees paid in advance.

6.   Additional Termination Provision

ASCAP shall have the right to terminate this license upon thirty days written notice if there is any major interference with, or substantial increase in the cost of ASCAP's operations as the result of any law in the state, territory, dependency, possession or political subdivision in which LICENSEE is located or in which LICENSEE presents Special Events, which is applicable to the licensing of performing rights. In the event of such termination, ASCAP shall refund to LICENSEE any unearned license fees paid in advance.

7.   Notices

ASCAP or LICENSEE may give any notice required by this Agreement by sending it by United States Mail, generally recognized same-day or overnight delivery service, or by transmitting the notice electronically to the other party's last known facsimile number or e-mail (or similar electronic transmission) address. Each party agrees to notify the other of any change of address.

8.   Applicable Law

The meaning of the provisions of this Agreement shall be governed by and construed in accordance with the laws of the State of New York, without regard to its conflict of laws principles.

IN WITNESS WHEREOF, this Agreement has been duly executed by ASCAP and LICENSEE on
_____.

AMERICAN SOCIETY OF COMPOSERS,   LICENSEE
AUTHORS AND PUBLISHERS

By: _____   By: _____

Title: _____   Title: _____
                                           Fill in capacity in which signed:
                                               (a) If corporation, state corporate office
held;
                                               (b) If partnership, write word "partner"
                                           under signature of signing partner; (c) If
                                           individual owner, write "individual owner".

ASCAP 2002 RATE SCHEDULE
SPECIAL EVENTS, ©ASCAP

The license fee for Special Events shall be the greater of $100 per year (Minimum Annual Fee) or the fees computed on the following basis:
-- for Special Events with mechanical music only, use Schedule I;
-- for Special Events with live entertainment only, use Schedule II;
-- for Special Events with mechanical music and live entertainment, use Schedules I and II;
-- for Benefit Events, use Schedule III only.

SCHEDULE I.   MECHANICAL MUSIC (See definition below.) The daily license fee for mechanical music shall be $75.

SCHEDULE II.   LIVE ENTERTAINMENT (See definition below.)

Admission or Similar Charge. For performances of Live Entertainment where there is a direct or indirect admission, cover, entertainment, minimum or similar charge the Live Entertainment fee shall be 1.75% of "Live Entertainment Costs".

No Admission or Similar Charge. For performances of Live Entertainment where there is no direct or indirect admission, cover, entertainment, minimum or similar charge, the Live Entertainment fee shall be 1% of "Live Entertainment Costs".

SCHEDULE III.   BENEFIT EVENTS

Capacity	Fee per Event
1 - 5,500	$ 10.00
5,501 - 10,000	$ 36.00
10,001 - 20,000	$ 77.00
20,001 - 60,000	$ 128.00
over 60,000	$ 255.00

DEFINITIONS

Mechanical Music means music which is performed at the premises by means other than by live musicians who are performing at the premises, including, but not limited to (A) compact disc, audio record or audio tape players (but not including "jukeboxes"); (B) videotape, videodisc or DVD players; (C) the reception and communication, at the premises where the Special Event is held, of radio or television transmissions which originate outside the premises and which are not exempt under the Copyright Law.

Live Entertainment means music which is performed at the premises by musicians, singers or other performers, including disc jockeys, video jockeys, karaoke hosts.

Live Entertainment Costs means direct and indirect expenditures paid by LICENSEE for all Live Entertainment for the performance of live music including, but not limited to, such payments made to any disc jockey, video jockey or karaoke host, in connection with LICENSEE'S activities at the premises. The term "live music entertainment costs" shall include:

(i)   Salaries and wages for performers of live music and disc, karaoke or video jockeys (collectively "Performers").

(ii)   The value of any accommodations or services which are made available to any entity or person rendering or presenting live music entertainment activities as part of the consideration for such entertainment services.

(iii)   Direct cost of instrument rental or purchase utilized by live entertainment performers.

(iv)   Payments to booking agents, outside production companies or payments to other parties who provide such services relating to the performance of live music entertainment.

Benefit Event means a Special Event which is not exempt from copyright liability under Section 110(4) of the United States Copyright Law, and which is held to raise money for a specific, bona fide, charitable institution or cause not affiliated in any way with LICENSEE, to which all the proceeds from the Special Event, after deducting the reasonable costs of producing the Special Event, are donated. Where the total seating capacity of a location has been altered to accommodate a particular performance, the term "Capacity" shall mean the total number of seats made available for that particular performance.

ANNUAL LICENSE FEE FOR CALENDAR YEAR 2003 AND THEREAFTER

The minimum annual, daily and benefit fees hereunder for each calendar year commencing 2003 shall be the minimum annual, daily and benefit fees for the preceding calendar year adjusted in accordance with the increase in the Consumer Price Index, All Urban Consumers - (CPI-U) between the preceding October and the next preceding October.

ASCAP LICENSE AGREEMENT - Conventions, Expositions, Industrial Shows, Meetings and Trade Shows for 2002, ©ASCAP

Agreement between American Society of Composers, Authors and Publishers ("SOCIETY"), located at:

2690 Cumberland Parkway, Suite 490
Atlanta, GA 30339-3913

and

("LICENSEE"), located at:

as follows:

1. Grant and Term of License
(a) SOCIETY grants and LICENSEE accepts for a term commencing   , and continuing thereafter for additional terms of one year each unless terminated by either party as provided in this Agreement, a license to perform publicly or cause to be performed publicly, in the United States, its territories and possessions, at "functions" presented in conjunction with each LICENSEE "event" and not elsewhere, non-dramatic renditions of the separate musical compositions now or hereafter during the term of this Agreement in the repertory of SOCIETY, and of which SOCIETY shall have the right to license such performing rights. The term "event" as used in this Agreement shall mean a conference, congress, convention, exposition, industrial show, institute, meeting, seminar, teleconference, trade show or other similar scheduled activity of LICENSEE of not more than fourteen days duration.

The term "function" as used in this Agreement shall mean any activity conducted, sponsored, endorsed or approved by, or presented by or under the auspices of LICENSEE as part of or in conjunction with any LICENSEE event which is open only to "attendees."

The term "attendees," as used in this Agreement, shall mean all individuals who register or pay to attend a LICENSEE event.

(b) This Agreement shall enure to the benefit of and shall be binding upon the parties hereto and their respective successors and assigns, but no assignment shall relieve the parties hereto of their respective obligations under this Agreement as to performances rendered, acts done and obligations incurred prior to the effective date of the assignment.

(c) Either party may, on or before ninety days prior to the end of the initial term or on or before thirty days prior to the end of any renewal term, give written notice of termination to the other. If such notice is given, the license shall terminate on the last day of such initial or renewal term.

2. Limitations on License
(a) This license is not assignable or transferable by operation of law, devolution or otherwise, except as provided in Paragraph "1(b), " and is limited strictly to the LICENSEE, to LICENSEE's event(s) and to the "premises" where each function shall be presented. The term "premises" as used in this Agreement, shall mean all locations used for functions at LICENSEE's events.

(b) This license does not authorize the broadcasting, telecasting or transmission by wire or otherwise, of renditions of musical compositions in SOCIETY's repertory to persons outside of the premises where each function shall be presented. Nothing in this Paragraph "2(b)" shall be deemed to limit LICENSEE's right to transmit renditions of musical compositions in SOCIETY's repertory to attendees in connection with teleconferences pursuant to Paragraph "1(a)" of this Agreement.

(c) This license shall be limited to performances of music during functions conducted, sponsored, endorsed or approved by, or presented by or under the auspices of LICENSEE as part of or in conjunction with LICENSEE's events which are open only to attendees.

(d) This license is limited to non-dramatic performances, and does not authorize any dramatic performances. For purposes of this Agreement, a dramatic performance shall include, but not be limited to, the following:

(i) performance of a "dramatico-musical work" in its entirety;

(ii) performance of one or more musical compositions from a "dramatico-musical work" accompanied by dialogue, pantomime, dance, stage action, or visual representation of the work from which the music is taken;

(iii) performance of one or more musical compositions as part of a story or plot, whether accompanied or unaccompanied by dialogue, pantomime, dance, stage action, or visual representation;

(iv) performance of a concert version of a "dramatico-musical work."

The term "dramatico-musical work" as used in this Agreement, shall include, but not be limited to, a musical comedy, opera, play with music, revue, or ballet.

3. License Fees

In consideration of the license granted in this Agreement, LICENSEE agrees to pay SOCIETY the applicable license fee for each event as set forth in the rate schedule attached to and made a part of this Agreement, based on "LICENSEE's Operating Policy." The term "LICENSEE's Operating Policy," as used in this Agreement, shall mean all of the factors which determine the license fee applicable to each event under the attached rate schedule.

4. Reports of Events and Payment of License Fees

(a) If LICENSEE presents four or fewer events per year, LICENSEE shall submit to SOCIETY, no later than thirty days after the presentation of each event:

(i) written notice of the event, on forms supplied free of charge by SOCIETY, stating the date of the event, the address of the premises and the LICENSEE's Operating Policy; and

(ii) payment of the applicable license fee.

(b) If LICENSEE presents five or more events per year, LICENSEE shall submit to SOCIETY no later than January 31, April 30, July 31 and October 31 of each year:

(i) written notice of each event presented during the preceding calendar quarter, on forms supplied free of charge by SOCIETY, stating the date of the event, the address of the premises and the LICENSEE's Operating Policy for each event; and

(ii) payment of the applicable license fee for all events presented during the preceding calendar quarter.

(c) SOCIETY shall have the right, by its authorized representatives, at any time during customary business hours, and upon thirty days written notice, to examine the books and records of account of LICENSEE to such extent as may be necessary to verify any statements of LICENSEE's Operating Policy rendered pursuant to this Agreement.

(d) SOCIETY shall consider all data and information coming to its attention as the result of the submission of statements of LICENSEE's Operating Policy or as the result of any examination of LICENSEE's books and records hereunder as completely and entirely confidential.

(e) In the event LICENSEE shall fail to pay any license fees when due to SOCIETY, LICENSEE shall pay a finance charge on the license fees due of 1 1/2 % per month, or the maximum rate permitted by law, whichever is less, from the date such license fees should have been paid.

(f) In the event that LICENSEE's payment of fees under this Agreement causes SOCIETY to incur a liability to pay a gross receipts, sales, use, business use, or other tax which is based on the amount Of SOCIETY's receipts from LICENSEE, the number of licensees of SOCIETY, or any similar measure of SOCIETY's activities, and

(i) SOCIETY has taken reasonable steps to be exempted or excused from paying such tax; and

(ii) SOCIETY is permitted by law to pass through such tax to its licensees, LICENSEE shall pay to SOCIETY the full amount of such tax.

5. Breach or Default

Upon any breach or default by LICENSEE of any term or condition herein contained, SOCIETY may terminate this license by giving LICENSEE thirty days written notice to cure such breach or default, and in the event that such breach or default has not been cured within said thirty days, this license shall terminate on the expiration of such thirty day period without further notice from SOCIETY.

6. Interference with SOCIETY's Operations

In the event of:

(a) any major interference with the operations of SOCIETY in the state, territory, dependency, possession or political subdivision in which LICENSEE is located, by reason of any law of such state, territory, dependency, possession or political subdivision; or

(b) any substantial increase in the cost to the SOCIETY of operating in such state, territory, dependency, possession, or political subdivision, by reason of any law of such state, territory, dependency, possession or political subdivision, which is applicable to the licensing of performing rights,

SOCIETY shall have the right to terminate this Agreement forthwith by thirty days written notice, and shall refund to LICENSEE any unearned license fees paid in advance.

7. Notices

All notices required or permitted hereunder shall be given in writing by certified United States mail sent to either party at the address stated above. Each party agrees to inform the other of any change of address.

IN WITNESS WHEREOF, this Agreement has been duly executed by SOCIETY and LICENSEE, this _____   day of _____, _____.

AMERICAN SOCIETY OF COMPOSERS,   LICENSEE
AUTHORS AND PUBLISHERS

By: _____   By: _____
Title: _____   Title: _____
                                                                              (Fill in capacity in which signed:
                                              (a) If corporation, state corporate office held;
                          (b) If partnership, write word "partner" under signature of signing partner;
                                          (c) If individual owner, write "individual owner" under signature.)

2002 RATE SCHEDULE - CONVENTIONS, EXPOSITIONS, INDUSTRIAL SHOWS, MEETINGS AND TRADE SHOWS

For purposes of computing license fees under this Rate Schedule, the number of Attendees shall include all persons who have registered or paid to attend LICENSEE's event, but shall exclude those persons required to produce LICENSEE's event, service contract personnel, temporary personnel, accredited members of the media, and one-half of the number of persons serving as exhibitor personnel.

Fees Per Event For Calendar Year 2002

1. If "mechanical music" is performed, the fee shall be $.064 times the number of Attendees per event, based on the greater of the number of "Attendees" reported by LICENSEE to SOCIETY pursuant to this Agreement or the number as reported in *Tradeshow Week Data Book* published by Tradeshow Week or any other publication. The term "mechanical music" shall mean music presented by means other than live musicians, e.g., records or tapes.

2. If live music is performed, the daily fee shall be the aggregate total applicable fee calculated in accordance with Subparagraphs 2(a) and 2(b) of this Rate Schedule, provided, however, that the aggregate fee for live music shall not exceed $705 per day.

(a) If live music is performed in the main meeting room or on any exhibition floor at LICENSEE's event, the daily fee shall be:

Number of Attendees	Daily Live Music Fee
250 or less	$ 35
251 - 500	70
501 - 750	105
751 - 1,000	140
1,001 - 1,500	175
1,501 - 2,000	210
2,001 - 3,000	285
3,001 - 4,000	355
4,001 - 5,000	425
5,001 - 7,500	495
7,501 -10,000	565
10,001 or more	705

(b) If live music is performed at function(s) occurring elsewhere than in the main meeting room or on an exhibition floor of LICENSEE's event, the fee shall be as shown in Subparagraph 2(a) of this Rate Schedule, provided that the number of Attendees for these function(s) shall be the aggregate number of persons for whom the rooms or areas in which such function(s) occur are set up, or, if the rooms or areas are not set up for specific numbers of persons, the fire capacity of such rooms or areas.

3. If both mechanical and live music are performed at LICENSEE's event, the fee shall be the total applicable fees for mechanical and live music, in accordance with Paragraphs 1, 2(a) and 2(b) of this Rate Schedule.

4. The minimum fee payable hereunder shall be $70 per event and the maximum fee payable hereunder shall be $5,650 per event, provided, however, that if neither live music nor mechanical music is performed at an event, then no fee shall be payable under this Agreement for such event.

Fees Per Event For Calendar Year 2003 and Thereafter
1. For calendar year 2003 and each calendar year thereafter, the license fees shall be the license fees for 1992, adjusted in accordance with any increase in the Consumer Price Index, All Urban Consumers - (CPI-U) between October 1989 and the October preceding the calendar year in question.

2. Such adjustments to license fees shall be rounded as follows:
    (a) For mechanical music, to the nearest one-half cent;
    (b) For live music, to the nearest $5.00;
    (c) For the minimum fee payable, to the nearest $10.00; and
    (d) For the maximum fee payable, to the nearest $50.00.

**ASCAP, 2690 Cumberland Parkway, Suite 490, Atlanta, GA 30339-3913 1.800.505.4052,
1.770.805.3475 (Fax)**

 MUSIC PERFORMANCE AGREEMENT

Business Multiple Use License

|36|

LI-02/02-36

http://www.bmi.com

1. DEFINITIONS
(a) Location: each premises operated and owned or leased by you or your subsidiaries which is used primarily as an executive or general office or as an industrial facility as listed or to be listed on Schedule A.
(b) Executive or general office: a location where LICENSEE conducts its managerial or administrative functions.
(c) Industrial facility: a premises used for manufacturing plant or warehouse and related purposes.
(d) Off-site location: a premises other than the location address under the location's sole control and attended solely by the location's employees, their families and social acquaintances, and intra-corporate invitees.
(e) Employees: all full-time and part-time persons employed at a location.
(f) Subsidiary: an entity wholly-owned by LICENSEE.

2. BMI GRANT
BMI grants you a non-exclusive license to perform or allow to be performed at the licensed locations and off-site locations all musical works of which BMI shall have the right to grant public performance licenses during the term of this Agreement. This grant of rights includes but is not limited to music performed: (1) over telephones in the form of music-on-hold; (2) as live music or recorded background music; (3) in fitness and aerobics facilities; (4) in audiovisual presentations in business meetings; (5) over teleconferencing at the licensed locations; (6) in television and radio programming received by LICENSEE on the locations; and (7) performances of music by interactive software, whether (a) delivered by media such as CD-ROM, CD-I, diskette or cartridge, or (b) rendered by multimedia hardware, such as computer-driven handheld devices.

This license does not include: (a) the right to present the music in any way which may be a use of the "grand rights;" (b) the right to broadcast, telecast, cablecast or otherwise transmit the performances outside of the licensed locations, except to the extent that music on telephone hold lines originating at a licensed location is audible at remote premises on telephone lines as part of "music-on-hold;" (c) performances of music by a jukebox; (d) any performance of music by interactive software, delivered by on line service, such as interactive cable, interactive TV, computer network, telephone or satellite. In all cases the term "premises" shall specifically exclude (1) any retail establishment owned or leased by LICENSEE; (2) any location which is used by LICENSEE for a trade show, convention or exposition; and (3) any hospital or similar facility.

LICENSEE may be responsible for securing other rights including, but not limited to, synchronization and mechanical rights.

BMI may withdraw from the license your right to perform any musical work as to which a legal action has been brought or a claim made that BMI does not have the right to license the work or that the work infringes another work.

3. INDEMNITY BY BMI
BMI agrees to indemnify you, your officers and employees against any and all claims that may be made against you with respect to the performance of any music licensed under this Agreement at the time of your performances. You agree to give BMI immediate notice of any claim, to deliver to BMI any related papers and to cooperate with BMI in the matter, of which BMI will be in full charge. BMI will, upon reasonable written request, advise you whether specific musical works are available for performance, if you provide the title and the writer/composer of each musical work.

4. BREACH OR DEFAULT/WAIVER
If there is any breach or default by you of this Agreement, BMI will have the right to cancel it, but the cancellation will become effective only if the breach or default continues thirty (30) days after the date of BMI's written notice to you. The right to cancel is in addition to any other remedies which BMI may have. BMI may enforce any of its rights under this Agreement at any time even if it has not done so earlier.

5. ARBITRATION
All disputes of any kind arising in connection with the terms of this Agreement shall be submitted to the American Arbitration Association in New York, New York under its rules then in effect. The arbitrators will be selected as follows: each of us will, by written notice to the other, have the right to appoint one arbitrator. If, within ten (10) days after such notice by one of us, the other one does not, by written notice, appoint another arbitrator, the first arbitrator will be the only arbitrator. However, if we each appoint an arbitrator, the two arbitrators will appoint a third arbitrator. If ten (10) days pass after the second arbitrator's appointment and the two arbitrators cannot agree upon the third arbitrator, then either of us may, in writing, request the American Arbitration Association to appoint the third arbitrator. The arbitration award shall be entirely binding on both of us and judgment may be entered in any appropriate court. The award shall include an amount for the costs, expenses and attorneys' fees of arbitration, which shall be paid by the losing party.

Schedule A

Name and address of each location for which a fee is paid, and highest number of employees at that location.

Locations DBA	Address	City	State	Zip	Highest # of employees for the report year	Subsidiary name (If Applicable)

Total Employees:

Enter Total here and on Page 3 of this Agreement in space provided

IF MORE SPACE REQUIRED, ATTACH SHEET(S)

6. NOTICES

Any notices to be given are to be in writing and will be deemed given on the day they are sent by ordinary first-class U.S. mail to the other of us at its above mailing address or any different address which either of us later designates in writing. Any notices you send to BMI will be addressed to the attention of the General Licensing Department. Any notices BMI sends to you will be addressed to the attention of the person signing this Agreement for you unless you advise BMI to address notices to someone else.

7. FEES

(a) You agree to pay BMI for each employee for the first year of this Agreement fees as follows:

LICENSE FEE SCHEDULE

NOTE: The tiers are successive, not cumulative. For example, 800 employees would be covered by 250 in the first tier, 250 in the second tier and 300 in the third tier.

NUMBER OF EMPLOYEES	FEE PER EMPLOYEE
First 250	62 cents
251 - 500	49 cents
501 - 10,000	37 cents
10,001 - 20,000	32 cents
20,001 - 75,000	26 cents
75,001 and Over	17 cents

(b) Subject to Subparagraphs 7 (a), (c), (d) and Paragraph 8, you agree to pay to BMI for each contract year an estimated fee as an advance of the actual fee. Based upon your projection, you estimate that your highest number of employees at all of the locations listed on Schedule A during the first contract year will be _____ and your estimated fee will be _____. **The minimum annual fee for 2002 is $154.**

The first annual fee is due within 30 days of your signing this Agreement.

(c) The amount of the fee per employee and minimum fee for the second and subsequent contract years of this Agreement shall be an adjustment of the first year's fee per employee and minimum fee based upon the percentage increase or decrease in the United States Consumer Price Index (National, All Items) between September 2001 and September of the year preceding each anniversary date of this Agreement. The license fees based upon the number of employees shall be computed to the nearest cent and the minimum fee to the nearest dollar. BMI will advise you in writing of the amount of each new fee.

(d) The estimated fee for the second and following contract years will be the actual fee for the previous contract year and will be due and payable no later than 30 days after the beginning of each contract year.

8. REPORTING

(a) At the same time as the payments required by Paragraph 7 are due, you agree to furnish BMI (on forms available from BMI) with a report, certified either by an officer or by your auditor, setting forth any information regarding the subject matter of this Agreement which BMI may reasonably require, including, without limitation:

   (i)   the highest number of employees for the year reported at each licensed location;

   (ii) the name and address of each location for which a fee is paid;

   (iii) the name and address of each subsidiary and the locations of that subsidiary to be licensed hereunder

(b) If, after processing the annual report, the actual fee is greater than the license fee already paid by you for the contract year, you agree to pay BMI the difference, within (30) days of the mailing by BMI to you of an adjusted statement.

(c) If, after processing the annual report, the actual fee is less than the license fee already paid by you to BMI for the contract year, BMI agrees to credit the difference between the actual and estimated license fees to your account, and if such adjustment occurs in the last contract year of the Agreement, BMI shall refund said sum promptly.

9. CANCELLATION OF ENTIRE CATEGORY

BMI shall have the right to cancel this Agreement along with the simultaneous cancellation of the Agreements of all other licensees of the same class and category as LICENSEE, as of the end of any month during the term, upon sixty (60) days advance written notice.

10. OFFER OF COMPARABLE AGREEMENT

If BMI, during the term of this Agreement and for the same class and category as yours, issues licenses granting rights similar to those in this Agreement on a more favorable basis, BMI will, for the rest of the term, offer you a comparable agreement.

11. MISCELLANEOUS

This Agreement is our entire understanding, will not be binding until signed by both of us, and no waiver or change will be valid unless in writing and signed by us. This Agreement is signed by the authorized representatives of each of us. Your rights are not assignable. This Agreement, its validity, construction and effect, will be governed by the laws of the State of New York. The fact that any parts of the Agreement may be found by a court of competent jurisdiction to be void or unenforceable will not affect the validity or enforceability of any other parts. The headings are for convenience only and are not a part of the Agreement.

12. TERM OF AGREEMENT

The first term of this Agreement begins on the first day of *(month/year)* _____ and ends on the last day of *(month/year)* _____ (a "contract year"). It will continue annually unless cancelled by either you or BMI at the end of the first term or any following one (1) year term by giving thirty (30) days advance written notice to the other of us.

AGREEMENT

AGREEMENT, made at New York, N.Y. on *(Date will be entered by BMI upon execution)* _____
between BROADCAST MUSIC, INC. ("BMI"), a New York corporation with its principal offices at 320 West 57th Street, New York, N.Y. 10019, and the entity described below ("LICENSEE" or "you"):

PLEASE RETURN THIS ENTIRE SIGNED LICENSE AGREEMENT TO:
BMI, 10 MUSIC SQUARE EAST, NASHVILLE, TN 37203

ENTER LEGAL NAME:

_____
(Name of Corporation, Partnership, or Individual Owner)

ENTER TRADE NAME:

_____
(Doing business under the name of)

LICENSED PREMISES

_____
(Street Address)

_____
(City)   *(State)*   *(Zip)*

_____
(Telephone No.)   *(Fax Number)*

_____
(Contact Name)   *(Title)*

CHECK APPROPRIATE BOX AND COMPLETE

☐ Individual Ownership _____

☐ LLC ☐ Corporation _____
         (State of Incorporation, if different from Licensed Premises)

☐ LLP ☐ Partnership _____
         (Enter names of partners)

☐ Other _____

Fed. Tax ID # _____

MAILING ADDRESS

_____
(Street Address)

_____
(City)   *(State)*   *(Zip)*

_____
(Telephone No.)   *(Fax Number)*

_____
(Contact Name)   *(Title)*

<table>
<tr>
<td>

TO BE COMPLETED BY LICENSEE
By signing this Agreement you agree that the foregoing is a true and accurate representation of your Music Policy.

I have read and understood all of the terms and conditions herein and my signature below is evidence of this.
(SIGN HERE – PLEASE INCLUDE PAYMENT)

_____
Signature

_____
Print Name / Title

</td>
<td>

FOR ADMINISTRATIVE USE ONLY
TO BE COMPLETED BY BMI
BROADCAST MUSIC, INC.

</td>
</tr>
</table>

FOR BMI USE ONLY

Account No.   COID

® BMI and the Musicstand symbol are registered trademarks of Broadcast Music, Inc.

Festivals / Special Events

Account #

39FSE

LI-01/03-39FSE

http://www.bmi.com

THIS AGREEMENT, made at New York, N.Y. entered into on *(Date will be entered upon execution)* _____ between BROADCAST MUSIC, INC., a corporation organized under the laws of the State of New York (hereinafter called BMI) with principal offices at 320 West 57th Street, New York, N.Y. 10019, and

ENTER LEGAL NAME _____

(Name of Corporation, Partnership or Individual Owner)

ENTER TRADE NAME _____

(Doing business under the name of)

CHECK APPROPRIATE BOX AND COMPLETE   ☐ **Corporation**   ☐ **Partnership** (Enter names of partners)   ☐ **Individual Owner**

_____
(State of Incorporation)

BUSINESS ADDRESS	**MAILING ADDRESS**
(Street Name)	*(Street Name)*
(City) *(State)* *(Zip)*	*(City)* *(State)* *(Zip)*
(Telephone No.) *(Contact Name)*	*(Telephone No.)* *(Contact Name)*
(Title)	*(Title)*

1. DEFINITIONS

(a) "**Facility**" shall include, but not be limited to, a hall, stadium, auditorium, civic center, coliseum, theatre, amphitheater, museum, library, stage, restaurants/nightclubs or similar venues whether enclosed or not, where an attraction may be presented, located within the United States of America, its territories and possessions.

(b) "**Festival(s)**" shall mean any attraction(s) lasting 7 hours or more over one day or longer, not to exceed 14 days duration, at which musical acts are engaged to perform. Festival(s) in this agreement *do not extend to concert series, or like performances*, with more than three (3) occurrences throughout any contract year.

(c) "**Special Event(s)**" shall mean any attraction(s) with limited occurrence throughout any contract year, not to exceed three (3) such occurrences per contract year. These attractions shall include variety shows (excluding circuses), pageants and other similar spectator events (including events sponsored by charitable organizations or for charitable purposes) that include music, whether or not music is the principal type of entertainment.

(d) "**Seating Capacity**" shall mean the total number of seats permanently affixed in the facility where the attraction is presented plus any temporary seats added within the facility for a particular attraction. If the total number of seats available for the attraction shall be less than that of the permanent seating capacity of the facility, "seating capacity" shall mean the total number of seats available for the particular attraction. If a facility does not have permanent seating, "seating capacity" shall mean the total number of persons attending a particular attraction. If a facility has lawn seating, then "seating capacity" shall mean the total number of seats permanently affixed in the facility, in addition to total lawn seating capacity as determined by the local Fire Marshall.

(e) "**Entertainment Costs**" shall mean the total monies expended for a festival or special event by LICENSEE or LICENSEE's authorized representatives and shall be limited to main attractions and supporting acts, and all monies paid (including the cost of room, board and transportation) to performers, supporting musicians, booking agents, and agents of the performers. The term "entertainment costs" shall not include normal stage props and equipment unless the entity or person rendering or presenting entertainment services specifically requires specialized stage props and equipment.

(f) "**Benefit Event**" shall mean a public entertainment, performance or social event held to raise funds for a specific person or cause in which all proceeds less direct expenses are donated to charity.

2. BMI GRANT

(a) BMI hereby grants to LICENSEE, for the term of this Agreement, a non-exclusive license solely to perform, present or cause the performance of, as part of festivals or special events, **including recorded music** performed in conjunction with attractions before, during or after the intermissions thereof, all the musical works as to which BMI shall have the right to grant public performance licenses during the term hereof. Such license shall be restricted to performance of music in the manner described herein, and is granted in consideration of payment of the license fees as set forth herein and is subject to all of the terms and conditions hereof. This license does not include: (i) dramatic rights, the right to perform dramatico-musical works in whole or in substantial part, the right to present individual works in a dramatic setting or the right to use the music licensed hereunder in any context which may constitute an exercise of the "grand rights" therein; or (ii) the right to simultaneously broadcast, telecast, cablecast, or otherwise transmit (including by the Internet or on-line service) the performances licensed hereunder to persons outside of the facility in which they originate; (iii) performances of music by means of a coin-operated phonorecord player (jukebox).

(b) BMI reserves the right at its discretion to withdraw from the license granted hereunder any musical work as to which any legal action has been instituted or a claim made that BMI does not have the right to license the performing rights in such work or that such work infringes another composition.

3. TERM OF AGREEMENT

The initial term of this Agreement shall begin on _____ and end on December 31, _____ and shall continue thereafter for additional periods of one (1) year each, unless cancelled by either party at the end of said period or any subsequent period, upon not less than sixty (60) days advance written notice by regular U.S. mail to the other party. Each one (1) year period is a "contract year". BMI shall have the right to cancel this Agreement along with the simultaneous cancellation of the Agreements of all other licensees of the same class and category as LICENSEE, at the end of the initial term or as of the end of any month during any subsequent renewal term, upon sixty (60) days advance written notice.

4. FEES

(a) LICENSEE agrees to pay BMI a fee for each performance of a festival/special event computed on the basis set forth in **Schedule A** of this Agreement, or, in the case of any festival(s) or special event(s) held as a benefit event, LICENSEE agrees to pay BMI a fee for each performance computed on the basis set forth in **Schedule B** of this Agreement.

(b) The minimum fees billed and payable for:

  (i) Schedule A Festivals/Special Event: <u>minimum fees</u> shall be **$150 per Festivals/Special Event per year.**

  (ii) Schedule B Benefit Event: <u>minimum fees</u> shall be **$150 per year or total Schedule B fees,** whichever is higher.

  (iii) If LICENSEE has both Schedule A Festival/Special Event and Schedule B Benefit Event, then Schedule B Benefit Event fees shall be computed in accordance with Schedule B and not subject to a Schedule B minimum fee.

(c) When an attraction is believed to be comprised entirely of musical compositions for which BMI shall not have the right to grant public performance licenses, LICENSEE may, at its option, submit a schedule, including writer and publisher information, for all those musical compositions performed at said attraction, *including opening acts and recorded music, if any*, and in those instances in the opinion of BMI, where all of the musical compositions performed at said attraction are ones to which BMI does not have the right to grant public performance licenses, no fee shall be due and payable to BMI. In the event no schedule is submitted to BMI, LICENSEE must pay the applicable fee for said attraction pursuant to Schedule A, or in the case of a festival or special event held as a benefit event, LICENSEE must pay the applicable fee for said attraction pursuant to Schedule B of this Agreement.

5. REPORTING OF FESTIVALS OR SPECIAL EVENTS/PAYMENT

(a) During each contract year of this Agreement, LICENSEE estimates that it will present:

CHECK APPROPRIATE BOX ➡

☐ One festival or special event per year (herein called "**Class 1 Presenter**") or

☐ Two or three festivals or special events per year (herein called "**Class 2 Presenter**")

(b) If LICENSEE is a **Class 1 Presenter**, LICENSEE shall submit its first report for the period beginning on the first day of this Agreement and ending December 31st of same year. The first report shall be estimated for period beginning on the first day of this Agreement. The license fee payable pursuant to said report shall be payable in full upon execution of this Agreement by LICENSEE. For all calendar years following the period of this first report, LICENSEE shall submit its report and make payment to BMI no later than twenty (20) days following the occurrence of the festival or special event. Should LICENSEE fail to report and submit payments to BMI within thirty (30) days after the specified date, then BMI will apply estimated billings to the account based on the prior year's figures for such LICENSEE. Any difference between the actual and estimated fee shall be payable at that time. If LICENSEE overestimated its first period's fee, then LICENSEE's account shall be credited with the difference.

(c) If LICENSEE is a **Class 2 Presenter**, LICENSEE shall report and pay quarterly. The first report shall be estimated for the period beginning on the first day of this Agreement and ending March 31st, June 30th, September 30th or December 31st, whichever comes first in same year. The license fee payable pursuant to the first estimated report shall be payable upon execution of this Agreement by LICENSEE. Within twenty (20) days after the end of the first estimated report period, LICENSEE shall submit its report setting forth the festival(s) or special event(s) which actually were presented during that period. Any difference between the actual and estimated fee shall be payable at that time. If LICENSEE overestimated its first period's fee, LICENSEE's account shall be credited with the difference. For all subsequent quarterly periods, reports and payments shall be due on the twentieth (20th) day of January, April, July and October of each year of this Agreement for all festival(s) or special event(s) presented during the prior calendar quarter. Should LICENSEE fail to report and submit payments to BMI within thirty (30) days after the specified date, then BMI will apply estimated billings to the account based on the prior quarters figures for such LICENSEE.

(d) As required in this paragraph, LICENSEE shall furnish BMI, when it makes payment of license fees pursuant to this Agreement, with a report on forms available from BMI, signed by an officer or auditor or otherwise authorized signatory of LICENSEE, covering performances of attractions occurring during the applicable reporting period. Such report shall include the date(s) of the festival or special event, name of each festival or special event, facility name (including address, city and state) where the attraction took place, and LICENSEE's total entertainment costs. In the case of a benefit event(s), such statement shall include the date(s), name(s) of the festival or special event held as a benefit, facility name (including address, city and state) where the attraction took place, seating capacity and the designated benefactor. A statement shall be furnished to BMI by LICENSEE for *each reporting period* during the term of this Agreement, *regardless of whether or not any performances occurred during that period.*

6. EXAMINATION OF BOOKS AND RECORDS

(a) BMI shall have the right to verify such data or information that is required to be furnished by LICENSEE pursuant to Paragraph 5, by BMI's authorized representatives, at any time during customary business hours, and upon thirty (30) days advance written notice, examining those portions of LICENSEE's books and records of account to such extent as may be necessary to verify any and all statements and/or accountings made hereunder. BMI shall consider all data and information coming to its attention as the result of any such examination of LICENSEE's books and records confidential.

(b) In the event BMI discovers an inaccuracy in any information reported by LICENSEE pursuant to Paragraph 5, either through an examination of LICENSEE, or otherwise, and as a result it is revealed that LICENSEE underpaid license fees to BMI, and the correct license fee is not paid to BMI within thirty (30) days of BMI's notice to LICENSEE of the inaccuracy or underpayment, then LICENSEE shall pay a late payment charge on the additional license fees due as a result of the examination(s) of one and one-half percent (1 ½%) per month, or the maximum rate permitted by law, whichever is less, from the date(s) the license fees should have been paid pursuant to this Agreement. If such payment is still not received within ninety (90) days of BMI's notice to LICENSEE of the inaccuracy or underpayment, then the license granted by this Agreement shall be terminated by BMI immediately.

7. LATE PAYMENT CHARGE

BMI may impose a late payment charge of one and one-half percent (1 ½%) per month from the date any payment is due hereunder on any payment that is received by BMI more than one month after the due date.

8. OFFER OF COMPARABLE AGREEMENT

In the event that BMI, at any time during the term of this Agreement, shall, for the same class and category as that of LICENSEE, issue licenses granting rights similar to those in this Agreement on a more favorable basis, BMI shall, for the balance of the term, offer LICENSEE a comparable Agreement.

9. INDEMNITY BY BMI

BMI agrees to indemnify, save harmless and defend LICENSEE, its officers and employees, from and against any and all claims, demands or suits that may be made or brought against them or any of them with respect to the performance of any material licensed under this Agreement. This indemnity shall be limited to works which are licensed by BMI at the time of LICENSEE's performances. BMI will, upon reasonable written request, advise LICENSEE whether particular musical works are available for performance as part of BMI's repertoire. LICENSEE shall provide the title and the writer/composer of each musical composition requested to be identified. LICENSEE agrees to give BMI immediate notice of any such claim, demand or suit, to deliver to BMI any papers pertaining thereto, and to cooperate with BMI with respect thereto, and BMI shall have full charge of the defense of any such claim, demand or suit.

10. BREACH OR DEFAULT/WAIVER

Upon any breach or default of the terms and conditions of this Agreement, BMI has the right to cancel this Agreement, but any such cancellation shall only become effective if such breach or default continues thirty (30) days after the date of BMI's written notice to LICENSEE. The right to cancel shall be in addition to any and all other remedies which BMI may have. No waiver by BMI of full performance of this Agreement by LICENSEE in any one or more instances will be a waiver of the right to require full and complete performance of this Agreement thereafter or of the right to cancel this Agreement in accordance with the terms of this Paragraph.

11. CANCELLATION BY LICENSEE

If LICENSEE permanently ceases to present attractions, this Agreement and LICENSEE's obligation to BMI shall thereupon terminate, provided, that LICENSEE shall, within ten (10) days thereafter, give written notice of such termination to BMI, setting forth the effective date thereof, and that LICENSEE shall submit all reports and pay to BMI all fees due hereunder until said effective date.

12. NOTICES

All notices, if any, under this Agreement will be in writing and deemed given upon "mailing," when sent by ordinary first-class U.S. mail to the party intended, at its mailing address above stated, or any other address which either party may designate. Any such notices sent to BMI shall be to the attention of the Vice President, General Licensing Department at 10 Music Square East, Nashville, TN 37203. Any notice sent to LICENSEE shall be to the attention of the person signing this Agreement on behalf of LICENSEE or such other person as LICENSEE may advise BMI in writing.

13. ARBITRATION

All disputes of any kind, nature or description arising in connection with the terms and conditions of this Agreement, not subject to the jurisdiction of the BMI Rate Court, shall be submitted to the American Arbitration Association in the City, County and State of New York, for arbitration under its then prevailing arbitration rules. The arbitrator(s) are to be selected as follows: Each of the parties shall, by written notice to the other, have the right to appoint one arbitrator. If, within ten (10) days following the giving of such notice by one party, the other shall not, by written notice, appoint another arbitrator, the first arbitrator shall be the sole arbitrator. If two arbitrators are so appointed, they shall appoint a third arbitrator. If ten (10) days elapse after the appointment of the second arbitrator and the two arbitrators are unable to agree upon a third arbitrator, then either party may, in writing, request the American Arbitration Association to appoint the third arbitrator. The award made in the arbitration shall be binding and conclusive on the parties and judgment may be, but need not be, entered in any court having jurisdiction. Such award shall include the fixing of the costs, expenses and attorneys' fees of arbitration, which shall be borne by the unsuccessful party.

14. MISCELLANEOUS

This Agreement is the entire understanding between the parties, will not be binding until signed by both parties, and cannot be waived or added to or modified orally, and no waiver, addition or modification will be valid unless in writing and signed by the parties. This Agreement is executed by the duly authorized representative of BMI and LICENSEE. The rights of LICENSEE are not assignable. This Agreement, its validity, construction and effect, will be governed by the substantive laws of the State of New York. The fact that any provisions are found by a court of competent jurisdiction to be void or unenforceable will not affect the validity or enforceability of any other provisions. All headings on this Agreement are for the purpose of convenience and shall not be considered to be part of this Agreement.

Schedule A
License Fee Schedule for Each Festival/Special Event

The Festival/Special Event License Fee Rate shall be one and one half percent (1 ½%) of LICENSEE's Total Entertainment Costs for each Festival/Special Event or $150.00 *for each Festival/Special Event,* whichever is higher.

Schedule B
License Fee Schedule for Each Benefit Event

1. Schedule B Benefit Event fees shall be *$150 per year or total Schedule B fees,* whichever is higher.
2. If LICENSEE has both Schedule A Festival/Special Event and Schedule B Benefit Event, then Schedule B Benefit Event fees shall be computed in accordance with Schedule B and *not subject to a Schedule B minimum fee.*

Seating Capacity	Fee Per Benefit Event	Seating Capacity	Fee Per Benefit Event
0 to 250	$15.00	7,501 to 10,000	$125.00
251 to 750	$18.00	10,001 to 15,000	$190.00
751 to 1,500	$28.00	15,001 to 20,000	$260.00
1,501 to 2,500	$45.00	20,001 to 25,000	$315.00
2,501 to 5,000	$67.00	25,001 to 40,000	$345.00
5,001 to 7,500	$90.00	40,001 and over	$480.00

IN WITNESS WHEREOF, this Agreement has been executed by the duly authorized representatives of BMI and LICENSEE as of the date above written.

TO BE COMPLETED BY LICENSEE
By signing this Agreement you agree that the foregoing is a true and accurate representation of your Music Policy.

I have read and have understood all of the terms and conditions herein and my signature below is evidence of this.
(SIGN HERE - PLEASE INCLUDE PAYMENT)

_____
Signature

_____
Print Name / Title

_____
Account #

FOR BMI USE ONLY

FOR ADMINISTRATIVE USE ONLY
TO BE COMPLETED BY BMI
BROADCAST MUSIC, INC.

_____
COID

Music Performance Agreement	**Meetings, Conventions, Trade Shows and Expositions**	Account #	**45**
			LI-01/11-45
			http://www.bmi.com

AGREEMENT, made at New York, N.Y. on *(Date Will Be Entered by BMI Upon Execution)* _____ between BROADCAST MUSIC, INC. (hereinafter called BMI), a state of New York corporation with its principal offices at 320 West 57th Street, New York, N.Y. 10019 and the entity described below and referred to thereafter as "LICENSEE" or "You:"

ENTER LEGAL NAME _____
Name of Corporation, Partnership or Individual Owner

ENTER TRADE NAME _____
(Doing business under the name of)

SELECT ONLY ONE BOX AND COMPLETE ☐ Corporation ☐ *Association* ☐ **Partnership** *(Enter names of partners)* ☐ **Individual Owner** *(indicate residence address below under Business Address)*

(State of Incorporation)

(Partner Names) ☐ **Limited Liability Company**

BUSINESS ADDRESS   **MAILING ADDRESS**

(Street Address)   *(Street Address)*

(City) *(State)* *(Zip)*   *(City)* *(State)* *(Zip)*

(Contact Name) *(Title)*   *(Contact Name)* *(Title)*
(Telephone No.) (   )   *(Telephone No.) (   )*

1. DEFINITIONS

(a) "**Event**" shall mean a convention that includes an assemblage of delegates, representatives and/or members of an organization(s) convened for a common purpose, a meeting which includes individuals assembled together for purposes of communicating information to each other (i.e. panels, seminars, symposiums, convocations, conferences, caucuses, forums, assemblies, congresses, institutes) or otherwise transacting business, an exposition at which products and services are displayed, or a trade, industrial or consumer show, or other activity of LICENSEE of not more than fourteen (14) consecutive days. An "**Event**" shall mean a concert which is sponsored, conducted, endorsed or approved by LICENSEE, unless the concert is open to members of the general public who are not affiliated with the LICENSEE.

(b) A "**Function**" shall include activity conducted, sponsored, endorsed or approved by LICENSEE occurring in connection with an Event, including, but not limited to, meals, plenary sessions, breakouts, meetings, receptions, concerts, cocktail parties, dinners, dances, dinner-dances, variety shows, seminars, or any other similar spectator or participatory activity.

(c) "**Attendees**" shall mean the number of persons present where any live, recorded or audio-visual music is performed or played at each of LICENSEE's Events whether or not any admission charge, registration fee or other payment is required to be made in connection with the attendance, but shall not include those required to produce the event, such as LICENSEE's employees working at the Event, exhibitor personnel, administrative, service contractor and temporary personnel, or credentialed members of the press. In the case of a trade show or convention where live or recorded music is performed on the exhibit floor, the number of Attendees shall be the total number of persons registered at the trade show / convention. If no music is performed on the exhibit floor, the number of Attendees shall mean the total attendance at each Function held during the trade show or convention at which music is performed; provided, however, that in no event shall the number of Attendees for a given trade show or convention exceed the total number of persons registered at the trade show / convention. In the case of a meeting which does not have an exhibit floor and consists only of a series of Functions, the number of Attendees shall be the total attendance at each Function at which music is performed, with the number not to exceed the total registered attendance of the entire meeting.

2. BMI GRANT

(a) BMI hereby grants to LICENSEE a non-exclusive license to perform, present or cause the live and/or recorded performance during Events of all musical works of which BMI shall have the right to grant public performance licenses during the term hereof. This license does not include: (i) dramatic rights, the right to perform dramatico-musical works in whole or in substantial part, the right to present individual works in a dramatic setting or the right to use the music licensed hereunder in any other context which may constitute an exercise of the "grand rights" therein; or (ii) the right to broadcast, telecast or otherwise transmit, including via the Internet or on-line service, the performances licensed hereunder to persons outside of any premises at which an Event occurs.

(b) LICENSEE may be responsible for securing other rights including, but not limited to, synchronization and mechanical rights.

(c) BMI may withdraw from the license your right to perform any musical work as to which a legal action has been brought or a claim made that BMI does not have the right to license the work or that the work infringes another work.

3. TERM OF AGREEMENT

The initial term of this annual agreement begins on January 1, _____ and shall end on December 31, _____ and shall continue annually unless canceled by either you or BMI at the end of the initial term or any following one (1) year term by giving thirty (30) days advance written notice to the other of us. BMI shall have the right to cancel this agreement along with the simultaneous cancellation of the agreements of all other licensees of the same class and category as LICENSEE, as of the end of any month during the term, upon sixty (60) days advance written notice. If there is any breach or default by you of this agreement, BMI shall have the right to cancel it, but the cancellation shall become effective only if the breach or default continues thirty (30) days after the date of BMI's written notice to you. The right to cancel is in addition to any other remedies which BMI may have. BMI may enforce any of its rights under this agreement at any time even if it has not done so earlier.

4. FEES

LICENSEE agrees to pay BMI for each one year term of the agreement a license fee based upon the following:

Calendar Year	Per Attendee Rate
2002	$.05

(a) For each year after the year 2000, the per attendee rate shall be an adjustment of the rate for the previous calendar year based upon the percentage increase or decrease in the United States Consumer Price Index (National, All Items) ("CPI") between September of the year which is two years before such year and September of the preceding year, rounded to the nearest penny (for example, the rate for the year 2001 shall be an adjustment of the rate for the year 2000, based upon the percentage difference in the CPI between September 1999 and September 2000). BMI shall inform you of the adjusted rate by the end of each calendar year.

(b) The minimum annual fee billed and payable for 2002 shall be $110 per year. The minimum annual fee for each year after 2002 shall be an adjustment of the minimum annual fee for the previous calendar year based upon the percentage increase or decrease in the CPI between September of the year which is two years before such year and September of the preceding year, rounded to the nearest five dollars.

(c) You agree to pay to BMI for each calendar year the total fee due. The minimum annual fee ($110) only is due simultaneously with your execution and return of this agreement. The remainder of the actual license fee for each calendar year shall be due within thirty (30) days from the beginning of the following calendar year, upon submission of the report required in paragraph 5, along with the minimum annual fee for the following calendar year.

(d) The license fee for each calendar year shall be based upon LICENSEE's actual total number of Attendees for that calendar year as set forth on the report required by Paragraph 5. If such report reveals that the actual fee due BMI for that report's calendar year is greater than the minimum annual fee previously paid, LICENSEE shall pay the difference at the same time it submits the report and pays its minimum annual fee for the following calendar year.

5.   REPORTING OF EVENTS

At the same time as the payment for the second and subsequent calendar years is due, you agree to furnish BMI (on forms available from BMI) with a report setting forth:

     (i)   the total number of Events held during the previous calendar year;

     (ii)   the total number of Attendees at all Events held during the previous calendar year; and

     (iii) the total license fee for the previous calendar year and the minimum annual license fee for the current calendar year.

6.   VERIFICATION OF / FAILURE TO REPORT

(a) BMI is entitled to verify the information submitted by LICENSEE in its report under paragraph 5, by any source, including the examination of LICENSEE's books and records. As such, LICENSEE is required to retain such books and records for a period of not less than three years after the calendar year contained in LICENSEE's report, copies of which books and records shall be turned over to BMI upon its request. If after such examination, BMI is still unable to verify said information, BMI shall be entitled to unilaterally assess LICENSEE a reasonable annual fee using any source.

(b) In the event LICENSEE fails to submit a report as required under paragraph 5 within thirty (30) days after BMI has given LICENSEE written notice of its failure to do so, BMI shall be entitled to unilaterally assess LICENSEE a reasonable annual fee using any source, including an examination of LICENSEE's books and records as set forth above.

7.   INDEMNITY BY BMI

BMI agrees to indemnify you, your officers and employees against any and all claims that may be made against you with respect to the performance of any music licensed under this agreement at the time of your performances. You agree to give BMI immediate notice of any claim, to deliver to BMI any related papers and to cooperate with BMI in the matter, of which BMI shall be in full charge.

8.   ARBITRATION

All disputes of any kind arising in connection with the terms of this agreement shall be submitted to the American Arbitration Association in New York, New York under its rules then in effect. The arbitrators shall be selected as follows: each of us shall, by written notice to the other, have the right to appoint one arbitrator. If, within ten (10) days after such notice by one of us, the other one does not, by written notice, appoint another arbitrator, the first arbitrator shall be the only arbitrator. However, if we each appoint an arbitrator, the two arbitrators shall appoint a third arbitrator. If ten (10) days pass after the second arbitrator's appointment and the two arbitrators cannot agree upon the third arbitrator, then either of us may, in writing, request the American Arbitration Association to appoint the third arbitrator. The arbitration award shall be entirely binding on both of us and judgment may be entered in any appropriate court. The award shall include an amount for the costs, expenses and attorneys' fees of arbitration, which shall be paid by the losing party.

9.   NOTICES

Any notices to be given are to be in writing and shall be deemed given on the day they are sent by ordinary first-class U.S. mail to the other of us at its above mailing address or any different address which either of us later designates in writing. Any notices you send to BMI shall be addressed to the attention of the General Licensing Department. Any notices BMI sends to you shall be addressed to the attention of the person signing this agreement for you unless you advise BMI to address notices to someone else.

10. MISCELLANEOUS

This agreement is our entire understanding, shall not be binding until signed by both of us, and no waiver or change shall be valid unless in writing and signed by us. Your rights are not assignable. This agreement, its validity, construction and effect, shall be governed by the laws of the State of New York. The fact that any parts of this agreement may be found by a court of competent jurisdiction to be void or unenforceable shall not affect the validity or enforceability of any other parts.

TO BE COMPLETED BY LICENSEE	FOR ADMINISTRATIVE USE ONLY
By signing this Agreement you agree that the foregoing is a true and accurate representation of your Music Policy.	TO BE COMPLETED BY BMI BROADCAST MUSIC, INC.
I have read and have understood all of the terms and conditions herein and my signature below is evidence of this. **(SIGN HERE - PLEASE INCLUDE PAYMENT)**	
_____ Signature	
_____ Print Name / Title	

FOR BMI USE ONLY

Account No.   COID

BMI

® BMI and the Musicstand symbol are registered trademarks of Broadcast Music, Inc

SESAC PERFORMANCE LICENSE

Agreement made by and between SESAC, Inc. ("SESAC") 421 West 54th Street, New York, NY 10019 and

|_____| ("LICENSEE")
(Legal Name of Owner)

Address |_____| Phone |_____| Fax |_____|

City |_____| ST |___| Zip |_____| E-Mail |_____|

A ⃝ Corporation ⃝ Partnership ⃝ Sole Proprietorship (check one) State of Incorporation (if applicable) |_____|.

SESAC and LICENSEE hereby mutually agree as follows:

1. GRANT OF RIGHTS: Effective as of |January 1| |2001| (the "Effective Date") SESAC grants to LICENSEE the non-exclusive right and license to publicly perform live or "recorded" non-dramatic renditions of the musical compositions, the performance rights to which SESAC controls and/or is empowered to license (the "Compositions") solely on and in connection with the operation of:

Name:|_____|

Address |_____| City |_____| ST |___| ZIP |_____|
(the "Premises").

This right and license is subject to the limitations set forth at Paragraph 2 herein below. As used herein, "recorded" means performances originating on the Premises by phonorecord and/or audio or audio/visual tapes and discs, and the reception of audio broadcast transmissions on the Premises by means of television or radio receivers or loudspeakers.

2. LIMITATIONS OF RIGHTS: The Rights granted pursuant to Paragraph 1 above shall specifically exclude:

A. the right to perform, broadcast, televise or otherwise transmit the compositions to any location other than the Premises (unless and to the extent otherwise expressly permitted in Schedule "A");
B. the right to grant the Rights to any third party;
C. "Grand Rights" in and to the Compositions ("Grand Rights" include, but are not limited to, the right to perform in whole or in part, dramatico-musical and dramatic works in a dramatic setting);
D. performances of the Compositions (i) which are part of a background music service originating from any location including the Premises, for which performance license fees are otherwise paid, regardless of the means by which such performances are transmitted on or to the Premises, (ii) by coin-operated phonorecord players ("jukeboxes"), as defined in 17 U.S.C. § 116(e)(1) (repealed), and/or (iii) transmitted by computer on-line services or electronic bulletin boards and received on the Premises (unless and to the extent otherwise expressly permitted in Schedule "A").

3. TERM OF LICENSE:

A. The term of the Agreement shall be for an initial period that commences upon the Effective Date and continues for a period of one (1) year (the "Initial Period"). Thereafter, the Agreement shall automatically continue in full force and effect for successive additional periods of one (1) year ("Renewal Period(s)"). SESAC and /or LICENSEE shall have the right to terminate this Agreement as of the last day of the Initial Period or as of the last day of any Renewal Period(s) upon giving written notice to the other party by certified mail, return receipt requested, at least thirty (30) days prior to the commencement of any Renewal Period(s). The Initial Period and Renewal Period(s) are sometimes collectively referred to herein as the "Term."

B. Notwithstanding anything to the contrary contained herein, SESAC shall have the right to terminate this Agreement: (i) at any time upon written notice to LICENSEE in the event LICENSEE is adjudicated bankrupt, or a petition in bankruptcy is filed with respect to LICENSEE, or LICENSEE is declared or becomes insolvent; or (ii) upon thirty (30) days written notice by reason of any law, rule, decree, or other enactment having the force of law, by any authority, whether federal, state, local, territorial or otherwise, which shall result in substantial interference in SESAC's operation or any substantial increase in the cost of conducting its business.

4. LICENSE FEE:

A. As consideration for the Rights granted herein, LICENSEE shall pay to SESAC the annual "License Fee" then in effect in accordance with the "Fee Schedule" set forth in Schedule "A" attached hereto.

B. In the event that SESAC is determined by the taxing authority or courts of any state in which LICENSEE conducts its operation to be liable for the payment of a gross receipts, sales, use, business use or other tax which is based on the amount of SESAC's receipts from LICENSEE, then LICENSEE shall reimburse SESAC, within thirty (30) days of notification therefore, for LICENSEE's pro rata share of any such tax derived from receipts received from LICENSEE.

C. SESAC shall have the right to impose a late payment charge of one and one-half percent (1.5%) per month for any License Fee payment that is more than thirty (30) days past due. In the event that SESAC incurs any costs or fees in connection with the collection of any amounts past due to SESAC hereunder, then LICENSEE shall be responsible for paying such amounts to SESAC.

D. Effective January 1 of each calendar year, the License Fee may be increased by an amount equivalent to the percent increase, if any, in the Consumer Price Index - All Urban Consumer (CPI-U) as published by the Bureau of Labor Statistics, U.S. Department of Labor, between the most recent October and the preceding October.

5. MISCELLANEOUS:

A. In the event LICENSEE fails to pay the License Fee when due or is otherwise in default of any other provision of this Agreement, then SESAC shall have the right to terminate this Agreement in addition to pursuing any and all other rights and/or remedies available if LICENSEE has not cured such breach within thirty (30) days following SESAC's written notice of such default.

B. SESAC shall have the right to withdraw from the scope of this License, upon written notice, the right to perform any musical composition licensed hereunder as to which any action has been threatened, instituted, or a claim made that SESAC does not have the right to license the performance rights in such composition.

C. This Agreement shall be binding upon and inure to the benefit of SESAC's and LICENSEE's legal representatives, successors, and assigns, but no assignment shall relieve SESAC or LICENSEE of their obligation under this Agreement. LICENSEE shall notify SESAC in writing within thirty (30) days of any change of ownership or control of LICENSEE's operations.

D. This Agreement shall be governed by and subject to the laws of the State of New York, applicable to agreements made and to be wholly performed in New York. This Agreement supersedes and cancels all prior negotiations and understandings between SESAC and LICENSEE in connection with the Premises. No modification of this Agreement shall be valid or binding unless in writing and executed by SESAC and LICENSEE. If any part of this Agreement shall be determined to be invalid or unenforceable by a court of competent jurisdiction or by any other legally constituted body having the jurisdiction to make such determination, the remainder of this Agreement shall remain in full force and effect. No waiver of any breach of this Agreement shall be deemed a waiver of any preceding, continuing or succeeding breach of the same, or any other provision of this Agreement.

IN WITNESS THEREOF, the parties have caused this Agreement to be duly signed as of _____

(Please insert today's date)

LICENSEE   **SESAC, Inc.**

BY: X _____   BY: _____
(Please sign here)

_____   TITLE: _____
(Type or print name)

TITLE: _____   S E S A C

Schedule "A"
MUSIC IN BUSINESS - 2001
New Media, On Site & External Performances

I. Premises "Premises," as used in the SESAC Performance License effective | January 1 | | 2001 | (the "Agreement") to which this Schedule "A" is attached, shall be defined as all locations owned, operated, or leased by LICENSEE in the United States, its territories and possessions and the Commonwealth of Puerto Rico, which are used as executive or general offices, as manufacturing plants, warehouses, or for related purposes, and locations under LICENSEE' s sole control and attended by LICENSEE' s employees, their families, social acquaintances, and intra-corporate invitees. " Premises" shall also include areas leased by LICENSEE, such as an exhibit booth; banquet hall; or meeting or seminar room at a convention, meeting, or trade show at which LICENSEE is an exhibitor. **The authorization under this license shall also extend to events sponsored by LICENSEE at conventions, meetings, trade shows, or shareholder functions.**

As used herein, " Premises" excludes any area owned, operated, or leased by LICENSEE, which is normally open to the general public, such as retail or entertainment facilities. As used herein, " Premises" excludes any online service provider, or any company whose primary business functions are conducted via the internet. Facilities owned, operated, or leased by LICENSEE that use copyrighted music and for which SESAC offers another type of license are excluded from this agreement.

II. Fee Schedule/License Fee.

A. The annual License Fee shall be based upon the number of Employees as noted below:

Number of Employees		License Fee for calendar year 2001
200,000	And over	$18,104
175,000	- 199,999	$ 15,518
150,000	- 174,999	$ 12,931
125,000	- 149,999	$ 10,345
100,000	- 124,999	$ 7,759
75,000	- 99,999	$ 5,173
50,000	- 74,999	$ 2,586
25,000	- 49,999	$ 1,552
15,000	- 24,999	$ 1,293
10,000	- 14,999	$ 1,035
5,000	- 9,999	$ 776
1,000	- 4,999	$ 414
500	- 999	$ 207
Under	500	$ 103

Number of Employees [   ]

This license will authorize **audio and/or audio/visual musical performances** (radio, records, tapes, compact discs, videocassettes, laser discs, television, and similar media), and **live musical performances**. This license will also authorize performances via **music on hold** systems operated by LICENSEE, and **video- or tele- conferencing.** This license will also authorize **transmissions on or through a Web Site, Bulletin Board Service, Intranet and other interconnected computer network** at the Premises. This license will not authorize transmissions of broadcasts on or through a Web Site, Bulletin Board Service, Intranet or other interconnected computer network, of broadcasts or webcasts of the programs or services of any television station, television network, radio station, radio network, cable station, cable network, cable system, satellite program distributor, or any similar operation.

B. As used herein, " Employee" shall mean the total number of full-time and part-time persons employed by LICENSEE as of September 1 of each calendar year. If LICENSEE has been in operation less than one year prior to the effective date of this agreement, then, for the Initial Period of this license, " Employee" shall mean the total number of full-time and part-time persons employed by LICENSEE at the Premises as of the Effective Date of this agreement.

C. LICENSEE shall pay the license fee to SESAC upon execution of this Agreement, with license fees due and payable in advance. The initial license fee payment shall be a pro-rated amount calculated using the then current license fee rate(s) from the Effective Date through the end of the current billing period. Subsequent payments shall be made annually in one (1) payment on or before the first day of January, for the billing period of January 1 through December 31 of each calendar year of the Term.

D. Upon execution of this License, LICENSEE shall provide SESAC with a report detailing the number of Employees as of the effective date of this License. Thereafter, on or before October 1 of each calendar year, in the event that a change in the number of LICENSEE's Employees results in a change in fee category, LICENSEE shall submit an updated report of the number of Employees. License fees will be adjusted effective the following January 1. SESAC retains the right to obtain these figures through independent industry sources and make appropriate adjustments to the license fee.

E. Notwithstanding anything to the contrary contained in this Agreement, upon written notice to LICENSEE, SESAC shall have the right to adjust the rates set forth in the Fee Schedule. In the event that LICENSEE's License Fee increases as a result of such adjustment to the Fee Schedule, LICENSEE shall have the right to terminate this Agreement as of the date such increase is to take effect. LICENSEE must give SESAC written notice of such termination by certified mail, return receipt requested, not later than thirty (30) days after written notice of such increase is sent to LICENSEE by certified mail. This paragraph shall not apply to paragraph 4.B or 4.D of the Agreement.

III. This Schedule is incorporated and made part of the Agreement. Unless otherwise indicated, all capitalized terms in this Schedule "A" shall have the same meaning as set forth in the Agreement.

APPENDIX 7

Technical Production Documents

Although you, the event manager, will probably not be directly involved with the technical aspects of entertainment production, it is critical that you understand the basic elements so that you can evaluate vendors who do have expertise in this area. This appendix includes a sample request for proposal (RFP) for lighting equipment, a cue sheet that is used by the technical staff to provide the proper sound and lighting elements for the production, and a sample stage setup plot for an event.

Sample Request for Proposal (RFP)

Show: Big party
Venue: Vegas C.C.

Load in: 2/22/03 8am
Load out: 2/26/03 1am

Contact info
Bill To
BigTime Producer

Production Rigger

Lighting Design & Staging Coordinator
Company Name
Company Contact Information

Notes

- All conventional instruments to be supplied complete
  (pipe clamp, safety cable, color frame) unless otherwise noted

- All moving lights to be supplied with necessary hanging hardware
  and safety cable unless otherwise noted

- All equipment must be in excellent working and visual condition

- All changes, substitutions, and/or deletions MUST be approved
  by lighting designer

- All rigging changes, substitutions, and/or deletions MUST be approved
  by production rigger

- Vendor to supply spares for all equipment

- Designer assumes no responsibility for structural or electrical safety and
  engineering and will make changes as needed to accommodate such
  requirements

- **This is not a complete order. It is the Vendor's responsibility to ensure all**
  necessary parts are supplied to make system operate properly.

Truss and Rigging

Truss
1- 20' diam circular truss 12"x12"x20'
40- 12"x12"x10' BLACK
35- 20"x20"x10'

Rigging Hardware
30 ½ ton chain hoists
all hoist control, distro and rigging

Lighting

Conventional
50- lekos (lens TBD)
50- Par 64 1K MFL
50- Par 641K NSP
16- 6' MR-16 zip strips
16- 8' 2K Fresnels

Moving Lights

Control/Dimming

1- DMX splitter 6 way
1- 96 x2.4k Dimmer
1- Moving light distro

Expendables
45- sheets gel (type TBD)
6- Black rolls black Gaffer tape
3- Rolls white Gaffer tape
6- Rolls black electrical tape
1- small spool tie line

Misc.
 2- water-based hazers
 2- 1.2K followspots
1- cable package
 Trucking to and from venue

Cue Sheet Sample (Television Film)

Film Name: *This Business of Music*
Production Company: Krasilovsky & Gross
Original Air Date: December 19, 1999
Length of Film: 90 minutes

Abbreviations: BI = background instrumental; BV = background vocal; TC = theme close; VV = visual vocal

Cue #	Title	Composer	Publisher	How Used	Time
1 Medley consisting of					
	Signature	Jane Doe	Backbeat	BI	0.07
	Juniper	Jane Doe	Backbeat	VV	5.37
	Cowboys	Mike Roe	Apex	BI	0.34
2 Medley consisting of					
	Juniper	Jane Doe	Backbeat	BI	0.09
	Cowboys	Mike Roe	Apex	BI	0.45
	Juniper	Jane Doe	Backbeat	BI	0.38
3	Boy and Bird	Irv Max	ABC	BV	1.25
4	Kestrel	Bob Smith	ABC	BI	0.40
5 Medley consisting of					
	Juniper	Jane Doe	Backbeat	BI	0.15
	Signature	Jane Doe	Backbeat	BI	0.15
	Cleo	Bob Smith	HappyTunes	VV	1.25
6	Air Theme	Mary Loe	Apex	TC	0.30

The Hall of Fame Show Stage Setup • Mark Sonder Productions

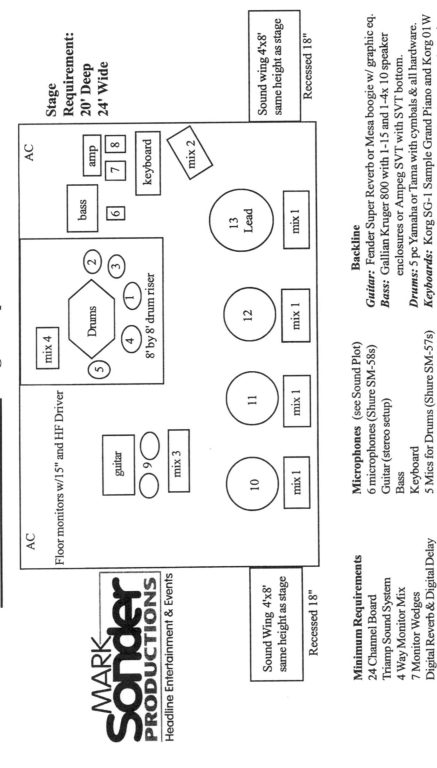

Stage Requirement: 20' Deep 24' Wide

AC

Floor monitors w/15" and HF Driver

AC

bass

amp

6

7 8

keyboard

mix 2

mix 4

Drums

8' by 8' drum riser

1 2 3 4 5

guitar

9

mix 3

10

mix 1

11

mix 1

12

mix 1

13 Lead

mix 1

Sound wing 4'x8' same height as stage

Recessed 18"

Sound Wing 4'x8' same height as stage

Recessed 18"

MARK Sonder PRODUCTIONS
Headline Entertainment & Events

Minimum Requirements
24 Channel Board
Triamp Sound System
4 Way Monitor Mix
7 Monitor Wedges
Digital Reverb & Digital Delay
Two (2) 20 amp circuits (AC)

Microphones (see Sound Plot)
6 microphones (Shure SM-58s)
Guitar (stereo setup)
Bass
Keyboard
5 Mics for Drums (Shure SM-57s)
6 wireless microphones

Backline
Guitar: Fender Super Reverb or Mesa boogie w/ graphic eq.
Bass: Gallian Kruger 800 with 1-15 and 1-4x 10 speaker enclosures or Ampeg SVT with SVT bottom.
Drums: 5 pc Yamaha or Tama with cymbals & all hardware.
Keyboards: Korg SG-1 Sample Grand Piano and Korg 01W FD plus keyboard amplifier for personal monitor.
Four (4) music stands with music stand lights.

Glossary

Addendum   Textual matter that is added to a publication, usually at the end.

ADI   Area of dominant influence, the geographic area or market reached by a radio or television station. It is used by advertisers and rating companies to determine the potential audience of a station.

Agency   A business or service authorized to act for others. The place of business of an agent.

Agent   A person, regulated by the AFM, AFTRA, SAG (Screen Actors Guild), or AEA (Actors' Equity Association) who finds or receives offers of employment for talent and negotiates the contracts for his or her clients. (Clients are the artists, including musicians, vocalists, and taped or live actors and actresses, who are only paid for the area where they render service.) An agent works on a commission basis, normally 10 to 20 percent of the artist's earnings for a given engagement. An agent can work through an agency. Individually or as a company, agents can represent many artists.

American Society of Composers, Authors and Publishers   ASCAP is a PRA (public rights association); also known as a PRO (public rights organization) or PRS (public rights society).

Amperage   A measure of the amount of current flowing in an electric circuit. Amperage equals wattage divided by voltage.

Area of dominant influence   ADI is the geographic area or market reached by a radio or television station. It is used by advertisers and rating companies to determine the potential audience of a station.

ASCAP   See *American Society of Composers, Authors and Publishers.*

Audiovisual production   The activities required to accommodate an audience's need to see and hear.

Automated lighting   Sometimes referred to as *intelligent lighting,* these sophisticated computer-controlled lights can change color, gobos, and focus by remote control.

Baby boomers   People born between 1946 and 1964.

Backlighting   A method of lighting whereby the light source is placed behind the item or area being lighted.

Backline   Instruments and associated equipment required for a performance.

Bible for events   Generally a three-ring binder with different tabs for all of the needed information for an event. Also called the *Production Book* or *Operations Manual.*

Blanket license   A license that allows the music user to perform any or all of the four million musical works in ASCAP's or BMI's repertory as much as he or she likes. Licensees pay an annual fee for the license. The blanket license saves music users paperwork, trouble, and the expense of finding and negotiating licenses with all of the copyright owners of the works that may be used during a year and helps to prevent the user from even inadvertently infringing on the copyrights of ASCAP's or BMI's members and the many foreign writers whose music is licensed by ASCAP or BMI in the United States (see also *per program license*).

BMI   See *Broadcast Music, Inc.*

Brainstorming   A group technique for stimulating creative ideas that are not initially judged for merit.

Breakeven dollars   The dollar volume a business must do to reach $0 net profit.

Breakeven point   The point at which the variable and fixed costs equal the revenue for an event. The variable costs and revenue are both contingent on the number of units sold.

Breakeven units   The number of units a business must sell in order to reach $0 net profit.

Broadcast Music, Inc.   BMI is a PRA (public rights association); also known as a PRO (public rights organization) or PRS (public rights society).

Business manager   A nonregulated person charged with taking care of the financials and investing artists' earnings. Usually earns a commission of 2 to 6 percent of the artist's earnings.

Caricature   A representation, especially pictorial or literary, in which the subject's distinctive features or peculiarities are deliberately exaggerated to produce a comic or grotesque effect.

Cash flow statement   A standard business accounting report that shows money coming in and money going out, providing a snapshot of the earner's money or cash position at a specific point in time.

Certification   A certificate stating that a person has met certain competency requirements in an industry.

Chops   (Colloquialism.) The knowledge, experience and maturity—the wherewithall—to perform or produce at a certain level.

CIMP   Certified Internet Meeting Professional, awarded by the Connected International Meeting Professionals Association.

CMM   Certified Meeting Manager, awarded by Meeting Professionals International.

CMP   Certified Meeting Professional, awarded by the Convention Industry Council.

Contract   An agreement between two or more people, one party (or parties) agreeing to perform certain acts, the other party (or parties) agreeing to pay for or give other consideration for said performance. A contract places an obligation on one party to do something and an obligation on the other party to reward the services that were rendered.

Contractor   A person hired to hire additional personnel required for the fulfillment of an engagement. Under the AFTRA Code, a contractor is required for all engagements of nonroyalty groups of singers consisting of three or more. In additional, the contractor must be a performing member of the singing group, unless his or her sex precludes the use of the contractor's services. An AFM contractor must be used if 12 or more sidemen are employed for any session. This contractor may be a performer.

Convention and Visitors Bureaus CVBs are organizations that operate in cities, focusing on attracting visitors to their cities, especially through meetings and conventions.

Copyright The legal right granted to an author, composer, playwright, publisher, or distributor to exclusive publication, production, sale, or distribution of a literary, musical, dramatic, or artistic work.

Corporate entertainment company A company/producer/person who makes the match between client and entertainer; can often produce the entire meeting or event in regard to the entertainment; procures artists from many different agencies; negotiates and/or realizes the rider; finds headline, regional, and local entertainment; has a complete catalog of entertainment entities other than musical in its roster. Also called an entertainment management company.

Cost of sales The direct cost of selling goods or services.

CPPM Certified Planner of Professional Meetings, awarded by the Connected International Meeting Professionals Association.

CSEP Certified Special Events Professional, awarded by the International Special Events Society.

Cue sheet A document that technicians use to record the visual or audio signals on stage, which tells them that a lighting, sound, or stage change should occur.

CVBs See *Convention and Visitors Bureaus.*

Deal memo An abbreviated form of a contract. An offer from a talent buyer to an artist outlining the details for a contract, if the offer is accepted. Once accepted, this memo is legally binding.

Design The incorporation of a themed message along with audiovisual, entertainment, and musical elements.

Destination management company DMC; a professional management company specializing in the design and delivery of events, activities, tours, staffing, and transportation, utilizing local knowledge, expertise, and resources.

Dimmer A device that controls the intensity or brightness of a lighting source.

DMC See *Destination management company.*

Downlighting A method of lighting whereby a light source is placed above, or at a higher level, than the item or area being lighted.

Downstage Front of the stage, closest to the audience.

Dramatic or grand rights, or dramatic performances ASCAP and BMI members do not grant ASCAP or BMI the right to license dramatic performances of their works. Although the line between dramatic and nondramatic performance is not clear and depends on the facts, a dramatic performance usually involves using the work to tell a story or as part of a story or plot. Dramatic performances, among others, include the following:

- Performance of an entire "dramatico-musical work." For example, a performance of the musical play *Oklahoma* would be a dramatic performance.
- Performance of one or more musical compositions from a dramatico-musical work accompanied by dialogue, pantomime, dance, stage action, or visual representation of the work from which the music is taken. For example, a performance of "People Will Say We're in Love" from *Oklahoma* with costumes, sets or props, or dialogue from the show, would be dramatic.
- Performance of one or more musical compositions as part of a story or plot, whether accompanied or unaccompanied by dialogue, pantomime, dance, stage

action, or visual representation. For example, incorporating a performance of "If I Loved You" from the musical *Carousel* into a story or plot would be a dramatic performance of the song.

■ Performance of a concert version of a dramatico-musical work. For example, a performance of all the songs in *Oklahoma,* even without costumes or sets, would be a dramatic performance.

The term *dramatico-musical work* includes, but is not limited to, a musical comedy, oratorio, choral work, opera, play with music, revue, or ballet.

ASCAP has the right to license "nondramatic" public performances of its members' works—for example, recordings broadcast on radio, songs or background music performed as part of a movie or other television program, or live or recorded performances in a bar or restaurant.

Dramatic, or grand, rights are licensed by the composer or the publisher of the work.

Employee   An individual, hired by an entity, who is given direction, control, and supervision.

Entertainer   One who performs for the purpose of providing amusement and enjoyment for others.

Entertainment   Activity performed for the amusement and enjoyment of others.

Executive producer   The person ultimately in charge of the financial success of an event.

Fair   An exhibition, as of farm products or manufactured goods, usually accompanied by various competitions and entertainment.

Festival   (1) A day or period of time set aside for feasting and celebration. (2) An organized series of acts and performances.

Fête   An outdoor festival.

Fixed costs   Expenses that do not change (in the short term) as sales rise.

Force majeure clause   A clause in a contract that protects both parties in the case of cancellation due to an act of God or other uncontrollable circumstance. Also *force majesture.*

Fresnel   A light that projects a soft-edged beam, which can be varied in size from narrow focus to wide flood. Excellent for lighting general areas, dance floors, backdrops, foliage, and decorative vignettes.

Gap analysis   A process that assesses the differences between expectations and results and then utilizes those differences to create positive organizational changes.

Gated event   An event that requires tickets in order to attend.

Gel   An term used to denote the filters placed into a light beam to add color or change the shape or characteristics of the light beam. Hundreds of colors and styles are available.

Generation X   People born between 1965 and 1976.

Generation Y   People born between 1977 and 1997.

Gig   An engagement, job, or performance date.

Gobos   Also known as templates or patterns, these are most often flat metal "stencils" that fit within a theatrical spotlight, or automated light, to project images such as clouds, corporate logos, geometric patterns, or any number of stock or custom images. Recently, heat-resistant glass and the ability to color glass gobos have increased the designer's options for creativity. Many ready-made stock gobos are available.

Gross profit   The money left after cost of sales is deducted from revenue.

Gross profit margin   Percentage of sales that is left after the cost of sales has been paid (gross profit divided by revenue).

Impresario   One who sponsors or produces entertainment.

Incentive program   Events organizations (incentive houses) use incentive programs to reward top-performing employees. The rewards may be as simple as awards given at a special awards ceremony, on the low end, to an extravagant, all-expense-paid week-long trip to an exotic destination.

Income statement   A standard business accounting report that provides an overview of income and expenses over a certain period of time and groups items by revenue or expense category.

Independent contractor   An individual who is engaged to do a job or perform an act but who maintains direction, control, and supervision him- or herself as to how the job or act is carried out.

Jingle house   A company set up for the purpose of creating musical commercials for radio or television formats.

Leko   The slang term for an ellipsoidal spotlight. This theatrical fixture projects a hard-edged beam of light, which can be shaped by built-in shutters or an iris, as well as by using a gobo. This fixture is useful for illuminating specific areas where control of the light beam is needed. Excellent for lighting single performers and architectural, and décor details.

License   A legal document needed to practice certain regulated professions or occupations.

Lick   (Colloquialism.) A passage from a musical performance that can be mimicked.

Light tree   Any of the many types and styles of vertical poles on which light fixtures may be hung.

Live Webcasting   Webcasting in which the video/audio signal is streamed in real time and remote viewers watch the feed just as they would watch a satellite or television feed.

Management   A company of managers.

Manager   A person responsible for day-to-day career development, personal advice and guidance, and planning the long-range direction of an artist's career. Managers generally receive commissions of 15 to 25 percent of the artist's gross earnings, plus reimbursement for travel and other out-of-pocket expenses. A manager can work through a management office. Individually or as a company, a manager generally represents one to five artists. Also called a *personal manager*.

Mechanical music   Recorded, taped music.

Mechanical rights   The rights to record and distribute (without visual images) a song on a phonorecord for private use. Mechanical rights or a mechanical license must be obtained in order to lawfully make and distribute records, CDs, and tapes.

Meeting   A gathering for business, educational, or social purposes. Associations often use the term to refer to a combination of educational sessions and exhibits. Includes seminars, forums, symposiums, conferences, workshops, and clinics.

Mitigation   To mitigate is to moderate a quality or condition in force or intensity; alleviate or relieve; to become milder; to act in such a way as to cause an offense to seem less serious.

Music publisher   An entity that works with songwriters to market and promote songs, resulting in exposure of the songs to the public and generating income. Music publishers "pitch" songs to record labels, movie and television producers, and others who use music, then license the right to use those songs and collect fees for such usage. The fees are then split with the songwriters.

Net profit   The money left over after all expenses have been paid (gross profit minus fixed costs).

Net profit margin   Net profit expressed as a percentage of revenue (net profit divided by revenue).

Networking   An informal system whereby persons having common interests or concerns assist each other, as in the exchange of information or the development of professional contacts.

One-off performance   A unique performance that is scheduled to occur only once. An "off-tour" date.

Operations Manual   Generally a three-ring binder with different tabs for all of the needed information for an event. Also called *the bible* or the *Production Book*.

Outsourcing   Hiring external companies or individuals who can handle certain functions of an event more efficiently than the event planning organization can.

Par cans   A 150 W to 1000 W lighting instrument that acts like a floodlight, providing an even light over a specific area; frequently seen in a polished aluminum version, hanging in large groups from ground support or a flying truss system.

Parade   A moving pageant including floats, bands, individual entertainers, and dignitaries.

PDA   See *Personal digital assistant*.

Performing rights   The rights granted for performances of songs in public.

Performing Rights Organization   PRO; in the United States, PROs include ASCAP, BMI, and SESAC.

Per program license   A license similar to a blanket license in that it authorizes a radio or television broadcaster to use all the works in the ASCAP or BMI repertory. However, this license is designed to cover use of ASCAP or BMI music in a specific radio or television program, requiring that the user keep track of all music used. In addition, the user must be certain to obtain rights for all the music used in programs not covered by the license.

Personal digital assistant   PDA; a small electronic device used to keep a calendar, address book, and other notes for an event.

Pinspot   This fixture projects a very narrow beam of light and is ideal for lighting table centerpieces, specific décor elements and details, and food displays on buffets.

Premises   Location of event, even if there are many locations.

Private date   An event held by invitation only; not open to the public. No print, TV, or any media advertising. Tickets are not available to the public. Artists' rates for this type of event are typically much higher than for a "gated" or public event. Examples include corporate, association, incentive, governmental, fund-raising, social, and special events.

PRO   See *Performing rights organization*.

Production Book   Generally a three-ring binder with different tabs for all of the needed information for an event. Also called *the bible* or the *Operations Manual*.

Production schedule   A detailed outline of all of the activities that will occur at an event, before, during, and immediately after.

Product placement   Utilizing motion pictures, television, and Broadway to showcase a product.

Promoter   An entrepreneur who takes the full financial risk of an event, show, or concert. Can be local, regional, national, or international in scope. Also called a *concert promoter* or *talent buyer*.

Public performance   An event that occurs in a place open to the public or at any place where a substantial number of persons outside a normal circle of a family and its social acquaintances are gathered. A public performance also occurs when the performance is transmitted by means of any device or process (for example, via broadcast, telephone wire, or other means) to the public. In order to perform a copyrighted work publicly, the user must obtain performance rights from the copyright owner or his or her representative.

Record label   A record label (or record company) makes, distributes and markets sound recordings (CDs, tapes, etc.). Record labels obtain from music publishers the right to record and distribute songs and, in turn, pay license fees for the recordings.

Registration   The formal act of registering personal information and professional or occupational qualifications with an organization.

Request for proposal   An RFP is the publication, by a prospective purchaser, of details of the required product or services in order to attract offers by vendors or planners to supply their products and/or services. A request for proposal (also called, in Britain, an *invitation to tender*) is the beginning of the selection process.

Retransmission   A transmission of a performance is the sending of a performance by any device or process (for example, radio, TV, cable, satellite, telephone) and received in a different place. A retransmission is a further transmission of that performance to yet another place.

Return on event entertainment   ROEE; the implicit and explicit benefits of having entertainment at an event.

Revenue   Money that a business receives for the products or services it sells. Also called *gross sales*.

RFP   See *Request for proposal*.

Rider   A clause or provision that is attached to a contract and should be considered part of the contract.

Risk   Any condition or occurrence that may affect the outcome of an event.

Risk management   The safeguarding of people, property, assets, and public image. The function of risk management is to reduce the probability of loss.

ROEE   See *Return on event entertainment*.

Service mark   The same as a trademark, except that it identifies services instead of products.

Sight line   The line of sight from the audience to the stage; desirably, unobstructed.

Sound recording   A sound recording is distinguished from a song itself in regard to copyright. The copyright in a song encompasses the words and music and is owned by the songwriter or music publisher. A sound recording is the result of recording music, words, or other sounds onto a tape, record, or CD. The copyright encompasses what you hear: the artist singing, the musicians playing, the entire production. The sound recording copyright is owned by the record label. The copyright in the musical work itself is owned by the music publisher, which grants the record label a "mechanical" license to record and distribute the song as part of the record.

Special event   A one-time event staged for the purpose of celebration; a unique activity.

Sponsorship   A cash or in-kind fee paid to a property (typically in sports, arts, entertainment, or causes) in return for access to the exploitable commercial potential associated with that property.

Stage left   The left side of the stage (from the performer's perspective).

Stage management   The people charged with alerting speakers or performers ahead of time and preparing them by bringing them to the stage holding area; physically assisting with stage changeovers; taking performers to and from green rooms; cueing performers, speakers, and others who will be using the stage; and keeping the show flowing. They should always be in voice contact with the production manager either by intercom or radio.

Stage right   The right side of the stage (from the performer's perspective).

SWOT analysis   An analysis of *s*trengths, *w*eaknesses, *o*pportunities, and *t*hreats for an event.

Synchronization or "synch" right   A right that involves the use of a recording of musical work in audiovisual form; for example, as part of a motion picture, television program, commercial announcement, music video, or other videotape. Often, the music is "synchronized" or recorded in timed relation with the visual images. Synchronization rights are licensed by the music publisher to the producer of the movie or program.

Talent buyer   A person or company that procures talent. Can be local, regional, national, or international in scope.

Technical staff   Used in shows incorporating sound, light, staging, AV, music, entertainment, and production; the people with sufficient understanding and proficiency who are responsible for providing services in all these areas to run the show.

Theme   An idea or a subject that unifies an event.

Throw   The distance a light beam must travel from the fixture to the item or area being illuminated.

Throw distance   The length of space between the projector and the screen. Consists of a combination of the projector's lens diameter and the screen width.

Top 40   Shortened from Billboard Top 40. A weekly published listing, in different formats, of the top-grossing records.

Trademark   A commercial listing that designates a manufacturer or a word, name, symbol, sign, slogan, label, or device that distinguishes one party's goods from another's.

Traffic flow   The stream of people, props, or technical equipment occurring on the stage from the start of the show to the end.

Truss   A structure that is internally braced so as to be able to span distances without bending. Trusses may be "flown" (hung from above) or floor supported (held up by vertical columns) and are used to support lighting fixtures, drapery, backdrops, and scenery. Many different styles and types are available.

Up lighting   A method of lighting whereby the light source is placed below, or at a lower level, than the item or area being lighted.

Upstage   The rear part of a stage, away from the audience.

Variable costs   Expenses that rise with sales.

Vicarious liability   Liability imposed on persons *other* than the person who performs a wrongful act.

Videoconferencing   An interactive use of video, computing, and communication technologies to allow people in two or more locations to meet—either one-on-one or in groups of up to a dozen people or so—without being physically together. Video can be streamed over the Internet or broadcast via television monitors.

Video on demand Webcasting   VOD; Webcasting that is available after the actual event and can be viewed anytime from anywhere.

Wash   Lighting effect using one or more fixtures to generally illuminate an area without emphasis on any particular focal point.

Web conferencing   Videoconferencing without the video—or, put another way, teleconferencing with the addition of the Web for interactive presentations, using PowerPoint, Excel, or other documents. Telephone and/or PC microphones can transmit audio.

Webcasting   Broadcasting audio and video signals over the Internet.

Index